HISTORY

Of The

GERMAN ELEMENT IN VIRGINIA

By Herrmann Schuricht

TWO VOLUMES IN ONE

With Indexes By
Anita Comtois

Originally Published
Baltimore, Maryland
Volume I: 1898
Volume II: 1900

Reprinted
Two Volumes in One
With Added Indexes
Genealogical Publishing Co., Inc.
Baltimore, 1977

Reprinted for Clearfield Company Inc. by
Genealogical Publishing Co. Inc.
Baltimore, MD 1989

Library of Congress Catalogue Card Number 77-82334
International Standard Book Number 0-8063-0783-8

Made in the United States of America

HISTORY

OF

THE GERMAN ELEMENT IN VIRGINIA.

BY

HERRMANN SCHURICHT.

VOL. I.

DEDICATION.

THIS work is dedicated to all German-Americans, who, with a loyal attachment to the land of their choice, combine a pious remembrance to the native land of their forefathers: those brave pioneers, who helped to develop the great resources of the New World and to make these United States of North America an abode of liberty and happiness. The history of Virginia — the mother of States — records many names of Germans who have acted their parts well in the work of civilization and deserve honorable recognition.

In particular this book is devoted to

The Society for the History of the Germans in Maryland, aiming to ascertain the merits of the German settlers, and to guard the same from oblivion.

Respectfully,

THE AUTHOR.

TABLE OF CONTENTS.

Vol. I.

Page

INTRODUCTION.

PERIOD I.

THE COLONIAL TIME TO THE END OF THE 18th CENTURY.

INTRODUCTION.

THE PARTICIPATION OF GERMANS IN THE DISCOVERY OF AMERICA.

THE PROGRESS of civilization has been advanced by no other historical event more powerfully than by the rediscovery of the New World, and no other race has alike promoted European culture in America, than the Germanic. Among the Europeans of Germanic origin, who have participated in the gigantic work of civilization in America, the Germans have quietly and little noticed done their share.

Virginia—with the sole exception of the settlements of the Norse or Northmen in "Vinland,"—was the first scene of Germanic life in North America. The name "Vinland" the New England States derived from the discovery of the native grapevine by the German Dietrich Tyrker, from the Rhine, who as teacher and guardian, sailed in the year 1001 with the sons of Eric the Red from Greenland to the coast of the North American continent. The world is indebted for the knowledge of the Norse discovery to the German Rev. Adam von Bremen, born at Meissen in Saxony, and died in the year 1076. In his "History of the Church," he reports statements received from Swein, King of Denmark and others; and Icelandic records and traditions confirm his narration and speak of Markland, Helluland and Vinland, which comprised the territory from Labrador to Massachusetts and part of Rhode Island. In the year 983 Red Eric (Erik Rauda) and Herjulf, compelled to fly from Iceland, sailed with a number of colonists to the distant coast of Greenland. Sailing around Cape Farewell, through their efforts the southern extremity of the western coast of Greenland was speedily settled, as is proved by many runic inscriptions. In 986 Herjulf's son Bjarn or Bjarni discovered by accident the great American continent in the neighborhood of Boston and the news of his discovery reached Norway, where Eric's son Leif stayed at the court of King Olaf Tryggvason to acquire a scientific education. Hearing of the beautiful land situated in the southwest of the ocean, Leif resolved to sail in quest of it and returned to Greenland in company with his German teacher, Dietrich Tyrker, from the Rhine. He purchased Bjarn's ship, manned it with 35 sailors and reached first a snowy and rocky coast, which he named Helluland (rocky land.) Coasting the mainland for many miles he and his companions sighted a rich woodland which they termed Markland, and finally reached an island and the mouth of a large river which originated from a lake. There they wintered, and Dietrich Tyrker, the guardian of Leif, explored the country and discovered the native Grape-Vine. Accordingly, they called this part of the land Vinland.—Two years later Leif and his brother Thorstein or Thorvald undertook another expedition to Vinland. Leif founded a village, "Leifsbudir," and in the spring of 1003 a part of his followers sailed farther south and discovered a very rich country. Attacked by the native savages or Skraellingers, the expedition returned to Greenland in 1005; but in the year 1006 Torfin built in Vinland a town which he called "Torfinsbudir," and Freydis a daughter of Red Eric, Halg, Finnbog and others importing colonists from Norway, the settlement prospered. In 1121 Bishop Erich inspected the colony—and for three centuries a commercial connection was kept up between Vinland, Greenland and Norway, until decay began. The hostility of the natives and "the black death," carried off most of the settlers, and finally with the unfortunate colonists all knowledge of Vinland died out. (Compare: "Der anregende Einfluss der Deutschen auf die Entdeckung der neuen Welt," von H. A. Rattermann, Seite 9 und 10,—Cincinnati, 1892; and Worthington's: "History of the United States.")—However, after the rediscovery of the Western Continent by Christopher Columbus in 1492, a permanent English settlement was effected as stated, in 1607 on Virginian soil; and although in some instances the old mother colony has been surpassed by later seats of European culture in America, its history presents a most interesting picture of the progress of civilization in the new world and the part the Germans have taken in it.

Germany had reached the climax of its commercial power at the end of the middle ages. The Hanseatic Union reigned in the Northern seas, and the Kings of Scandinavia and Britain submitted to her superiority. But during the last decades of the fifteenth century symptoms of a rapid decline became apparent. England and the Netherlands made strenuous efforts to compete in the commerce of the world: Particularism began to loosen the ties upon which the strength and power of the Hanse rested, and finally grand events as the rediscovery of America by Christopher Columbus, and the maritime route opened to East India by Vasco de Gama, not only furnished Spain and Portugal with immense amounts of gold and silver, but changed the ancient routes of commerce and opened new markets. The Mediterranean Sea lost much of its importance, and Italy, called in Germany: "Das Haus im innern Hofe der Welt," — ceased to be such. All the western European nations acquired transatlantic possessions, established colonies and enjoyed the benefit of the new Era, but the German Hanse and the Italian republics, — the masters of the seas, — did not participate, endeavoring in vain to force the world's traffic back in its old channels. The Hanseates were driven from the emporium; the wealth of the German nation suffered severely, and religious wars, massacres and persecutions inflicted upon their commerce and industry deep wounds. Mining in Germany proved less profitable after the capture of gold and silver by the Spaniards, followed by the discovery of many rich mines of precious metals in South America and Mexico, and finally the cruel "Thirty years' war, 1618–1648" wholly destroyed the national welfare. Entire villages disappeared, cities were reduced to ruin, pestilence and famine swept away those who had escaped the sword, and culture and morality fled this terror without precedent. It is not surprising, that in the midst of their national calamity the German princes did not possess the means or even the inclination to organize the great mass of fugitives, that tried to regain happiness and peace on the other side of the ocean

However, the great period of discoveries and the consequent migration of nations, did not commence unprepared or *without German assistance.* These important events were preluded in a fair way by pioneers and guides, and many of them were of German origin. Even Columbus had his German advisers who assisted him in the rediscovery of the lost or forgotten part of the Globe. Of the numerous German thinkers and explorers, who are known to have helped in the great event, only one principal figure shall be mentioned.

Martin Behaim, born 1459 at Nuremberg, is frequently asserted to be *the first rediscoverer of America*, and he is undoubtedly entitled to great merit with regard to the discovery of the Western Hemisphere He undertook extended voyages, visited Venice and Antwerp, and was introduced in the year 1480 to King Alphons V, of Portugal. Fifty years before the most distant station in the West, the Azores or Western Islands, Fayal and Pico, had been settled by "German–Flandrian traders," a colony had been organized and rapidly enlarged. About 1490 it amounted to several thousand inhabitants. Martin Behaim visited these islands, became acquainted with the Governor, the noble knight Jobst von Hurter, Seigneur of Mörkirchen, and married his daughter Johanna. He was a great cosmographer, mathematician and inventor of nautical instruments. He improved the old astrolabium to an instrument for measuring altitude, "the quadrant." Behaim also took part in the exploring expeditions of the Portuguese Admiral Diego Cano along the western coast of Africa and was knighted in recognition of his meritorious services. In the year 1492, after various voyages and having penetrated far into the unknown western seas, he returned to his native city in Germany, designed various maps and construed there the first globe of the earth: "Globus oder Erdapfel," which is preserved to this day in the German Museum at Nuremberg, as one of the most interesting relics and as a monument of German ingenuity. On his globe a cluster of islands: "Antilia" is marked, which represent America as it was known to him, and it is asserted that Portugal afterwards founded her claim on Brazil before the Papal tribunal of arbitration upon the statement, that Martin Behaim in the year 1483, when in the service of the Portuguese Crown, discovered the western continent. The chronicle of Nuremberg: "Nuremberger Weltchronik, of the year 1494," also says: "These two men, Behaim and Diego Cano, with the assistance of our Lord, reached the other part of the globe, having crossed the western ocean and the equinox, where facing the east the shadow fell southward and to their right. Therefore, they opened by their merit a new part of the earth which had been unknown." Giovanni Baptista Riccioli, an Italian historian, reports in his Geographiae et Hydrographiae Reformata, "Columbus received valuable information regarding his plans in the house of Martin Behaim." Furthermore, the Spanish historians, Herrera and Muñoz, and the Portuguese Barros state: "That Martin Behaim viewed Pernambuco and discovered Brazil previous to Columbus and Vespucci," and "Columbus would not have ventured on his voyage if Behaim had not given him the directions." To some degree these assertions are confirmed by Alexander von Humboldt, who never made a statement without good proof. He says: "Columbus probably knew Behaim at Lisabon, where both resided from 1480 to 1484." It is known also, that De Perestrello, the father-in-law of the great Genuese, called on the German explorer at Nuremberg in order to get his opinion and advice regarding the probability of discovering a western route to India. The knowledge that Behaim possessed of a western continent, is also affirmed by the historical report, "That Magelhaens used a map drawn by the German geographer, when he sailed around Cape Horn."

These statements of the great deeds of a German explorer do not lessen the enormous merits of Christopher Columbus, for it remains his glory, to have opened the fabulous lands of the Far West to civilization. However ungrateful single men may be, the totality of mankind acknowledge and honor its benefactors, their grand services are preserved and bequeathed from generation to generation. Columbus experienced the ingratitude of his contemporaries, but in the heart of posterity his name is printed in golden letters, *and like him all those are entitled to grateful recognition, who guided him on the path of glory.*

Many more names and circumstances might be related to prove the intellectual part the Germans have taken in the rediscovery of the New World. German literary men like Nicholaus Kopernikus, (Kopernik) born at Frauenburg in Prussia, Georg Purbach or Peurbach, an Austrian, Johannes

Regiomontanus, properly Johannes Mueller or Molitor, born at Koenigsberg in Franconia, and others, were celebrities of the highest rank in astronomy, mathematics and geography. They were predecessors of Behaim and Columbus, and have materially enlightened the knowledge of the world. "They not only are," says Lichtenberg, "the restorers of astronomic knowledge in Germany, but actually the founders of astronomic science in Europe," and the French scholar Gassendi proclaims, that, "without Purbach or Regiomontanus probably no Columbus and Kopernikus would have arisen."

Germans afterwards took the lead in publishing the discoveries of Columbus and Vespucci. In the year 1506 under the nom de plume, "Martinus Hylacomilus," Martin Waldseemueller or Waltzemueller, born at Freiburg in Baden, was *the first* to express in his Cosmographiae Introductio etc., the opinion, that Columbus had discovered a new continent; in 1515 Johannes Schoener at Nuremberg, published his map under the title, "De America, quarta orbis parte"; in 1508 Jobst Ruckhammers or Ruchamers, "Neue unbekanthe landte und eine newe weldte in kurtz vergangener zeythe erfunden," appeared at Nuremberg and this was *the first book* to give extensive reports about the then known discoveries. Jobst Ruchammer in his book published 1507 in Lubeck, also gave to the New World the name of "America," and the first map of the world which mentioned this name appeared in the "Cosmographie" of Petrus Apianus, that is, Peter Bienewitz, born 1495 at Leissnig, in Saxony.

Later on Spain, England, France, Holland and Sweden employed German intelligence, capital and labor to secure colonies in America and make them prosperous. Charles V, King of Spain and Emperor of Germany, borrowed eleven million florins of the German banker Welser, at Augsburg; King Francis I, of France, received from the same firm two million florins, and the Kings of England, Henry VIII and Edward VII in 1546 and 1547 contracted large loans with the Augsburg Banking House. Welser himself bought Venezuela, which his family owned until 1558 and he commissioned Alfinger or Dalfinger, Federmann and Georg von Speyer, to explore the country along the Magdalen and Orinoco rivers. The governments of the forenamed kingdoms commissioned numerous agents to engage German colonists and artisans for their American provinces.

The Dutch government appointed the German Prince von Nassau-Siegen, governor of Brazil from 1624 to 1648, and Holland as well as Sweden entrusted the Germans, Peter Minnewit, of Wesel on the Rhine, 1626, and Johann Printz von Buchau of Holstein, 1643, with the occupation and administration of their colonies on the Hudson and Delaware rivers. Even among the *first settlers in Virginia* were several Germans and they helped materially to explore and cultivate the land and to establish moral and lawful life.

The political and social conditions of England before and during the middle ages were in a deplorable state, its commerce and industry were dependent on foreign countries, principally the Hanseate Union and Italy. But during the reign of Edward III, in the first half of the 14th century, a greater activity is observable and in the 15th century domestic commercial associations struggled to take the imports and exports into their own hands. The first steps to organize a royal naval force were taken at the time of Henry VII in 1485 to 1509. Only five years after the first voyage of Columbus, the King enabled John Cabot and his son Sebastian to cross the ocean in order to make new discoveries in the interest of England and to find a northern route to India. These two courageous seamen descried the North American continent, the coasts of Labrador or Newfoundland, 14 months earlier than the famous Genuese, and they sailed in 1498 from Labrador to Virginia and to the Albemarle sound in North Carolina. But they failed to find a northern route to Asia and to bring back to England expected treasures of gold and silver. Nearly half a century elapsed before Martin Frobisher succeeded to repeat Cabot's plans. By the influence of Ambrose Dudley, Earl of Warwick, he obtained two small ships of Queen Elizabeth, sailed through unknown waters until he entered Baffin Bay in 1576. Here he heaped up a pile of stones and took possession of the country for the British Crown. Among other things which he collected he brought back a stone containing traces of gold: This fact soon became generally known and created a wild gold fever in England. The thirst for gold was the cause of two other naval expeditions under the command of Frobisher, but after sustaining innumerable perils incident to arctic regions, the ships returned to England without the coveted result and the spirit of enterprise would have gone asleep, had not Francis Drake of Devonshire, during the war between England and Spain, 1577 to 1579, sailing through the straits of Magellan and coasting along the Pacific shore ransacked the Spanish colonies, Chili and Peru, and captured a Spanish vessel loaded with treasures.

Sir Walter Raleigh, a great favorite with Queen Elizabeth, obtained for his brother-in-law, Sir Humphrey Gilbert, the concession to form permanent settlements in the sub-tropical region of North America. Sir Humphrey sailed in the year 1583 to Newfoundland, which he reached on August 5th. He there erected the English arms and assigned certain lands to the fishermen of other nations agreeing to pay an annual ground rent. This was the first commercial treaty of the English in America.

In connection with this expedition the *first information of German participation* is preserved. The historian George Bancroft reports, that an expert miner who accompanied Sir Humphrey, was *an honest and pious Saxon* and very industrious. It was the general opinion, that the appearance of the mountains indicated mineral wealth and the Saxon asserted upon his life, that there was an abundance of silver ore. He gathered specimens and the precious ore was loaded on board of one of the ships, but it was wrecked and the Saxon with his cre and all her crew perished.

Sir Walter Raleigh himself was no more successful than his brother-in-law. He received of Queen Elizabeth a patent for an extended territory, lying between Florida and Canada, which in honor of his maiden Queen he called Virginia. Two ships, commanded by experienced officers, sailed in April 1584 from London conveying one hundred and eighty colonists to the New World. Raleigh's first attempt to plant a colony, was on Roanoke Island in Palmico Sound, but the settlers proved incompetent, they made no effort to till the soil, but wasted their time hunting for gold. They believed that the Roanoke river had its head waters in the "golden rocks" of the fabulous Eldorado. Not realizing their expectations, they were disheartened and returned to England. Fifteen only consented to stay and await the arrival of fresh colonists, but of these daring adventurers nothing was afterwards heard. Those returning home had learned the use of tobacco and imported into the motherland the custom of "drinking tobacco," as it was called.

In the year 1587 Raleigh again sent out a fleet, but it was equally unsuccessful. Fortunately for the American interests English trading vessels sailed occasionally across the Atlantic, also visiting Virginia and returning with valuable cargo. The favorable results of these commercial expeditions kept alive the desire to colonize the coast of North America.

Finally James I, in 1606 divided his American country into two districts, nearly equal in extent, and granted to a company of wealthy London merchants a patent of the southern part, situated between the 34th and 40th degree northern latitude. This "London Company" had the foundation of a colony for its object and it sent out in 1607 an expedition under the command of Christopher Newport, an experienced navigator. On the 26th day of April, 1607, they reached the Chesapeake Bay and at the mouth of a beautiful river, which they called the James in honor of the King, they laid the foundation of the first permanent English settlement at Jamestown in Virginia. This event is the starting point of the history of the mother colony of the United States of North America and at the same time *of the part the Germans took in establishing American civilization.*

Thus, after a period of one hundred and ten years after the time that Cabot discovered the North American continent, and after many misfortunes and disappointments, the Germanic element had planted the seedcorn from which was to grow the most glorious republic of the world. Whenever, at the present time, the name America is mentioned, we think little of the Latin race or the countrymen of Columbus, but of the Germanic immigration, that is the English and the Dutch, who, with the assistance of Germans, Scandinavians and others, gave to North America its truly Germanic character. In other words, we admire the growing empire of the world, the homestead of liberty, the United States of North America, as the standard bearer of civilization in the New World. Beside Virginia many other States have been organized in the Union as seats of modern culture, commerce and industry, art and science have developed, millions of men have found on the virgin soil of America new homesteads and enjoy the benefit of liberal institutions, which for the first time give to the old world an idea of true freedom. These are the blessings for which America and in fact all mankind are indebted to the Germanic pioneers in the New World.

PERIOD I.

The Colonial Time to the End of the 18th Century.

CHAPTER I.

The Settlement of Tidewater Virginia.

"IN the history of German immigration to the English colonies of North America during the last century Virginia takes a prominent share," says the late Vice-Governor of Illinois, Gustav Koerner,[1]) and he might have dated this statement back to the earliest time of colonization.

The early immigration of Germans to Virginia differs essentially, it must be admitted, from that under the leadership of Wm. Penn and Franz Pastorius to Pennsylvania, for unlike these it was not organized or compact. With the forenamed there came at once a large number of Germans to the New World, numerous additions followed and they kept together and founded German settlements which have preserved their national character to this day. But into Virginia the Germans immigrated singly, without a leader of their own nationality and without connection among themselves. Not until the beginning of the eighteenth century a German mass-immigration commenced from North Carolina, Pennsylvania, New Jersey and the Fatherland. The first comers scattered during the first decades of the colony over all its various sections, and yet the influence of this immigration proved of the greatest value to the development of Virginia or "Attanough Komouch," the Indian name of the country.

1.) „Das deutsche Element in den Ver. Staaten von Nord-Amerika," von G. Koerner, Seite 403. Cincinnati, Ohio, 1880.

The civilization of all countries began with the tilling of the soil or agriculture, and this was the case too in the old mother colony. It is generally admitted, that no part of the United States possesses greater natural advantages for the production of cereals, vegetables and orchard fruit than the "Old Dominion!" Situated in the most favorable latitude of the temperate zone, with variety of soil and enormous mineral resources, richly watered and with the best harbors on the Atlantic coast, it was well qualified to become the starting point of English colonization. But already in selecting the locality of the first settlement, the English colonists were injudicious by choosing a low and unhealthy section.

Early in 1607 the London Company sent out Captain Christopher Newport, with three small ships, the Susan Constance, the Discoverer and the God-speed, coming with one hundred and five men to establish a colony. Before the departure from England a form of government was prepared and all power was vested in a body of seven councillors, whose names were: Edward Maria Wingfield, president, and Capt. John Smith, Christ. Newport, John Ratcliffe, John Martin, Bartholomew Gosnold and George Kendall. The original intention was to settle on Roanoke Island, but a storm drove the little fleet into the Chesapeake Bay and it sailed up the "Powhatan River" to which the adventurers gave the name of "James." Upon its banks, about fifty miles from its mouth, they established the settlement "Jamestown." Unfortunately most of the settlers were English noblemen and adventurers, not fond of work and even despising it, and therefore, they were but little qualified to do the hard labors of pioneers. "Vagabond gentlemen" as they are called in some American histories for schools,[2 & 3]) they had no families and came in search of wealth, expecting when rich to return to England and to commence anew a life of dissipation. They imported into America nothing but their prejudice and faults, and even President Wingfield soon showed himself a heartless scoundrel. Not much good could be expected of such elements for the new colony.

---

2) "American History for Schools," by G. P. Quackenbos, p. 43. New York, 1877.

3) "History of the United States of America," by Ch A. Goodrich and W. Seavy, p. 31. N. Y. 1867.

Mr. Cooke[4]) who lived in Virginia on the old homestead of his ancestors and who took an earnest interest in the history of his native State, describes the precaution with which the ships of the daring seamen approached the coast and the landing of Newport's expedition as follows:

Before them was the great expanse of Chesapeake Bay, the "Mother of waters" as the Indian name signified, and in the distance the broad mouth of a great river, the Powhatan. As the ships approached the western shore of the bay the storm had spent its force, and they called the place Point Comfort. A little further, at the present Hampton, they landed and were hospitably received by a tribe of Indians. The ships then sailed on up the river, which was new-named James River, and parties landed here and there, looking for a good site for the colony. A very bad one was finally selected, a low peninsula half buried in the tide at highwater. Here the adventurers landed on May 13th, 1607, and gave the place the name of Jamestown, in honor of the King. Nothing remains of this famous settlement but the ruins of a church tower covered with ivy, and some old tombstones. The tower is crumbling year by year, and the roots of trees have cracked the slabs, making great rifts across the names of the old Armigers and Honourables. The place is desolate, with its washing waves and flitting sea-fowl, but possesses a singular attraction. It is one of the few localities which recall the first years of American history, but it will not recall them much longer. Every distinctive feature of the spot is slowly disappearing. The river encroaches year by year, and the ground occupied by the original huts is already submerged."

Mr. Cooke gives in his pretty description a fair picture of the unfitness of the first immigrants, and also unintentionally shows a characteristic difference between the English and the Germans, that exists to this day. His complaint concerning the unmitigated decay of the mementoes of such an important event, as the first settlement in Virginia was, is fully justified and deserves honorable mentioning, but this demonstrates also how

---

4) "Virginia," A History of the People, by John Esten Cooke, p. 19. Boston, Mass., 1883.

irreverent and little ideal the Anglo-Americans are in such matters in contrast with the Germans, who perhaps less smart and enterprising in the practices of life are of deeper feeling and reverence. Not until 1891 were the first steps taken to preserve the few remaining ruins of old Jamestown to posterity. Congress appropriated ten thousand dollars to prevent the further destruction of the island, and an embankment with ripraps has been built along the northern end, but the work is badly done, and already the bank is beginning to be undermined. Like "red tape" this characteristic difference between the two principal elements of the population is to be observed in the history of the Union and particularly of Virginia.

It is also not to be left unmentioned, that *the oldest printed publication* about Virginia is a German one. A chronological list of works up to Capt. Smith's death, 1631, published in "The English Scholar's Library," Birmingham, 1884, page cxxxii, names in the very first place: "1590–1650 Levinius Hulsius, A Collection of Voyages. In German-Frankfort." Furthermore, on page cxxxiv is stated, "In 1617, Hulsius, the German collector, translated Smith's description for his voyages and reengraved the map (drawn by Captain Smith); but the names in the lower corners were omitted, and Smith's title, the verses concerning him and some of the explanations were given in German. In regard to Capt. Smith's map, printed by Georg Low in London, is said in the same publication, "The original condition of the map bears in the lower left-hand corner, Simon Pasacus, sculpit," which appears to be a latinized German name.

Upon the banks of James river the colonists met with peaceable and hospitable Indians. Powhatan, the chief of the native confederacy, resided at Werowocomoco on the shores of York River. In the beginning friendly relations existed between the colonists and the savages, and Captains Newport and Smith in exploring the country up the James River and eastward to York River, frequently visited the kind-hearted chief in his wigwam. Capt. Smith[5]) reports also, "the savages often visited us kindly."

5.) "The Three Travels." Adventures and Observations of Capt. John Smith. Vol. I, p. 151. London edition, 1629, and republished at Richmond, Va., 1819.

In June 1607 Captain Newport sailed for England, leaving the smallest of his ships behind him and soon the colonists began to experience a variety of calamities. They were, as has already been stated, poorly fitted to struggle with life in the wilderness, neglecting to cultivate the soil and wasting their time in unsuccessful searches for gold. Among them, as stated in Capt. Smith's reports to the London Company, were only four carpenters and twelve laborers,[6]) and most of them were "Dutchmen."

A list of the "first planters" gives the following probably anglicized names of the four carpenters: William Laxon, Edward Pising, Thomas Emry and Robert Small, and in 1609, Adam and Francis, two stout Dutchmen, are mentioned. No distinction was made in those days between the appellations "Dutch" and "Deutsch or German." Germans and Hollanders came to England and America by way of the same Dutch harbors. However, Capt. John Smith, speaking of the natives of Holland in his "Description of New England," always calls them Hollanders *and not Dutch.* From a recommendation to the Council of Virginia[7]): "To send *to Germany* and Poland for laborers," it can safely be concluded, *that those carpenters and laborers were Germans, and that they have built the first dwelling houses in Virginia.* This conjecture appears the more plausible, as the other immigrants were not skilled to this work. Furthermore Capt. Smith had travelled through Poland *and Germany* and knew the Germans as an industrious and reliable people. He also ordered three of his "German" carpenters as he distinctly calls them and as will be further related, to build a house for the Indian Chief Powhatan, and that he made great efforts to persuade them to return, when they preferred to remain with the natives.

In "Hening's Statutes at Large," Vol. I, p. 114–118; dated July 24th, 1621, instructions drawn up by the Council, also refer to the care to be taken of Frenchmen, Dutch, Italians and others, and clearly indicate the presence of emigrants from various nations.

6.) "The English Scholar's Library." pp. 94 and 130. Birmingham, 1884; and "Historical Collections of Virginia," by Henry Howe, p. 24. Charleston, S. C., 1849.

7.) "The English Scholar's Library," pp. 194, 195, 196, 197, 444 &c. Birmingham, 1884; and "The Three Travels," by Capt. John Smith. Vol. I, p. 202. Richmond, Va., 1819.

The documents giving the names of the first comers are incomplete, but contain a number of German family names. In the letter to the Council, before mentioned, Capt. John Smith speaks with distinction of one *Capitaine Richard Waldo* and a *Maister Andrew Buckler*. The lists of the arrivals from 1607 to 1609, expressly confirm the presence of Dutch and Poles[8]) and contain the following names of German sound: *John Herd, Henry Leigh, Thomas Lavander, William, George* and *Thom. Cassen, Wm. Unger, Wm. May, Vere, Michaell, Peter Keffer*, a gunner, *Wm. Dowman, Thomas Feld*, apothecary, *Rose, Milman, Michaell Lowicke, Hillard, Nath. Graues*, (probably *Krause*,) etc. In a list of the names of the adventurers of Virginia, contained in a printed book edited by the treasurer and Council in 1620,[9]) we meet also with names of German sound as, *David Borne, Wm. Beck, Benjamin Brand, Charles Beck, George Bache, J. Ferne, J. Fenner, L. Campe, Abraham Colmer, John Francklin, Peter Franck, J. Geering, G. Holeman, J. Heiden, G. Herst, N. Hide, J. Harper, Christ. Landman, John Landman, H. Leigh, H. May, J. Miller, J. Martin, J. Mundz, Rich. Morer, Rich. Paulson, N. Salter, A. Speckhard, Henry Spranger, Dr. Wm. Turner, Rich. Turner, J. Treuer, J. Tauerner, R. and H. Venne, J. Weld, John Waller* and many doubtful names.

Provisions were scarce and of poor quality, sickness spread among the settlers, and before the beginning of winter 1607 one half had perished. Worse than all these misfortunes, the neighboring Indians, alarmed by the intrusion and unkind treatment of the whites, became jealous and hostile and refused to furnish supplies of corn, etc.

Fortunately in this desperate position Capt. Smith proved to be the right kind of man to meet the emergency and so deserves the predicate given to him, "the father of Virginia." He succeeded to quiet the savages, to persuade them to provide his starving followers with provisions and thereby saved the rest of the colonists from certain starvation.

However, upon his return to Jamestown, he discovered that President Wingfield was about to leave the colony with some of

---

8.) "The English Scholar's Library," pp. 108, 129 and 446. Birmingham, 1884; and "The Three Travels." Adventures and Observations of Capt. John Smith. Vol. I, pp. 153, 172, 173, 181, 203 and 205, from London edition of 1629, republished at Richmond, Va , 1819.

9) The Generall Historie of Virginia" etc , by Capt. John Smith. Vol. II, pp. 43 – 56. Richmond, Va., 1819.

his partisans and the most valuable stores on Capt. Newport's ship bound for the West Indies. He forced the treacherous President to stay, and Wingfield being disposed of, Capt. Smith was appointed to his office and restored order. He trained his English companions to swinging the axe in the woods and to till the soil, declaring that, "he who would not work, should not eat."

Soon new troubles arose with the Indians and Capt. Smith planned with *Capitaine Waldo*, (this name indicates that the Captain was a German or German descendant,) "upon whom he knew he could rely in time of need,"[10]) to subdue them. Not being very conscientious in regard to the means for accomplishing his design, he resolved to lurk the unsuspecting Powhatan into his power. In one of his reports he mentions, that he proposed to the Indian chief to erect for him a dwelling house after the European pattern and that he ordered three of his *German carpenters* and two Englishmen, "having so small allowance and few were able to do anything to purpose,"[11]) to do the job. He instructed these artisans to act also as spies and assist him to accomplish his object to get the Indian chief in his power. But the Germans learned to esteem the Indians and particularly the well meaning Powhatan, and finally they gave warning to the chief and resolved to stay and live with the sons of the wilderness. It seems that these men had endured many privations amidst the English, for Capt. Smith says, "it would have done well, but to send them and without victualls to work, was not so well advised nor considered of, as it should have been.'[12]) When Capt. Smith heard of this socalled treachery of the German workmen, he angrily remarked as "Fama" reports, "damned Dutch," and accordingly he ought to be looked upon as the author of the illbred predicate which is to this day in use by ill meaning people. Wherever different nationalities are mixed together, there will be some rivalry, and American life illustrates this fact from Capt. Smith's time to the present. It seems too, from the captain's statements, that the

10.) "The Three Travels." Adventures and Observations of Capt. John Smith Vol I, p. 204, from the London edition, 1629, and republished at Richmond, Va., 1819; and "The English Scholar's Library," pp. 130 and 447. Birmingham, 1884.

11.) Do. Vol. I, p. 205.

12.) Do. Vol. I, p. 193; and "The English Scholar's Library," p. 122. Birmingham, 1884.

"Dutchmen" had "English" confederates[13]) and it is well known, that dissatisfaction and discord split the colonists in adverse parties.

The intrigue of Capt. Smith reawakened the suspicion of the natives, and the bad feeling was increased to bitter hatred by the following occurrence. The Indians[14]) had raised an abundant harvest, but to secure a portion of it was no easy task for the colonists. Smith, however, determined to undertake it and in company with five companions he descended the James as far as Hampton Roads, where he landed, and went boldly among the savages, offering to exchange hatchets and coin for corn, but they only laughed at the proposal and mocked the strangers by offering a piece of bread for Smith's sword and musket. Smith, always determined to succeed in every undertaking, abandoned the idea of barter and resolved to fight. He ordered his men to fire upon the unarmed natives, who ran howling into the woods, leaving their wigwams, filled with corn, an easy prey of the English, but not a grain was touched until the Indians returned. In a short time sixty or seventy painted warriors, at the head of whom marched a priest bearing an idol, appeared and made an attack. The English gave fire a second time, made a rush, drove the savages back and captured their idol. The Indians, when they saw their deity in possession of the English, sent the priest to humbly beg for its return. Smith stood with his musket across the prostrate image and dictated the only terms upon which he would surrender it; that six unarmed Indians should come forward and fill his boat with corn. The terms were accepted, the idol given up, and Smith returned to Jamestown with a boat load of supplies, but leaving behind him enraged enemies.

Capt. Smith soon afterwards made several trips of exploration, thinking it possible to discover a passage to the Pacific. On one of these expeditions, while sailing up the Chickahominy river, he was attacked by a party of Indians and taken prisoner. His captors carried him before their chief Powhatan and after a long consultation he was condemned to die. The executioners rushed forward and dragged their victim to a large stone on which it

---

13) "The Three Travels." Adventures and Observations of Capt. John Smith. Vol. I, p. 218, from the London edition, 1629, republished at Richmond, Va., 1819.

14) "History of West Virginia," by Virgil A Lewis, p. 29 Philadelphia, 1889.

had been decided his head should be crushed. His head already rested on the stone, still shown at the old Mayo farm near Richmond, and the two warriors had raised the club to strike the fatal blow, when Pocahontas, the favorite daughter of the chief, threw herself upon the captive and implored her father to spare the life of the prisoner. Powhatan yielded to the maiden's prayer. Smith was released and in a few days concluded a bargain with the old chief, by which he was to receive a large tract of country in exchange for two cannon and a grindstone, which were to be sent from Jamestown. Accompanied by a guard of twelve men he arrived there after an absence of seven weeks, and under the pretext of instructing the Indian guardsmen in the use of the cannons, discharged them into the trees, at which the savages were so frightened, that they would have nothing to do with them. The grindstone proved so heavy, that they could not carry it, and finally they returned with only a number of trinkets.

Pocahontas, a girl of thirteen years of age, loved the captain dearly. She afterwards embraced the Christian faith and was baptized Rebecca. After the return of Smith to England in 1609, a young English settler, John Rolfe, assured her that Smith died and persuaded her to marry him. Three years later the couple visited England and she was received with great ceremony at the royal court. There she met with Captain Smith and it is said, that she died heart broken finding herself the victim of deceit. She left one son, who was educated in England and who then returned to Virginia, where several of the most prominent families claim to be his descendants.

The poetical Pocahontas tale has been related here in full, to prove the correctness of the assertion made previously in regard to the lack of devotion to the memoirs of history on part of Anglo-Americans. No prominent American poet has taken hold of this admirable story, but the German-American teacher, Johann Straubenmueller, published in German in 1858 at Baltimore, Md., a poem entitled: "Pocahontas or the foundation of Virginia." It is an astonishing fact, that more German-American, and even German poets, as for instance, Friedrich von Schiller[15]) and Nicolaus Lenau,[16]) have selected American

15) „Nadowessier's Todtenlied," by Friedrich von Schiller.

16.) „Der Indianerzug," „Die drei Indianer," etc., by Nicolaus Lenau.

myths and Indian life for their poetry and saved those precious pearls from falling into oblivion, than native American poets. The original painting of Pocahontas, a picture which has long been sought for and which is now ascertained to be in Norfolk, is probably too the work of a German artist, Nicolaus Locker.[17])

After friendly relations were again reestablished between Smith and Powhatan, the captain tried to induce the German carpenters sent to the Indian chief to return to Jamestown. He granted them full pardon and detailed a Swiss, by name William Volday, to persuade them, but his messenger also preferred to stay with the Indians and only one German, named *Adam*, availed himself of the captain's offer.[18]) Capt. Smith then charged the Dutchmen, — or the cursed countrymen of the Swiss Volda or Volday, as he called them, — to have conspired with the Spaniards to destroy the colony. In an interesting historical publication, "Die unbekannte neue Welt oder Beschreibung des Welttheils Amerika, by Dr. O. D., Amsterdam, 1673," of which a copy is in possession of Rev. Eduard Huber, Baltimore, Md., the unwise and oppressive treatment the Germans suffered by the English and their consequent enmity, is confirmed. On page 161 of this Dutch book is stated, "They (the Englishmen) had also many troubles with the High-Germans (Hochdeutschen,) which having been badly treated, joined the Virginians (the Indians) to destroy the English settlement." Thus it appears, that the grievances experienced, induced the German colonists to actions of a hostile character and that in those early days of the colony a want of harmony created a deplorable national calamity, which has continued in some degree to this day.

Being unable to induce the German mechanics to return to Jamestown, Capt. Smith persuaded Thomas Douse and Thomas Mallard "to bring the Dutchmen and the inconstant savages in such a manner amongst such ambuscades, as he had prepared, that not many of them should return from the peninsula."[19]) But Douse failed to accomplish his design.

---

17) "The English Scholar's Library," page 136. Birmingham, 1884.

18) "The Three Travels." Adventures and Observations by Capt. John Smith Vol. I, pp. 231, 232. Richmond, Va., 1819.

19.) "The English Scholar's Library," page 477. Birmingham, 1884.

In the spring and again in the fall of 1608 Capt. Newport arrived with provisions and new immigrants. Among the newcomers were a number of Poles and Germans, brought over with the purpose to manufacture pitch, tar, glass, sope-ashes, etc., but most of the new settlers were of the same sort as their predecessors, who in spite of the remonstrances of Smith, wasted their time in search of gold. Capt. Smith complained of the habits and character of the men sent out and entreated the council, "when they send out again, rather to send but thirty carpenters, husbandmen, gardeners, fishermen, blacksmiths, masons and diggers of tree roots, well provided, than a thousand of such as they had." The bad state of affairs continued and after two years of existence, there were but forty acres of cultivated land in the colony.

In the year 1609 the London Company obtained a new charter, granting enlarged territory and putting the management of affairs of the colony in the hands of a governor assisted by a council. Lord Delaware was appointed governor, after Capt. Smith, by the accidental explosion of a bag of gunpowder, had been wounded and obliged to return to England. Besides Jamestown, that was strongly palisaded, containing some fifty or sixty houses, he left five or six other forts and plantations. It was an unlucky day for the colony when Capt. Smith departed, — his actions had not always been free of harshness and cruelty, — but the circumstances that surrounded him may serve for his excuse, — and when he had left, disorder, sickness and famine ensued. The winter of 1609 to 1610 was properly termed "the starving time." Of the 490 persons whom Smith left, only sixty survived, and it may safely be accepted, that most of the survivors belonged to the industrious, sober working class from the European continent, while the English fortune seekers, carrying on a dissipate life, perished. Capt. Smith stated,[20]) "the adventurers never knew what a day's work was, except the Dutchmen and Poles, and some dozen others. For all the rest were poor gentlemen, tradesmen, serving men, libertines and such like, ten times more fit to spoil a commonwealth, than either begin one, or but help to maintain one."

20) "The Three Travels." Adventures and Observations. Vol. I, p. 241. Richmond, 1819.

The Indians, no longer afraid, began to harass the unfortunates, who concluded to desert the settlement and to sail to Newfoundland. Nearing the mouth of the James river, they descried a fleet entering Hampdon roads. It was Lord Delaware with new colonists and provisions, and the disheartened fugitives were persuaded to return to the abandoned Jamestown. The new arrivals were of a better class and by the judicious management of the governor the future of the colony wore a brighter aspect.

Among the new settlers were many Dutch and Germans, they plowed the soil, corn was raised in abundance and no further famine again endangered the lives of the colonists. Tobacco and cotton were extensively cultivated for export, and tobacco was used as money, being worth about 75 cents a pound. Capt. Waldo, before mentioned and highly esteemed by Capt. Smith, went to England and persuaded the merchants to commence mining in Virginia. But the mines he had found did not prove rich and he was treated as an impostor and died most miserably.[21]) The remains of an iron furnace[22]) are found in Chesterfield County, five or six miles below Richmond, described by Berkeley in his History of Virginia as being worked in 1620. Very likely these iron works were established by Capt. Waldo. In the Price-Lists of 1621 iron is marked at twelve pounds sterling per ton, but in 1622 the Chesterfield furnace was broken up by the massacre of the Indians under the chief Opechancanough.

Ill health soon obliged governor Delaware to give up the administration of the colony and he was succeeded by Sir Thomas Dale. The last act of governor Dale marks an era in the history of Virginia. Ever since the foundation of the colony all property was held in common, the settlers worked together and the products of the harvest were deposited in a common storehouse and distributed by the council. Governor Dale now introduced the policy of assigning to each settler a few acres of land to be his own, and the advantages of this system soon became apparent in the general improvement.

---

21) "The Three Travels." Adventures and Observations. Vol. I, p. 241. Richmond, 1819.

22.) "The Hand-Book of Virginia," p. 64 Fifth Edition Richmond, Va, 1886.

In the year 1611 the colony counted 200 inhabitants and the settlements extended on both sides of the James. In several of the reports to the London Company the presence of Germans is confirmed and they show, that the administration appreciated diligent labor and endeavored to encourage immigration from France, Germany, Switzerland, and Holland. The intolerance of the clergy and of the worldly rulers in Europe furthered the realization of this plan.

Before 1619 the colonists had no part in the making of the laws by which they were governed, but in that year, under the administration of Sir George Yeardley, a representative government was established, and in order to further ensure the permanency of the colony through the establishment of family life, one hundred and fifty agreeable young women, poor but respectable, were brought over. They were sold to the planters in marriage bound at the cost of their transportation expenses, at the price of one hundred pounds of tobacco, and the demand exceeding the supply, other transports were furnished and the price advanced to 150 pounds. This almost comic transaction proved of the highest merit, as domestic and moral life was its result and even the restless adventurers relinquished the fondled hope of returning to the mother land.

It is very probable that many of the German settlers married English women and thereby became anglicized.

Acquisitions of a different and decidedly unfavorable character were also made to the population of the colony. One hundred criminals were, by the order of King James, sent over to be sold for a term of years as servants to the planters, and this beginning created a desire on part of some of the colonists to employ labor and the opportunity to gratify it came only too soon.

In 1620 a Dutch ship from Africa touched at Jamestown and landed twenty negroes, who were sold for lifetime as slaves, and thus the abominable institution of slavery was introduced, spreading gradually over the entire territory of the English colonies — and it became the curse of the inhabitants. In the beginning slavery was only silently tolerated, but in the course of time slave holding, slave breeding and slave trade were protected by law. However, the great majority of the colonists were opposed to the institution and especially to the importation of negroes, and only through the influence of the large land-owners, mostly English lords, was slavery forced on Virginia. Twenty-three statutes were passed by the House of Burgesses *to prevent the importation of slaves,* but all were vetoed by the English government. The general education was purposely neglected and even from the pulpit slavery was declared to be a divine institution.[23]) The Church was urged to keep the mass of the people in a state of ignorance, for fear, that with the progress of intellect the right of humanity might be recognized. Sir William Berkeley, who was appointed governor in 1641, said in the year 1671 in a report to the English government, "I thank God there are no free-schools or printing, for learning has brought disobedience and heresy and sects into the world, and printing has divulged them and libels against the best government. God keep us from both!"—And in fact, not until 1736 was the first newspaper published in Virginia.[24]) In 1730 a prohibitory law was issued, forbidding the German printer *John Buckner,* who had set up *the first printing press* in the mother colony, to publish in print the laws of the government." A school law was not passed by the Assembly until 1796, and it was never carried out. In 1818 and 1846 additional laws were passed, but unfortunately,[25]) as in the case of the law of 1796, it was left optional with the counties to adopt or reject it, and the result was a failure to secure any State system. The census of 1860 showed only 85, 443 pupils in 3778 schools, so-called, though many were but private classes in which some public fund pupils were instructed. Not until the year 1870 was the present excellent public school law inaugurated in Virginia and at once the enrolment showed for that year 157,841 pupils in all schools, — an immense advance on any previous year.

Slave holding also had most injurious effects on the development of industry and commerce. As long as the mass of a people is without an own income, — as long as all the pro-

---

23) "Geschichte der deutschen Schulbestrebungen in Amerika," by Herrmann Schuricht, p. 4. Leipzig, 1884.

24) Compare, "History of Printing," by Thomas.

25.) Report of the Commissioner of Education for 1876, p 401. Washington, government printing office, 1878.

ducts of the soil are the property of a few, —there is no market except for farm produce and no exchange for surplus. This is shown by statistics. Of imports, the share of the South as compared with the free states before the war of secession, was like 40 to 321, and this proves, that a very small portion of the southern commerce was in southern hands. There certainly would have been tenfold more commerce and manufacture in Virginia and the other southern states, if there had been intelligent, industrious and patriotic free laborers, receiving pay for their work and spending their money for the necessaries and luxuries of life. But for slavery, Virginia would to-day be, as it was in 1790, the most populous state of the Union, as well as the most wealthy and influential. Slavery still had another disastrous effect, — it has the tendency to degrade free labor and to render the free laborer worthless. The habit of giving preference to slave-labor has operated to the prejudice of free labor. It has caused the population of little means to grow up in idleness, to think labor degrading, to be incapable of earnest regular work, and it kept away immigration of white workingmen, because they disliked to be looked down upon and treated as negroes.

The German settlers, whose number was much larger than is generally conceded, were with very few exceptions opposed to slavery, — resulting to their great disadvantage. The slaveholders consequently distrusted the Germans and a new feeling of animosity towards them sprang up. Their political influence was curtailed, and the majority of them submitted in order to secure toleration and peace. In this way a valuable civil element was almost excluded from building up the future state, — but only in political respects and not in its social and economical life. In farming and in commerce the Germans became important factors, as will be shown hereafter. But outside of slavery there was another obstacle in the path of quick development of the colony, that impeded foreign and particularly German immigration.

"The feudal system," says Mr. Ben. Perley Poor,[26]) "was transplanted to Virginia from England and the royal grants of

---

26.) "History of Agriculture of the United States," by Ben. Perley Poor, U. S. Agricultural Report of 1866, p. 505.

land gave the proprietors, — mostly favorites of the King, — baronial power. One of these grants or "patents," as they were called, gave the patentee the right to divide the said tract or territory of land into counties, hundreds, parishes, tithings, townships, hamlets and boroughs, and to erect and build cities, towns, etc., and to endow the same at their free will and pleasure, and did appoint them full and perpetual patrons of all churches, with power also to divide a part or parcel of said tract or territory, or portion of land, into manors and to call the same after their own or any of their names, or by other name or names whatsoever; and within the same to hold court in the nature of a court baron, and to hold pleas of all actions, trespasses, covenants, accounts, contracts, detinues, debts, and demands whatsoever when the debt or thing demanded exceed not the value of forty shilling, sterling money of England, and to receive and take all amercements, fruits, commodities, advantages, perquisites and emoluments whatsoever, to such respective court barons belonging or in any wise appertaining and further, to hold within the same manors a court lect and view of frank pledge of all the tenants, residents and inhabitants of the hundred within such respective manors, etc."

The power being thus vested in the hands of a few lords, desirable immigrants did not come in large numbers as had been expected. Convicts and a great many indentured white servants, Irish and Scotch prisoners of war, were sent over from England in and after the year 1621, — but after a generation or two all these elements became blended into a homogeneous mass of "cavaliers,"— aristocratic because they had an inferior race beneath them.

Still, in spite of all the mismanagement and unlucky circumstances, the colony extended its lines and soon after immigration began to penetrate into the interior.

Until the death of Powhatan in 1618 the settlers lived fairly in peace with the natives, but after his brother Opechancanough (speak Ope-kan-kano) became the head of the confederate tribes, the relations changed. Eyeing with suspicion the increasing numbers of the palefaces, he laid a murderous plan in 1622 for their total extermination.

Mr. Virgil A. Lewis[27]) describes the cruel massacre, which also caused the death of many a German settler, as follows: "In order to avoid suspicion, he, Opechancanough, renewed the treaty of peace with governor Wyatt, and only two days before the blow was to be struck he declared that the sky should fall before he would violate the terms of the treaty. The friendly relations were continued up to the very day, even to the fatal hour. They borrowed boats from the English, brought in venison and other provisions for sale and sat down to breakfast with their unsuspecting victims. The hour arrived. It was twelve o'clock noon on the 22nd day of March, 1622, when every hamlet in Virginia was attacked by a band of yelling savages, who spared neither age, sex nor condition. The bloody work went on until 347 men, women and children had fallen victims at the barbarous hands of that perfidious and inhuman people." The "Colonial Records of Virginia," published by order of the Senate, Richmond, Va., 1874, contain a list of all those that were massacred by the savages, and this document gives the following names of Germans, besides a very large number of doubtful names, but of probably German origin: *Robert Horner*, *Samuel Stringer*, *Georg Soldan*, *Th. Freeman*, *Edw. Heyden*, *Edw. Lister*, *John Benner*, *Thomas Sheffeld* and *Robert Walden*.

Had not a converted Indian, who lived with a man named Pace, revealed the plot and so put the people of Jamestown and neighboring settlements on their guard, and therefore in a state of defence, every settlement would have been laid in ruins and the inhabitants put to the tomahawk. So the plan failed. There were yet 1600 fighting men in the colony and the Indians were made to pay dear for their perfidy. The English pushed into the wilderness, burning wigwams, killing every Indian that fell into their hands, and destroying the crops, until the foe was driven far into the interior. Confidence was once more restored, and a feeling of security brought a return of prosperity; immigration revived and at the end of the year the population numbered 2500."

Especially one class of the English immigrants caused the dissatisfaction and provocation of the natives, namely the *pio-*

27.) "History of West Virginia," by Virgil A. Lewis, pp. 46, 47. Phila, Pa., 1889.

neers, who strongly contrasted with the cavalier planters and the regular settlers.[28]) Generally speaking, they were the younger sons, unlucky gamesters, turbulent spirits, rejected lovers and disbanded soldiers, who turned their backs on civilization to live an untrammeled life in some fertile mountain gap or rich river bottom. Game was plentiful and they were hunters and trappers rather than farmers, sending their peltries to market and only cultivating enough land to supply their immediate wants. This unrestrained life became a passion and frequently led to conflicts with the Indians, who claimed the forests as their hunting ground, — and the peaceful and active farmers on the frontier, mostly Germans, suffered much on this account.

The London Company had not gained any profit by the colonization of Virginia so far. She had sent over more than 9000 persons at an expense of about 100,000 pounds sterling, — many of the immigrants perished, others had joined the Indians or left the country, — and after eighteen years of existence the colony counted only 2500 inhabitants, and the annual export scarcely amounted to 20,000 pounds.

King James too was little pleased with these meagre results, and when the Indian troubles commenced and the very existence of the colony was endangered, he dissolved the company and in 1624 Virginia was declared a royal province. The Colonial Assembly was however allowed to exercise its former power, and by and by the importance of Virginia was felt. A thousand immigrants arrived in the single year 1627 and took to farming whereever fertile land invited them.

The "Colonial Records of Virginia" contain lists of the living and dead in Virginia on Feb. 16th, 1623, that give the following German names: *William Welder*, *Margaret Berman*, *Henry Coltman*, *Mrs. Coltman*, *Petters*, *Richard Spurling* (*Sperling*), *John Landman*, *Daniel Vergo*, *Wm. Boocke*, *Walter Priest*, *Henry Turner*, *Edw. Bricke*, *Elizabeth Salter*, *Ch. Waller*, *Georg Graues*, *Th. Spilman*, *Th. Rees*, *John Rose*, *Wm. Stocker*, *Wm. Kemp*, *George Fryer*, *Peter Staber*, *John Filmer*, *John Rachell* and *Margarett Pollentin*, *Adam Rumell*, *Nicholas Wesell*, *John Salter*, *Cornelius* and *Elizabeth May* and child, *Wm. Cappe*, *Peter*

28) "History of the Agriculture of the United States," by Ben. Perley Poor, Agricultural Report of the U. S., p. 506, Washington, 1867.

Longman, Robert Winter, Richard Spriese, Sam. Foreman, Daniel Francke, Rich. Ranke, Vallentyne Gentler, Th. Horner, Cathrin Cappe and a very large number of doubtful names.

Tobacco had become the staple product of Virginia and efforts were made to also encourage other branches of rural industry. Cotton was first planted in 1621 and its cultivation was now promoted. King James I, prompted doubtless by his antipathy to "the Virginia weed," as he termed the tobacco plant, and having understood that the soil naturally yielded store of excellent mulberries, gave directions to urge the cultivation of silk and to erect silk-mills. Men of experience were brought over from France, Switzerland and Germany, and premiums were offered to encourage the raising of the silk-worm, and later also that of indigo, hops and other agricultural staples; but fresh disturbances interfered.

The war with the Indians just ended, the political and religious troubles in England, the immorality of the royal court, the corruption of the office holders, the animosity of the tories and wighs, the contest between the church and its opponents, and finally the establishment of a republican government by Cromwell, exercised their convulsive influences even upon distant Virginia.

After the restoration of Charles II to the throne of his beheaded father, he failed to fulfill the expectations of his people, who were in hope that the king, who had gone through a school of misfortune, would give his country peace and prosperity. But Charles II soon lost the confidence and respect of his subjects. He was incapable of resolute action and self-sacrifice, without trust in humanity or virtue. "He was a drunkard, a libertine, and a hypocrite, who had neither shame nor sensibility and who in point of honor was unworthy to enter the presence of the meanest of his subjects."[29])

To have the throne occupied for a quarter of century by such a man as this one, was the surest way of weakening that ignorant and indiscriminate loyalty to which various people have often sacrificed their dearest rights, and to shake the faith in the

29) "History of Civilization in England," by Henry Thomas Buckle. Vol. I, p. 280. New York, 1870.

continuance of public welfare. Charles II deceived the Protestants by favoring the Catholics, and he rushed England into unlucky wars. He wounded the national pride of his people by the sale of Duenkirchen to Louis XIV of France, and by the defeat in the war with Holland. England, which had advanced during the republican administration to the first naval power of Europe, had to endure the mortification, that a Dutch fleet under de Ruyter sailed up the Thames and alarmed the city of London by the thunder of its cannon. In the treaty of Dorn Charles II agreed to adopt the Catholic faith and to support the claim of the King of France on the Spanish throne with his fleet and army, while on the other hand Louis XIV obliged himself to pay subsidies and to land an army in England in case of revolution. Henry Thomas Buckle says,[30]) "Politically and morally there were to be found in the government all the elements of confusion, of weakness and of crime. The king himself was a mean and spiritless voluptuary, without the morals of a Christian and almost without the feeling of man. His ministers had not one of the attributes of statesmen and nearly all of them were pensioned by the crown of France."

The English possessed a great deal of national self-esteem and all the disgrace that the king brought over Great Britain wounded them deeply. The same effect was visible in the English colonies and finally resulted in outbursts of indignation. This was particularly the case in Virginia, where a great number of disgusted English and Scotch refugees had settled, while the immigrants from the European continent possessed no special attachment to the English throne and advocated American independence. The rights of the mass of the colonists were everywhere restricted. Sir William Berkeley, who had held the office of governor by the will of the people, and who had administered the colonial affairs in a liberal manner, was confirmed by Charles II in 1660, but thereupon commenced a rule of despotism and oppression, — the affairs of the Church were placed in the hands of vestries, — and the Assembly composed of aristocrats made themselves permanent. Prospects grew dark!

---

30) "History of Civilization in England," by Henry Thomas Buckle. Vol. I, p. 275. New York, 1870.

During the time of the Commonwealth in the year 1651, Parliament had extended its authority to America, and in an act required all the exports from the colonies to England to be carried in English or colonial vessels. Virginia expected after the Restoration, in acknowledgment of her loyalty, some special marks of the king's favor, but by compulsory laws, as the above mentioned, she was required to look to England as her sole market for her exports and to receive from England alone her imports. In 1672 duties were even imposed upon articles carried from one colony to another, and these aggressions drove the colonists finally to insurrection.

But the great natural wealth of the land assisted, in spite of restrictions and obstructions, the progress of Virginia. Among the various strange and surprising things which the settlers found on Virginian soil, were a great variety of wild grape vines, and the London Company determined, as early as 1630, to make some experiments with the culture of the European canes through French and German experts. The favorite drinks of the English were, at that time: portwine, sherry and madeira, and it is easy to understand, that they desired to produce wines of this character in Virginia. Premiums were offered to encourage the cultivation of vines, but the delicate European sorts did not resist the injuries of climate and insects, and the results were unsatisfactory.

At about the same time a German-Bohemian named *Augustine Herrmann*, from Prague in Bohemia, came to Virginia.[31]) His name is mentioned also with distinction in the annals of other North-American colonies, as, New Amsterdam, now New York,—New Jersey and Maryland, and in fact the Dutch colonies are principally entitled to claim him as theirs, but his services in regard to Virginia are of such great merit, that his name ought for all time to be given a place of honor in her history.

There is very little known about the early life of Herrmann, — even the year of his birth is only judged to be 1605. It seems that he came to Virginia in 1629, for in a petition addressed to the Dutch governor Stuyvesant, dated 1654, he says: "Without

31) "Deutsch-Amerikanisches Magazin," H. A. Rattermann. Numbers 2 and 4. Cincinnati, O., 1886.

specially praising myself, *I am the founder of the Virginia tobacco trade*, and it is well known that in a short time great advantages for the public welfare have been called forth thereby." This assertion of Herrmann has never been controverted, and as a memorial of the deputies of the Dutch West India Company, dated November 16th, 1629, speaks of "a large quantity of tobacco, which now has become an important article of trade,[32]) it may safely be accepted that the above statement in respect to the time of his arrival in Virginia is correct.

Later Herrmann removed to New Amsterdam and began business of his own and as agent for Peter Gabry & Co., Amsterdam. He was also a wholesale dealer in wine, bought and sold furs, Virginia cotton and tobacco, which he exported to Holland. It is proved by documents that he received the last named articles, by the intervention of *Georg Hack* in Northampton, Va., whose wife was a sister of Mrs. Herrmann, né Jeanetie Verlet, from Utrecht, and who frequently visited her relatives in New Amsterdam. In exchange for Virginia products Herrmann supplied his brother-in-law with all kinds of imported goods.

Georg Hack apparently was a man of energy and influence, who took an active part in politics. He was one of the subscribers to the so-called "engagement of Northampton,"[33]) dated March 25th, 1651, by which the county declared itself in favor of Parliament, respectively of Cromwell and the republic. This action of Hack deserves special mention, as most Virginians were at that crisis loyal royalists and bitterly opposed the "Navigation Act" enforced by the British Parliament. This law, as has been stated, prohibited export and import except to and from England and was necessarily a severe blow to the foreign trade established by Hack's brother-in-law. Georg Hack appears therefore as a man of character, who would rather sacrifice the interests of his relative and his own, than depart from his principles.

Herrmann on the other hand defended the interests of the Dutch with energy and soon gained respect and influence. Several times during the period of the Commonwealth, he was

---

32) L. van Aitzema, "Historie van Saken van Staet en Oorlogh, in ende omtrent de Vereen Nederland, etc." 4° edition Vol. II, p. 912. An English translation is to be found in: "Documents relating to the colonial history of New York." Vol. I, pp. 40–42.

33.) "Virginia Historical Register." Vol. I, p. 163.

sent as ambassador by governor Stuyvesant to Virginia and Maryland, and his reports are still preserved in the state archive of New York at Albany.[34])

Besides his creditable doings as merchant and statesman, he gained fame in another way. He advocated, as early as 1659, in a letter to governor Stuyvesant: an accurate geographical survey of the English and Dutch colonies,[35]) and he was possessed of the talent and knowledge to undertake the difficult work himself. He was well posted in literature, spoke the most important languages: German, English, Dutch, French, Spanish and Latin, and he was an efficient draughtsman, mathematician and surveyor. Edwin R. Purple calls him[36]) "a man of good education, a surveyor by profession, talented in sketching and a draughtsman, — a smart and enterprising business man, — a rare and noble man, — and an admirer of this country."

Probably the map of the New Netherland, printed by Nicolaus Jan Visscher and contained in von der Donk's book, "Beschreyvings van Nieuw Nederland," published at Amsterdam in 1655, was drawn by Herrmann, as it is certain, that the view of New Amsterdam, which is also contained in the book, originates from him. Beyond all doubt he has drawn in 1670 the "map of the English and Dutch colonies," which was published by the government in 1673 and embraces the section between the line of North Carolina and the Hudson river. Although incorrect in several respects, it gives a very comprehensive picture of the land, mouths of rivers and inlets of the sea. Virginia is particularly well drawn, and Herrmann must have explored the tidewater-region very carefully. The map shows the likeness of its designer with the inscription, "Augustine Herrmann, Bohemian," and a vignette with the inscription, "Virginia and Maryland as it was planted and inhabited this present year 1670. Surveyed and exactly drawn by our own labor and endeavor of Augustine Herrmann, Bohemiensis," and at the side of which are represented a young Indian with bow and arrow, and an Indian girl.

It is of great interest that Herrmann's map also gives some German names of places in Virginia, as: Scharburg and Backer's

---

34) "Dutch Manuscript." Vol. XVIII, p. 96.

35) "Deutsch-Amerikanisches Magazin." Copy 4, pp. 535 to 536.

36) "The New York Genealogical and Biographical Record." Vol. IX, pp. 57 to 58.

Creek. This is almost proof, that in the very infancy of the colony German settlements existed. Augustine Herrmann died in 1686.

It appears also that Germans occupied high political offices, before and during the governorship of Sir Wm. Berkeley. One *Richard Kempe* was secretary of the land office of Henrico in 1624, member of the council of Virginia in 1642, president of this body in 1644, and during the time Sir Berkeley visited England, *acting governor*. The name Kempe is undoubtedly German, but some historians write him "Kemp," and claim erroneously that this form of the name is English. Yet Kemp, as well as Kempe, are to this day German family names and the land-registers of Henrico of 1624[37]) contain many signatures in Rich. Kempe's own handwriting—and with but one exception he signed "Kempe." Furthermore all biographies of the English colonial governors[38]) give the name of their native land, county and birthplace, with the sole exception of R. Kempe's biography, and this omission also speaks for his German origin. Surely there is no full evidence that R. Kempe was a German, but the probabilities are in favor of it.

During the same period some Germans rendered very valuable services by exploring the unknown country in the interior.

Johannes Lederer was the first explorer of the Alleghany mountains, and he is one of the brightest figures in the early history of the German element in Virginia. The German-American historian H. A. Rattermann, of Cincinnati, O., deserves credit for the preservation of the great deeds of Lederer,[39]) and an extract from his researches may find room at this place.

In the year 1668 Johannes Lederer came to Jamestown and offered his services to governor Berkeley. "A son of the Alps," as he said, "he had come to explore America." He was a scientific man and familiar with several languages, especially the classical, and he expressed the desire to explore the mountain region. Governor Berkeley readily equipped an expedition to

---

37.) "Land Patents No I," preserved in the land office, Capitol Building, Richmond, Va.

38.) "Virginia and the Virginians," by Dr. Brook, Secretary of the Historical Society of Virginia.

39.) "Der erste Erforscher des Alleghany Gebirges: Johannes Lederer," by H. A. Rattermann, "Deutscher Pionier." Jahrgang 8. Cincinnati, O., 1876.

accompany him. Lederer undertook three trips, but failed to discover an easy passage through the mountains, which the governor wished for. During his last expedition his companions became disheartened and deserted him, while he ventured to continue his researches with only an Indian guide, who served him as interpreter. At his return he was ill-treated, — his companions, ashamed of their cowardice, circulated false reports about him, — and finding even his life endangered, he fled to Maryland. Sir William Talbot, governor of the colony, received him kindly, and upon his suggestion he wrote an account of his trips in Latin, which was printed in English in London in 1672 with a map of the country drawn by the author. This interesting little book was entitled: "The Discoveries of John Lederer, in Their Several Marches From Virginia to the West of Carolina and Other Parts of the Continent, begun in March, 1669, and Ended in September, 1670, Etc., with Map, London, 1672." and contains 27 pages, 4°. A copy of it is preserved in the library of the U. S. Congress at Washington City. It is the first scientific report about the geology, botany, animals and native tribes of the extensive district as far as Florida, seen by the courageous German, and it deserves special acknowledgment in a German-American history, giving evidence, that the first exploration of the Alleghanies was the work of a German.

Very little is known of Lederer himself and no reports are left of his later career and end. The family name of Lederer is well known in Austria and Germany. At Wittenberg in Prussia, Grossenhain in Saxony, Marburg in Hessia, Vienna and Innsbruck in Austria, etc., several members of this illustrious family occupied high positions. Some Lederers held diplomatic offices in the United States of America. One, Baron Alois Lederer, was Consul General of Austria and Toscana at New York, and his son Carl was ambassador at Washington City in 1868.

Lederer's map, which appeared with his book, gives only an inaccurate picture of the country, but it must be taken in consideration that his instruments had been carried off by his faithless companions. It shows the land from Virginia to Florida.

In those early times maps only gave general outlines, and all parts not explored had to be guesswork. This may be illustrated by the following.

"A Map of Virginia discovered to ye Hills," 1651, gives to the American continent from the southern cape of Delaware to "the sea of China and the East Indies," a width of less than 300 miles. — On Hennepin's map of 1683, Lake Erie extends to the southern line of Virginia, making the entire state of Ohio part of the lake. — A map of Wm. Delisle, published by Joh. Justin Gebauer and affixed to Bruzen la Martinier's "Introduction à l'histoire de l'Asie, de l'Afrique et de l'Amerique, etc.," Paris, 1735, presents nothing of the Ohio river and places the source of the Wabash near the Erie in Pennsylvania. — More accurate is a map: "Nouvelle France," by Charlevoix, 1743. — The "Carte de la Virginie et du Maryland, dressée sur la grande carte anglaise de Messrs. Josue Fry[40]) and Pierre Jefferson par Robert de Vaugondy, Géographe ordinaire du Roi," 1755, gives a fair picture of the lands along the coast of the Atlantic, but the section on the other side of the Blue Ridge and the Alleghanies is very inaccurately drawn, — and the same may be said in respect to the old map designed by Augustine Herrmann.

Another German explorer of Virginia is mentioned by Klauprecht, the chronicler of the Ohio valley,—by John Esten Cook,—and by Stierlein in his history of Kentucky and the city of Louisville: the German *Capt. Heinrich Batte,* who in 1667 crossed the Alleghanies and reached the Ohio river.

All these historical facts show that the colonial governments have used German scientific men to open the wilderness to civilization, and the history of North Carolina, the neighboring state of the Old Dominion, furnishes further evidence.

In 1663 a German Swiss, *Peter Fabian,* from Bern, accompanied an expedition sent out by the English North Carolina Company. The report of this exploring expedition appeared in London in 1665 and bears the signatures of its leaders: Anthony Long, Wm. Milton and Peter Fabian. The last named was certainly the author of the report and the scientific man of the expedition, as is shown by the estimates of distances in *German*

---

40) Mr. Josue Fry has drawn several maps of North America, and his name — Fry, or Frei, or Frey, — indicates that he was a German or of German descent.

S. Kercheval, the historian of the Shenandoah Valley, says (History of the Valley of Va., Winchester, 1833, p. 81): "There were a mixture of Irish and Germans on Cedar Creek and its vicinity: the *Frys*, Newells, Blackburns, Wilsons, etc., were among the number."

and not in English mileage. The report, for instance, states: "On Friday, the 16th, we heaved anchor by north-west wind and sailed up River Cape-Fair 4 or 5 *German* miles, where we came to anchor at 5 to 7 fathoms."

Before the end of the seventeenth century the administration of the Swiss Canton Bern planned to establish colonies in North America with the surplus of her population. *Franz Ludwig Michel*[41]), — English historians misname him Mitchell, — was sent to Pennsylvania, Virginia and North Carolina, and John Lawson, the first historian of North Carolina, relates in his book: "A new voyage to Carolina, etc.," printed at London, 1709, and published in German by M. Vischer, Hamburg, in 1712, — that he met on his voyage to the Carolinas the German explorer, who was well acquainted with the land and its people.[42]) Michel again came to North Carolina in 1709, accompanied by *Baron Christopher von Grafenried*, of Bern, at the head of 1500 emigrants from Switzerland and the Palatinate, (die Pfalz in Germany), — all of whom were Germans. Many of these people afterwards settled in Virginia, as will be related further on.

Towards the close of the seventeenth and in the beginning of the eighteenth century, under the leadership of Claude Philippe de Richebourg, another numerous immigration of French Huguenots and German Calvinists or Reformists from Elsace and Loraine took place. These newcomers were industrious and pious people and they scattered successively over the tide-water district, middle Virginia and the Shenandoah valley, but most of them settled in the counties of Norfolk, Surry, Powhatan and Prince William. In the Shenandoah valley they met with a numerous German element and these French Huguenots were perfectly Germanized.

In 1671, by issue of the first law of naturalization, immigration was materially supported. This law prescribed that any

---

41) "Die Deutschen in Nord-Carolina." Historische Skizze von General J. A. Wagener, Charleston, S. C., publicirt in: "Der deutsche Pionier," Jahrgang III, Seite 328 etc. Cincinnati, Ohio, 1871.

42) "Beitrag zur Geschichte der Deutschen in Nord- und Süd-Carolina," von H. A. Rattermann, publicirt in: "Der deutsche Pionier," Jahrgang X, Seite 189. Cincinnati, Ohio, 1878.

foreigner could be naturalized upon application to the Assembly and by taking the oath of allegiance to the King of England, and that thereafter he should be entitled to hold public office, carry on business, own real estate, etc. The first Germans who applied for naturalization papers were *Joseph Mulder*, *Heinrich Weedich*, *Thomas Hastmenson*, *John Peterson* and *Hermann Keldermann* in 1673.

The number of German settlers during the first century of the existence of the colony was, as has been stated, much larger than is commonly admitted, and some Anglo-American historians unfairly ignore or belittle the share the Germans have taken in the development of Virginia, desiring to represent it as an "entirely English colony." But the old mother colony was from the very beginning *in its character cosmopolitan*, only founded by English enterprise. The following investigations will prove how incorrect and devoid statements of such "manufacturers of history" are.

The Land Patents (Registers) at the land office of Virginia, Capitol building, Richmond, Va., name as early as 1624 to 1635, or during the third decade of the colony, besides many doubtful names, the following German ones: Johann Busch, Thomas Spilman (Spielmann), John Choohman (Schumann), Ph. Clauss, Zacharias Crippe, Christopher Windmill (Windmueller), Henry Coleman (Kohlmann or Kuhlmann), John Loube (Laube), John and Mary Brower (Brauer), Georg Koth, Thomas Holeman (Hollmann or Hoelemann), Robert Ackerman, etc.

The oldest volume of the county-records, kept at Henrico Courthouse at Richmond, Va., referring to inheritances, criminal investigations, etc., mentions as prosecutors, defendants and witnesses among many names that may just as well be English as German, the following Germans:

1677—William Hand, Th. Gregory, John Bowman (Baumann.)

1678—Margarete Horner.

1679—John Gunter (Guenther), Katherine Knibbe, Georg Kranz and Thos. Risboc, — the last two in German letters.

1680—Thom. Brockhouse (Brockhaus), Georg Archer, John Harras and W. T. Eller, — the last three in partial German writing.

1681—J. Tanner, Edm. Bollcher, Rob. Bolling, Th. Grouse (Krause), and in German writing: John Feil.

1682-86—Doll, Rich. Starke, Mary Skirme, Henry Shurmann (that is: Schuermann, — in later entries the same man signs: Sherman), — Thos. Ruck, Joshua Stap (probably Stapf), and in German letters: Will. Blachman.

Taking in consideration the small number of white settlers, these German names in the registers and records of a single county, which was at the time still predominantly inhabited by Indians, are proof that the German immigration was numerally worthy of notice.

The limits of the counties of Norfolk and Princess Ann originally from 1637 to 1691 formed "Lower Norfolk County." Edward W. James mentions in his "Antiquary" among the earliest landowners the following names of German sound: Samuel Boush, John Weblin, Thos. Wishart, Capt. James Kempe, Wm. Wishart, Thos. and Wm. Brock, Robert Waller, Jeremiah and Matthew Forman, L. Miller, Abrah. Mesler, Robert Fry (schoolmaster of Norfolk Borough), Wm. Plume (member of the Common Council, Norfolk Borough), John Boush (Mayor of Norfolk Borough 1791), Daniel Bedinger (member of a Court of Aldermen), and others.

The population was, as has been mentioned, heavily oppressed during the government of Sir Berkeley, and dissatisfaction was spreading. The English high-church by its intolerance greatly furthered the rebellious spirit. The peaceable Quakers were especially made to suffer. However, the immediate cause of the outbreak of the revolution was the renewed depredations of the Indians in revenge for the treacherous murder of some of their chiefs.

Alarmed and disgusted by the inefficient measures for defence taken by governor Berkeley, the indignant settlers rose in opposition in 1676. They asked permission to arm and defend themselves and to appoint Nathaniel Bacon, a patriotic young lawyer, their leader. This the governor, fearing to put arms in the hands of the discontented men, and jealous of

Bacon's popularity, refused; while the savages continued to commit many outrages on the planters. Bacon now put himself at the head of his followers, defeated the Indians and then turned round against the governor, who had declared him a traitor. He drove Sir Berkeley and his adherents from Jamestown and the town was partly destroyed. Bacon died suddenly, and there was not a second man brave and worthy enough to take his place. Berkeley recovered his power and wreaked vengeance on the patriots by confiscations and executions until the thoughtless and profligate King Charles II declared: "The old fool has taken away more lives in that naked country, than I for the murder of my father!" — However, Bacon's rebellion, as this revolution is called, foreshadowed the great war of Independence and the end of English tyranny. It is a remarkable coincidence, that Drummond, one of the supporters of Bacon, was beheaded on the same spot where a hundred years later Lord Cornwallis surrendered to the superior tactics and strategy of George Washington and his German general von Steuben, assisted by the French allied army.

In 1677 governor Berkeley was discharged from office and for the space of 31 years the king granted the colony to Lords Culpepper and Arlington. The first named was appointed governor for life. He came over in 1680, but trying only to get as much money as possible out of his province, another rebellion was threatening, when the king, for fear of its results, revoked the grant and recalled Culpepper. His successor, Lord Howard, was little better, he also deemed Virginia his "milk cow," and it is really surprising that in spite of all the ill-treatment and mismanagement the colony prospered. In the year 1671 there were 40,000 white inhabitants in Virginia, and at the end of the seventeenth century the population nearly reached 100,000.

CHAPTER II.

The Organization of the Colonies of Maryland and Pennsylvania and the German Sects.

TOWARDS the close of the seventeenth century events took place in the country north and east of Virginia, that had decided influence on the growth of German life in the old mother-state.

In England Roman-Catholics were exposed to persecution and most barbarous punishments were inflicted upon them. With the thirty-nine articles of the Anglican High Church a political organism was created, that lacked true religious sentiment, real Christian love and ideal theory of life. The hatred towards the dissenters, Catholics and Protestant sects, led Lord Baltimore, one of the most influential Catholics in old England, to look for some place of refuge in the New World, where those of his creed might follow their worship unmolested. He first tried Newfoundland, but found the climate too severe, and then he tried Virginia, but found its English people more intolerant than in England. Finally he obtained, in 1632, from King Charles I a large tract of land, east of the Potomac and extending along the coast of the Chesapeake bay, to which he gave the name of Maryland, in honor of the queen Henrietta Maria. Although Lord Baltimore was an ardent Catholic, he made his land an asylum for all those pursued and unfortunate. The historian Bankroft says: that from France there came Huguenots, from Germany, Holland, Sweden, Finnland and probably too from Piedmont, the children of misfortune. — Emigrants accordingly soon flocked to the province from Europe and the English colonies. But before long difficulties arose. Virginia claimed that Lord Baltimore's grant belonged to her, and Clayborne, a member of the Jamestown Council, who had already established two trading posts in Maryland, opposed the authority of Lord Baltimore. A bloody contest followed, and religious trouble and war between the Protestants and Catholics, caused by the intolerant and ambitious Puritans and Episcopalians, soon clouded the fair dawn of the rising colony. In England the reign of the Stuarts had been superseded by the new rulers William and Maria, and Lord Baltimore, hesitating to recognize the new government, was in 1691 entirely deprived of his privileges and Maryland became a royal province. Not until 1715 did the fourth Lord Baltimore recover the government — and religious freedom was again restored. During this long period of disturbance the number of the discontented enlarged considerably and many, especially a great number of German colonists, left Maryland and wandered to the fertile valleys in the mountain region of Virginia.

Pennsylvania was also colonized towards the close of the seventeenth century, but religious quarrels and English presumption fostered like results. To enjoy freedom of religion many Germans had emigrated to Pennsylvania. They had endured the dangers and hardships of a long sea-voyage, and they were not disposed to allow themselves to be again deprived of the liberty gained by such sacrifice.

"Religious motives," writes Professor O. Seidensticker,[43]) "caused the prosecuted Puritans and Quakers to go in search of an asylum to the New World. For these reasons the Germans left the Fatherland. Only three creeds, the Catholic, Lutheran and Calvin, were granted the right of tolerance within the German empire by the treaty of Westphalia. Whoever was moved by scruples of conscience to give to his Christian belief some different shape or to interpret the Bible in another way, persecution was his lot. Such secular Christians, prosecuted and abused without mercy, were plentiful in Germany towards the close of the seventeenth century. The inoffensive *Mennonites* found only in a few states a precarious admittance,—the pious *Schwenkfelder* had to endure the most terrible treatment, and even the *Pietists*, the followers of Jacob Spencer, who only endeavoured a more earnest and conscientious devotion to religion within the bounds of the Lutheran creed, were abused and denounced as dangerous inno-

43.) "Die erste deutsche Einwanderung in Amerika und die Gründung von Germantown im Jahre 1683," by Oswald Seidensticker, p. 28. Philadelphia, Pa , 1883.

vators. The *Mystics* of various nuances, who had adherents among the literary men as well as among the people, the authorities would have liked best to shut up in lunatic asylums or prisons."

Besides the sects named in the above citation, German *Quakers, Anabaptists, Dunkards* or *Tunkers* and *Moravians* or *Herrnhuter*, participated in the colonization of Pennsylvania; — in Maryland, in Cecil County, at the Bohemian river, more than one hundred *Labidists* settled, and later on the mountain region of Virginia was mainly opened to civilization by German *Lutherans, Calvinists, Mennonites, Dunkards, Quakers* and *Moravians*.[44 and 45])

Wm. Penn, the son of an English admiral, whom the English government owed a large sum of money, received instead of payment a large grant of forest land west of the Delaware. Charles II recommended to name this territory "Sylvania," that is, forest land, but finally he prefixed to it the name of Penn and baptized it "Pennsylvania." Wm. Penn had embraced the doctrines of the Quakers or Friends, who were bitterly prosecuted in England, and he resolved to make his American domain an abode for his Quaker brethren and a free colony for all mankind. Very correctly he is considered the talented and noblest leader of his sect, — his highest ambition was to advance the happiness of his fellow men. Even if, as has been asserted, he had aimed to convert his extended landed property into money, it must be acknowledged that he carried out his plan in a disinterested way, advancing an ideal design.

In Germany some Quaker communities existed at Crefeld and Kriesheim near Worms, and akin to them were the Mennonites and Anabaptists. Friendship and equality of all men were the leading doctrine of the Quakers, who originated in England in 1647 through the teachings of John Fox. They believe, that he who implores the Holy Ghost by fervent prayer, will share in divine revelation. Their worship is simple, without the ringing of bells they assemble in a plain

44) "Die ersten deutschen Secten in Amerika," von L. P. Hennighausen. Belletristisches Journal, No. 1972, Seite 10 und 11. New York, 1890.

45) "F. D. Pastorius' Pennsylvanien," von Friedrich Kapp, Crefeld, 1884.

meeting-house without altar and pulpit, without the sound of an organ or vocal music. In solemn silence and with covered heads they await for a member of the congregation to be moved by the Holy Ghost and to preach to them. They refuse to take oath and consider war wrong even when waged in self-defence, they condemn all worldly amusements and luxuries, use the article thou and thee no matter whom they address, keep their hats on even in presence of the king, and dress very plain.

Louis P. Hennighausen, of Baltimore, Md., writes about the German Quakers: "William Penn visited and preached to them in 1672 and 1677. They had been oppressed and persecuted in their old Fatherland. Imprisonment, scourging, heavy fines and confiscations was their lot. In some states of northern Germany the magistrates paid a reward of five florins for the information of the whereabouts of a Quaker. The Friends at Crefeld, in June 1683, bought of Wm. Penn 18,000 acres and those of Frankfurt 25,000 acres. In 1683, on the 6th of October, the first thirteen families from Crefeld were landed at Philadelphia. Two days later they selected the land for their settlement, on the 24th it was surveyed, on the 25th the homesteads were divided and the building up of Germantown was begun at once. Many more Germans, especially from Kriesheim, followed and in a few years Germantown had become a flourishing city. In an English book, printed at Philadelphia in 1692, George Frames sings:

> The Germantown of which I spoke before,
> Which is at least in length one mile or more,
> Where live high German people and low Dutch,
> Whose trade in weaving linnen cloth is much,
> There grows the flax. —

The German Quakers had been converted to the new creed by English missionaries and in their new adopted home they found good friends. William Penn, the proprietor of the province, frequently visited them, — preached to them in the German language and always remained their true friend. In 1686 they erected the first meeting-house in Germantown and Franz Daniel Pastorius was their leader and preacher. Pastorius, who also was the first mayor and delegate of the town, was a man of lofty character and classical education. He had in Germany been invested with the title of 'Doctor of Jurisprudence,' and he spoke English, French, Spanish and Latin. These Germans were not uneducated people, as they have falsely been represented to be. Among them were Heinrich Herrmann Kuester, who preached in German and English, — Philipp Theodor Lehmann, secretary of Wm. Penn, — van Bebber, Hendriks, Cassel, Brothers of den Graff and other men of education and wealth. The most glorious and famous action of these German men was: *their solemn protest against slavery,* published in English on April 18th, 1688."

A great many colonists also came from England to Pennsylvania. They belonged to different sects, who had lived in hatred and discord in their native land, and they imported unpleasant feelings of jealousy, intolerance and pretention into the abode of peace founded by the noble Penn. They were only on one point of one mind, and that was their envy and antipathy towards the prosperous Germans, who were rapidly increasing in number. The English settlers called them "*foreigners,*" and a very deplorable spirit of native presumption grew up. This spitefulness of the two nationalities was heightened when the Germans issued their protest against the institution of slavery.

The Mennonites and Anabaptists originally were closely connected. Both disputed the legality and efficacy of the christening of children, which they condemned as being in contradiction of the Holy scripture. The Anabaptists were rather troublesome people and religious fanatics, they desired the restoration of the empire of Christ on earth, community of property, belief in sacred revelation, etc., and they soon came in conflict with the civil authority and law. Consequently they were bitterly persecuted. But they deserve high credit for having unfolded the banner of constant progress or perpetual reformation — and to have enforced, like the Quakers, rigid morality and recognized equality of mankind. Nicolas Storch was the founder of this sect, born at Zwickau in Saxony, he was in 1521 assisted by Marcus Stubner and Thomas Muenzer.—The followers of Menno Simmons in the Netherlands called themselves Mennonites. Simmons was a Catholic priest at Witmarsum, when in 1535 several Anabaptists and among them his own brother, were executed. This event made a deep impression on his mind, he left the Roman Catholic Church and joined the Anabaptists, taking charge of one of their congregations at Groeningen. Simmons reorganized the Dutch Anabaptists, disapproving all religious and political agitation. He was opposed to christening children, but declared the baptism of adults to be indispensible — and he desired to restore the original character of the Christian Church. Taking oath, warfare, public offices, law-suits and divorces were rejected by him. Although his followers were very peaceable people, they were confounded with the fanatic Anabaptists, who engaged in a bloody conspiracy at Muenster, and persecution followed. In 1662 twenty-five fugitive Mennonites were already landed at the mouth of the Delaware, but nothing is known of their fate. However, many more followed, and from 1709 to 1730 the Mennonite immigration was very great. They mostly settled in Lancaster county, Pa., and from there they spread, about the middle of the 18th century, to Virginia and finally over the great West.

Another kind of Anabaptists are the Dunkards (Tunker or Dunker). Alexander Mark was the founder of this sect. The Dunkards were not tolerated in their native state: "the Palatinate," but they prospered in America. The nickname of Tunker was given them because they perform the act of baptism by immersion, but they call themselves Brethren and in America "the German Baptist Brethren." Immersion with them is a symbolic purification and revival. They resign all worldly amusements, and only admire a truly Christian character and life, they are highly esteemed for their morality and reliability. A promise given they hold sacred. The first twenty families of this sect arrived from Crefeld in Pennsylvania anno 1719. Their number soon increased and communities of Dunkards were organized[46]) 1723 at Germantown, 1724 at Coventry, Chester Co., 1732 at Oley, Berks Co., 1733 at Great Swamp, Buck Co., 1735 at Cocalico, Lancaster Co., 1736 at Weisseichenland, Lancaster Co., 1738 at Klein-Conewago, York Co., 1741 at Conewago, York Co., 1748 at Tulpe-

46) "Ephrata," by Dr. Oswald Seidensticker, page 27. Cincinnati, O., 1883.

hocken, Berk Co., 1756 at Gross Swatara, Lancaster Co., 1757 at Swatara, Berk Co. But soon they divided into various groups like the Ephrata-sect or Beisselians in 1724. Commonly they are classed as "Old Conservatives," who consider ignorance as less dangerous to the welfare of the soul than the possession of a treasure of worldly knowledge, — and the "Progressive," who are in favor of public education.[47])

The gentle Moravians immigrated into Pennsylvania and Georgia in the fourth decade of the 18th century and proved to be a valuable acquisition. They soon came to Virginia from Tennessee and Ohio. In 1741 Count Nicolaus Ludwig von Zinzendorf, the founder of this sect, arrived in America, where he intended to propagate his creed. The theological principle[48]) of the Moravians has its nucleus in the expiatory death of Christ. From this they derive an ascetic theory of life — but also a grave religious seriousness and reverence. Dogmatical cunning and distinctions of creed they treat with indifference, the serenity of mind they value most. This devotion is to them no tiresome toil, but a pleasure; the death wounds of Christ do not frighten but enchant them. If the Moravian faith is of confined view in several respects, it has nevertheless infused the deadening dogmatics of Protestantism with new life; proclaiming: that those will not be excluded from salvation who have no knowledge of the gospel. Count Zinzendorf first endeavored to unite the various sects in Virginia, Maryland and Pennsylvania into one community, but unsuccessfully, and then he directed his attention to the conversion of the Indians. The Moravians devoted special care to education. Their schools at Bethlehem, Litiz and Nazareth were counted among the very best in Pennsylvania. Some of their regulations[49]) are very peculiar and were the cause that they were regarded as peculiar people. The strict separation of the sexes during juvenile years, the match-making by the old folks with disregard of mutual affection of the betrothed, the use of lottery tickets as decisions of God, the tasteless costumes of the women, were among these strange regulations.

47.) "Geschichte der deutschen Schulbestrebungen in Amerika," by Herrmann Schuricht, page 5. Leipzig, 1884.

48) "Die Geschichte der Pädagogik," by Dr. Karl Schmidt, Vol. II, page 386. Coethen, 1861.

49) "In der neuen Heimath," by Anton Eickhoff, page 139. New York, 1884.

These few remarks about the most important German sects, will suffice to characterize the early German immigration to Pennsylvania, Maryland and Virginia. The nature of the Lutheran and Calvin church are supposed to be familiar to the reader, but the great part they have played in the civilization of the colonies, will receive in this history full mention in its place.

The religious motives of the early German immigration to Pennsylvania and the adjoining colonies are very well defined by the following public statement of Christian Saur, printer and publisher at Germantown, published in 1754.

" Pennsylvania is a land, the equal of which you cannot hear nor read of in all the world; many thousand people have come here and are still coming here for the sole reason to enjoy its kind government and freedom of conscience. This noble liberty is like a decoy bird or bait which draws men first to Pennsylvania, and if good lands get scarce, they move into the adjoining English colonies, and these English colonies are settled by many immigrants from Germany to the advantage of the Crown on account of Pennsylvania."

CHAPTER III.

Topographical Survey of Virginia.

THE State of Virginia, after the excision of West Virginia, is divided, with reference to the surface and natural character of the land and extending from East to West, into the following grand divisions:

Tidewater Virginia - - - - - -	11,350	sq. miles.
Middle Virginia - - - - - - - -	12,470	"
Piedmont District - - - - - -	6,680	"
The Valley - - - - - - - - -	7,550	"
The Section of the Blue Ridge - -	1,230	"
The Appalachian District - - - -	5,720	"
Total,	45,000	sq. miles.

The *Tidewater Division* extends from the Atlantic ocean to the lower falls of the Appomattox, James and Rappahannock rivers, and is divided by the large tidal rivers and the waters of Chesapeake bay into nine principal and a large number of secondary peninsulas. An imaginary line drawn diagonally across the State and touching the cities of Petersburg, Richmond, Fredericksburg and Alexandria, will represent this section. In this belt the winter is mild, snow seldom covers the ground for any length of time, and in summer a large portion of it is refreshed by the sea breeze. Near the line of North Carolina is the swamp and fever-district of Virginia and the fear of "Malaria" keeps away settlers from this unhealthy section. The navigable water-ways give the inhabitants special advantages and make the "low country," as it was called, a very desirable part of the State. Hampton roads and Norfolk bay present the finest and deepest harbors on the Atlantic coast. Here the early settlers established themselves, and here are found those elegant mansions and baronial estates for which Virginia was once celebrated. The coast district absorbed most of the

English immigration and the people of some counties, especially those adjoining Maryland, show to this day, the strongly marked individuality of the English, retaining in a marked degree the manners and expressions of the mother country a century or more ago.[50]) Not very flatteringly says a correspondent of the Handbook of Virginia: "There is nothing lacking here but people, new people, new ideas. We are as intelligent and industrious as most people, but we need new life to pull us out of the grooves and ruts and turn us into different and more progressive channels." The tidewater country being favored with a semi-tropical climate has a great variety of agricultural and garden products, it is the land of peanuts, sweet potatoes, melons, delicious fruit and all sorts of vegetables. The reputation of Virginia tobacco was built upon the product of this region, in colonial times it was the staple product, but now it is only raised to a limited extent in some of the tidewater counties. The tobacco grown at "Varina" on the James river had a special high reputation, and the name of the place is said to have been given to it because of the quality of the tobacco grown there, resembling that of Varinas in Cuba. "The waters of the Chesapeake are of themselves[51]) a bountiful source of supply and a mine of wealth to the people immediately on its shores. There is no other sheet of water in the country that supplies such an abundance of excellent fish and oysters. Travellers from Europe, especially the Germans, who visit Virginia, generally remark upon two things in particular, one is the habitual waste of bread, and the other that they see so few beggars or paupers."

Middle Virginia, is a wide undulating plain, crossed by many rivers, bordered by alluvial bottom-lands. It extends to the range of hills parallel to the Blue Ridge and about 20 miles distant from it. This is the great tobacco region of Virginia, and the cereals and fruits of the temperate climate are cultivated here. The extensive and negligent cultivation of tobacco and corn has exhausted much good land, but careful management soon restores to it its original productiveness. This district also suffered greatly during the late war, for it was the main battle

50.) "Handbook of Virginia," 5th edition, by the Commissioner of Agriculture, page 26. Richmond, Va., 1886.

51.) "Physical Survey of Virginia," by Wm. F. Maury, pp. 6—8. Richmond, Va , 1878.

ground. However, this healthy and most improvable region gradually regains its former condition. The forest growth changes as we ascend from the tidewater division to Piedmont, the cypress disappears and the cedar, pine and holly, the gum, oak, chestnut, hickory, tulip tree, walnut, locust, maple, sycamore and other timber become more and more frequent. The mineral resources are very extensive, besides coal this country yields: gold, silver, copper, sulphur, and iron ores in great abundance, and for architectural purposes fine gray granite, brown stone, slate for roofing, limestone and marble are worked. The population corresponded during the 17th and 18th centuries with that of the tidewater region, but it had a visible tincture of German. Since the end of the war enterprising settlers from Europe and from the North and West, have come here, and within the last ten years a marked improvement is manifested in the general appearance of the country.

The Piedmont Division, as its name implies, lies at the foot of the Blue Ridge mountains, and extends from the Potomac to the Dan river. It is a delightful country — for climate, beauty of landscape, variety of scenery, natural fertility of soil, water courses contributing to practical purposes as well as to beauty of scenery, this section is surpassed by few, if any other sections in the United States, and it may justly be called: "the orchard and vineyard of Virginia." The highest mountains are the picturesque peaks of Otter — 3874 and 4000 feet high, and if the atmosphere is clear the mountains are enveiled in a violet tint or vapor, like the Alps on the line of northern Italy and Switzerland. The climate is, as has been stated before, mild and invigorating. Piedmont is in fact the best sanitarium in the United States, east of the Mississippi. The population is of a cosmopolitan character — and to her industrious German element this section is indebted for much of its prosperity.

The Valley is a portion of the great central Appalachian valley, that extends for several hundred miles from Canada to Alabama, a broad belt of rolling country, enclosed between lofty mountain ranges, diversified by hills and valleys with many winding streams of water. The Blue Ridge is on the east, and the Kitatinny or Endless Mountains on the west.[52]) The Valley is the American land of red soil — and it enjoys and deserves the reputation of great fertility. The various grasses for hay and pasture, the natural blue grass lands, make the valley the home of the stock raiser and dairy man. Washington, the noble and great son of Virginia, remarked about this rich section: "In soil, climate and productions, in my opinion, it will be considered, if not considered so already, as the garden of America." For a century and a half human labor has especially improved it and made it the most flourishing part of Virginia. Randolph Harrison, Commissioner of Agriculture, said[53]): "A large portion of the valley was settled by Pennsylvania Germans in the early history of the State. These people brought with them their frugal habits, their conservative systems and modes of farming, which served to keep it what nature made it to be — one of the most desirable tracts of country in the United States." Besides her farming advantages the valley possesses many mineral springs of excellent waters of their nature and many minerals are found there. This district is naturally divided in the following sub-divisions: the Shenandoah valley, the Jamesriver valley, the Roanoke valley, the New River and Kanawha valley, and the Holston or Tennessee valley.

The Blue Ridge Division or New River Plateau is enclosed between the two widely diverging ranges of the Blue Ridge and comprises the counties of Floyd, Carroll and Grayson. Its mean elevation over the sea is about 2600 feet, and the soil is covered by timber and grass. These counties send to market herds of fine healthy cattle, flocks of sheep, much high prized tobacco, wheat, dried fruit, etc., and some of the finest apples produced in Virginia. The mineral resources are very great, but undeveloped, and offer profitable investment to enterprising capitalists.

The Appalachian Country is a rough mountain district thinly populated. It is composed of a number of parallel mountain chains, with trough-like valleys between them, the moun-

52) "Virginia, a Geographical and Political Summary," by the Board of Immigration, page 8. Richmond, Va, 1876.

53) "Handbook of Virginia," Fifth edition, by the Commissioner of Agriculture, p. 110. Richmond, Va, 1886.

tains often extending for fifty miles or more as an unbroken, single, straight, lofty ridge, with an equally uniform valley alongside: sometimes the mountains recede and the valleys widen.[54]) This district belongs to the Mississippi valley, for the waters are all drained off into that river, either by the tributaries of the Ohio or the Tennessee rivers. It is rich in timber, coal and iron and also has some mineral springs of sanitary value.

The New State of West Virginia, to which a later chapter of this history is devoted, resembles in its western part the last described district, — it is underlaid with coal, rich in timber, though upon the mountains it is still chiefly an untrodden wilderness, — and the eastern counties are in respect to surface, resources and population similar to the Shenandoah valley.

These short geographical remarks will serve to gain a view of the different divisions of Virginia and to facilitate a correct understanding of the following historical account.

---

54) "Virginia, a geographical and political summary," by the Board of Immigration. p 8, etc. 1876

CHAPTER IV.

Causes of the German Immigration into Virginia During the Eighteenth Century.

IN the early part of the eighteenth century a large number of Germans immigrated as well into Virginia as into Pennsylvania and were the instrument by which the immense natural resources of the colony were developed and a regular and sound state of affairs was created. In the numerous petty States of the German empire, at the end of the seventeenth and in the beginning of the eighteenth century, most deplorable conditions prevailed and the suffering of the people was nigh unbearable. The cruelty of the despotic rulers had already driven thousands of peaceable citizens from their homes and across the ocean, — to Virginia also Germans had come and the number of the fugitives from the German Fatherland increased yearly. Particularly southern Germany — and there especially the once flourishing Palatinate, sighed under the hardships and devastations of repeated wars, the tyranny of extravagant princes, and the hateful struggle for supremacy of the various Christian confessions. In the seventeenth century the despotism of the Elector of the Palatinate had forced his people to change its creed three times, first to the Lutheran, then to the Calvinist, again to the Lutheran and finally a second time to the Calvinist faith. This occurrence is certainly abhorrible as the most unwarranted oppression of the liberty of thought and conscience. Louis XIV of France, invaded the German country and destroyed its last resources. The French marshal de Turenne devastated this beautiful section of Germany from 1673 to 1676 — and in 1689 Durat ordered the population of nearly half a million people to leave their homes within three days. In the midst of winter, without shelter or food, many died. The cities of Phillipsburg, Frankenthal, Mannheim, etc., were reduced to ashes, fields and vineyards were devastated and the magnificent castle of Heidelberg was demolished. After all these trials the enemy at home took the place of the French tormentor. Elector Johann Wilhelm, 1690–1716, an able pupil of the Jesuits and an unbounded prodigal, aimed to take advantage of the animosity between the Lutherans and Reformists for forcible conversion to Catholicism, and his successor, Karl Philipp, persecuted all Protestants in fanatic fury and forced emigration on many.

Similar conditions prevailed in the entire German empire and particularly in the countries of the lower Rhine, Hannover and Thurinia. To make the national misfortune complete, French taste, luxury and corruption spread among the higher classes of society, and morality and propriety of conduct disappeared. Thus Germary grew faithless to its true character and bowed to foreign influence. Helpless and poor, in constant fear of death, the mass of the people took refuge with its inmost feeling and thought, saving to themselves self-respect and the belief in human equality. Under ruins and mould, behind prison-walls, germinated the seed-corn of true humanity and sound philosophy. Amidst its disgrace the heart of the German nation commenced to embrace the real theory of life and liberty, and the plain and pious peasant and citizen learned to value the art of reasoning in place of quiet submission to despotism. More sects were organized and each of them, even when adopting odd methods, gave evidence of mental impulse and independent reasoning. Their followers adhered to it manly and neither persecution nor exile forced them to desert their belief.

The German emigrants to America, having gone through such a school of bitter trials, imported firmness of character and had the willingness and qualification of doing the hard labor of pioneers. Faithful to their conviction they proved themselves in the New World conducive to the public good, obedient to law — and yet firmly devoted to the principles of liberty.

In the year 1702 Queen Anne ascended the English throne. Moved by the sufferings of the German people and recognizing their qualifications for the colonization of her American provinces, she patronized German immigration to Pennsylvania, New York, the Carolinas, Virginia, etc. At the same time several of the German Swiss cantons, like Bern, Basel, Appencell, St. Gallen, etc., undertook to colonize the surplus of their population in South and North Carolina and Virginia.

Among those unfortunate Palatines who had been robbed by the French plunderers and then forced to emigrate, was Rev. Josua von Kocherthal.[55]) In January 1708 he applied to the English resident at Frankfurt a./M., Mr. Davenant, to furnish him and several families, numbering in all 61 persons, with money and passports to travel to England. Davenant asked his government for instructions — and the request was declined. However the Palatines managed to reach London and being without means of support, Queen Anne granted to each of them one shilling per day. The news of their kind treatment soon spread in Germany and intensified the longing to escape the sufferings at home. At the same time English emissaries travelled in the German States to induce wealthy people to emigrate to America, and these men distributed pamphlets and books containing the most enticing descriptions of the resources, fertility and beauty of the New World. On the 4th of February 1709 Montague offered in the English parliament a bill for the naturalization of foreign Protestants, which was passed without opposition. This new law purposed to induce the rich French Huguenots to emigrate to the English colonies, — but the poor people of southern Germany considered it as an invitation extended to them too. In the spring of 1709 the exodus was very great, so much so that in June more than 10,000 Germans had arrived in London, and at the end of the year their number is said to have been 32,500. Most of them were homeless, poor but good and useful working people. Frank's "Frankfurter Mess Kalender" reports for instance, that from Easter to the fall of 1709 about 6520 German Protestants reached London, of which 1278 were men with families, 1238 married women, 39 widows, 384 young men, 106 maidens, 379 boys and 374 girls over 14 years

55) "Geschichte der deutschen Einwanderung in Amerika," by Friedrich Kapp, p 79. N. Y. 1868.

of age and 2672 children of different age. The professions among them were represented by 1083 farmers and vintagers, 90 carpenters, 34 bakers, 48 masons, 20 cabinet-makers, 40 shoe-makers, 58 tailors, 15 butchers, 27 millers, 7 tanners, 4 stocking-weavers, 6 barbers, 3 lock-smiths, 13 blacksmiths, 46 linen and woolen-weavers, 48 coopers, 13 cast-wrights, 5 hunters, 7 saddlers, 2 glaziers, 2 hat-makers, 8 tile-makers, 1 cook, 10 teachers, 1 student and 2 engravers, in short they were of the working and middle classes. But on account of their large number they soon became a burden to the English government and the native population,—however they were cared for as far as possible. The queen paid daily 160 pounds sterling for their support, in all parts of Great Britain collections were started for the benefit of "the poor Germans." The linnen weavers were taken to Scotch and Irish factories, the young girls received employment in families, — many young men took service in the army and navy, and all others were taken to camp at Black Heath near Greenwich until they could be transported to America. But many of those in camp, it is said several thousands, died of fever.

More than 3000 were sent to New York, about 600 to North Carolina, and several shiploads to *Virginia*. E. Willard says[56]): "Six or seven thousand arrived during the year 1710 and settled in the province of New York, Pennsylvania, Virginia and Carolina."

A German letter by David Topp, dated: Lemgo, January 5th 1711, is preserved in the State Library at Richmond. The name of the person addressed is missing, — but the contents of the letter indicate that he was a clergyman — and it gives evidence of the continued immigration of Germans. The pious mode of thinking of the German people and the deplorable conditions which prevailed in Germany at that time, are also illustrated by this interesting document. We copy the following from it: "Wir können nichts weiter alsz das wir wünschen, der Herre Herr, welcher ihn so wunderbahrlich bisz dahin geführet, der wolle ihn fernerweit in seiner christ-

---

56) "History of the United States," by E. Willard, pp. 134, 135. New York and Chicago. 1871.

lichen resolution und Gelassenheit stärken, festigen und gründen: ja Er wolle ihm Gnade geben, sich selbst und viele andere Menschen stark zu machen an den inwendigen Menschen, das Sie durch seine Lehre und Leben dasz eitele Wesen dieser Welt und die theuerwerthen ewigen schätze in dem himlischen Sion unterscheiden und erwehlen lernen." — — — and furthermore to elucidate the wretched condition in the German empire: "Hier in Lemgo neiget sich alles kräfftig zum untergange und werden wir unvermerket unserm Landesherrn gantz subject, wie dan hier in Teutschland die Herrschaften alle souverain, und die unterthanen alle sclavisch werden, Gott ändere die Gemüther und bessere die Zeiten, sonst wird alles desperat werden. Das beste ist dasz fast zehen jahr her noch so wohlfeile Zeit allhier gewest; wir wüssten gern wasz bei ihnen vor getreide wächset und ob es wohl hoch im preisse sei, worauf *da so viel Familien jaehrlich dazu kommen,* und wie und womit sich dieselben alle ernehren, ob Sie alda Häuser finden oder bauen, ob Sie die Heyden oder Wilden mit der Zeit vertreiben oder bekehren, oder was es für arth menschen da gebe und wie Sie leben. Ich bitte nochmahlst um weitläufige Nachricht und schliesse damit." —

The treatment on sea was rough, many died and found their graves in the ocean. Very characteristic is an old German-American verse:

"Sie wurden in enger Koje kalt —
Gelangten nie zum Port —
Man hat sie auf ein Brett geschnallt
Und warf sie ueber Bord."

Just as correctly says Koesting[57]):

"In einem Hafen Englands, angesichts
Bebuschter Kreidefelsen, lag, umschwaermt
Von Moeven und Schaluppen, angewaermt
Vom Sonnenglanz des jungen Morgenlichts,
Ein segelfertig Schiff, fuer wen'ge Stunden
Noch mit dem Ufer durch ein Brett verbunden.
Auswand'rer draengten sich auf dem Verdeck,
Verschuechtert Volk, von fluchenden Matrosen
Nicht besser als sein ungeschlacht Gepaeck

57.) "Der Weg nach Eden," by Karl Koesting, p. 59. Leipzig, 1884.

Behandelt. Schweigend liessen sie sich stossen ;—
Bloss Deutsche waren's, die sich nicht erbosten, —
Sie kamen frisch aus einer Hoelle her,
Drum scheuten sie kein Fegefeuer mehr.
Auch war man laengstens in fuenf Wochen ja
Im Land der Sehnsucht: in Amerika!"

By sickness and bad food a great many of these poor brave people were taken away and never gained the shores of the land of their craving. In the year 1743 a vessel arrived in Hampton Roads, Va., with German immigrants, — 200 in number they had left England, but 160 died on sea — and only 40 landed on Virginia soil.[58])

It would be unjust to hold the English government responsible for the ill treatment the emigrants had to endure at sea, for it was prompted by the very best intentions towards the German colonists. The government granted to each German 40 acres of land, the necessary agricultural implements and provisions for one year, — but many limitations to these liberal conditions subjected them to the mercy of the governors and selfish officials — and thus frustrated the good intentions of the royal government. The well-known ardent tenacity of the German colonists outlived these distressing difficulties, and by endurance and hard labor they proved a blessing to the colony.

---

58) "In der neuen Heimath," by Max Eickhoff, p 202. New York, 1884.

CHAPTER V.

German Settlements in Middle Virginia and Piedmont.

IN the year 1714 Governor Alexander Spotswood founded a German settlement in that part of the colony which was in 1720 named after him: the county of Spotsylvania. The occasion for this measure was the partial failure of Franz Ludwig Michel and Baron Christopher von Graffenried, both from Berne in Switzerland, to establish a colony in North Carolina. This conclusion is evident by reading the "Spotswood Letters" published in Vol. I of "Collections of the Historical Society of Virginia." On page 116 is stated: that in 1709 the lord proprietors had sold to Christopher Baron von Graffenried 10,000 acres of land on the Neuse and Cape Fear rivers at the rate of £10 for each 1000 acres. A great number of Palatines and Swiss followed him to North Carolina and founded New Berne. But during the massacre of the Tuscarora Indians they became disheartened, for many families were murdered and Baron Graffenried himself was taken prisoner. This tragic event occurred in 1711. After the baron's release he sold his land to Th. Pollock and with a number of Swiss and Palatines he removed to Virginia, where he settled in the forks of the Potomac. Besides, other causes necessitated this re-emigration. Many colonists were disappointed by not receiving the promised title for 200 acres of land to each family, and the unwholesome location of Graffenried's possessions may have influenced many of them to select some other country wherein to settle. "New Berne" — says Dr. Johann Daniel Schœpf in his account of his travels during the last century[60]): "is situated on a point of land em-

59.) "Historical Collections of the Historical Society of Virginia," p. 137.

60.) "Dr. Schoepf's Amerika," or compare: "Der Sueden," d.-a. Wochenschrift, I Jahrgang, p. 3. Richmond, Va., 1891.

braced by the rivers New and Trent. The beds of these rivers are very deep, but the shores are low and subject to frequent inundations. For these reasons the country does not enjoy a salubrious climate and pure air, and in fall many people die by sickness. The mortality of the children especially is very great, in fact twice as great as in the Northern States."

A number of colonists parted altogether with Baron Graffenried. They wandered up the New river to the fertile valleys at the southern slopes of the Alleghany mountains in Virginia, where the present counties of Wythe, Pulaski, Montgomery and Craig are located, and they built another New Berne in Pulaski.

Others, who had followed Baron von Graffenried to the forks of the Potomac, encountered renewed, unlooked for difficulties. Their leader went there upon written instructions of the queen to the governor of Virginia: to assign to him that section without pay, — but older claims on the land interfered. In a letter dated July 26th 1714, Governor Spotswood says himself: that a number of German Protestants came to Germanna on his inducement. They immigrated to Virginia with Baron Graffenried, who was in possession of a letter from the queen, by which he, Spotswood, received instructions to assign to these people tracts of land. Most of these Germans were miners, writes the governor, and he exempted them for several years from payment of taxes, to encourage others of their countrymen to settle in Virginia. Graffenried,[61]) utterly disgusted by the failure of his plans, gave up all further efforts at colonization, — but Governor Spotswood and some other "gentlemen," as is stated in the Spotswood-letter of July 21st 1714, cared for the deserted colonists. Governor Spotswood induced a number of them to enter his service and he erected, with their assistance, on the shores of the Rapidan, between the Russel- and Wilderness-runs: "ironworks" and the town *Germanna*; the balance of the immigrants settled in the present counties of Stafford, King George and Westmoorland. In Stafford county a German settlement was built up at Germanna Ford. Even at the present

61.) Several descendants of Graffenried are living in North Carolina and Virginia. One Dr. Joseph de Graffenried represented Luxemburg in the Assembly from 1805 to 1816 and W. B. de Graffenried was a member of the Petersburg Virginian Volunteers organized October 21st 1812, he served with honor during the war until May 5th 1813.

time occasionally traces of those German settlers are found. Mr. J. Kohler of Richmond is in possession of a Luther-medal bearing the date of 1720. It was ploughed up in Stafford county and was encrusted with earth. It is about the size of a silver-dollar, and is in a fine state of preservation. Upon the obverse are in bass-relief bust portraitures of Luther and Melanchton, with the legend, D. Martin Luther, Philip Melanchton. On the reverse is depicted the Diet of Worms, in Session, and the legend:

Ein gut bekentnis vor vielen zeugen
1st Tim., 6, 12.

Augsburg Con. Memoria Renov.
1730.

The date marks the two hundredth anniversary of the adoption of the Augsburg confession, which was compiled by Melanchton and endorsed by Luther.

By direction of Governor Spotswood dwelling houses, a church, a court-house and a residence for himself were built at Germanna and surrounded by palisades for protection against the Indians. The English historian Hugh Jones[62]) also reports, that the governor employed servants and negroes to clear the land all round, in order to give settlers a good opinion of this little populated country and to encourage their countrymen to join them. There is no doubt but that this historical remark refers to the Germans — and appreciative of their industry Sir Spotswood also encouraged *direct immigration from Germany.* The relations between the governor and the German colonists were of the very best kind. They called Virginia in his honor: "Spotsylvania"—and he was at home with them. He was so much charmed by this laborious and peaceable people, that he married a young German lady by name "Theke" and born in Hannover. Col. Byrd, the founder of Richmond, describes in his "Progress of the mines" the family life of the governor and his attachment to his wife and many children, in picturesque language.

The reports concerning the first direct immigration from Germany to the settlements on the Rapidan are somewhat contradicting. Dr. Slaughter puts it to 32 families, while other

62) "The Present State of Virginia," by Hugh Jones. London, 1724.

historians speak of two separate parties[63]) of which the first numbered 12 families and is said to have arrived in 1714, and the second counted 20 families and reached Germanna in 1717. However, both statements agree in the main point: the total number of 32 families. Dr. Slaughter also says: the first settlers had a quarrel with the ship-captain over their passage money and cites other authority to show that some time after the settlement of Germanna the condition of the colonists was deplorable in the last degree. Governor Spotswood, under date of 1714, writes to Ye Lords Commissioners of Trade: "The act for exempting certain German Protestants from ye payment of Levys is made in fav'r of several Familys of that Nation, who upon the encouragement of the Baron de Graaffenried came over hither in the hopes of finding out mines (they were engaged principally in mining in their native land), but the Baron's misfortunes obliged him to leave the country before their arrival. They have been settled on ye Frontiers of Rappahannock and subsisted chiefly at my charge and on the contributions of some gentlemen that have a prospect of being reimbursed by their labors." — Later "complaints" were made against Spotswood which involved various charges and which in a letter to the "Lord Commissioners of Trade and Plantations" he answers at length. In refuting the charge that he had built two forts, one at the head of the James river and one at the head of the Rappahannock, at the expense of the country only to support two private interests, he says: that as to the Germanna settlement, there were about forty Germans, men, women and children, who quitted their native country upon the invitation of Baron Graaffenried, and that both in compassion to these strangers and in regard to the safety of the country he placed them together on a piece of land where he built them habitations, and subsisted them until by their own labor they were able to provide for themselves.

Touching a charge that he "denied" to let his Majesty's subjects take up land,—at the same time gave leave or order to another person to take up 12,000 acres to be patented in the

63) Compare Senator Lovenstein's Oration at the "German Day" celebration in Richmond, October 6th, 1890, published in the "Richmond Dispatch" and "Richmond Times," October 7th, 1890.

name of John Robinson to his (Spotswood's) own private use and leased the same to "ye Germans,"—he says: that the patents being signed by the governor it would be improper to grant one to himself. He also claims, that the Germans were not insensible to the kindness he had shown them, and that instead of being his tenants they might have been his servants in view of the passage money — 150 £s. they owed him. The date of these answers is 1716.

The consensus of authority is that Spotswood bent his every energy to the development of the resources of the colony, but as has been seen: he did not escape harsh criticism. Reference has been made to his land "deal" with Robinson, but that was not his only "deal" in which the German interest figured. In 1722 he granted to Richard Hickman 28,000 acres of land, the consideration for which, as the books of the Register of the Land Office show, was monetary alone. In 1732 the same land was "confirmed" to Spotswood upon the averment of Hickman: that it had been held in trust for Spotswood.

"In the following period, from 1720 to 1732," so report the "Halleschen Nachrichten," "the number of high German Protestants from the Palatinate, Wuertenberg, Darmstadt and other places, increased. Many came, too, from the State of New York to Virginia, who had been transported there from England during the reign of Queen Anne. They spread and settled in all parts of the province. Some of those who arrived about the middle of this period, were accompanied by preachers like Reverends Hinkel, Falkner, Stoever, etc."

Although plain people, these early German pioneers were not wanting a certain degree of education. The fact alone, that in their company German preachers and schoolmasters came to the virgin woods of Virginia, confirms this assertion, and old documents: the Land Registers and County Records, show that nearly all of them could read and write. Several of their descendants have filled the highest state offices. Among the pioneers who arrived in 1714 was Johann Kemper from Oldenburg, who settled afterwards in the German colony in Madison county, and in 1717 married Alice Utterback. Their son, John Peter Kemper, in 1738 married a daughter of the

German parson Dr. Haeger[64]) and one of their descendants is James Lawson Kemper at Orange Court House, who had command of one brigade of Picket's celebrated division in the battle of Gettysburg, and was dangerously wounded at the heroic attack of the so-called "Round Top"; but he recovered from his wounds and from 1873 to 1878 he was governor of the State. The biography of General and Governor Kemper follows in a later chapter. — The German inhabitants of Germanna were generally esteemed and some of them were appointed to important offices. In 1748 a commission was entrusted with a revision of the colonial laws and the German, Benj. Waller of Germanna, was a member of that body.

Gerhard Hinkel or Henkel, as his descendants call him, was an old man of seventy-five years when he came to Virginia as the *first* German preacher.[65]) It seems that he was a Saxon by birth, for he had held the position of court chaplain to Duke Moritz Wilhelm of Saxony-Zeitz until this prince confirmed to the Catholic creed and exiled him. Hinkel then occupied a preachership at Zweibruecken in the Palatinate — and at the time when the Elector Karl Philipp attempted to exile the confessors to the Lutheran and Calvin confessions, he became the leader of the fugitive Palatines and accepted the ministry of their church in Germanna, Virginia. The German-American historian, H. A. Rattermann of Cincinnati, O., examined Hinkel's daybook, which is in possession of Dr. Geo. C. Henkel at Farmersville, O., and reports: "The church was named the 'hopeful church' (Hoffnungsvolle Kirche), for its members were inspired with hope that they might be allowed with the assistance of the Lord to worship the Savior Jesus Christ undisturbed, according to the teachings of the late Dr. Luther and the statutes of the confession of Augsburg." — In an historical sketch of the Shenandoah valley[66]) Andreas Simon relates: that Rev. Hinkel was a descendant of Count Hinkel von Poeltzig, to whom America is indebted: to have induced Rev. Heinrich Melchior Muehlenberg, the patriarch of the

64.) Compare "Virginia and Virginians," by Dr. R. A. Brook. Richmond, Va, 1888.

65.) "Deutscher Pionier," Vol. 12, No. 2, page 66. Cincinnati, O., 1880.

66.) "Der Westen," Sunday issue of Ill. Staats-Zeitung, May 29, 1892. Chicago, Ill.

Lutheran Church in America, to make it, after 1742, the field of his meritorious activity.

These statements are also confirmed by some of the Spotswood Letters, not yet mentioned.[67]) In a report, dated May 1712, the governor says, that Baron von Graffenried, with several Swiss families, came to the forks of the Potomac to settle there and that he was greatly disappointed, having expected to receive the lands as a gift from the Queen. In another letter, dated February 7, 1716, Spotswood mentions that about forty Germans, men, women and children, had left North Carolina with Baron Graffenried, because he could not fulfill his promises to them and on account of a horrible plot of the Tuscarora Indians for extermination of the entire white population. The governor added, that he had houses built for them some miles distant from Germanna and that he was furnishing them with provisions until they could provide for themselves. He also says: that he does not expect to be unjust, requiring them to repay his advances. — The above mentioned "Mines and Ironworks" were erected in the " Wilderness," the bloody battlefield of the late war of secession, situated between Germanna and Fredericksburg— and the "Handbook of Virginia"[68]) says about them: "The oldest furnace in America of which we have any certain knowledge, was 'Spotswood' in the county Spotsylvania, described by Col. Byrd in the Westover Manuscript a century and a half ago." At the present time iron ore is still produced there by the Wilderness Mining Co., five miles south from Parker's station.

The existence of Germanna seems to have been not of long duration. The German inhabitants who were appointed overseers on Spotswood's plantations or employed in his mines and at the iron furnace, finally had to claim large sums for unpaid wages, and in place of payment he transferred to them large tracts of land on Robertson river, a tributary of the Rapidan, in the present county of Madison. Others acquired farms in a similar manner in Spotsylvania, Culpepper and Stafford counties. Dr. Slaughter, the historian above mentioned, furnishes history,

67.) Collections of the Historical Society of Virginia, Vol. I.

68) "Handbook of Virginia," by the Commissioner of Agriculture. 5th edition, p 82. Richmond, Va , 1886.

tradition, and names, which go to show that a colony from the Germanna immigrants settled *Germantown*, in Fauquier county. In the middle of the eighteenth century, writes Col. Byrd,[69]) "Germanna consisted of the residence of Governor Spotswood and a dozen and a half of half decayed houses, formerly occupied by German families."

On the modern maps of Virginia, Germanna cannot be found, but on "a map of the internal improvement of Virginia," by C. Crozet, published by Ritchie & Dannavent, Richmond, Va., 1855, the "Germanna Mills" are mentioned, located in the north-eastern corner of Orange county, and exactly in the place where the town of Germanna was once erected. On the maps: "Carte de la Virginie," par Robert de Vaugondy, 1758, "A map of the British and French Dominions," by J. Mitchell, "A map of the most inhabited part of Virginia," by J. Frey and P. Jefferson, and "A map of the country between Albemarle Sound and Lake Erie," the town Germanna is named and besides the following localities with German names in Spotsylvania and adjoining counties: Hedgeman, Hedgeman's River, Germantown, Fredericksburg and Buckner.[70])

Governor Spotswood was the first to cross the "Blue Ridge" on horseback.[71]) Desirous to learn more of the wilderness west of the mountains, he equipped a party of 30 horsemen, employed some Indian guides, and heading in person, left Williamsburg in August 1716. They were well supplied with provisions and invigorating drink. At Germanna they rested for a few days and thence they travelled by way of Mountain Run to the Rappahannock, which they crossed at Somerville's Ford. Advancing on the left shore of the river, near Peyton's Ford, they recrossed and proceeded to near the present site of Stannardsville in Green county, whence they passed through

69.) Compare: "The Westover Manuscript," printed by Edmond and Julian Ruffin, Petersburg, Va., 1841.

70.) Buckner is a German family name, and in Virginia it reaches back to the earliest days of the colony. Many members of this family were men of prominence. One, Major Richard Buckner, was collector in Williamsburg in 1710; M. Buckner was Colonel of the 6th Virginia regiment during the War of Independence; but special credit is owing to the German printer, John Buckner, who in 1730 set up the *first printing press* in Virginia.

71.) Compare: "History of the Valley," by Sam'l Kerchevall. Woodstock, Va., 1850; and "Der Einfluss der Deutschen auf die kulturgeschichtliche Entwickelung des amerikanischen Volkes," by H. A. Rattermann, "Deutscher Pionier," 1876, No. 3, page 106.

the Blue Ridge by way of Swift Run Gap into the beautiful valley. Crossing the Shenandoah river a few miles north of where Port Republic is located, near what is known as River Bank in Rockingham, the intrepid governor pushed onward to the west across the Shenandoah valley and through the mountain defiles, until on the 5th of September 1716, on one of the loftiest peaks of the Appalachian range, probably within the limits of what is now Pendleton county in West Virginia, they halted. Governor Spotswood ordered the bugle to be sounded, speeches were made, provisions and delicious beverages partaken of, and the health of King George I was toasted. The highest peak of the mountains was baptized "Mount George," and another "Mount Spotswood or Alexander," in honor of the governor, but nobody can tell to-day what mountain tops were thus honored. Failing to discover any indication that the Mississippi originated in this part of the country, as had been thought likely, the party returned to Williamsburg and in glowing terms described the country they had visited. For the purpose of inducing emigration to the great western valley and the mountain sides with mystical hygeian fountains from which flowed the life-giving water, — the governor established the "Trans-mountain Order, or Knights of the Golden Horse Shoe," presenting to each of those who had accompanied him a miniature golden horse-shoe with the inscription: "Sic jurat transcendere montes" (thus he swears to cross the mountains). These decorations were given to all who would agree to comply with the inscription.

The German colony on Robinson river, west of the present town of Madison, prospered under the kind government of Sir Alexander Spotswood. The colonists were laborious and pious people. In 1735 they founded a congregation with Rev. Johann Kaspar Stoever as parson, who also took charge of the church at Germanna, upon Rev. Henkel's acceptance of a call to the congregation near the Yadkin river in North Carolina. The Germans in Madison county at first erected a large log-house in a glen amid the virgin wood, where never before a pale-face had risked to wander. The church registers which until 1810 were written in German, show that two sentinels, armed with muskets, were posted at the entrance of the meeting-house, to guard the farmers, their wives and children while at worship from surprise by the Indians. These guards — and likewise the parson — received their pay in tobacco, which was the tender of those times.

In the year 1739 Rev. Stoever travelled to Germany in order to raise money for building a church, a parsonage with *school rooms* and to establish a *library.* The instruction in school afterwards was given by the venerable parson himself and it comprised: religion, reading, writing, and arithmetic. This achievement of Rev. Stoever cannot be praised to highly, *for his school was the first authentical school for white children in the Old Dominion.*

The "few old field-schools,—log huts in the fields or woods," — of which John Esten Cook makes mention in his book: "Virginia," — and which he says to have existed as early as 1634, — are too obscure to be taken in consideration and scarcely possessed a claim on the high title of: "Schools." This opinion is confirmed in an article referring to Virginia: "Early Education in the South," published in the "U. S. Educational Report," 1895 to 1896, Vol. I, page 269: "In this period of nearly one hundred and seventy years (1608—1776) we find nothing to remind us even of the beginnings of the American common schools, save, perhaps, the action of neighbors in the support of a 'field school,' or neighborhood arrangement, temporary in its character, but the outgrowth of a popular desire for the schooling of the children."

Some historians, and even the German-American: Friedrich Kapp — in his "History of the Germans in the State of New York, — have represented the German immigrants of that period as of low intellectual and moral standing. Kapp, for instance, says: "Even in religious respects there was a great difference between our countrymen and the English settlers. The English brought to America as an indispensable part of their inventory the schoolhouse and the church, while the Germans struggled for their maintenance before they thought of educating their children, if in fact they possessed any interest for such duty." — The most vicious "Knownothing" could not have defamed the early German immigrants any more and offended the truth in a more startling manner, than

Friedrich Kapp. The majority of the Germans left their dear Fatherland and came to America for religious causes, — while in Virginia, as has been stated, the English Governor Berkeley recommended to the clergy: "to preach less and to pray more" — and expressed the hope: "that within a hundred years to come *no public school* would exist in the colony." The impetuous Bacon fully characterized the English educational standing in Virginia, addressing to Gov. Berkeley the damaging query: "What arts, sciences, schools of learning or manufactures hath been promoted by any now in authority?" The Germans brought with them their preachers and schoolmasters — and they built churches and schools at once! The facts, that they were plain, modest, but not wealthy farmers and artisans, that they did not possess the conventional forms and social polish of the English aristocracy, and that their inefficiency in the English language obliged them to stand back in public life, can certainly not degrade them in intellectual or moral respects. It must not be overlooked that the colonial government employed *German intelligence* to explore the country. In contradiction to F. Kapp says Kercheval[72]), the historian of the Shenandoah Valley: "It is remarkable that throughout the whole extent of the United States the Germans, in proportion to their wealth, have the best churches, organs and grave-yards."

Some dark shadows fall upon the glorious early history of the German colony in Madison county. Rev. Stoever had been very successful in the money collecting in the old Fatherland, and after the erection of the "Hopeful Evangelic Lutheran Church," etc., a considerable surplus was left, which was invested in the purchase of 700 acres of land and a *number of slaves.* This is one of the rare cases, wherein Germans departed from their dislike of the institution of slavery. — Soon after confessional differences displaced harmony. Count Zinsendorf, the head of the Herrenhuters (Moravians), came to Virginia and he tried to convert the Lutherans and Reformists. Some members of the Hebron-congregation commenced to waver and Rev. Stoever was obliged to defend his young parish with

72) "History of the Valley of Virginia," by Samuel Kercheval, p 260 Woodstock, Va., 1850.

energy. Some wandering preachers like Kurz, Goering and others caused similar disturbances, and from 1740 to 1796 the "infamous" Karl Rudolph, as Rev. H. M. Muehlenberg[73]) called him, persuaded members of the churches at Madison and Germanna to join the Baptists. A community of Dunkards (Tunker) was organized by the side of the Lutheran, but in 1780 they emigrated to Pennsylvania under the leadership of their preacher, Johannes Tanner. It is doubtful if Tanner was the correct name of the man. Some believe[74]) that his real name was Danner or Gerber.

These disturbances induced Rev. Stoever to look for support and by his influence the German Lutheran communities, which had been organized successively at Fredericksburg, New Market, Strasburgh, Winchester, Woodstock, etc., joined the "Lutheran Synod of Pennsylvania."

The Hebron church in Madison still exists and possesses antique, sacred vessels, which it received from friends in Germany,—but the greatest ornament and the pride of the church is the German organ, imported a hundred years ago and transported from Philadelphia to Madison on ox-drays.

Rev. Wm. Zimmermann anglicized this old German church and translated and changed also his own German name to "Carpenter." However a loving and proud remembrance of their German origin still exists among the members of the Hebron community, but the use of the German language has died out. He, who at the present time attends the service in the old Lutheran church, will meet there the descendants of the brave pioneers who immigrated into this Virginia wilderness nearly 200 years ago. Most of these German-Virginians are wealthy and highly respected people. Several of them have held the highest offices in the county and have represented it in the Legislature.

About the middle of the eighteenth century many Germans settled in Orange, Culpepper, Rappahannoc, Fauquier, Loudon, Prince William, Page, Green, Albemarle, and Louisa counties. Among the many German emigrants, who came to

73) Compare: "Hallesche Nachrichten," p. 264.

74) Compare: "Deutscher Pionier," No. 12, p. 68.

America in the early period of the eighteenth century, were Andrew Waggener with his five brothers.[75]) Edward with another brother settled in the present county of Culpepper in 1750. They joined Col. Washington as volunteers in his expedition against Fort Du Quesne in 1754 and marched with the First Virginia Regiment to the fatal scene of Braddock's defeat, where Edward fell among the dead. Andrew again took part in defence of the frontier against the Indians, was commissioned Captain and placed in command of Fort Pleasant. In 1765 he purchased land at Bunker's Hill, then in Frederick, now in Berkeley county, where he dwelled until the outbreak of the Revolution, when he once more entered the army and served to the end of the war. He bore a major's commission and was in the battles of Valley Forge, Princeton, Trenton, and Yorktown. Major Waggener was a personal friend of General Washington and a frequent guest of the first President.

It is an erroneous though commonly current belief that the above named counties are of exclusive English constitution. The names of German settlers and of their homes have been frequently changed, their origin has been forgotten and the Germans now living in the State know very little about it and often admire as the result of English "smartness" what has often been the fruit of German labor. This may be illustrated by the following.

In 1886 the author bought his farm in the north-west corner of Louisa county, adjoining Albemarle and Orange counties—and in former years and particularly during the late war, he had noticed many traces of German life in this section of Virginia. The name of the real estate agent who sold him the farm was Yaeger (Jaeger), one of his nearest neighbours, named Crittenberger, was a descendant of a Hessian taken prisoner in the War of Independence, his butcher calls himself Schlosser, his provision dealer Scholz, his dry goods merchants Baer and Marcus, etc., and it was therefore but natural to conjecture, that Germans had already participated in the first settlement of these counties. To ascertain the facts he went to the county seat Louisa and asked the county clerk,

---

75.) "History of West Virginia," by Virgil A. Lewis, pp. 499 and 500. Philadelphia, Pa. 1889.

Mr. Porter: "Do you know if any Germans have been among the earliest settlers?" — The clerk, with a smile and some emphasis, replied: "No Sir, — Louisa county is an entirely English county." — Upon the writer's request Mr. Porter showed him the Land Registers and he himself opened the oldest volume, beginning with the year 1742. After looking with surprise at the peculiar law style of the writing, the official remarked: "D . . . . . if that don't look Dutch!"—The first county clerk, an Englishman, was no penman, as his uncultivated signature denotes — and very likely he employed a German assistant to do the writing. Among the first entries in the Register are the following German names, besides many of uncertain origin: I. Boesick, Robert Hesler, F. Hehler, Benj. Arndt, Armistead, (Armstaedt), Flemming, Kohler, Noack, Brockman, Buckner, Starke, Spiller, etc., and in several cases "Fredericksville Parish" was mentioned as their place of residence. "Where is Fredericksville Parish located?" inquired the writer of the clerk — and after a little hesitation he was told: "That was a German settlement in your part of the county."

This occurrence and the fact that some German villages were founded in Louisa during the present century, about which some later chapter will report, illustrates how little is known about the true history of Virginia. No one will dispute that the Old Dominion is of English foundation, but it must be credited that German toil has materially assisted to make it vital and prosperous. The Germans themselves are to blame, if they are not duly credited for the part their ancestors took in the furtherance of this English colony. Many disowned their German nationality and claimed English or Scotch parentage, expecting to improve their social recognition thereby. This deplorable trait of character of many German immigrants has since disappeared, owing to the ascendance to a powerful united German empire, gaining the respect of all other nations, — but before 1870 it clouded the history of German emigration in Virginia and elsewhere.— The names of some of the oldest families in Fluvanna, Goochland, Powhatan, and Hannover, — although the English and French elements dominate in these counties, — indicate that Germans belonged to the first settlers.

In the year 1733 Col. Wm. Byrd from Westover founded the cities of Richmond and Petersburg. In his diary[76]) he reports, in his quaint manner: "When we returned home we laid the foundation of two large cities, one at Shacco's to be called Richmond and the other at the falls of the Appomatox river to be named Petersburg. These Major Mayo offered to lay out into lots without fee or reward. The truth of it is, these two places being the uppermost landing of James and Appomattox rivers, are naturally intented for marts where the traffic of the outer inhabitants must centre. Thus we did not only built castles, but also cities in the air."— Peter Jones[77]) was one of the associate founders—and to him, as the proprietor of the land, Petersburg is indebted for its name. In the year 1742 the Assembly of Virginia passed "an act establishing '*the town of Richmond*' and in 1769 the town of '*Manchester*.'" It is not known who built the first house in the State Capital, but different statements agree that the first sale of land by Col. Byrd was to a German and that the oldest building in the city: "the old stone house on Main street," still standing, was built by a German about 1737. Capt. Wm. Byrd, the son of Col. Byrd, sold the respective lot to Samuel Scherer, who afterwards deeded it to Jacob Ege, — and the property remained in the possession of this German family until a few years ago. — Another report is presented in "The Richmond Dispatch" of January 12th, 1896, as follows: "The 'Stone House' is, without doubt, the oldest building in Richmond, and its erection probably antedates the laying out of the town.

"In 1737 the half-acre lot No. 32, fronting on Main between what are now Nineteenth and Twentieth streets, was conveyed by deed from William Byrd and wife to Samuel Ege, and from the amount of the consideration mentioned in the deed, it is presumed there were improvements then on the

76.) "The Westover Manuscript," Petersburg, Va, printed by Edmont & Julian Ruffin, 1841.

77.) "Richmond in By-gone-days," p. 14, — reminiscences of an old citizen, — Richmond, Va., 1856.

lot. It is very probable that the Stone House had been standing on this lot long before the date of this deed. — — — It is reasonable to conjecture that Fort Charles was located on the present site of the old Stone House, and that the stones of the fort were used by Colonel Byrd in the construction of the house used as his quarters. If this be so, the old Stone House may be said to have existed in some shape for about 250 years."

"In 1687 Colonel Byrd patented 956 acres of land on the north side of James river, between Shockoe creek and Gillie's creek, the same land which was afterwards laid out as the town of Richmond. The quarters of Colonel Byrd were doubtless upon this land, and were probably near the fort."

This statement differs in several points with that first mentioned,—but both agree: that the property came in the possession of the German family: Ege, at the time of the foundation of Richmond. — In 1782 Richmond numbered 1,031 inhabitants, of whom 563 were whites, — but it cannot be ascertained how many were Germans. — The oldest land records of *the city of Petersburg* in Dinwiddie county date back to 1784, and among the first entries from 1784 to 1786 sales to the following Germans are recorded: W. Steger, A. Grammer (county clerk,) Fritz Ott, Edw. Stoller, Lewis Starke, Th. Walke, Ch. Seder, Henry Sadler, Joseph Weisiger, Dr. Balmann, John Fischer, Wm. Stabler, Robt. Massenburg, Rich. Gregory, V. Maick, W. Maynard, W. Steinbeck, Daniel Fisher, Frederick Adler, Th. Matthes, etc.

It is claimed also that the first owner of the land, upon which the city of *Lynchburg* in Campbell county was built, was a German Quaker and that from him John Lynch, an Irishman, in whose honor the city received its name, bought the property.

In order to complete the historical reports the following is here placed, although it does not refer to Middle Virginia, but to the Tide-water district.

The cities of *Norfolk* and *Portsmouth*, situated on the western and eastern shores of Elizabeth river, were founded in the beginning of the eighteenth century. There is no doubt but that the German element was represented at both places at this early period. French Huguenots and German Reformists arrived and settled in Norfolk county during and after the reign of Queen Anne,—and several transports of Germans from the Palatinate were landed at Hampton roads. Some of these immigrants stayed in the coast district—and others, as Hugh Jones confirms, penetrated into the interior to the neighborhood of the Blue Ridge. In 1705 Norfolk was recognized as a town and Portsmouth in 1752. German merchants prospered in both places, which count to the best harbors on the Atlantic coast, — and they kept pace with the development of commerce to the present day.

The founders of *Smithfield*, in the county "Isle of Wight," were Germans. In 1772 they built a Lutheran church, which was continued until 1836, — and it has lately been restored and consecrated.

From 1735 to 1740 another German Swiss immigration from North and South Carolina, Georgia and Switzerland, settled along the southern line of Virginia, on Dan and Roanoke rivers, in the counties of Pittsylvania, Halifax and Mecklenburg. A small book[78]), probably printed at Basel in Switzerland in 1737, shows that some speculative, unscrupulous Swiss had induced hundreds of their countrymen, especially from the cantons Bern, Appenzell and Neuenburg, to emigrate and settle in unwholesome, sterile sections of Georgia and the Carolinas. The book describes the mean deception and sufferings of the unfortunates and it invites them to come to Virginia. It appears that the "Helvetische Societaet" had purchased 30,060 acres of land, located in a curve of the Roanoke river under 36° 30′ north latitude and 78° 15′ west longitude, and it gives a highly colored description of the "*Eden*," thereby arousing suspicion: that this enterprise was also of a speculative kind. The aforementioned district enjoys the fertility, climate and other conditions necessary to the highest development and invited immigration. Information concerning the number of Swiss settlers near the Roanoke is no longer accessible, but a statement made in the book is of interest: "that there gained considerable wealth in a short

78) "Neu gefundenes Eden, oder ausfuehrlicher Bericht von Sued und Nord Carolina, Pennsylvania, Maryland und Virginia." — In Truck verfertigt durch Befelch der Helvetischen Societaet 1737. — Republished in "Der Westen," Chicago, Ills, November 6th, 1892, to January 29th, 1893.

time a few Swiss and some Frenchmen — by cultivating hemp and flax." — Col. Byrd, in his "Journey to the land of Eden," on Roanoke river[79]), confirms what has been said of the character of the land. — It is also confirmed by the publication of the Helvetian Society: "that many French Reformists, respectively people from Alsace and Loraine (now: die Reichslande), owned large plantations along James river, particularly above the James-river-falls (Powhatan and Goochland counties), who had left France fugitive on account of their religious faith."

---

79) "Richmond in By-gone days," p. 52 Richmond, Va, 1856

CHAPTER VI.

Settlement of the North Western Mountain Region of Virginia by Germans and German-Pennsylvanians.

ABOUT two decades after the foundation of the German settlements on the Rappahannock and Rapidan rivers, a large emigration of Germans to the north western mountainous region of Virginia began, and it soon spread from the Maryland line to the Ohio river into the present States of Kentucky, and Tennessee and North Carolina. However, the main limit was the beautiful and fertile Shenandoah Valley in Virginia.

Tradition has it[80]) that a man by name John Van Matre, a Dutchman from the Hudson, was the first white man who traversed the South Branch Valley, the Wappatomica of the Indians. He was an Indian trader and made his headquarters with the Delawares, whence he journeyed far to the south to trade with the Cherokees and Catawbas. On his return to New York he advised his sons, if ever they should remove to Virginia, to secure lands on the South Branch, being the best he had seen in all his travels. Acting upon this advice Isaac Van Matre, one of his sons, visited the frontier of Virginia about the year 1727, and he was so much pleased with the lands described by his father, that in 1730 he and his brother John accepted from Governor Gooch a patent for 40,000 acres, which they located and surveyed the same year.[81]) But the Van Matre's did not undertake to cultivate their large territory.

---

80) "History of the Valley of Virginia," by S. Kercheval, page 46. Woodstock, Va.

81) "History of West Virginia," by Virgil A Lewis, page 59. Philadelphia, Pa , 1889.

The greater part of the valley between the Blue Ridge and the little North Mountain has an extension of 45 miles from the Potomac, it was a blooming prairie, with the exception of some narrow fringes of timber bordering the creeks and rivers abounding in fish. Game was abundant: buffaloes, elks, deer, the bear, panther, wolves, foxes, beaver and wild fowl. It was, in fact, a tract of land inviting settlers, and the most exaggerated reports concerning it were circulated in Pennsylvania. Still the German farmers in Pennsylvania would not have given up their homes in exchange for it, had not different circumstances made them untenable; especially the frequent raids of the Indians in revenge of encroachments on part of the English. They devastated the German settlements and forced the farmers to re-emigrate. In Rupp's collection of more than 30,000 names of immigrants in Pennsylvania, it is reported, that on May 10th, 1728, the settlers in Colebrook Valley in Pennsylvania petitioned Governor Gordon to protect them against the inroads of the Indians, who had already attacked the settlements near Falkner's Swamp and Goschenhoppen. But no help was granted, and the disappointment of the German farmers was intensified by religious intolerance and various oppressions on part of the English. The laws of Pennsylvania promised religious freedom, and adherents of almost every sect and confession were settled there: Quakers, Mennonites, Dunkards, Moravians, Lutherans, Calvinites, Presbyterians, Episcopalians, Inspireds, etc. The result of such a number of heterogeneous elements was jealousy and mutual hatred. The German settlers suffered the most, and the desire arose in their hearts: to live in a country where they might worship the Lord unmolested in conformity with their conviction. They hoped to find such a place in the Shenandoah Valley in Virginia.

Justus Heid or Joist Hite, as his name is spelled in English documents, was one of the subscribers to the above mentioned petition to the Governor of Pennsylvania, and becoming highly disgusted by the indifference of the government, he gave rise to the first immigration of Pennsylvania-Germans to Virginia. He purchased a portion of the lands of the Van Matres in 1732, and he with his family, his sons-in-law: George Bowman, Jacob Chrisman and Paul Froman with their families, and W. Duff,

Peter Stephan or Stephens with others,—in all sixteen families,—left York, Pa., crossed the Potomac, the "Cohongoruta" of the Indians, two miles above the present site of Harper's Ferry, and thence proceeding up the valley they halted near where Winchester now stands. To Joist Hite therefore belongs the honor of having planted first the standard of civilization in the mountain region of Virginia. The Governor of Virginia confirmed his purchase of land, which afterwards was well known as "Joist Hite Grant," on account of a lawsuit which Lord Fairfax entered against Joist Hite and which continued in the courts for a period of fifty years.

Hite settled on Opequon, about five miles south of Winchester. Peter Stephens and some others founded Stephansburg or Stephensburg; George Bowman *i. e.* Baumann, made his home on Cedar Creek; Jacob Chrisman *i. e.* Christmann, located near what has ever since been known as Chrisman's Spring, about two miles south of Stephensburg, and Paul Froman *i. e.* Frohmann, built his dwelling in Froman's Run, which derives its name from him. Within the next two years the following German pioneers arrived: Robert Harper, from whom Harper's Ferry derived its name; Thomas Schaefer viz. Shepherd, the founder of Shepherdstown; Thomas Swearinger, James Foreman, Edw. Lucas, Jacob Hite and others. The historian Kercheval reports, that the first settlers of Winchester, in Frederick county, were Germans, but that in the year 1738 only two cabins had been erected. This statement appears to be contradicted by Klauprecht, the historian of the Ohio valley: he states that only two years later, in 1740, two German inhabitants of Winchester, named Thomas Mehrlin and John Salling, started on a bold trading-trip into the Indian country, and from this may be judged that Winchester was at that time a small village. Col. John Hite[82]) in 1753, a son of Justus Heid and distinguished by his bravery during the Indian war, built near Winchester a house of limestone, which was at that time considered to be the most elegant residence west of the Blue Ridge, and still stands, preserved in good condition.

82.) "Lord Fairfax von Virginien," historische Skizze von Andreas Simon in "Der Westen," Chicago, 1892.

The Hite family soon gained high respect and compromised close relationship with the most respected Anglo-Americans. The widow of Jacob Hite, for example, was a sister of Col. J. Madison of Orange county, and the aunt of James Madison, President of the United States.

Quite a large number of Quakers or Friends settled on Opequon and held regular meetings here as early as 1738. Kercheval reports: "An enterprising Quaker by name of Ross, obtained a warrant for surveying 40,000 acres of land along Opequon, north of Winchester and up to Apple-pie-ridge," and their numbers constantly increased.

German settlements were also established in the upper valley. In 1733 Jacob Stauffer or Stover, an enterprising German, as Kercheval calls him, received a land grant of 5000 acres on the south branch of the Gerando or Shenandoah river. Tradition says that in order not to forfeit his claim, Stauffer represented every animal that he possessed as a settler and as the head of a family, giving a name to each of them. On his land he laid out Staufferstadt, afterwards renamed through the influence of two inhabitants born in Alsace, Anton and Philip Mueller: Strasburgh. — Shenandoah and Rockingham counties were prematurely settled by Germans from Pennsylvania, who were joined by trans-atlantic immigrants[83]) of the same nationality. They adhered to their vernacular dialect and simplicity of manners, still retained in some families. In the counties of Warren, Page, and Augusta the German element was also largely represented from the beginning. Prof. M. F. Maury of the Virginia Military Institute says[84]): "This county, Augusta, as well as Rockingham, Shenandoah and Frederick, was settled up in a great measure by Germans, and the population has retained its German character." — One of the first settlers of Page county was a German named Ruffner, whose descendants will be mentioned repeatedly in this history. Dr. W. H. Ruffner, who was the first State School Superintendent

83.) "Virginia: Her Past, Present and Future," by Samuel M. Janney. Rep. of the Commissioner of Agriculture for 1864, page 27. Washington, 1865.

84.) "Physical Survey of Virginia," by Prof. M. F. Maury, page 121. Richmond, Va., 1878.

of Virginia and his son A. H. Ruffner at Lexington, Va., informed the author: "That the first Ruffner came to Virginia a hundred and fifty years ago and owned a large tract of land on the Hawksbill creek, near Luray. According to the family history he was the son of a German baron who lived in Hanover." The name of this pioneer is commemorated in "Ruffner's Cave," in close neighborhood to the famous Luray Cave.—Wm. Millars founded a settlement on South Fork, above Front Royal, in Warren county. Many other German pioneers found homes in the Valley, as the Schmuckers from Michelstadt in the Odenwald, Jaeckly, Jung, Bender, F. Huber, Becker (changed to Baker), Westerhoefer, Kunz, Sauer (changed to Sower), von Weber, Casselmann, Hott, Fink, Funkhauser, Moler, Weier (Bernhard Weier or Wyer, a hunter, discovered in 1804 the beautiful Wyer's Cave), and the Koiners from Winterlingen in Wuertemberg. "Koiner's Church" is the oldest Lutheran meeting house in the valley and was built by Kaspar Koiner (originally Keinadt or Kunath), Martin Busch and Jacob Barger (Berger). Michael Koinath and his wife, Margarethe, *né* Diller, are the ancestors of the well-known Koiner family in America and both are buried in the little grave-yard at Koiner's church. Some of their descendants settled in Augusta county and several of them attained high honors in civil service and in times of war. The name Keinadt or Kunath has been anglicized in many different ways,—there are in Virginia: Koiner, Koyner, Coyner, Coiner, Kiner, Cuyner and Cyner. This disfiguration of German names makes it very difficult to prove the German origin of many families. In Frederick county, for instance, the Kloess family was settled, that changed the name to Glaize, and Peter Kuntz of Winchester called himself Coontz.

Several German immigrants crossed the Alleghanies and built their cabins on the New, Greenbrier and Kanawha rivers. The insecurity of titles in the lower valley was the motive prompting them to select so distant homesteads. A large portion of north-eastern Virginia was claimed by Lord Fairfax, as has been stated. In 1681 a grant had been made to Lord Hopton and others by King Charles II of what is known as the "Northern Neck." The patentees sold it to Lord Culpepper, to whom it was confirmed by letters patent of King James II in 1688. This enormous land grant, which was afterwards known as the "Fairfax Patent," included all the territory "bounded by and within the heads of the rivers Tappahannock, *i. e.* Rappahannock, and Quiriough, *i. e.* Potomac river, the course of said rivers as they are commonly called and known by the inhabitants, and description of their parts and Chesapeake Bay," — and it descended from Lord Culpepper to his only daughter, Catherine, who married one Lord Fairfax, from whom it entailed upon their eldest son, Thomas. Lord Thomas Fairfax came to Virginia in 1745, and in 1748 he employed George Washington, then seventeen years of age, to survey and lay out into lots the part of the estate situated in the Valley and Alleghany mountains, that the proprietor might collect rents and give legal titles. About thirteen miles southeast of Frederickstown, as Winchester was called at that time, the Lord built his residence: "Greenway Court," where he lived until his death in 1782. Leaving no issue to inherit his vast estate, he bequeathed it to Rev. Denny Martin, his nephew in England, who left it by will to General Philip Martin. Finally the title of the Fairfax lands was purchased by Chief Justice Marshall, Raleigh Colston and General Henry Lee. Thus the settlement of the Valley was influenced by excitement caused through the lawsuit of Lord Fairfax against Joist Hite in 1736, as has been stated, and the suit continued in the Courts until 1786, when every one of the original parties to it were resting in their graves.[85–87]).

Andreas Simon says in his historical sketch: "Lord Fairfax of Virginia": "How kindly in other respects Lord Fairfax was inclined towards his German neighbors is clearly shown by the fact, that he presented on May 15th, 1753, the 'German Reformed Congregation,' which had been organized about twelve years previously in the environs of Winchester, with a lot for building a church, and that he made a like donation to the

---

85) "Historical Collections of Virginia," by Henry Howe, page 235 Charleston, S. C., 1849.

86) "History of the Valley of Virginia," by Sam Kercheval, pp 138—140. Woodstock, Va, 1850.

87.) "History of West Virginia," by Virgil A. Lewis, pp. 60—62. Philadelphia, Pa, 1889.

German Lutherans of the town. The crumbled walls of a small church near Kernstown are still shown to visitors as the ruins of the first named building. The deed of gift drawn up in this case gives the names of Philip Busch, Heinrich Brinker, Daniel Busch, Jacob Sauer and Friedrich Conrad. The parson who first preached in the little church, built of logs, was Rev. Bernhard Wille. The Lutheran Congregation built on the donated land a new church building, the cornerstone of which was laid on June 16th, 1764. In Norris' "History of the lower Valley" the following names are given as the founders and members of the church: Thomas Schmidt, Nicholas Schrack, Christian Heiskell, David Dieterich, Christoph Wetzel, Peter Holferstein, Georg Michael Laubinger, Heinrich Becker, Jacob Sibert, Jacob Braun, Stephan Frainecker, Christoph Altrich, Tobias Otto, Eberhard Doring, Andreas Friedle, Emanuel Burger, Christoph Heintz, Donald Heigel, Jacob Trautwein, John Sigmund Haenli, Johannes Laemmle, Johannes Leutz, Christian Neuberger, Georg Schumacher, Michael Roger, Michael Waring, Christoph Lamber, Samuel Wendel, Michael Gluck, Julius Spickert, Balthasar Poe, Jacob Koppenhaber and Heinrich Weller. Johannes Caspar Kirchner at that time had charge of the ministry of the community, Ludwig Adam was the sacristan and Anton Ludi the schoolmaster. Rev. Christian Streit was appointed parson in the year 1785 and continued in this capacity until his death in 1812. As long as he preached in German a German parochial school existed. Lord Fairfax supported all the various churches in the Valley and was a regular visitor of the Episcopal church at Winchester and of Cunningham's Chapel. Rev. Sebastian, a Pennsylvanian German, was rector of the church from 1766 to 1777, when he followed the example of his colleague, the Rev. Muehlenberg of Muellerstadt, or Woodstock, and exchanged the robe for the uniform to fight for American liberty.

The German Lutheran church at Woodstock was a rough log building, but during the time of office of the Rev. Muehlenberg a large and pretty church was erected. Abraham Brumbacher made a present of the lot and by deed of gift transferred it to Abraham Keller, Lorenz Schnapp, Georg Feller, Jacob Holzmann, Friedrich Staufer, Philip Hoffmann, Heinrich Froebel (Fravel), Henry Nelson, Burr Harrison, T. Beale and Joseph Pugh. Other German Lutherans came to the Valley during the life of Lord Fairfax, like Peter Mauck, Johann Friedrich, V. Helm, Johann Georg Dellenauer, Philip Glass, Jacob Beck, August and Valentin Windel, Christoph Windel, Johann Hermann, Heinrich Mueller, Philip and Michael Bauscher, Hugo Paul, Johann Sturmann, Simon Linder, Jacob Christmann, etc.

It has been stated that most of the German immigrants to Virginia were prompted by religious reasons, — but it is very difficult to give at the present time a complete description of their church organizations and their numbers. The political issues, the Anglo-American naturalization and lack of a high national self-esteem are the causes that the descendants of the German settlers have retained little knowledge or recollection of the merits of their forefathers. The German Lutherans, Mennonites, Calvinists, Dunkards, etc., forced their way up the Valley and furnished a high percentage of the population of Rockbridge, Botetourt, Roanoke, Craig, Montgomery, Pulaski and Wythe counties. In the four last mentioned counties they met with the Swiss who emigrated from North Carolina. Capt. R. B. Moorman, of Roanoke, wrote the author: "Rockbridge, Botetourt, Roanoke, Craig, Montgomery and Pulaski present a grateful field to the German-American historian." — German churches existed at the close of the eighteenth century at: Wheeling, Shepherdstown, Winchester, Kernstown, New Market, Strasburgh, Woodstock and in Augusta, Botetourt, Roanoke, Pulaski and Wythe counties. Salem, in Roanoke, was for a long time the exclusive domain of the Lutherans. Quite a number of German churches, chapels and meeting houses, — especially of Dunkards, — probably existed in the remote valleys of the mountains.

The most reliable information we possess about the Lutheran congregations in the Valley. Kercheval, the historian of the Valley, says: "The number of the Lutheran congregations is said to be at least one hundred; that of the Reformed, it is presumed, is about the same." — The first Lutheran parson at New Mecklenburg, or Shepherdstown, was Rev. Bauer, in the year 1776, and his successors were: Reverends Wiltbahn, Nicodemus, Georg Jung, and Weymann. The community afterwards was joined with that of Rev. Christ. Streit, of Winchester, who was the first native Lutheran minister in America.[88]) The Lutheran congregation at Woodstock remained, after the Rev. Muehlenberg joined the army, without a permanent pastor, but was visited at times by pastors from other towns, as, for instance, in the spring of 1775 by Heinrich Moeller, in the fall of 1776 by C. F. Wiltbahn, in 1786 by Jacob Goering, from York, Pa., and by his brother-in-law, the Rev. I. D. Kurtz, in 1792 by Christian Streit, of Winchester, and 1793 by J. D. Jung, of Martinsburg. Other reverends may have preached to them during the following years, until in 1806 Samuel Simon Schmucker was elected pastor and remained in his office for forty years. He delivered his sermons solely in the Pennsylvanian German dialect, but with his successor, I. F. Campbell, the English language was introduced. The following are the names of the pastors to the present day: J. P. Cline (Klein), S. Keller, J. A. Snyder, H. Miller, and A. A. J. Bushong.— The New Market parish was administered by descendants of the first German preacher in Virginia: Gerhard Henkel, of Germanna. The names of the pastors are: Paul Henkel, Ambrosius Henkel, David Henkel, and Socrates Henkel. In a later chapter of this history some publications of Ambrosius, Paul and Socrates Henkel will receive special mention. In the year 1793 Dr. Georg Daniel Flohr came to Virginia, and resigning his medical studies, he devoted himself, under the tutorship of Rev. Carpenter at Madison, to theology. Dr. Flohr[89]) afterwards acted as pastor among the German settlements on New River and particulary at the Swiss colony at New Bern, Pulaski county. In the adjoining county of Wythe a German Lutheran church was sustained at Wytheville, which was established[90]) in 1792 on land donated by Stophel Zimmermann and John Davis, and was jointly owned by the Lutheran and the Reformed congregations.

The "Wytheville Dispatch" of April 9th, 1897, contains an

88.) "Church Growth in America," by Rev. J. E. Bushnell, Roanoke, Va., from the Lutheran Quarterly, April, 1888.

89.) "The American Lutheran Pulpit," pp. 121 to 122.

90.) "Historical Collections of Virginia," by Henry Howe, p. 5:4 Charleston, S. C. 1849.

historical article written by Rev. Alex. Phillippi, D.D., and published by request of the Lutheran Pastor's Association of Wythe County. Rev. Phillippi reports: "After 1732, the Germans, mostly from Pennsylvania, came in considerable numbers to the lower Valley of Virginia and slowly extended themselves into the south-western part of the State, so that at the time of the outbreaking of the Revolutionary War, several considerable settlements had been formed in what is now Wythe and adjoining counties. These settlements, after the close of the war, received numerous additions from Pennsylvania, Maryland and the lower valley of Virginia. The early Germans who came to Wythe County, with few exceptions, had some means, and were a hardy, industrious, moral, intelligent, Christian people. The Bibles, some very costly and beautiful copies, which they brought with them, are still found in possession of their posterity, with many other useful and religious books, had a place in almost every family. Schoolhouses, which for the time were also used as places of public worship, were among the first and most expensive buildings erected. With few exceptions these people were Protestants, nearly equally divided between the Lutheran and the German Reformed Churches. For reasons not fully understood at this day, these colonists failed to secure and bring with them into their new homes pious and capable pastors and teachers, — and for twenty-five or more years religion and education were not only greatly neglected in these feeble and scattered communities by incapable and immoral, godless leaders." — Rev. Phillippi also mentions that German Lutheran churches were established: one mile north of Wytheville the St. John's Lutheran church and twelve miles west St. Paul's church, — and that in 1796 Rev. Leonard Willy became pastor between Cedar Grove, of Smyth County, Kimberling, St. Paul's and St. John's congregations of Wythe County. — In 1799 Rev. George Flohr, before mentioned, accepted a call to the Lutheran churches in south-west Virginia and located several miles north of Wytheville. His ministry ended with his death in 1826 and his remains lie buried in St. John's cemetery.

According to Prof. O. Seidensticker[91]) some faithless mem-

91) "Ephrata,"—eine amerikanische Klostergeschichte von Dr. Oswald Seidensticker. Cincinnati, 1883.

bers of the German convent "Ephrata" in Pennsylvania, organized by the sect of the Siebentaeger or Beisselianer, a kind of Dunkards, left in the year 1745 and founded a settlement on New River which they named "Mahanaim." Repeated attacks of the Indians obliged the settlers to flee,—some were carried away prisoners by the savages — and all traces of Mahanaim are lost. A number of fugitive lay-brothers selected the beautiful Shenandoah valley for their home, but it appears they were not pleased with it. In a letter published in the eighteenth century by Leibert and Billmeyer at Germantown, Pa., Peter Blaeser complains to his friend, the printer Mich. Billmeyer, that he and others, on account of their virtuous habits of life, are called by the nickname "Strabler," and a German verse sounds thus:

"Der Koth in Virginia den Satan gehecket,
Damit er die Stillen im Land hat beflecket,
Hat dort her ein Stueck in Cacusa geschmissen
Allwo er noch greulich thut stinken und fliessen."

Their monastic life and peculiar habits probably excited the displeasure and criticism of their neighbors, causing their own dissatisfaction.

Several Germans, it has been stated, penetrated into the wild regions of the Alleghanies. As early as the middle of the eighteenth century about twelve miles west of Franklin, in Pendleton county, the frontier fort "Seybert" was erected, which was attacked by a party of Shawnees under their vile chief "Kill-buck" in May 1758[92]), when garrisoned by only thirty or forty men. The following account of the affair is given by De Hass: "Finding neither threatening words nor bullets of any avail, the cunning savages, after two days' trial, resorted to strategy and unhappily with most fatal success. They made various propositions to the besieged to give up, and their lives should be spared. — The promise of safety lured the unfortunate victims from their duty, they yielded quiet possession of the fort, but of their number all were massacred but eleven, who were carried to the Indian town as prisoners." — Kercheval states that Capt. Seybert was murdered by Kill-buck imme-

92.) "History of West Virginia," by Virgil A. Lewis, pp 566 to 567. Phila., 1889.

diately after the surrender and that his son was among those carried away prisoners. — Among those who first attempted a settlement within the present limits of Tucker county in 1776 was one Simms, who was also killed by the Indians. — Many German families counted to the pioneers of Pocahontas county, like the Harpers, Grines, Sharp, etc., and Peter Lightner, who built the first mill on Knapp's Creek. — It is of special interest that the first owner of the lands of White Sulphur Springs in Greenbrier county probably was a German. During the year 1774 the Shawnees, the predominant tribe of western Virginia, were gradually subdued by the ever encroaching colonists from eastern Virginia, and having suffered a signal defeat at Point Pleasant, they began to abandon the country, but not entirely, for by frequent marauding parties with tomahawk and scalping knife they fully attested their attachment to their ancient hunting-grounds. It has been before mentioned that the family Zimmermann at Madison changed its name to "Carpenter," and that several of its members migrated again farther west and to Kentucky. The road they travelled was the same which was afterwards chosen for the construction of the "Stage-road" to the Kanawha and Ohio rivers, and it traversed the territory of the famous Sulphur Springs. One, Nathan Carpenter,[93]) came there in 1774 and selected the charming valley of White Sulphur Springs for his home. It was patented to him under what is called a "Corn Right;" but a band of marauding Indians forced him and other settlers to retreat to a stockade fort, where the town of Covington now stands, and during a fight with the savages he was killed. His wife Kate and their children took refuge for some time in a neighboring mountain, overlooking the springs from the south, which ever since has been called Kate's Mountain.

At the same period a German Hebrew immigration party settled in the western parts of Virginia[94]). The numerous Sephardic and Portuguese Jewish element in the Old Dominion was now gradually surpassed by the German, and a new era in

---

93) "White Sulphur Springs in Greenbrier County," p. 9. A. Hoen & Co, Baltimore, Md.

94) "Materialien zur Geschichte der Juden in America," von S. Wiener, Belletristisches Journal, p. 11. New York, January 8th, 1891.

the development of Jewish life commenced. A great number of Jews at that time came from Lancaster, Pa., and built up their homes on the fertile lands near the Ohio river. — Other German colonists also came to this section of Virginia. The Deckers were the first white settlers near Morgantown, in Monongahela county, W. Va., of those days. Alexander Withers reports in his "Chronicles of Border Warfare," that in the autumn of 1758 Thomas Decker and some others built their cabins on the Monongahela where Decker's Creek joins this river, — but that he was murdered by the Indians in 1759. Soon afterwards other German immigrants came and Michael Kerns was one of the founders of Morgantown. John Decker was the last white man killed by an Indian in Brooke county; W. Boner, E. Rittenhouse, M. Decker, Capt. van Buskirk, etc., counted to the early colonists. John Wetzel, the Siverts, Earlywines, Tush, Capt. Baker, Col. Beeler, etc., domiciled in Marshall county in 1769, and are all well known on account of their bravery and sufferings during the Indian war.

The German immigrants also crossed the Blue Ridge and settled in Loudoun, Fairfax, Prince William, Stafford, Fauquier, Rappahannock and Culpepper counties, where they met with their countrymen come there from the South. Confirming this emigration from the Valley to Middle Virginia, Col. Thomas Whitehead, Commissioner of Agriculture in Virginia, says[95]): "Let Virginia distribute her population. Let those who have none, or very small tracts, in the Valley and Piedmont, go to the Southside and Middle Virginia, and they will succeed, *as did the Tunkers*, who went from the Valley — selling at high prices — to Prince William, where they bought low, and are improving and making former waste fields to blossom. Facts to sustain this position are in possession of this department."

The habits and the mode of life of the German pioneers in the Virginia mountains were simple and modest. Their style of living and their industry were the causes of their prosperity and enlarged wealth. Another circumstance added to their success. "We see in the population only a small infusion of the

---

95) "Report of the State Board of Agriculture of Va." p. 142. Richmond, Va., 1888.

old Virginia element," — states an official document[96]) — "being composed chiefly of Germans and Scotch-Irish, — naturally this is the most fertile region of the State, and *as it was only partially subjected to the blighting influence of slavery, it has ever been the most prosperous.*" — It is proven by facts, that the *German* farmers in the Valley and the Alleghanies, with few exceptions, owned *no slaves.* The majority of them, especially the Mennonites, Tunkers and Quakers, considered slavery inhuman and displeasing the Lord, and mainly the English were slaveholders. The above mentioned document bears therefore honorable testimony to the German farmers of the Valley and mountains of Virginia. On account of the notorious antipathy of the Germans towards slavery, the number of negroes has always been smaller there than in other parts of the State. According to statistical reports, in 1877, the negro population in the Alleghany district amounted to only seven per cent., in the Valley to sixteen per cent., but in the Piedmont and Coast district from forty-seven to fifty-one per cent. of the total population.

Another reason why the German farmers prospered more than their English neighbors, was that they did not care to possess excessively large estates, but farms comparatively small, — just large enough that an active farmer could with the assistance of his family work them well. On their acres, thus carefully tilled and manured, they raised better and larger crops, than the Anglo-American planters on their plantations of thousands of acres with the help of negro labor. The culture of these vast estates often was carried to the point of exhaustion. The Handbook of Virginia[97]) very correctly says of the German farmers of the last century: "These people brought with them their frugal habits, their conservative systems and modes of farm management, which served to keep it what nature made it to be, one of the most desirable tracts of country in the United States." This statement is confirmed, too, in the reports of Dr. Johann David Schoepf in his description of Virginia a hundred years ago. He says: "They distinguish themselves by

96.) "Status of Virginia Agriculture in 1870,"—U. S. Report of Agriculture for 1870, pp. 271 to 272. Washington, 1871

97.) "Handbook of Virginia," Fifth Edition, p. 110. Richmond, Va., 1886.

their diligence and steadiness. Their fellow-citizens concede that they possess these merits, — but only few are inclined to follow their example."

Concerning the customs and mode of life of the German colonists, Kercheval gives the following interesting details.[98])

"The first houses erected were log cabins, with covers of split clapboards, and weight-poles to keep them in place. There were, however, a few framed and stone buildings erected previous to the war of the revolution. As the country improved in population and wealth, there was a corresponding improvement in the erection of buildings. When this improvement commenced, the most general mode of building was with hewn logs, a shingle roof and plank floor, the plank cut out with the whip-saw. Before the erection of saw-mills, all the plank used was worked out in this way. The timber intended to be sawed was first squared with the broad-ax, and then raised on a scaffold six or seven feet high. Two able-bodied men then took hold of the saw, one standing on top of the log and the other under it. The labor was excessively fatiguing and about 100 feet of plank or scantling was considered a good day's work for two hands. — The dress of the early settlers was of the plainest materials, generally of their own manufacture. Previous to the war of the revolution, the married men generally shaved their heads, and either wore wigs or white linen caps. When the war commenced, this fashion was laid aside, for wigs could not easily be obtained, nor white linen for caps. The men's coats were generally made with broad backs and straight short skirts, with pockets on the outside having large flaps. The waistcoats had skirts nearly half-way down to the knees and very broad pocket flaps. The breeches were so short as barely to reach the knee, with a band surrounding the knee, fastened with either brass or silver buckles. The stocking was drawn up under the knee-band and tied with a garter (generally red or blue) below the knee, so as to be seen. The shoes were of coarse leather, with straps to the quarters, and fastened with either brass or silver buckles. The hat was either of wool or fur, with a round crown not exceeding three or four inches high, with a broad brim. The

8) **"History of the Valley," by S. Kercheval, pp 203—208 Winchester, Va., 1833**

dress for the neck was usually a narrow collar to the shirt, with a white linen stock drawn together at the ends, on the back of the neck, with a broad metal buckle. The more wealthy and fashionable were sometimes seen with their stock, knee and shoe buckles set either in gold or silver with brilliant stones. — The female dress was generally the short gown and petticoat, made of the plainest materials. The German women mostly wore tight calico caps on their heads, and in the summer season they were generally seen with no other clothing than a linen shift and petticoat — the feet, hands and arms bare. In hay and harvest time they joined the men in the labor of the meadow and grain fields. Many females were most expert mowers and reapers. — The natural result of this kind of rural life was, to produce a hardy and vigorous race of people. It was this race of people who had to meet and breast the various Indian wars and the storms of the revolution. The Dutchman's barn was usually the best building on his farm. He was sure to erect a fine large barn, before he built any other dwelling house than his rude log cabin. There were none of our primitive immigrants more uniform in the form of their buildings than the Germans. Their dwelling houses were seldom raised more than a single story in height, with a large cellar beneath; the chimney in the middle, with a very wide fire-place in one end of the kitchen, in the other end a stove-room. Their furniture was of the simplest and plainest kind; and there was always a long pine table fixed in one corner of the stove-room, with permanent benches on one side. On the upper floor garners for holding grain were very common. Their beds were generally filled with straw or chaff, with a fine feather bed for covering in the winter. Many of the Germans have what they call a drum, through which the stove-pipe passes in their upper rooms. It is made of sheet-iron, something in the shape of a military drum. It soon fills with heat from the pipe, by which the rooms become agreeably warm in the coldest weather. A piazza is a very common appendage to a Dutchman's dwelling house, in which his saddles, bridles, and very frequently his wagon or plow harness, are hung up. The Germans erect stables for their domestic animals of every species: even their swine are housed in the winter season. Their barns and stables are well stored with provender, particularly fine hay: hence their quadrupeds of all kinds are kept throughout the year in the finest possible order. The German women, many of them are remarkably neat housekeepers. There are some of them, however, extremely slovenly, and their dwellings are kept in the worst possible condition. The Germans are remarkable for their fine bread, milk and butter. They consume in their diet less animal flesh, and of course, more vegetables, milk and butter, than most other people. Their "Sour Krout" in winter constitutes a considerable part of their living. They generally consume less and sell more of the product of their labor, than any other class of citizens. A Dutchman is proverbial for his patient perseverance in his domestic labors. Their farms are generally small and nicely cultivated. In all his agricultural pursuits his meadows demand his greatest care and attention. His little farm is laid off in fields not exceeding 10 to 12 acres each. It is rarely seen that a Dutchman will cultivate more than about 10—12 acres of Indian Corn any one year. They are of opinion that the corn crop is a great exhauster of the soil and they make but little use of corn for any other purpose than feeding and fattening their swine."

Kercheval also relates (pp. 79—80): "With few exceptions, they strictly inhibited their children from joining in the dance or other juvenile amusements common to the Germans. — In their marriages much ceremony was observed and great preparations made. Fatted calves, lambs, poultry, the finest of bread, butter, milk, honey, domestic sugar, wine, if it could be had, with every article necessary for a sumptuous feast in their plain way, were prepared in abundance. Previous to the performance of the ceremony (the clergyman attending at the place appointed for the marriage), four of the most respectable young females and four of the most respectable young men were selected as waiters upon the bride and groom. The several waiters were decorated with badges, to indicate their offices. The groomsmen, as they were termed, were invariably furnished with fine white aprons beautifully embroidered. It was deemed a high honor to wear the apron. The duty of the waiters consisted in not only waiting on the bride and groom, but they were required, after the marriage ceremony was performed, to serve up the wedding dinner, and to guard and protect the bride while at dinner from having her shoe stolen from her foot. To succeed in it, the greatest dexterity was used by the younger part of the company, while equal vigilance was manifested by the waiters to defend her against the theft; and if they failed, they were in honor bound to pay a penalty for the redemption of the shoe. This penalty was a bottle of wine, or one dollar, — and as a punishment to the bride, she was not permitted to dance until the shoe was restored. The successful thief, on getting hold of the shoe, held it up in great triumph to the view of the whole assemblage, which was generally pretty numerous. This custom was continued among the Germans from generation to generation, until since the war of revolution."

In consequence of the growing prosperity of the German colonists, a number of towns and villages, as stated before, were founded, and to this day many names of inhabited places, rivers and mountains recall to memory the times of the German pioneers. The following review of the German foundations during the eighteenth century bears evidence of the share they have taken in establishing the welfare of the State.

In the year 1737 some German families settled, as has been reported, where soon after *Frederickstown* or *Winchester*, as it is now called, was laid out. *Stephansburg* in Frederick county, now Stephensburg, was founded by Peter Stephan in 1758, who with Justus Heid came to Virginia in 1732. *Kernstown* was built on the land of Adam Kern. *Stauferstadt* or *Strasburgh*, in Shenandoah county, derived its original name from its founder, Peter Staufee, or Stover, who laid it out in 1761. In the same year Jacob Mueller established *Muellerstown*, which was afterwards called *Woodstock*. Its founder laid out 196 lots on 1200 acres of land, and every one of these lots was purchased by Germans. *Shepherdstown*, formerly *Mecklenburg*, in what is now Jefferson county in West Virginia, is the oldest German town in this part of the Valley; it was incorporated in 1762 and inhabited by German tradesmen. *Harpers Ferry*, also in Jefferson county and famous in history as the scene of John Brown's Insurrection, commemorates the name of a German, Robert Harper, who settled near by in 1734. — *Wheeling*, in

Ohio county, was first laid out in 1770 in town lots by Col. Ebenezer Zane and 1795 it was made a town by act of the Assembly. *West Liberty*, also in Ohio county, was established by legislative enactment in 1787 on the lands of Reuben Foreman. — From Christian Peter, who came to Monroe county, now West Virginia, in 1770, the village *Peterstown* takes its name and also the mountain range which now forms the dividing line between the Old Dominion and West Virginia. — *Martinsburg*, the present county seat of Berkeley, W. Va., was made a town in 1778 on the lands of General Adam Stephan, Stephen, or anglicized Steven, — and *Darkesville*, in the same county, commemorates the name of the brave General W. Darke, the son of Pennsylvanian German parents. Other places which have been founded chiefly by Germans are: *Lexington*, Rockbridge county, in 1777, — *Amsterdam*, Botetourt county, by Pennsylvanian German Tunkers, — *Harrisonburg*, Rockingham county, 1780, — *Lewisburg*, Greenbrier county, 1782, — *Clarksburg*, Harrison county, 1785, — *Charlestown*, Kanawha county, 1786, — *Frankfurt*, in Hampshire county, 1787, by John Schloss, J. Adler, H. Whitemann, Jacob Brockhardt and other Germans, — *Middletown*, now Gerrardstown, in honor of David Gerrard, (*i. e.* Gerhard) in 1787, — in 1788 *Front Royal*, in Frederick county, by S. Vanmeter, H. Front, Th. Hant, etc., — *Beverly*, in Randolph county, in 1790, on the lands of Jacob Westfall, — in 1791 *Keisletown*, formerly *Kieselstadt*, Rockingham county, — *Berryville*, in Clarke county, by Benj. Berry and S. Strebling in 1798. The county of *Alexandria*, with the city of the same name, belonged to the estates of Lord Fairfax, and promised to become an important harbor and trading place before the Capital of the Union — Washington city — was founded on the opposite shore of the Potomac. At Alexandria the river is more than one mile wide and at the landing place thirty feet deep. It is not certain how many Germans participated in the founding of the city, but Dr. Julius Dienelt, of Alexandria, informed the author of this book, that he found in the County Records the following German names: Peter Wagener, county clerk from 1776 to 1797, and within the period from 1787 to 1794: Michael Steiber, Michael Gerther, Johann Hess, Georg Christian Otto, Johann Schneider, Wilhelm Bocher, Tobias Zimmermann, Josias

Spier, Adam Ebert, Adam Faizer, Joh. Christ. Kempff, Th. Hederich, Jac. Beltinger, and Joseph Thomas.

This list of places established by Germans, or chiefly with their assistance, is incomplete; it gives only a number of examples with special reference to the Valley, and the reader is referred to two other lists in Volume II, chapters thirteen and sixteen.

The two German mass-immigrations to Middle Virginia and to the north-western mountain region differ essentially in one feature. The settlers on the Rappahannock river and in Piedmont, at the time of Governor Spotswood, stood at first in a serviceable dependency, until they secured independence and property, — but the German colonists of the Valley and Alleghany mountains were wealthy people and purchased lands, and those who came from Maryland, Pennsylvania and New York brought practical experience in pioneer-work with them. The poor German immigrants, mostly farm-hands and craftsmen, who had bound themselves to serve for the amount of their travelling expenses to America, were landed in large numbers at Philadelphia and New York, but showed little willingness to hire out to southern slave-holders. Dr. Schoepf says about them: "They possess to much pride to work with and among the negroes, who in Virginia and the Carolinas are almost exclusively the only laborers."

This disinclination to be placed on one level with the colored people has kept away to the present day white laborers,—especially those of German nationality,—from the southern States. "We do not want to be treated like negroes, to work for low negro-wages and to be reduced to negro rations of corn and bacon," — these are the arguments which white laborers still use to justify their prejudice against the South.

CHAPTER VII.

The French and Indian War and Indian Devastations.

THE development of the German settlements in Virginia was much impeded by the growing difficulties and quarrels between the French and English in regard to the boundaries of their colonies. The English, in 1750, actually occupied only a narrow strip along the coast of the Atlantic, about 1000 miles in length, but they claimed all land from New Foundland to Florida as having been discovered by the Cabots. The French territory extended around the English colonies, from Quebec to New Orleans and upward to the great lakes, supported by a cordon of forts. The French based their claim on the ground of the exploration of this vast territory by French travellers. Both nations claimed the region west of the Alleghany mountains, along the Ohio river, and this was the cause of the great struggle, known in history as the French and Indian War. The rights of the natives on the land of their ancestors were completely ignored by both contestants. A grant made by the English crown, in 1749, of 800,000 acres on the Ohio to the Ohio Company, brought matters to a crisis. The enraged Indians sent to the agent of the Ohio Company the pertinent query: "Where is the land of the Indians? The English claim all on one side of the river, the French all on the other, where does our land lie?" — The French erected new forts in the northwest of Pennsylvania and took possession of an English post in what is now western Ohio, and carried the garrison off prisoners. Unfortunately the English did not understand to gain the friendship of the natives, consequently most of the

Indian tribes united with the French, — and suddenly fell upon the exposed German settlements along the Ohio, committing acts of horrible cruelty.

The King of England had granted the Ohio Company the aforesaid privilege for the purpose of planting settlers beyond the Alleghanies — and to monopolize the fur-trade, and soon the Company aimed to extend its traffic eastward into the country of the "Six Nations." German men were entrusted with the important and dangerous mission to negotiate with the Indians and to conclude treaties with them.

In 1748 the savages threatened to invade the settlements and *Konrad Weiser* was sent to Logstown to appease them by exhortations and presents.[99]) — "The two Weisers, father and son," says Friedrich Kapp[100]), figure among the most illustrious Germans who came to America during the last century." — Johann Konrad Weiser, the father, was born at Grossaspach in Wuertemberg, and arrived at New York in 1710, with the influx of the emigrants from the Palatinate. He remained up to his death in 1746 the leader and defender of the German settlers in the Shoharie Valley against the corrupt and extorting English officials. His son Konrad was only fourteen years old when he landed at New York, and after his father had settled in the Shoharie Valley, he was given in charge of the Indian chief Quagnant, who was a friend of Weiser, Sr. — Living among and with the natives Konrad became acquainted with the Indian languages, the customs and the way of reasoning of the children of the wilderness. This knowledge of the character, the idiom and the mode of viewing things of the Indians, afterwards made Weiser the sought for adviser and mediator of the two races — and the natives esteemed him as a justly reliable friend. He came in 1737, upon the request of Governor Gooch, for the first time to Virginia, to undertake the difficult mission to arrange an armistice with the chiefs of the "Six Nations," and finally a defensive alliance with the Cherokese and Catawbas. Not less important was his mission to Logstown in

99) "In der neuen Heimath," Seite 231, von Anton Eikhoff. New-York, 1884.

100) "Geschichte der Deutschen im Staate New York," von Friedrich Kapp, — Seite 134. New York, 1868.

1748, to which we already referred. On his journey he had to travel through a wilderness full of perils, over rough mountains to the Ohio and then to Logstown: to confer with the enraged Indians, to persuade them not to unite with the French, and at the same time to gather full particulars as to the strength and position of the French forces and fortifications. He succeeded well with his hazardous mission. Friedrich Kapp[101]) states: "The personal knowledge of the situation of things on the Ohio and in the western portion of the English settlements Weiser used six years later in Albany to great advantages, where the deputies of seven colonies had a conference with the chiefs of the "Six Nations," purposing to form an alliance against the French. It was one of the most important periods in the history of the colonies; it was the time of the beginning of the French war, and the first cooperation of the colonies, hitherto acting separately and frequently in discord. The colonists desired to secure the alliance of the Indians and to this end tried to convince them that the French had committed numerous encroachments in the Ohio valley and the western Indian territories. Among other speakers Vice-Governor de Lancey, of New York, addressed the savages and in the course of his speech remarked: "It is very lucky that Mr. Weiser, who has arranged matters with your nations in Virginia and Pennsylvania and who is also thoroughly acquainted with the whole situation, is present. Listen to his statements which will throw full light on all the difficulties." Then Weiser stepped forward and in the Mohawk language gave a detailed description of the outrages and intrusions in the Ohio valley committed by the French, and known to him as an eye-witness. His address made a deep impression on the Indian chiefs — and in a few days an alliance was arranged between the English and the Six Nations.

Although Konrad Weiser never made Virginia his permanent home, he rendered to it such eminent services, that his name deserves a prominent place in the history of the Old Dominion.

101.) "Geschichte der Deutschen im Staate New-York," von Friedrich Kapp,— Seite 140—141. New-York, 1868.

In 1751 *Christopher Gist, Geist* or *Guest*[102]), another distinguished German of Frederick, Virginia, was appointed agent of the Ohio Company. He was despatched to the Tuigtuis Indians, living near the present Piquia in Ohio, to secure their partisanship for the Virginia cause. Gist's travels through the land north of the Ohio river lasted from October 31st, 1750, to May 1751; he then returned to Virginia to organize the settlements which the Ohio Company had projected on the Kanawha river. In 1753, when Major George Washington was entrusted by Governor Dinwiddie with the dangerous mission to the French commander on the upper Ohio to deliver a protest against his advance and to demand his withdrawal from the Ohio valley, he chose for one of his companions Christopher Gist.

The great struggle was now at hand, — Virginia prepared for war, and in 1754 the hostilities commenced. The war was waged for years with varying success. The exposed German settlements on the frontier suffered greatly by the Indian allies of the French, until France could no longer protract the struggle and by a treaty, ratified in 1763, she gave up all her American territory, including the upper Ohio region, to the English.

England and the colonies owed this victory to a great extent to an agreement concluded with the Iroquois Indians by the German *Christian Friedrich Post*, a Moravian.

"On the 25th of August" — writes Klauprecht — "the same day that England's great ally in Europe, King Frederick II of Prussia, defeated the Russians in the fierce battle of Johnsdorf, the modest champion of England, the Moravian Post, stood on the battlefield and within the range of the enemies' cannon, in full sight of Fort Du Quesne (Pittsburg) and the flying lily-banners of France, he persuaded the Indian warriors, surrounding him, to break with their allies."

During this long war several Germans gained high military distinction. Captain *Adam Stephan* or *Stephen*, who

---

102.) "Geschichte des grossen amerikanischen Westens," von H. A. Rattermann, — Seite 28. Cincinnati, 1875.

practiced medicine at Neu Mecklenburg (Shepherdstown) Va., from 1747 to 1754, organized a company of German volunteers in the vicinity of Harper's Ferry, and advanced with Washington to the West. He fought with valor in the battles at Great Meadows, Fort Necessity and General Braddock's disastrous defeat; and he was promoted to the rank of Lieutenant-Colonel and given command of Fort Cumberland.

Colonel *Wilhelm Drake* was another German officer of fame. He had come, when a child, with his German parents to Neu Mecklenburg, and only nineteen years of age he participated in Gen. Braddock's campaign. Colonel George Washington in a report, dated Great Meadows in May 1754, also stated: that under his command there served the Ensign Carl Gustav von Splitdorf and Lieutenant Edmund Wagner, who was killed in battle.

Peace was restored and the French army gone, but peaceful times did not follow. The enlarged power of the English, who now held possession of all the territory extending to the great lakes, and who now occupied the forts built by the French, the French settlers who dwelled around the northern lakes, and who were still opposed to the English rule, a large emigration of colonists to the fertile prairies of the west, excited the apprehension and fury of the Indians in the West, and nearly every tribe from New England to the western extremity of Lake Superior united in a conspiracy against the white intruders. Pontiac, the bold and sagacious chief of the Ottawas, was at the head of the united savages. On June third of 1763 the redskins simultaneously attacked the English outposts and forts, and all but Fort Pitt, Niagara and Detroit fell into their hands. The frontier settlements in Virginia and Pennsylvania were devastated and more than twenty thousand people were obliged to fly from their homes or to suffer a barbarous death. In all directions the conflagration of dwellings and crops illumined the sky.

The first of these blows,[103)] struck within the present limits of West Virginia, resulted in the total destruction of

103.) "History of West Virginia," by Virgil A. Lewis, page 106 Philadelphia, Pa. 1889.

the settlements in the Greenbrier valley, and within what now is Greenbrier county. All fled before the Indians and in Rockbridge county, where they had hoped to be in safety, many families were killed or taken by them. The Indians also carried destruction and death into the Shenandoah valley, especially in the present counties of Berkeley, Shenandoah and Frederick, making frequent inroads into the upper valley as far as a few miles off Staunton.

Many Germans were among the slaughtered, and indignation and despair forced the survivors to take up arms in self-defence. Among the forces that defended the western forts, not fallen into the hands of the enemy, there were also many Germans, officers as well as privates, and they assisted to check the progress of the savages to the South. Finally Sir Jeffrey Amherst, the English commander-in-chief, sent Colonel *Heinrich Bouquet* or *Henry Boquet*[104]), a native of Switzerland, born in the German Canton Berne, to the West to raise the siege of the beleaguered forts. His troops, organized in haste, were mostly Germans from Pennsylvania and Virginia. He was a soldier born and began his military career in Sweden and later he served in the Dutch army. In 1755 he was persuaded by the English ambassador, Sir Yorke, to enter the English-American service and was appointed major of a battalion of the "Royal American Regiment," consisting mostly of Germans. He served throughout the French and Indian war — and when ordered out against Pontiac's confederates, he defeated them in the fiercely contested battle of Bushy Run in Pennsylvania, arrived at Fort Pitt in August 1764 and forced the Indians on the twelfth day of November, 1764, at the forks of the Muskingum in Ohio, to make peace and cede two hundred and six captives, ninety of whom had been carried away from Virginia.

Touching scenes are related to have occurred at the delivery of the prisoners when husband and wife, parents and children, were reunited. Anton Eikhoff[105]) reports: "A

104) H. A. Rattermann says in "Deutscher Pionier," Vol. X, p 217: That Heinrich Bouquet's true name was "Strauss."

105) "In der neuen Heimath," von Anton Eikhoff, Seite 247. New York, 1884.

Virginia volunteer of Bouquets' army had been robbed of his wife and a two year old child by the Indians about six months before. How delighted was the afflicted soldier, when he could again embrace his beloved wife and a baby three months old, — but the two year old child was missing. The mother could only give the information that the child had been taken from her at the time they were captured. —A few days later however a child was brought into camp and it was thought to be the missing one. The mother was called, and she did not recognize it to be her own at first sight, but on closer examination she did and shouting for joy she drew it to her heart."

With the failure of Pontiac's plot the aggressive power of the Indians was broken, but they continued to make treacherous attacks in northern Virginia.

England had risen by the success of the French and Indian War, — respectively by its "seven years' sea war" (1756 to 1763) with France and Spain, — to the most important naval and colonial power, but she had also added largely to her debt. No sooner was peace restored and the colonies beginning to recover from the calamities of war and Indian devastations, then the English Parliament determined to make them repay by taxation what had been expended in defending them. The colonies, on the other hand, had always considered the aid rendered them by the motherland as insufficient, they charged the English government to have abused them for the benefit of her merchants and manufacturers and they thought England pretty well compensated for the cost of the war by the acquisition of the French territory and Florida. The colonial policy of Great Britain was in fact unscrupulously selfish, it treated the settlers as an inferior class of people, while the English High-Church constantly aimed to reduce free religious exercise. Thus the colonists became exasperated and the idea to form a union for redress of all grievances gained popularity.

In spite of this unsettled and alarming condition of political affairs, the German immigration to Virginia did not cease, although it was less numerous than in the beginning of the century. The following names may prove the correctness of this statement.

Adam Dutton, from Germany, settled in Wythe county and one of his sons, George Dutton, married the daughter of another German named Friedrich Copenhaver in Smith county, Henry Fleenor, also a German, was one of the first colonists in Rock Valley, — in Washington county the Pennsylvania Germans: Anton Horn, Giesler, Rodeker, Gobble, King (Koenig) and Krieger were domiciled, — and also in 1778 Jacob Hartenstine (Hartenstein), whose son, John Hartenstine, was a major in the Confederate army during the War of Secession. George Kerr immigrated into Northumberland, — Wm. Short in Surry county, George Hood (Huth) in Charles City county, Ed. Voss in Culpepper, etc. — and the names of various counties show, that the German immigration extended in all directions of the colony.

It must also be noted that George Washington esteemed the Germans highly as colonists. Having received from the English government, in acknowledgement of his services during the French and Indian war, in 1770, ten thousand acres of land south of the Ohio river, and by purchase secured a large tract of land on the Kanawha and Greenbrier rivers, he had in view to settle his estates with Germans. In February 1774 he wrote from Mt. Vernon to James Tilghman, in Philadelphia: "that motives of interest and of policy required a speedy, successful and inexpensive colonization of these lands, and that of all suggestions made to him, none promised better success: than the settlement of Germans from the Palatinate." He inquired how this plan could be carried out, and if it was advisable to send an intelligent German to Germany to invite immigrants, to control their embarkation in Holland, etc. He also addressed ship-owners like Henry Riddle in Philadelphia and offered to pay the travelling expenses to the Potomac and Ohio, to provide the settlers with victuals until a first crop had been gathered and to exempt them from payment of any rent for a period of four years if there was no house on the property at the time of taking possession of it. But these and other plans to colonize his estate were interrupted by the outbreak of the Revolutionary War.

CHAPTER VIII.

The War of Independence and the German Virginians.

No other period in the history of old Virginia gives better evidence of the devotion and loyalty of the German Virginians to American interests than the War of Independence, — and yet on account of circumstances, entirely beyond their control, they have received comparatively little recognition. When the cry was raised: to defend the rights and liberties of the country, the German colonists did not hesitate for one moment, they left their homes, their wives and children and followed the banner of Virginia's great son, George Washington. With his illustrious name are inseparably associated those of the German heroes: Baron von Steuben, Peter Muehlenberg, von der Wieden, and others, and it is very probable that without their advice and heroism victory would not have crowned the American arms. The German soldiers of the colonial army proved brave and reliable — but, because German allied troops fought in the English army, due credit has been denied them and even their integrity has been suspected. The German subsidiary troops, — the "d . . . . d Hessians," as they were called in Virginia — were only the involuntary, unfortunate victims of an abominable bargain, which *the English King had arranged with covetous German princes.* The German colonists are in no way responsible for this agreement, they were almost unanimously in favor of American independence, while the Anglo-Virginians were divided into two parties: *Whigs* and *Tories;* the former name applied to the patriots, the latter to the supporters of the royal cause. Historians who ignore or slander the patriotism and strong affection of the German-Americans and claim all glory for the Anglo-Americans and their French allies, are partial and therefore unjust. The German-American historian H. A. Rattermann says, with reference to the exaggerated glorification of the French merits[106]): "Lafayette visited America again and was pleased to be carried in triumph through the United States, while the greater Steuben had to compete with many difficulties to receive the lands which Congress had promised to him, and lived without ostentation in quiet retirement in the State of New York." — Steuben and Lafayette are two figures reflecting the character of their respective nations, — the former unselfish, sacrificing everything to a grand idea, — the other also immolating, but calculating to promote his "Gloire." — The Anglo-Americans, disposed to be misled by outer show, sympathized in a demonstrative manner with Lafayette, thus wounding the feeling of their German fellow-citizens.

Twelve decades have passed since the Revolutionary War began, and it is now impossible to do full justice to the merits of the Germans of that great time. Many facts are lost and forgotten, and the anglicizing of the German element in Virginia after the war, has contributed much to create this deplorable incompleteness. But even this resignment of home-reminiscences and of the language of their fathers shows, that the German Virginians were so fully devoted to the American cause: that they forgot the reverential piety they owed to their old Fatherland.

The colonies were without political connection before the Revolution. The people, originating from various nationalities, — separated by vast distances and the want of public roads for travel, — differing in habits and religion, — quarreling about the borders and titles of land, — and influenced by conflicting commercial and agricultural interests, — were only forced to combine by the tyranny and restrictions England imposed upon them. It was not a longing for republican liberty that led to the foundation of the Union, but chiefly endangered material interests. Particularly in the South the

106) "Der deutsche Pionier," Vol. VIII, Seite 18. Cincinnati, Ohio, 1876.

form of government was looked upon with much indifference, the colonists of English descent had no wish to renounce their allegiance to the British crown, and they cherished sentiments of filial devotion towards the motherland. The inclination and desires of the German population however were totally different. The German colonists were not attached to the British rulers by national ties or by gratitude for special favors, and cognizant of the sufferings and abuse that had driven their forefathers from Germany to America, they longed, in their quiet way, for political and religious freedom.

During the period from 1763 to 1775 England had imposed restraints upon the commerce and industry of the colonies, and these, with growing energy, had resisted. The British Parliament passed laws to impede the home trade and navigation of the colonies, juries were abolished, in 1764 the intention to raise a revenue from America was formally declared, and import duties were imposed on sugar, coffee, indigo, wine and silks. On March 22nd, 1765, the Stamp Act was passed, that ordained: that no written instrument should be legal unless the paper was stamped on which it was drawn, and which was to be purchased at an exorbitant price of the agents of the British government. Finally the colonists were directed to furnish to the British soldiery quarters and rations. The colonies had no representation in Parliament and claimed that taxation without representation is tyranny, and they were determined to resist any violation of their rights. King George III however said publicly: "That the obedience of the colonies would be enforced." Clouds gathered rapidly — and the storm threatened to break out. Resolutions were passed by the Colonial Assemblies of Virginia, North Carolina and Massachusetts to resist coercion.

Patrick Henry, a young lawyer, 27 years old, had gained great popularity by his arguments in a lawsuit against the clergy, known as "Parson's Cause," and by pleading on that occasion the cause of colonial rights with eminent eloquence. He was consequently elected a member of the Virginia House of Burgesses, and when the news of the passing of the Stamp Act reached the Old Dominion, he introduced in the House five resolutions, declaring that the right of taxing the colonies belonged to them and that laws like the Stamp Act were destructive of peace. His resolutions were violently opposed to, but finally adopted through the powerful eloquence with which Patrick Henry advocated them. In the heat of the debate he boldly asserted: "Caesar had his Brutus, Charles I his Cromwell, and George III — " "Treason! treason!" interrupted angry loyalists in different parts of the house. — "And George III" — repeated the speaker, his eye lighting up with the flame of patriotism — "and George III may profit by their example. If that be treason, make the most of it!"

The words of the young patriot kindled the slumbering hatred into the flame of revolution — and the German Virginians figured among his most ardent admirers.

Before these events in Virginia became known in Massachusetts, the general court of that colony had adopted measures to inaugurate a combined opposition to the oppressive acts of the English. A Colonial Congress was proposed and on the first Tuesday in October, 1765, the delegates of nine of the colonies met at New York. They drew up a "Declaration of Rights," claiming the privileges of legal born subjects of Great Britain, especially those of self-taxation and trial by jury. The Congress then prepared petitions to the King and to Parliament, assuring the loyalty of the people, — but also their determination to nullify the odious Stamp Act.

As the day approached on which the Stamp Act was to take effect, the popular feeling against it increased. The stamps sent from England were refused the landing or destroyed, — stamp officers were insulted and forced to resign, — associations under the title of "Sons of Liberty" were formed to resist the law and the members resolved to forego all the luxuries of life, rather than to purchase them from England, — the merchants agreed to import no English goods until Parliament should recall the hateful bill, and the first day of November, 1765, appointed for the law to go into operation, was observed as a day of mourning. The bells were tolled, the vessels displayed their flags on half-mast, people dressed in mourning, all business was suspended, and even from the pulpits the popular excitement received expression.

The authorities in England were at a loss how to proceed, they were scared by this energetic protest of the Americans, and the Stamp Act was repealed the following year. The English however still maintained : to have the full right to bind and tax the colonies.

Although the repeal of the Stamp Act was received with great joy in America, yet the clause asserting the supremacy of Parliament, excited the distrust of the colonists and they continued a jealous watch over the actions of the British government. Soon new taxes were levied on tea, glass, paper and painters' colors, and the officers of the navy were appointed custom house officers with duties to enforce the laws. The Assembly of Massachusetts, having addressed circulars to the other Colonial Assemblies, to invite them to cooperate and redress all common grievances, was dissolved.

Anticipating bitter opposition, troops were sent from England to enforce the laws. New York refused to furnish quarters and supplies to British troops, and the legislative power of the Assembly of this colony was suspended. The presence of the troops was regarded as an insult, — and the overbearing conduct of the soldiery provoked the people. In the year 1769 the Assemblies of Virginia and North Carolina were also dissolved. All these measures proved ineffective and the waves of dissatisfaction and hostility tossed higher and higher. Finally, on the 5th of March, 1770, the first bloody collision occurred at Boston, Mass. — Samuel Adams demanded, in the name of the infuriated citizens, of the Governor the withdrawal of the soldiers; he yielded, and the troops retired to Castle William. — In North Carolina the extortion, by corrupt and dishonest officials, — Governor Tyson included, — had caused a number of farmers to unite under the name of "Regulators," to resist oppression. In 1771 the Governor marched against the "rebels" and took a bloody revenge. Many fled to the West and others to Virginia, there increasing the number of the discontented.

When Benjamin Franklin published the correspondence between Governor Hutchinson, of Massachusetts, and Col. Olivier, thereby revealing the intention of Parliament to remodel the constitutional laws of Massachusetts, and when England, after the well-known tea-revolt in Boston, December 18th, 1773, interdicted all commercial intercourse with the port of Boston, and appointed General Gage Governor of Massachusetts and commander-in-chief of the royal troops in America, — the climax of public excitement was reached.

The cause of the people of Boston was espoused by all the colonies, and in Virginia the members of the dissolved Assembly formed an association and voted to recommend to the colonies a General Congress. The first of June, the day on which the port bill (versa Boston) was to take effect, was observed in Virginia as a day of fasting, humiliation and prayer, to implore God that he would avert the evils that threatened them and give them one heart and one mind to firmly oppose by all just and proper means every injury to American rights.

But foremost in the movement of resistance throughout Virginia were the German inhabitants of the Valley. Hon. J. M. H. Beale stated in a letter, published in the "New York Herald" and afterwards at Woodstock, Va., Nov. 30th, 1894, in the "Shenandoah Herald:" "They formed a distinct organization, as contradistinguished from its colonial, and invested power in a 'Committee of Safety,' the prerogatives of which were to erect opposition to the royal power in case of necessity.

"The meeting which took these initial revolutionary steps was held at Woodstock, on the 16th of June, 1774, one year before the celebrated Mecklenburg meeting in North Carolina, which occurred in June, 1775. The Rev. Peter Muehlenberg was chosen the moderator of the meeting, and afterwards, as chairman of the Committee on Resolutions, reported a number of spirited and appropriate resolutions, the tone of which was bolder than public opinion was then prepared to sanction. The following are a part of the noble sentiments then put forth by those patriotic lovers of liberty.

"That we will pay due submission to such acts of government as his Majesty has a right by law to exercise over his subjects, and to such only.

"That it is the inherent right of British subjects to be governed and taxed by representatives chosen by themselves only, and that every act of the British Parliament respecting the internal policy of America is a dangerous and unconstitutional invasion of our rights and privileges.

"That the enforcing the execution of the said act of Parliament by a military power will have a necessary tendency to cause a civil war, thereby dissolving that union which has so long happily subsisted between the mother country and her colonies; and that we will most heartily and unanimously concur with our suffering brethren of Boston, and every other part of North America, who are the immediate victims of tyranny, in promoting all proper measures to avert such dreadful calamities, to procure a redress of our grievances, and to secure our common liberties.'

"The other resolutions were common at that period, depreciating importation or exportation with Great Britain and the East India Company, who are called 'the servile tools of Arbitrary power.' The proceedings close by 'pledging themselves to each other, and to our country, that we will inviolably adhere to the votes of this day.' The Committee of Safety and Correspondence appointed for the county consisted of Rev. Peter Muehlenberg, chairman; Francis Slaughter, Abraham Bird, Tavener Beale, (father of the undersigned,) John Tipton, and Abraham Bowman, esqs., members.

"The proceedings of this meeting are published in full in the Virginia Gazette for August 4, 1774, a file of which paper is preserved in the Congressional Library at Washington City."

On the 4th of September, 1774, the First Continental Congress met in Philadelphia. All the colonies, except Georgia, were represented, and by an unanimous vote Peyton Randolph, of Virginia, was elected president. It was resolved to resist the oppression of England, to approve the conduct of Massachusetts, to entreat General Gage to desist from military operations, and finally to continue the Congressional Union until the repeal of oppressive duties by Parliament. Congress called upon the people to practice in the use of arms and to prepare to act in case of emergency, and yet only a few members of Congress had any idea of independence.

All attempts at reconciliation however proved futile. King George III, by nature arbitrary and stubborn, was bent on reducing his colonial subjects to submission by the sword. The determination of the King to oppress the Americans was so notorious, that when the war actually broke out, it was called in England "the King's War." Walpole's "George III," Vol. IV, p. 114, contains the following pungent remarks: "The war was considered as the war of the King personally. Those who supported it, were called the King's friends, while those who wished the country to pause and reconsider the propriety of persevering in the contest, were branded as disloyal." George III was a peculiar man and wrote this: "I wish nothing but good: therefore, every man who does not agree with me, is a liar and a scoundrel." The British Parliament was determined to make no concessions, and early in 1775 rejected a conciliatory bill introduced by Lord Chatham; thus the colonies were driven to the dread alternative of war, and Patrick Henry gave the signal, when in March, 1775, he uttered the memorable words before the Convention of Virginia, assembled at Richmond in the "Old Church": "As for me, give me liberty or give me death."

As early as the ninth of May, 1775, representatives of the people of North Carolina[107]), mostly Germans, assembled at Charlotte, Mecklenburg County, N. C., to formally renounce their allegiance to the King, and to make provisions for self-government. This was *the first declaration of independence, illustrating the German spirit and aim*, — while the men of the North were simply fighting for their rights as *subjects* of Great Britain.[108]) The demonstrations in North Carolina were of such character, that the Governor deemed it prudent to take refuge on a man-of-war in July, — only two months later the Governor of South Carolina followed his example, evacuating the City of Charleston, — and the Governor of Virginia, as will be explained later, also was compelled to fly on board of an armed vessel. Previous to these events, April 19th, 1775, the battle of Lexington, Mass., had been fought, the Second Continental Congress met at Philadelphia on May 10th, assuming the authority of a general government of the "United Colonies of

107.) "Der deutsche Pionier," Vol. III, May and June Edition. Cincinnati, Ohio, 1871.

108.) "American History for Schools," by G. P. Quackenbos, p. 141. New York, 1879.

America," and elected George Washington commander-in-chief of the American forces. On the 17th of June the battle of Bunker Hill was fought. The Americans were driven back, but they still besieged Boston, and in a few weeks Washington took command.

It is not the object to give a complete description of the War of Independence in this history, it aims to state the part Virginia, and the German Virginians in particular, took in this great struggle. All the foregoing and following historical details of a general character are simply intended to explain the action of the German Virginians.

Before further describing the course of events, another precursor of the Revolutionary War, — a new Indian war, in the year 1774, known as the "*Dunmore War*," — must be mentioned, during which the German settlers of the north-eastern mountain region of Virginia again suffered severely.

The treaty with the savages, which had not been violated since 1764, was broken by the English.[109]) Several Indians were murdered simply to gratify the desire for Indian blood, and they retaliated in their cruel savage custom. The first innocent victims of their rage were the members of a German family by name Stroud, living on Gauley river near its junction with the Great Kanawha. The murder of the family of Logan, chief of the Mingoes and an ally of the English during the French and Indian war, particularly exasperated the Indians. Logan swore to take bloody revenge and invited the cooperation of the Delawares and Shawnees to annihilate the treacherous Whites. The two Indian tribes hesitated to join him and he began the war alone, attacking the settlements on the Ohio river.

The Assembly of Virginia resolved to protect the colonists. Governor Lord Dunmore left the gubernatorial residence at Williamsburg with an army of about twelve hundred men, and General Andrew Lewis, of Augusta county, a Scotch descendant, was ordered to muster troops in the counties of Berkeley, Hampshire, Frederick and Shenandoah, principally populated by Germans. Germans and Scotch responded with patriotism to his call,

---

109) "History of West Virginia," by Virgil A. Lewis, page 113. Philadelphia, Pa., 1889.

and on October 6th, 1774, he arrived with his force of eleven hundred men at the mouth of the Great Kanawha. His little army consisted of two regiments, commanded by Colonels William Fleming, of Botetourt county, and Charles Lewis, of Augusta, — two companies from Culpepper and Bedford, — and a detachment from the Holstein settlement, now Washington county, at the head of which was Captain Shelby, a German Virginian. They erected a camp to await the arrival of Lord Dunmore's troops, but on October 9th a messenger arrived with orders from the Governor, commanding General Lewis to cross the Ohio, to dislodge the Indians in his way and to march towards the Indian villages on the Scioto, where the two divisions of the Virginian army should meet. On the 10th of October General Lewis started on his dangerous march and soon met with the Indians, who were determined to prevent the union of the two detachments. They were in superior force, the combined tribes of the Shawanees, Delawares, Mingos, Cayugas and Wyandottes, under the leadership of the famous chief Cornstalk.[110])

A general engagement occurred, extending from the banks of the Ohio to the Kanawha, distant half a mile from the junction of the two rivers. General Lewis, who had witnessed a similar scene at Braddock's defeat, acted with firmness and decision, and his men fought with admirable bravery. Colonel Lewis was killed, Colonel Fleming severely wounded, one half of the other officers and seventy-five men were slain and one hundred and forty wounded. The memory of the desperate battle of Point Pleasant still lives in a popular song among the mountaineers of Virginia:

"Let us mind the tenth day of October,
Seventy-four, which caused woe, —
The Indian savages they did cover
The pleasant banks of the Ohio."

The next day Colonel Christian, with three hundred men from Fincastle, Botetourt county, arrived at Point Pleasant and at once proceeded to bury the dead. The wounded were

110) "Geschichte des grossen amerik Westen," von H A. Rattermann, Seite 18 50. Cincinnati, 1875.

sheltered in the hastily thrown up walls of Fort Randolph, which was garrisoned by one hundred men, and then the brave Virginians crossed the Ohio in hot pursuit of the defeated savages. On the 24th of October they encamped on Congo Creek, near the present town of Pickaway, having received orders to advance no further, — and to the great disappointment of the little army, desirous to avenge the death of their fallen comrades, Lord Dunmore negotiated for peace with the Indians. Thus closed "Dunmore's War," but its unpopular end only hastened the outbreak of the great crisis in Virginia. The hostile mood of the Virginians induced the English government to instruct Lord Dunmore to remove all military stores and arms to places of security, — and on the 20th day of April, 1775, he seized a quantity of powder belonging to the colony, — kept at Williamsburg, — and conveyed it on board the man-of-war "Magdalen," anchored near Yorktown. When this act of the Governor became known, the colonial militia and all the people were highly exasperated. They took up arms and organized under the leadership of Patrick Henry. The cowardly Dunmore declared, that he would free all slaves and destroy Williamsburg by fire, if any harm should be done him or any English official. This threat only enraged the people still more, — about six hundred men from the mountain counties, *principally from German districts*, assembled at Fredericksburg, — and also in other sections of Virginia the citizens prepared to defend their rights. The attitude of the Virginians was so threatening, that in June, as has been stated before, Lord Dunmore fled on board a British man-of-war. This was the end of royal government in Virginia. The patriot Patrick Henry was made Governor: — now by will of the people.

Lord Dunmore tried to regain his lost authority and organized a troop of Tories, British soldiers and fugitive slaves, — but on December 9th, 1775, he was defeated at Great Bridge near Norfolk, — he retreated to this flourishing city and burnt it before the evacuation on January 6th, 1776. He attempted then to fortify himself on Governor's Island in the Chesapeake Bay, but General Andrew Lewis routed his force and Dunmore embarked again on an English vessel and after that time never returned to Virginia. — Several historians accuse Lord Dunmore to have wilfully provoked the "Dunmore War," in order to reduce the strength of the Virginians, — and there may be some truth in this assertion. It is undoubtedly true that England encouraged, during the War of Independence, the Indians to attack the settlements on the frontier. — The jurisdiction of Virginia, extended in 1776 to the Mississippi, comprising the present States of Kentucky, Tennessee, Indiana, Illinois and Ohio. Several bold pioneers, mainly Germans from Virginia and North Carolina, had emigrated to this wilderness, and the Indians, fearful of being deprived of their beloved hunting-ground, and stirred up by English emissaries, attacked the exposed settlements in Kentucky and West Virginia. In the spring of 1776 the Cherokees also began to invade the settlements in Tennessee, the Carolinas and Georgia, — and Virginia and North and South Carolina armed three expeditions to destroy the villages and fields of the savages. Towards the end of the year the defeated Indians were compelled to sue for peace. In 1777 other Indian tribes, again incited by English agitation, renewed the murderous invasion, and chiefly the German-Virginian homes on the Ohio and Monongahela were ravaged. England adopted the most barbarous measures of warfare against the patriots. It paid a premium to the Indians for every American scalp, making no distinction of sex or age. This detestable action had the most frightful results, as will be illustrated by the following statement.

Among the rich spoils[111]) that a New England expedition captured in February, 1782, from the Indians, there were eight packages with ten hundred and sixty-two scalps that these savages had taken within the last three years from American colonists in Virginia, Pennsylvania, New York and New England, and which they had intended to send to Governor Haldimand of Canada with the request to forward them to the King of England: "That he might look on them, be refreshed by their sight, and reward his Indian Allies for their loyalty with new domiciles."

---

111) "Geschichte der Deutschen im Staate New-York," von Friedrich Kapp, -- Seite 277—278. New-York, 1868.

In Marshall county, West Virginia, about four miles from Moundsville, a monument still reminds of the victims of the savage allies of Great Britain. The monument bears this inscription[112]): "This humble stone is erected to the memory of Captain Foreman (a German Virginian) and twenty-one of his men, who were slain by a band of ruthless savages — the allies of a civilized nation of Europe — on the 25th of September, 1777.

So sleep the brave who sink to rest
By all their country's wishes blessed."

The fights with the Indians continued to the end of the War of Independence, but side by side with pictures of fright they present scenes of comforting and admirable heroism, and not the least on part of German frontiermen.

In September, 1777, the savages[113]), their number variously estimated at from three hundred and eighty to five hundred warriors, abundantly supplied with arms and ammunition by the British Governor Hamilton at Detroit, besieged Fort Henry, now Wheeling, W. Va. The garrison, under command of Colonel Shepherd (Schaefer), a Pennsylvanian German, numbered only forty-two fighting men all told, counting those advanced in years as well as those who were mere boys. The supply of gunpowder in the fort was soon exhausted, and Colonel Shepherd resolved to send for a keg of gunpowder which was known to be in the house of Ebenezer Zane, about sixty yards from the gate of the fort. Three or four young men volunteered to undertake the desperate enterprise, but the Colonel informed them, that the weak state of the garrison would not justify the absence of more than one man, and that it was for themselves to decide who the one should be. Much time was consumed in the eager contention of the patriotic young men; it was feared that the Indians would renew the attack before the powder could be secured, and at this crisis a young lady, the sister of Ebenezer and Silas Zane, the German founders of Wheeling, came forward and desired

112) "History of West Virginia," by Virgil A. Lewis, page 667. Philadelphia, Pa., 1889.

113.) "History of West Virginia," by Virgil A. Lewis, page 155. Philadelphia, Pa. 1889.

that she might be permitted to execute the service. Elizabeth Zane was the name of this German Virginian heroine. She said to the men, who refused to consent to her reckless plan: "As the garrison was very weak, no soldier's life should be risked, and that if she were to fall her loss would not be felt." — Her noble undertaking was ultimately granted and the gate opened for her to pass out. When the brave girl crossed the open space to reach her brother's house, the Indians looked at her in surprise and by some unexplained motive permitted her to pass unmolested. As soon however as she reappeared with the keg of powder in her arms, — suspecting no doubt the nature of her burden, — they discharged a volley at her as she swiftly glided towards the fort, — but the fearless girl reached the gate unhurt.

The historian of West Virginia[114]) says very truly: "The pages of history may furnish a parallel to the noble exploit of Elizabeth Zane, but an instance of greater self-devotion and moral intrepidity is not to be found anywhere."

The wife of Ebenezer Zane and several other women in the fort, employed themselves in running bullets and patches for the use of the men, and their presence and good cheering words contributed not a little to turn the fortunes of the day. The next morning Captain Swearinger, — another German Virginian, — arrived with fourteen men in a perogue from Cross Creek and was fortunate enough to fight his way into the fort without the loss of a single man. Shortly afterwards Major Samuel McColloch, with forty mounted men from Short Creek, came to the relief of the garrison, and the Indians raised the siege and withdrew after setting fire to all the houses and fences outside the fort and killing about three hundred head of cattle. Of the forty-two men who were in the fort on the morning of the 27th, not less than twenty-three were killed and five wounded. Governor Patrick Henry expressed his sincere acknowledgment to Colonel Shepherd and his men for their heroic defence.

In September, 1782, three hundred Indians again attacked Fort Henry, but accomplished nothing, and about one hun-

114) "History of West Virginia," by Virgil A. Lewis, p. 161. Philadelphia, 1889.

dred of them marched to Fort Rice, on Buffalo Creek, which they expected to take without much opposition. This fort was made up of a few cabins and log-houses and was defended by *only six Germans,* — but this small garrison repulsed all the enemy's attacks and forced them to retreat. The names of these stout-hearted heroes are: Jacob Miller, George Lefler, Peter Fullenweider, Daniel Rice, Jacob Lefler and George Fellbaum, — the latter was killed. The last resting places of the others are forgotten, but the names of the six brave men are written down on the pages of history, — they are immortal.

Among the participators in General George Rogers Clark's celebrated campaign to Kentucky, Indiana and Illinois, the following German Virginian officers gained distinction: Captain Leonard Helm, of Fauquier county, and Major Joseph Bowman, of Frederick county, who was next in command to General Clark. Other names, mentioned in Wm. Hayden English's "Conquest of the Northwest of the River Ohio, 1778—1783, and Life of General Clark," are essentially German-Virginian, as: Honaker, Chrisman, etc. — General Clark himself was a native of Albemarle county, Virginia. No episode in the history of Virginia is more glorious than this. With one hundred and seventy ragged boys General Clark crossed rivers in the month of February, 1779, planted the Virginian Standard upon the banks of the Mississippi, — demanded and secured unconditional surrender, — and from that time the country of Illinois, Missouri, etc., was opened to civilization. — The great distances, the uncertainty, the wilderness, and the Indians made General Clark's expedition one of terrible hardship, and the adroitness with which Clark proceeded in reconciling both the Indians and French inhabitants and surprising the English posts: Kaskaskia and Vincennes, and the indomitable energy displayed by him and his soldiers in overcoming the rigors of winter and the terrors of rain and flood, cannot but command admiration.

Several years before the Revolutionary War General Morgan organized his famous corps of riflemen and took active part in the combats with the Indians. A large number of German Virginians from Winchester and its environs were among his men. Andreas Simon[115]) names the following: Johann Schultz, Jacob Sperry, Peter and Simon Lauck, Friedrich Kurtz, Karl Grimm, Georg Heisler, and Adam Kurz. Morgan's so-called "Dutch Mess"[116]) gained special fame by its attachment to the General and brave conduct. They accompanied him in all his adventurous expeditions against the Indians, in the disastrous campaign of General Braddock, in Arnold's expedition to Canada, and to the end of the War of Independence. The six members of the "mess" acted as aide-de-camp, — but never received or accepted an officer's commission. After the war they were rewarded with valuable lands near Winchester, which to this day are owned by their descendants.

It has been stated that the German Virginians were dissatisfied with the English rule and very much disposed to assist in the overthrow of British supremacy. "Der Staatsbote," a German paper published at Philadelphia, had many readers among the Germans of the Valley, and stirred the revolutionary spirit. Heinrich Ringer, at Winchester, and Jacob Nicolas, at Picket Mountain, Augusty county, were the Virginian agents of the paper. The edition of March 19th, 1776, contains an appeal to the Germans, beginning as follows[117]): "Remember that your forefathers emigrated to America to escape bondage and to enjoy liberty, and bore the greatest hardship and ill treatment. — Remember that where bondage existed in Germany, no bondsman was allowed to marry without the consent of his patron, and that parents and children were not treated much better than the black slaves in West India." — The article closes with the words: "Remember that the British Government and Parliament aim to establish similar and perhaps worse conditions in America."

The "Staatsbote" was like a fire-brand thrown among the German settlers — and they enthusiastically embraced the American cause. Their self-sacrifice and fidelity is worthy of lauda-

---

115,) "Der Westen," Chicago, Ills., 1892.

116.) "Der Süden," deutsch-amerikanische Wochenschrift, Jahrgang I, No. 2, Seite 4. Richmond, Va., 1891.

117.) "Deutsch-amerikanisches Magazin," von H. A. Rattermann, Band I, Heft 8, Seite 422. Cincinnati, 1886.

tion. L. A. Wollenweber[118]) for example relates the following instance of German devotion: "In 1751 Friedrich Ladner had emigrated from Pliningen, in Wuertemberg, to America and with his family settled a few miles south of Harper's Ferry. When the people rushed to arms *three of his sons* and *four of his grand-children* joined Peter Muehlenberg's regiment to defend their adopted fatherland."

In 1776 the Convention of Virginia resolved to recruit seven new regiments besides the existing, and among the commanding officers were the following with German names[119]):

2nd Virginia line:	Colonel Christian Febiger (1778—1783), Lieutenant-Colonel Charles Simms (1778—1779), and Colonel Wm. Darke (1791).
3d " "	Colonel G. von der Wieden (Weedon), Lieutenant-Colonel Ch. Fleming.
4th " "	Major Ch. Fleming.
6th " "	Colonel M. Buckner, Colonel Adam Stephan, Lieutenant-Colonel Chas. Simms (1777—1778).
8th " "	Colonel Peter Muehlenberg (1776-1777), Lieutenant-Colonel and after 1777 Colonel Abraham Bauman (Bowman), Major Keim, and in succession: Wm. Darke and Andreas Waggener.
9th " "	Colonel Ch. Fleming, Major Peter Helfenstein.
11th " "	Lieutenant-Colonel Christian Febiger (1776—1778).

Of other German Virginian officers of the Colonial army are known: Major Johannes Mueller, Mathias Heid, Abel Westphal, Daniel Kolb, Jacob Rucker and Isaac Israel[120]), — all but the

118.) "Deutscher Pionier," 2. und 3. Jahrgang. — Historische Novelle von L. A. Wollenweber, Cincinnati, 1870—1871.

119.) "Historical Register of the Officers of the Continental Army," by F. B. Heitman. Washington, 1893.

120.) "The American Jew as Patriot, Soldier and Citizen," by Simon Wolf. Philadelphia, 1895.

first two belonged to Muehlenberg's regiment. The Pension Registers in Washington also prove that German Virginians served in Maryland and Pennsylvania regiments.

A most striking example of patriotism was given by *Johann Gabriel Peter Muehlenberg*, the pastor of the Lutheran church at Woodstock, in the Shenandoah Valley. He was born at Trappe, Pa., in 1746, his father was the venerable patriarch of the Lutheran Church in America, the Rev. Heinrich M. Muehlenberg, — under his guidance he received an excellent education. In his youth he was a boy difficult to manage. Destined for the ministry, his father sent him to Germany to conclude his studies, — but Peter entered an apprenticeship to a mercantile house in Luebeck. He stayed there three years, working faithfully, — but his spirits were depressed by his close and monotonous duties. He abruptly left his place and enlisted in Hanover in a regiment of dragoons. Later on maturer judgment overcame his inclination towards the adventurous and he recommenced the study of theology, passed his examinations and after his return to America he received the vocation of pastor at Woodstock, Va. The young pastor gained the intimate friendship of George Washington and Patrick Henry — and took great interest in the struggle for independence and the preparations for war. His military antecedence was revived, and upon the recommendations of George Washington and Patrick Henry he was commissioned Colonel of the Eighth Virginia Regiment. In January, 1776, he preached his valedictory sermon. "From far and near the German farmers came with their wives and children," says Rev. Dr. Zimmermann,[121]) "and crowded the little church at Woodstock." — Muehlenberg implored the congregation to support the struggle for liberty and then he exclaimed: "Dear brethren and sisters, I feel truly grieved to announce that this is my farewell sermon, but if it is God's will I shall soon return to you. It is a sacred duty that calls me from you and I feel I must submit to it. The endangered fatherland, to which we owe wealth and blood, needs our arms — it calls on its sons to drive off the oppressors.

121.) "Vierhundert Jahre amerikanischer Geschichte," von Dr. G. A. Zimmermann, Seite 227—228. Milwaukee, Wisc., 1893.

You know how much we have suffered for years, — that all our petitions for help have been in vain,—and that the King of England shut his ears to our complaints. The Holy Scripture says: There is a time for everything in this world; a time to talk, a time to be silent, a time to preach and to pray, — but also a time to fight, — and this time has come! Therefore, whoever loves freedom and his new fatherland, he *may follow me!"*— After these inspiring remarks Rev. Muehlenberg uttered a benediction, and then he laid aside his priestly robe and buckled a sword about his waist. — A scene of indescribable enthusiasm followed — the entire assembly arose from the seats, and Dr. Luther's powerful hymn: "Eine feste Burg ist unser Gott," was intonated. Drums were beaten outside the church — and after the lapse of half an hour one hundred and sixty-two men and youths had enlisted to follow their parson. — This act of German-American patriotism has been immortalized by several German-American poets, like Dr. Victor Precht in his drama: "Kuerass und Kutte," and Prof. Wilhelm Mueller in his poem: "Die letzte Predigt.[122])

Muehlenberg's regiment was first ordered South and distinguished itself at Charleston, S. C., and in Georgia. Reduced greatly in number by loss on the battlefield and sickness, the commanding officer, Gen. Lee, having received orders to join the northern army, directed Muehlenberg, sick himself, to return to Woodstock with his invalides. He was prostrated by an attack of fever, but only a short rest was allowed him to recover his health; he was ordered to bring up the rest of his regiment from Savannah, to reinforce it with new members and to join General Washington's army in New Jersey. When Muehlenberg's regiment reached Washington's camp it was stronger than ever before, having gained many recruits in Maryland and Pennsylvania.

On February 21st, 1777, Muehlenberg was promoted by act of Congress to the rank of Brigadier-General, and besides his own regiment the Third and Fifth Virginia were placed under his command. Many Germans also belonged to these regiments.

122.) "Am Wege gepflückt," Gedicht-Sammlung von Wilh. Müller. Glarus in der Schweiz, 1888.

General Muehlenberg was a born military genius and Anglo-American historians have acknowledged his courage and talent. General Washington esteemed him highly — and the celebrated German generals: von Steuben and De Kalb, were attached to him by ties of friendship. — The battle of Brandywine on the 11th of September, 1777, was disastrous to the American army. A rout ensued and utter defeat was prevented only by the brave resistance of Muehlenberg's brigade, that checked the advance of the pursuing British army and enabled the retreating American and French forces to escape annihilation. — In the battle of Germantown, on October 4th, 1777, he defeated the opposing wing of the enemy's army, and when the centre and right wing of the Americans gave way, he again covered the retreat. His loss was severe, among the killed was Major Keim, — but the weakened regiments replenished their number by numerous deserters of the German subsidiary troops of the British army. — At Valley Forge he aided his friend, General von Steuben, to reorganize the demoralized army, and under his command he fought in 1780 in Virginia against the traitor Arnold, who pillaged the country along the James river. When Arnold harassed Petersburg, Muehlenberg, with a few hundred Germans, defended the bridge leading to the city, and when forced to withdraw, he retreated in good order. In his report to Congress Governor Jefferson spoke with the highest admiration of this war-like deed. — In the final decisive combats at Yorktown Muehlenberg's brigade stormed and took the redoubt on the left wing of the British fortification and thus assisted to force the surrender. In this glorious affair Colonel Bowman lost his life.

After the surrender of Yorktown, General Washington appointed Muehlenberg military commander of Virginia, and on the conclusion of peace the Lutheran community at Woodstock invited General Muehlenberg to resume his pastorate. Muehlenberg declined and said: "It would not be proper to again graft the pastor on the soldier," — and he returned to his native State, Pennsylvania. He was elected to Congress and died on October 1st, 1807. At Trappe, near his father's old church, a tombstone bears the following inscription:

"To the memory of General Peter Muehlenberg.
Born Oct. 1st, 1746, and died Oct. 1st, 1807.
He was brave in battle, wise in council, honorable in all his actions, a faithful friend and an honest man."

The reward with which the National Government presented him, was rather scanty in consideration of his noble services. His father wrote on September 6th, 1785, with unmistakable bitterness: "After the end of the war the S. T. government donated to him some thousand acres of land far off in the wilderness, which region is still in possession of the savage Indians and must either be purchased with money or taken by force of arms."

General *Gerhard von der Wieden* — or Weedon, as Anglo-American historians call him, — is another example of patriotic devotion. He was a native of Hannover and had served as an officer in the German army. He came to America with General Heinrich Bouquet and took part in the campaigns of the French and Indian war. After the treaty of peace was signed, von der Wieden settled at Fredericksburg, Va., where he married, took charge of the post office and established an inn. He took great interest in the political events of the time and enthusiastically advocated the American cause. At the outbreak of the Revolution von der Wieden was captain in the Third Virginia Regiment of Militia, and on February 13th, 1776, he was elected Lieutenant-Colonel, — on August 12th he received the appointment as Colonel of the reorganized First Virginia Regiment in the Continental Army, and on February 24th, 1777, he was promoted to the rank of Brigadier-General. On account of disregard in promotion he afterwards resigned his charge, but upon the urgent request of General Muehlenberg he again accepted a brigadier-generalship and finally commanded the Virginia militia at Gloucester Point during the siege of Yorktown. General von Steuben esteemed him as an experienced and valiant officer, and the Englishman, Dr. J. T. D. Smith, who travelled in America and published an account of his travels at London in 1784, bears the following testimony of his patriotic sentiments: "When I reached Fredericksburg I did put up at an inn kept by one Weedon, who is now a general in the American army and was zealous to fan the flame of insurrection."

General *William Darke*, already mentioned, was born at Lancaster, Pa., in 1736, and was but five years of age when he came to Virginia with his German parents, who settled near Shepherdstown. Here they were on the outermost bounds of civilization, and amid this solitude young Darke grew up to manhood. "Nature made him," — says Virgil A. Lewis, — "a noble man; he was endowed with an herculean frame; his manners were rough, his mind strong but uncultivated, and his disposition frank and fearless." — A spirit of daring and adventure induced him, when only aged nineteen, to join Braddock's army. During the War of Independence he rose to the rank of Lieutenant-Colonel, and in 1791 he commanded the Second Virginia Regiment. On the disastrous field on the banks of the St. Mary he evinced the utmost bravery. General St. Clair in his official report, written at Fort Washington on November 9th, 1791, says: "Colonel Darke was ordered to make a charge with a part of the second line, and to turn the left flank of the enemy. This was executed with great spirit and at first promised great success. The Indians instantly gave way and were driven back three or four hundred yards, but for want of a sufficient number of riflemen to pursue this advantage, they soon returned and the troops were obliged to give back in their turn." Colonel Darke's Virginians made a second charge, not less gallantly performed, but with sad results, and among the many killed was Captain Joseph Darke, the youngest son of the Colonel. Colonel Darke then returned to his home in Berkeley county, which he represented in the General Assembly, and in acknowledgment of his military services he received the title of General. He died on the 20th day of November, 1801, and "Darkeville," in Berkeley county, and "Darke county," in Ohio, commemorate his name.

General *Adam Stephan*, Stephen or Steven, already spoken of in Chapter VII, entered the Continental Army at the beginning of the war with rank as Colonel of the Sixth Virginia Regiment. On September 4th, 1776, he received a Brigadier-General's commission, and on February 12th, 1777, that of Major-General. He gained distinction in the battle of Brandywine, but his inclination to dissipation was his ruin. He was tried by a court-martial on the charge of intoxication at the battle of Germantown, — and was found guilty and discharged from the army in 1778. Nevertheless he enjoyed the respect of his countrymen and in 1788 was elected to represent Berkeley county in the Convention. He died near Winchester in November 1791.

Armand's Legion, that the Marquis de la Rouerie, with the consent of Congress, recruited in the summer of 1777 in America of men "who could not speak English," was originally commanded by Baron von Ottendorf, a Saxon by birth, and consisted chiefly of German Virginians of Augusta, Rockingham, Monroe, Frederick, Loudon and Berkeley counties. To this corps the independent cavalry company of Captain Paul Schott was afterwards added. All officers and privates of this squadron were Germans. H. A. Rattermann[123]) gives the following names: Johann Paul Schott, Captain, — Christian Manele and Georg Schaffner, Lieutenants, — Friedrich Liebe, Georg Duehn, and Georg Langhammer, Sergeants, — Friedrich Bergmann, David Breckle, and Johann Goedecke, Corporals, — and Johann Holzbrueck, Trumpeter. The history of *Captain Schott* is one of the most pleasing pictures of that stormy time and the historian Rattermann relates it as below:

"In the early part of the year 1776, a young man of slender stature, fascinating manners and highly educated, arrived at New York to see America and to inform himself about the Revolutionary War, already waged for three quarters of a year. English and Dutch letters of introduction to Governor Tryon represented him as Johann Paul Schott, First Lieutenant in the army of his Majesty Frederick II of Prussia and Adjutant of his Highness Prince Ferdinand of Brunswick, Lieutenant-General of the Prussian army. His soldierly manners and pleasing and correct conduct soon gained him the favor of the aristocratic circles to which he had been especially recommended. He spoke English fluently with only a slight German accent. He had crossed the ocean in a Dutch ship from Rotterdam, which probably sailed to New York, that port being in possession of the Tories, and with more assurance of safety to reach than either Philadelphia or Baltimore, not to speak of Boston, which was besieged at that

123.) "Der deutsche Pionier," Vol. VIII, Seite 57. Cincinnati, Ohio, 1876.

time by General Washington. Not desirous to stay at New York and watch only the British methods of war, he soon left for Philadelphia, being also provided with letters of introduction to several prominent American leaders. He was impressed by the deep concern which was exhibited by the patriots for their cause. He was so much inspired, that he resolved to draw his sword for American independence. Seeing that the colonists were much in need of arms, particularly cannon and ammunition, and possessed of a large sum of money, he determined to risk the hazardous enterprise to supply them with the requisites of war. During the summer of 1776 he sailed to St. Eustache, a small island of the Lesser Antilles, owned by the Dutch, where goods and military stores were sold and blockade-runners fitted out. Herr Schott chartered a schooner, freighted it with arms and ammunition, which he purchased, and then steered for the Coast of Virginia. At Hampton Roads he met the English fleet, which he deceived by raising the English flag and dressing his sailors like English marines. The British man-of-war allowed the schooner to pass unmolested, supposing it to be a transport ship of the fleet, — until it sailed beyond the line. Discovering their error, they signalled it to return, which was of course not obeyed, and then several volleys and finally a broadside were fired on the swiftly sailing vessel, but did it no harm. When Schott neared the land, the English uniforms, which he and his men had had no time to change, endangered their lives again. Although he had now raised the flag of the Colonies, several shots were fired from the American batteries, and by one of them the rigging of the schooner was torn. Hoisting a white flag, the Americans recognized them at last to be friends and amid cheers of welcome they landed at Norfolk. Schott sold his arms, etc., and upon his application to Congress he received a captain's commission, with the order to report at once to General Washington at New York. At the time he arrived at New York depression and gloom weighed heavily upon the army. Lord Howe's army had been reinforced by nine thousand Hessians and Brunswick troops under General Heister, and had attacked and defeated the American troops on Long Island, under Putnam. Lord Howe's object now was to get possession of New York and the Hudson — and he ordered the British fleet to sail up the North river to cut off the retreat of Washington's army to New Jersey. This was the situation on the 9th of September, when Capt. Schott reached camp. He found the commanding general at the battery, watching the English men-of-war. A powerful frigate first tried to go up the North river and General Washington gave the order to open fire, — but at that time the British on Governor's Island began to shell the Americans, and with great effect. Especially one English cannon was well served and did much harm. Schott, who had no chance to approach General Washington at this critical moment, observed an American cannon which was not served, and he quickly collected some soldiers, had the gun loaded, sighted it himself, and soon silenced the troublesome piece of ordinance on Governor's Island. General Washington had observed his brave deed and at once placed Captain Schott in command of a battery. He was afterwards authorized to recruit a company of German dragoons, — as already mentioned, — to appoint his officers and to use the *German language in command.* His squadron gained many laurels during the following years of the war. After the close of the war Captain Schott was made Judge of Luzerne county, Pa., and he died in 1829 at Philadelphia.

The defeats at Brandywine and Germantown and the evacuation of Philadelphia proved very demoralizing to the American army. At Valley Forge, on the Schuylkill river, twenty-two miles from Philadelphia, General Washington and his suffering men went into winter-quarters. They were encamped in comfortless huts, half-clad, frequently in need of the plainest clothing, without shoes or blankets. Sickness prevailed, and many friends of the cause lost confidence in General Washington. While he was fighting against famine and perils, General Conway, Inspector-General of the army, and a cunning intriguer, formed a plot with the officers to raise General Gates to the chief command in his stead. Even the life of Washington was endangered, and upon the advice of his Secretary and Adjutant, Reed, the son of German parents in New Jersey, — who replied to an offer made him by the British of wealth and titles for the future, if he would aid the royal cause: "I am not worth purchasing; but, such as I am, the King of England is not rich enough to buy me,"—he authorized Major Bartholomaeus von Heer and Captain Jacob Meytinger to organize a mounted German body-guard under the name of "Independent Troop of Horse," and he entrusted only this troop with the carrying of all orders from his head-quarters. Some German Virginians were among the members of this German-American body-guard, as: Friedrich Fuchs, of Woodstock, Corporal Ignatz Effinger, Friedrich Trecius and Heinrich Frank. — At this dark hour of the Revolutionary War, the greatest German-American of his time: *Baron Friedrich Wilhelm von Steuben*, who in the Seven Years' War had served under Frederick the Great, of Prussia, came to America and tendered his sword to the National cause. He was appointed to General Conway's office and soon made his skillful management apparent in every department. General von Steuben introduced a strict discipline after the Prussian pattern and a uniform system of tactics. For some time, says Washington Irving, there was nothing but drilling in the camp of Valley Forge, followed by evolutions of different kind. Officers and men were schooled. The troops were formed in line of parade, every officer in his place, and the Baron walked along the front examining every musket and controling that accoutrements and uniforms were in perfect order. In the start the Baron had to compete with a dislike of the foreigner and the difficulties of the English language, but his kindness, justice and earnest care for the welfare of the soldiers soon gained him general confidence and affection. General Washington rendered him all possible assistance. Milder weather, the recognition of the Independence of the United Colonies by France on the 6th day of February, 1778, and the news, that a French fleet was on its way to help them in their struggle, — gladdened the hearts of all, and confidence returned.

General von Steuben was born at Magdeburg and entered the Prussian army when but fourteen years of age. He distinguished himself in the campaigns of Frederick the Great, and was promoted to the rank of Adjutant-Major. After the inauguration of peace he left the Prussian service, declined a proposition to join the English army and sailed to America to offer his services to the patriots. After he received his commission as Inspector-General, and having reorganized the disheartened army, he took active part in the battle of Monmouth on June 28th, 1778. The British General, Matthews, making havoc on the James and Elizabeth rivers in the Old Dominion, burning trade- and war-ships, carrying off tobacco or whatever other booty he could make, von Steuben was appointed Commanding General of Virginia, and here he gained the highest distinction. He had just commenced to recruit and organize a force, when in January, 1781, the traitor Arnold with sixteen hundred men, and a number of armed ships, invaded Virginia. Steuben had only three hundred men to oppose him and he could not prevent that Arnold destroyed a large amount of property on both sides of the James river and occupied the city of Richmond without resistance. Meanwhile General Steuben had been reinforced by General Muehlenberg's Brigade and hastily gathered all attainable militia — altogether about four thousand men — and then he forced the British to retreat to Portsmouth. It was his cherished plan to capture Arnold and his entire force. General Washington approved of it and despatched General Lafayette with twelve hundred Continentals to join Steuben. A French fleet was also sent to cut off Arnold's retreat by water, but it was engaged and worsted by an English squadron and returned to Rhode Island. General Philipps then reinforced Arnold with twenty-five hundred men and took command of the troops. He advanced towards Richmond, pillaging the country. Lafayette now arrived in Virginia, but he could not prevent that Lord Cornwallis united with Arnold on the 20th of May, and then harassed the country by patroling out his light troops. General Wayne however came to the succor of Lafayette and they forced the English commander to fall back upon Yorktown, which he proceeded to fortify. The French fleet, with a large force under the Count de Grasse, arrived in the Chesapeake Bay, blocking the mouths of the York and James rivers. General Washington and Count Rochambeau, the French commander in the United States, concentrated the allied forces, amounting to sixteen thousand men, near Williamsburg, and on the night of the 6th of October General von Steuben commenced to draw his parallels around Yorktown. On the 11th of October he began the second line of approach, which he very rapidly completed before morning. General Washington had intrusted him with these important matters, knowing that he possessed more practical experience in the tactics of siege, than any other officer of his army. Two redoubts, Nos. 9 and 10, in advance of the English main works, greatly annoyed the American line by their fire, — and being within storming distance, General Washington resolved to have them silenced. The supposed best troops in the allied army were selected for the storming — and these were German and German-Virginian. The capture of Redoubt No. 10 was assigned to four hundred of Muehlenberg's Light Infantry under command of General Hamilton, — and on the French side Lieutenant-Colonel Prince Wilhelm von Zweibrücken, with four hundred grenadiers of the regiments "Royal Deuxponts" and "Gatenois," received orders to take No. 9. — Prof. John P. McGuire, of Richmond, Va., on the 15th of January, 1897, in a lecture delivered before the Association for the Preservation of Virginia Antiquities, gave the following description of the attack: "It is the evening of the 14th. The parties move into position; the Light Infantry, 'refreshed,' says a chronicler, 'with dinner and a nap.' Suddenly six shells blaze forth from the lines, sounding the signal and giving direction to the chargers. Hamilton and his men advance at double quick, with bayonets on unloaded muskets, Ginat's battalion in front. Laurens is detached to swing around the redoubt and prevent the escape of the garrison. Half way to the work they take the charging step. Not waiting for the sappers, Hamilton in the lead, with his friend, Nicholas Fish. Through and over the obstructions rush the brave Continentals. Over the ditch they go, and scale the parapet. In nine minutes from the start the redoubt is taken. In the nine minutes they lost thirty-four men killed and wounded." — Colonel Bauman suffered heroic death — and General Muehlenberg was slightly wounded. — "Keeping time with Hamilton's advance," — Prof. McGuire continued, — "Deuxpont's men move silently out, but at one hundred and twenty paces from the redoubt they hear a Hessian sentinel shout, 'Wer da?' Instantly the enemy fire. At twenty-five paces from the fort strong abatis stop the French until the sappers clear the way. Then the chaseurs dash on and mount the parapet. The British charge upon them. Deux-ponts orders his men to fire and counter-charge, and the works are theirs. It has cost them half an hour and ninety-two men." — Prince Wilhelm was among the wounded.

These brilliant feats of arms excited General Washington's enthusiasm and he exclaimed: "The work is done, and well done," and in his journal he wrote: "Few cases have exhibited greater proof of intrepidity, coolness and firmness than were shown upon this occasion."

Cornwallis, in an effort to escape by crossing the river, failed, and he sent a white flag to ask terms of surrender. General Steuben was at that time in command of the outline of the besieging armies, and while the negotiations dragged on, General Lafayette came with his division to relieve him, asserting also that the surrender of the English was to be made to him. Steuben remonstrated and maintained: that this demand was conflicting with the usage of war, and that the commander to whom the capitulation had been offered, was to remain in command until the terms of surrender had been accepted or refused, — and *General Washington decided in his favor.* Thus the British lowered their flag to General von Steuben. The whole remaining British force surrendered to the allies, — the land army to the Americans and the marine force to the French, and this glorious victory caused a cry of joy in every American heart.

After the end of the war Steuben continued for three years as Inspector-General of the army, but he resigned in disgust on the 15th of April, 1784, when Congress did not appoint him to the position of Secretary of War, for which he had applied, giving as reason: *that such an important office could not be bestowed on a foreigner.* Such is the gratitude of nations! Congress accepted the resignation of General von Steuben, expressed him the thanks of the Nation for his great services and presented him with a sword with golden hilt and a pension of $2500 a year. The States of Virginia, Pennsylvania, New Jersey and New York donated the great German-American with tracts of land.

General Steuben passed the rest of his days in quietude at his country-seat near Utica, N. Y. — "It is difficult," says the

Anglo-American historian Headly, "to value Steuben's merits to their full extent, but it is certain, that his arrival in our country marks a period in our revolution. The discipline which he introduced did wonders at Monmouth and made veterans of the soldiers who stormed Stony Point, — the eyes of the Government and of the officers were now opened and the army underwent a total reorganization." — Prof. O. Seidensticker writes of him: "Steuben's merits as the organisator of the army were of greater value for the revolutionary cause than a corps d'armée."

On November 28th, 1794, the German hero died. In Virginia, where he achieved his greatest triumph as General and military engineer, his memory is held sacred by his countrymen. In some later chapter it will be reported how they have honored the great German soldier.[124]) General Steuben, on his part, also remained a true friend of his countrymen. — He was president of the German Society of New York from September 12th, 1785, until his death.[125])

Not only on the bloody fields of battle have the German Virginians verified their love of liberty and their devotion to the American cause. Dr. Schoepf, the famed traveller, for instance, relates[126]): "In Manchester I visited Mr. Jacob Ruebsaamen, a German, who had formerly been in the mining and smelting business in New Jersey, but who erected a powder-mill in Virginia at the beginning of the war, — *the first one ever established in America.* The mill was afterwards destroyed by the British troops." — The pious German Quakers, Tunkers and Mennonites, who refused to carry arms for religious reasons, served the cause of liberty and independence in their unostentatious way. They raised provisions, and some historians state: that they hauled wagon-loads of grain to the camps for the starving soldiers. It was an act of injustice to doubt their sincerity. They were frequently treated very rudely. From

124) Compare: "The Life of Frederick Wilhelm von Steuben," by Friedrich Kapp. New York, 1869. — "Der deutsche Pionier," Jahrgang I: "Der Arm Washington's" von Kara Giorg (Dr. G. Bruehl) Cincinnati, 1869.

125.) "Das deutsche Element in den Vereinigten Staaten," von Gustav Koerner, Seite 96. Cincinnati, 1880 — "Geschichte der Deutschen in New York," von Friedrich Kapp, Seite 338. New York, 1868

126) "Der Süden," deutsch-amerikanische Wochenschrift, Jahrgang I, No. 18, Seite 4, Richmond, Va, 1891.

Pennsylvania, where they suffered most, troops of them were brought to Virginia as prisoners and held in confinement near Staunton.

During the whole time of the War of Independence only *one case of enmity* on part of the Germans in Virginia is known, — the Tories were mostly of English descent. In 1781, at the time when Lord Cornwallis invaded Virginia with a large army, John Claypole, a Scotchman by birth, and his two sons, who lived within the present limits of Hardy county, succeeded in drawing over to the British side a number of people domiciled on Lost river and the south branch of the Potomac, then in Hampshire, now in Hardy county. They refused to pay taxes and to furnish their quota of men to serve in the militia. Among them was John Brake,[127]) an old German of considerable wealth, who had a fine farm, mill and distillery about fifteen miles above Moorefield, and also many fat hogs and cattle. "*He was an exception in his political course to his countrymen,*" says Kercheval, "*as they were almost to a man true Whigs and friends to this country.*" His house was the place of rendevouz for the insurgents, who organized and made John Claypole their commander. The insurrection was soon suppressed and General Morgan took Brake prisoner and quartered his German sharpshooters at his house to live on the best that his farm, mill and distillery afforded. Three days later General Morgan returned to Winchester with his troops, and thus the Tory-insurrection ended. The parties themselves were aroused to shame by their conduct and several volunteered and aided in the capture of Cornwallis.

Virgil A. Lewis[128]) characterizes the Germans of the Valley as follows: "The lower portion of the Valley was occupied by the sturdy yeomanry of Germany. No European nation contributed a better class of emigrants than these. Arriving first in Pennsylvania, they pressed onward in search of fertile lands. These they found in the Shenandoah Valley, and almost the entire region of country where Harrisonburg now

127) "History of the Valley of Virginia," by S. Kercheval. Woodstock, Va., 1850.

128.) "History of West Virginia," by Virgil A. Lewis, pp 70 and 71. Philadelphia, 1889.

stands to Harper's Ferry was possessed by them before the beginning of the French and Indian war. During the struggle hundreds of them served with Washington and at its close the bones of many of them lay bleaching on the disastrous field of Monongahela. When the Revolutionary War came their sons were ready, and many of them filled the Virginia line in the strife for independence." — The importance of the German element in Virginia at the close of the eighteenth century is also demonstrated by the following historical fact: "On December 23d, 1794, the House of Delegates of Virginia resolved to publish *in German* the most important laws of the State — and in 1795 a translation by Gustav Friedrich Goetz was printed by Carl Cist in Philadelphia under the title: "Acten, welche in der General Assembly der Republik Virginien passirt worden sind."

CHAPTER IX.

GERMAN ALLIED TROOPS OF ENGLAND AS PRISONERS OF WAR IN VIRGINIA.

AT dawn of the 26th of December, 1776, General George Washington surprised and captured at Trenton, N. J., a Hessian detachment under Colonel Rahl, and most of these soldiers were taken to Virginia as prisoners of war. On their way there they were frequently threatened with violence by mobs, especially at Philadelphia, and upon General Washington's suggestion the magistracy of this city issued a proclamation to quiet the people. This public notice stated:

"One thousand Hessian prisoners reached our city yesterday, who were captured by His Excellency General Washington, in his successful expedition to New Jersey. The General has instructed this council to provide them with suitable quarters, and it is his earnest wish, that they may be well treated in order to make during their captivity such experience, that the eyes of their countrymen serving in the Royal British army be opened. These unfortunate men deserve our sympathy. They entertain no enmity towards us, they did not come voluntarily, but have been hired out without their consent by their despotic princes to a foreign monarch, etc."

This act of kindness of General Washington had good results, although it was not approved by many fanatic Americans. Indeed, the longer the war lasted, the more the feeling of hate towards the Hessian hirelings increased, especially among the lower class of the English population.

On October 17th, 1777, General Burgoyne surrendered on the plains of Saratoga, and the number of German prisoners of war was increased by seven thousand. General Morgan escorted a large detachment of them, Hessian and Brunswick troops, under General Friedrich Adolph von Riedesel, to Virginia: "A march of 650 miles," says von Eelking,[129]) "through a country full of hostile inhabitants, with no provision for health or comfort." The men were taken to Winchester, Staunton and Charlottesville, and the officers to Winchester and Charlottesville, and later on to Fredericksburg and Richmond.

The German troops[130]) that surrendered at Yorktown, Va., with Cornwallis, included the Crown Prince's regiment, two other Hessian regiments, and two from the Rhine. General Muehlenberg commanded the small escort, which accompanied the prisoners to their winter-quarters at Winchester, and later on part of them were sent to Frederick, Md., and Lancaster, Pa.

The German Virginians were much grieved by the deplorable part their captured countrymen were destined to take in the War of Independence, and the modern slave trade of German soldiers was most severely condemned by all intelligent people of Germany. Heroes of science[131]) like Kant, Arndt, Klopstock, Herder and Lessing, detested the unscrupulous dealings of some petty German princes and sympathized with America struggling for liberty.

Niebuhr wrote in his, "Geschichte des Zeitalters der Revolution:

"The more the subsidiary contracts were hated and cursed, the more sympathy was felt for America. The frame of mind was so much moved out of the natural line of direction, that the news of the capture of German troops by Washington in 1776, was received with general joy instead of regret."

And never any act was more scornfully criticized than this sale of soldiers by the noble-hearted and ideal Friedrich von Schiller, the favorite Poet of all Germans. In his tragedy: "Kabale und Liebe," he stigmatized it in the following scene.[132])

129.) "The German Allied Troops," (Die deutschen Hilfstruppen im Nord Amerikanischen Befreiungskriege, von Max von Eelking,) translated by J. G. Rosengarten, page 147. Albany, N. Y., 1893.

130.) "The German Soldier in the Wars of the United States," by J. G. Rosengarten, p. 83. Philadelphia, 1890.

131.) "Ueber den Soldatenhandel," von W. A. Fritzsch, in: "Deutsch-amerik. Magazin," Heft IV, pp. 589–593. Cincinnati, 1889.

132.) "Kabale und Liebe," von Friedrich von Schiller, 2. Act, 2. Scene.

An old chamberlain of the Duke brings a jewelry box, and Lady Milford, the mistress of the prince, refuses with contempt to accept the diamonds, learning that they have been paid with gold received for soldiers.

Chamberlain: "His serene highness sends his compliments and these diamonds just received from Venice."

Lady (opening the casket with surprise): "Say, sir, how much has the Duke paid for the jewels?"

Chamberlain (with a sad expression): "They cost him nothing."

Lady: "What? Are you crazy? Nothing? And why do you look at me so exasperated?—These immensely valuable diamonds cost him nothing?"

Chamberlain: "Yesterday 7,000 subjects left for America, they will pay for them!"

Lady (laying the jewel box hastily aside): "Man, what ails you? It seems you cry!"

Chamberlain (wiping his tears): "Two sons of mine are among them!"

Lady (grasping his hands): "But, they were not forced to go?"

Chamberlain (laughing grimly): "O Lord no! They all volunteered! There were a few saucy fellows who stepped to the front and asked the colonel, at what price our prince sells a team of men,—but our gracious sovereign ordered all the regiments to the parade ground, and had those fools executed. We heard the report of the rifles, we saw their brains spattered on the pavement, and the whole army shouted, Hurrah! To America!"

Lady (dropping on her sofa in terror): "O, Lord! And I heard nothing, had no knowledge of it!"

Chamberlain: "Yes, my lady, why did you go bear-hunting with our Duke, when the alarm was given? You ought not have missed the sight, when the shrill clang of drums announced that the time to part had come; and crying orphans followed their yet living fathers,—a mother in despair tried to spear her baby to a bayonet,—bride and bridegroom were rudely separated, and white-bearded men looked on in distraction, throwing their crutches to the boys to take them along also to the New World! And again the drums were beaten, that the all-knowing God might not hear our prayers. At the town-gate they turned around once more and shouted: "The Lord protect you, women and children! God save the prince! At the day of judgment we will meet again!"

Vis-a-vis to the moral indignation of the German people, as demonstrated by its best men, neither the victims, nor the tyrannized German nation, can be blamed for a bargain, which the English Government had effected with some covetous and profligate German princes. The Americans had still less cause for their spiteful conduct, and for making the Hessians a degrading byword, for belonging to the allied French forces were also German subsidiary troops, fighting shoulder to shoulder with the Continental Army. It was altogether unreasonable to abuse the disinterested German-Americans, who proved faithful to the American cause during the war even unto death!

The German allied troops, who served in Virginia under the French General: de Rochambeau, were, according to H. A. Rattermann's careful researches[133]):

1. Regiment "Royal Allemand de Deux-Ponts." (Koenigliches deutsches Regiment Zweibruecken.) Officers known:

Colonel Prince Christian, of Zweibruecken-Birkenfeld, Lieut. Colonel Prince Wilhelm, of Zweibruecken-Birkenfeld, Major Freiherr Eberhard von Eisebeck, and Capt. Haake.

2. One battalion of "Kur-Triersche Grenadiere," as "Detachement du regiment La Sarre," incorporated in the regiment "Saintonge," and commanded by Colonel Adam Philipp Graf (count) von Custine, of Lorraine.

3. Some rifle companies from Alsace and Lorraine, attached to the regiments "Bourbonnais" and "Soissonnais."

4. A large portion of the mounted Legion of the Duc de Lauzun. A muster roll of this Legion is preserved in the archives at Harrisburg, Pa.

133.) "Der deutsche Pionier," Jahrgang XIII, Seite 317, 360 und 430. Cincinnati, 1881.

Numerous German officers occupied prominent positions in Marquis de Rochambeau's army. Count von Wittgenstein commanded the second division.[134]) Count Axel von Fersen, of Swedish-Pommeranian nobility, chief of staff, — Baron Ludwig von Closen-Haydenburg, born near Wissingen in Bavaria, Adjutant of Gen. de Rochambeau, — Count von Holzendorf, a Saxon, — Baron von Exbech, — Capt. Gau, chief of artillery, — Count von Stedingk, born at Greifswalde,—Paul Friedr. Jul. v. Gambs, Adjutant of Baron de Viosmenil, born at Johannesberg, Bohemia,—Capt. Nortmann of Lauzun's mounted Legion,—and Prof. Lutz, of Strassburg, interpreter at headquarters.[135])

Taking an impartial view—the character of the serviceable position of the French-German allied troops fighting under General Washington, must be commented exactly the same as that of the "cursed Hessians" on the opposing side.

Furthermore it is to be remembered that a large number of deserters of the English-German troops, from Hessen-Cassel, Brunswick, Hessen-Hanau, Waldeck, Ansbach-Bayreuth, and Anhalt-Zerbst, joined the American army, and that the American Commander-in-chief as well as Congress encouraged the desertion of Germans from the British ranks. In 1778, Congress passed a resolution to organize a corps of German deserters, and in Virginia the officers of the German prisoners of war were separated from their men, that the latter might be more readily persuaded to enter the American service. Recruiting officers[136]) came into the camps, going into the barracks, promised thirty Spanish dollars hard money, of which eight dollars were paid down, and, even carried with them musicians, loose women and liquor to help them to induce the men to leave their colors. These facts show that the soldierly qualification of the German prisoners and their brave and good conduct, were fully known to the American authorities.

The Anglo-Virginians, at least those of better judgment, soon valued these men and also recognized their qualification

134.) "The German Soldier in the Wars of the United States," by J. G. Rosengarten, p. 115. Philadelphia, 1890.

135) "Der deutsche Pionier," Jahrgang XIII, Seite 319 und 320. Cincinnati, 1881.

136. "The German Allied Troops," by Max von Eelking, and translated by J. G. Rosengarten, p. 212. Albany, N. Y., 1893.

to become desirable colonists. General Washington owned large estates in western Virginia, and he wished, as stated previously, to settle his lands by Germans. After the close of the war a large number of German prisoners of war helped him to realize this plan. They drove the murderous Indians wholly from the Virginian soil, and opened the wilderness of the Alleghanies to the Ohio, and farther. The author met during the war of secession many farmers in Greenbrier, Fayette, Nicholas, and Pocahontas counties, whose fathers or grandfathers had been captured at Trenton or Saratoga, and one of his fellow-officers in Company D, Fourteenth Virginia Cavalry, organized at Greenbrier White Sulphur Springs, was a descendant of a Hessian.

The "Winchester Times" said about the German prisoners confined in and near Winchester,[137]) "they were skilled workers in leather, stone and iron-work, and the stone fences and comfortable stone-houses were built by them. They also acquainted the pioneer-settlers with the progress made in agriculture, etc."

Some of the private soldiers were at once allowed to go to work on the neighboring farms. Many of the owners were of German descent, and German speech and friendly hospitality gave their unfortunate countrymen great comfort. Several of them fell in love with the daughters of the old farmers, and married. These were allowed to ransom themselves for a fixed sum of eighty Spanish dollars[138]) and those who could not raise the amount and had no friends or relatives in the country to help them, usually found Americans to advance the money and agreed to labor for it a certain length of time. These were called "Redemptioners," and their bargains had a sort of legal sanction, they were made public at church and generally acknowledged as binding.

When the war was over Congress offered the German soldiers every advantage in case they remained in America, and the German princes, desirous to reduce their standing armies, gladly gave their men and officers leave to stay.

137.) "The Winchester Times," copied 1890 from "Daily Commercial," Memphis, Tenn., the report of an old Navy Officer born at Winchester, Va.

138.) "The German Alleid Troops," by Max von Eelking, translated by J. G. Rosengarten, p. 217. Albany, N. Y., 1893.

In many respects the long and weary imprisonment was a time of suffering and hardship to the captives. At Winchester the quarters gave no hope, as von Eelking reports, of a comfortable winter, — wretched huts of wood and canvass, roofless, without doors and windows, and located in a heavy forest growth, were assigned to them. The men were crowded close together twenty to thirty in a hut, and even the food was scanty and poor. The men confined near Staunton had similar hardships to endure, and the presence of a large number of captive British soldiers added to their discomfort. Staunton was at that time a small town of only thirty ordinary houses, and the prisoners had little intercourse with the inhabitants, as the barracks were some miles distant. These barracks were in an unfinished state when the Hessian and Brunswick troops arrived, and afforded no protection from cold and heat. The German captives repaired them, laid out gardens and chicken-yards, and the Virginians came to look at their arrangements and to make purchases. Good fighting-cocks were in special demand and ten to thirteen shillings were paid for them. Thus circumstances were improved, but the men complained of the big prices of all staples, that they could exchange their money only with a heavy loss of about 40 per cent. and that they heard and saw nothing of the world.

Baroness von Riedesel, who had accompanied her husband, General Friedrich Adolph von Riedesel, and about eighteen hundred men taken at Saratoga to Charlottesville, wrote to a friend in Germany: "The prisoners had at first to bear many trials. They lived in little log-houses without doors and windows, but they soon built better dwellings surrounded by gardens, and by their labor the place gained the appearance of a pretty little town." — Further reports von Eelking[139]): "They surrounded themselves with such comfort as could be provided, and occupied the time by building a church to which was annexed a graveyard, fitted up a theatre, had constant visitors from far and near, and brought new life into a desolate little country village." — General von Riedesel lived at Charlottesville like a native farmer. He built a block-house with furni-

139.) "The German Allied Troops," by Max von Eelking, translated by J. G. Rosengarten, pp. 149 and 152. Albany, N. Y., 1893.

ture made on the spot, worked in his garden, had horses and cows, and his wife made a capital housekeeper. Anburey, one of the British officers quartered here with the Saratoga troops, writes[140]): "This famous place we had heard so much of, consisted only of a courthouse, one tavern and about a dozen houses, all of which were crowded with officers. The soldiers camped in a wood near the town." — The road leading out of Charlottesville to the northwest, is to this day called "the Old Barrack's Road."

It is significant that Governor Thomas Jefferson took pleasure in associating with the German officers at Charlottesville and inviting them to his country-seat, Monticello. They were well educated men, and the Governor offered them the use of his library. In the evening he frequently indulged in music with those of musical efficiency. "His diposition to the arts of peace," says E. A. Duyckinck[141]), "in mitigation of the calamities of war, had been shown in his treatment of the Saratoga prisoners of war, who were quartered in the neighborhood, near Charlottesville. He added to the comforts of the men and entertained the officers at his table."

On the 8th of December, 1777, Congress granted the Hessian officers at Winchester their request to go to Fredericksburg, Va. They had gained the confidence of the Americans, so that each was allowed to choose his own time to move there. On the 13th they were all in Fredericksburg, and as there could not be found quarters for the whole number, some went to Falmouth, an attractive village on the other side of the Rappahannock river. They admired the stream and its shores, and their relations to the most distinguished families in the neighborhood were very pleasant. Lieutenant Wiederhold wrote in his diary[142]): "The ladies of the neighborhood showed us much kindness, they are lovely, polite, modest and of natural grace. Sixteen of them, and the most prominent ones, arranged a 'surprise party,' and 'surprised' the captain in his quarters

140.) "Albemarle," by W. H. Seamon, pp. 9 to 10. Charlottesville, Va., 1888.

141.) "Thomas Jefferson," Portrait Gallery of Eminent Men and Women, by E. A. Duyckinck, Vol. I, p. 280. New York, N. Y.

142.) "Lord Fairfax," by A. Simon, published in "Der Westen," Chicago, Ills , June 19th, 1892.

after he had been notified of it. The beautiful Virginia ladies had intended to stay only an hour, but they extended their visit from four o'clock in the afternoon to ten o'clock at night. Among the agreeable visitors were a sister and a niece of General Washington, and also one of his brothers. The German officers entertained their welcome guests with musical exercises, which the ladies sometimes accompanied by singing. Tea, chocolate, coffee, claret and cake were at hand." Wiederhold writes in addition: "In Europe we would not have earned much praise by our musical performance, but here we were admired like virtuosos. Sobbe played the flute, Surgeon Oliva the violin, and I the guitar. I think the Virginia gentlemen were a little jealous, that we were treated with so much amiability."

Finally the German prisoners were released, "and then," says Rosengarten, "they began to laugh at their recent experiences, to talk about the theatre, which had helped to shorten the weary hours of their exile and imprisonment." The scattered troops, including those in Virginia, were collected and gradually returned to Germany.

An abundance of books on the American war and the country were written by German soldiers of all grades and illustrated the resources and advantages America offers to settlers. Dr. Johann David Schoepf, surgeon of the Anspach-Baireuth troops, published, as mentioned before, a very instructive work about his travels in the South, especially Virginia.[143]) These publications attracted widespread attention throughout Germany and thus the very men, who had been sent across the ocean to help conquer the rebellious colonies, assisted to increase immigration and to advance the development of the new republic. An era of prosperity followed. Virginia, possessing the finest climate of the North American continent, with thousands of acres of broad, fertile, unoccupied lands awaiting the tiller's toil, thousands of acres of timber awaiting the woodman's axe, and thousands of veins of most valuable ores and coal only awaiting enterprise and capital, received its share of German industrious citizens. The large number of German prisoners, who stayed there after

143.) "Reise durch einige der mittlern und südlichen Staaten in 1783 und 1784." — Im Auszug wieder veröffentlicht in "Der Süden," Jahrgang I. Richmond, Va., 1891.

the close of hostilities, were soon joined by new comers from the old fatherland, giving the Old Dominion many families of note and of useful citizens. Hessia, the native State of the much abused "mercenaries," took in Virginia the lead of a growing tide of valuable German immigrants.

The large number of desirable citizens America received from the subsidiary troops is shown by the following figures:

The Brunswick contingent counted during the war 5,723 men and officers, and out of this number 1,200 men, 27 officers and chaplain Melsheimer remained in America. It is stated that of the troops of Hessen-Cassel, Hessen-Hanau, Waldeck, Anspach, Baireuth, and Anhalt-Zerbst, about 7,000 made Virginia, Maryland, Pennsylvania and New Jersey their permanent home. The official reports say that the total number of the German contingents was 29,166 men and that 11,853 were counted as lost.

CHAPTER X.

The Indian Hunters and the German-Virginian Emigration to the West.

THE barbarous warfare of the Indians had highly excited the peaceful German frontiermen and made several of them merciless avengers. History calls these sworn enemies of the natives: "Indian Hunters." A rifle over the shoulder, a tomahawk and a scalping knife in the belt, they rambled through the woods, and no savage, who came near them, was spared. Wild and bloody was their revenge, not consistent with humanity and law, and yet the enraged and suffering people sympathized with them. Tradition has surrounded them with a mist of romance. The following names of German Virginians, who figured in the border history as the most successful Indian hunters, are: Ludwig Wetzel, Georg Ruffner, Col. Peter Nieswanger, Jacob Weiser, Karl Bilderbach, and Johann Waerth; and in the Cumberland mountains in Kentucky and Tennessee: Michael Steiner, the ancestor of the Stoners, and Kaspar Mausher, afterwards colonel of the militia-force at the border. The most famous of the Indian hunters in the West was Ludwig (Lewis) Wetzel, whose name is perpetuated in Wetzel county, West Virginia. The German-American poet, Friedrich Albert Schmitt, (he died at Cincinnati, O.,) has sung his fame in several songs. He represented him as taking the following oath[144]):

144.) "Ludwig Wetzel, der Indianerjäger," von Friedrich Albert Schmitt. — "Deutscher Pionier," Band I, Seite 44. Cincinnati, 1876.

"Fuer den Erschlagenen Rache! Wir machen wieder gut,
Was uns gethan die Wilden: in ihrem eignen Blut!
Sei jede Rothhaut fuerder geweiht dem sich'ren Tod,
So wahr in gluehen Flammen dies Haus emporgeloht!

Am Grab des Vaters schwoeren wir Jenen Untergang!
Du Himmel, wollst es hoeren: es soll der Schlachtgesang
Den hier die Indianer geheult, um Rache schrein,—
Er soll ein grimmer Mahner zur ew'gen Rache sein!"

Ludwig Wetzel was the son of Johann Wetzel from the Palatinate, who was one of the first settlers on Big Wheeling Creek. When Ludwig was a boy of thirteen years, in 1787, the Indians burned down the log-house of his parents and killed his father, and Ludwig, with a gun-wound in his breast, was carried off prisoner together with his brother Jacob. The two boys succeeded in escaping and trained by their father in the use of arms, they devoted themselves to avenging his death. Ludwig especially inspired the red men with terror. "In all he took over thirty scalps of warriors," says de Haas[145]) "thus killing more Indians than were slain by either one of the two large armies of Braddock or St. Clair during their disastrous campaigns." — After the conclusion of peace with the savages he still continued his murderous work of revenge, and was consequently pursued and imprisoned at Fort Washington, near Cincinnati, — but the people sided with him and he was released. He went to Louisiana, where he was again arrested, but by means of deceit and with the assistance of his friends he escaped. He feigned to have suddenly fallen sick, was represented as having died, placed in a coffin and carried to a vault, from where he effected his flight the next night. He finally died in Texas.

A similar life full of adventures and hair-breadth escapes was led by all the Indian hunters, and yet they were admired by the people exposed to the murderous treachery of the natives. They were feared by the red men, — their mere presence was a protection — and thus they frustrated many a massacre.

145.) "History of the Early Settlement and Indian-Wars of Western Virginia," by Wills de Haas, p. 344. Wheeling and Philadelphia, 1851.

The repeated incursions of hostile Indians not only aroused the bloody avengers, the Indian hunters,—they also induced many German Virginians to emigrate further west. The distrust and animosity of the slave-holders, and the spiteful persecution of all dissenters by the English High Church, made life in Virginia unbearable to many. The German poet, Emil Rittershaus, very truly says:

"Die Heimath ist, wo man Dich gern erscheinen
und ungern wandern sieht," —

and Virginia had not offered such dear homes to those pioneers.

Enticing descriptions of the fertility of the soil in Kentucky, Ohio and Indiana helped to induce many desirable settlers to leave the Old Dominion. As early as the middle of the eighteenth century some German Virginians, either voluntarily or against their own free will, came to Kentucky. Collins[146]) relates, that the first white women who came to Kentucky, were Mrs. Maria Engels, from Virginia, with her children and her sister-in-law, Mrs. Draper, who had been taken prisoners and carried off by the Shawanees. The same historian also reports, that Mrs. Engel and the other German woman managed to escape, after the children had been separated from them, — and that they reached the Kanawha river in Virginia, encountering many accidents and troubles. Mrs. Engel afterwards returned to Kentucky with her husband and settled in Boone county, — others followed, — but principally during the War of Independence the German immigration increased. Many of the revolutionary soldiers found homes there. — In 1773 a society headed by one Robert McAfee,—among its members were several Germans,—left Botetourt county, Va., and wandered to Kentucky (Kain-tuck-ee.) Only one German name of those pioneers is preserved: Herrmann. Other German Virginians, who settled in Kentucky at the same time, were: Abraham Hite, Joseph and Jacob Sadowsky, Captain A. Schoeplein (anglicized: Chapline), etc. It was a life of privation and danger which these emissaries of European civilization had to endure. They held the frontier outposts against Indian barbarity. The U. S. Educational Report for

146.) Compare: Collins "History of Kentucky."

1895—96 says, Vol. I, page 317, with reference to them: "The settlers were not indifferent to the importance of schooling their own children, and went about the work in the rough-and-ready way only possible to their provincial life. Each of the fortified villages, which were the only places of safety from the depredations of the savages, set up its school. More than one of the brave pioneer schoolmasters met his death about his work; all taught amid an environment of difficulty and peril, that make the career of each a special romance. They took their meagre pay in tobacco and the produce of the country."

We previously mentioned the name of the speaker or preacher of a Tunker congregation, Johann Tanner, who left Virginia with his followers and emigrated to Pennsylvania. There he met with intolerance — and in 1785 he went and settled in Kentucky. The loss of his sons, Johannes and Eduard, who had been carried off by the Indians, caused him to move still further west and to make his home near New Madrid, in Missouri, which was a Spanish colony at the time. Several German families had accompanied him to Kentucky and settled at Farmers' Station, now Bullitsburg, as: the Dewees, the Matheus and Schmidt[147]), whose German names are varied to Mathews and Smith. New additions came from the Old German colony at Madison, Va. Ludwig Rausch, about 1800, had ventured through the dark virgin woods as far as Florence county, Ky., where he found very fertile lands. He returned to Virginia and praised the "Charming West," saying that he would make it his home. He departed again, built a log-house, tilled the land, and in 1804 he went to Madison for his betrothed wife. His success caused much excitement in the old German colony and the next year fourteen men with their families started for Boone county, Kentucky, namely: Solomon Hoffman and his wife, Elizabeth, with two children; Georg Rause and wife; Ephraim Tanner and wife Susanna; Johannes Haus and wife Emilie; Fried. Zimmermann and his wife Rosa; Johannes Rause and his wife Nancy; Benjamin Ayler, Simon Tanner, Johannes Biemann, Michael

147.) "Deutscher Pionier," Band XII, Seite 68. Cincinnati, Ohio, 1880.

Rausch, Jacob Rausch, Fried. Tanner, Josua Zimmermann and Jeremias Carpenter, i. e. Zimmermann. In the year 1806 they organized an ecclesiastical community and erected a church, which they called "the Hopeful," and in 1813 they induced the pastor: Wm. Carpenter, of the "Hebron Church" at Madison (as reported in Chapter IV) to remove there. Rev. Carpenter had studied theology and the classics under the tutorship of the Lutheran pastor Christian Streit, at Winchester, Va., after serving in the War of Independence in General Muehlenberg's division. More Germans arrived in northern Kentucky, and they founded the cities of: Frankfort, Lexington, Florence, Louisville, etc. The diocese of the Rev. Carpenter soon extended over all these settlements and into Ohio. Until 1824 he preached only in German,—the instruction in the schools was given in both English and German. His successor, Jacob Crigler (1834), who also came from Madison, Va., preached mostly in German and when urged to use the English language exclusively, because a number of English families had settled in Boone county, he resigned his office and accepted the pastorate of a German parish in Ohio. The English idiom soon made rapid progress among the Germans, and the American born reverends were the chief promoters of the change. The German descendants however preserved a faithful remembrance for the land and nation of their ancestors. Rev. Harbough wrote: "As a community we descend of the venerable parish on the Rapidan. We are therefore of German origin and we are proud of it. Our ancestors came from the land of Luther — and that gives us great satisfaction. We are not the ungrateful son who disowns and slights his mother."

It has already been said that the revolutionary soldiers furnished a large contingent of settlers to Kentucky and Ohio, this territory belonged at that time still to Virginia. The State of Virginia had presented the patriots with land and consequently there was about the year 1788 a heavy German influx to the "Virginia Military Lands" in Kentucky and Ohio. — "Woodford county in Kentucky," writes Collins, "was principally settled by emigrants from eastern and western Virginia." — Daniel Weissiger, who had lived at Norfolk and later at Staunton, is named as the founder of Frankfort, the Capital of the present State of Kentucky.[148]) Its name was given it by the German settlers, who came mostly from Frankfurt on the Main in 1786—87. — Major Bernhard Niederland, born of German parents in Powhatan county, Va., on February 27th, 1755, was the first land-owner at Lexington, Ky. — Major Georg Michael Bedinger, of Shepherdstown, Va., came to Kentucky in 1779, distinguished himself as a valiant officer in the battle on Blue Lick, August 19th, 1782, was elected delegate of Bourbon county to the first Legislature of the State in 1792, and a member of the United States Congress from 1803—7. — Georg Muter, of Madison, Va., was a member of the conventions in 1785, 1787 and 1788, elector of Woodford county in 1792, and was appointed First Chief-Justice of the new State.—Karl Springer, the father of the noble founder of the magnificent Music Hall at Cincinnati: Reuben R. Springer, came about the year 1788 from Botetourt county, Va., to Fayette county, Kentucky, and some time later removed to Frankfort. — The first physician of Frankfort was Dr. Louis Marschall from Virginia, father of Humphrey Marshall, — (he anglicized his German name), — noted in both the civil and military history of Kentucky. — Among the pioneer settlers of Bourbon and Pendleton counties numbered: Hans Waller, born at Germanna, Va., in 1749; Peter Demoss, who had served in Muehlenberg's regiment and founded Demossville; and Simon Luetzel, of Prince William county, Va. — Bracken county[149]) commemorates the name of the German surveyor, Matthias Bracken, who was sent to Kentucky in 1773 by Governor Dunmore and laid out the city of Frankfort. The German Virginian: Bernard Weier, Wyer or Weyer, who discovered the beautiful cave in the Shenandoah valley that bears his name: "Wyer's Cave," — settled in Highland county, Ohio.

These few historical facts show, that the German-Virginian immigration has done much for the development of Kentucky and Ohio. Indiana, Illinois, Tennessee and Missouri

---

148.) "Deutscher Pionier," Band XII, Seite 301. Cincinnati, Ohio, 1880.

149.) "Deutscher Pionier," Band XII, Seite 293—444. Cincinnati, Ohio.

also received a large portion of this desirable, industrious element[150]) and many of the most prominent families in those States are descended from these German pioneers, and it can be asserted, that by their assistance the great natural resources of the Great West of the Union became known and partially developed. Richard Edwards, in his valuable History of the Great West, characterizes that German immigration as follows:

"Wherever they are found, the Germans are remarkable by the possession of those elements of character which always contribute to their worldly prosperity. They are not as fast in their ideas as Young America, but they have more solidity of character, and are more constant and untiring in their pursuits and are generally more sure of gaining the race in life and arriving at the goal of fortune. They resemble the tortoise in the fable—slow, constant and successful!"

According to a statistical report[151]) 99,267 white and colored people emigrated from Virginia, previous to 1860, to Kentucky and Missouri, — and 163,644 to Ohio, Indiana, Illinois and Iowa.

150) Compare: Klauprecht's "Deutsche Chronik in der Geschichte des Ohio Thales," — Stirlin's "Der Staat Kentucky und die Stadt Louisville," — and Edward's "Great West and History of St. Louis."

151) "U. S. Report of the Commissioner of Agriculture," p. 44. Washington, D. C., 1863.

End of Volume I.

INDEX OF NAMES

Volume I

-N-O-

-P-Q-

-R-

-S-

-X-Y-Z-

GENERAL INDEX

A

B

C

D

E

F

G

H

I

J

K

L

P

Q

R

S

T

U

V

W

Y

Z

HISTORY

OF

THE GERMAN ELEMENT IN VIRGINIA.

BY

HERRMANN SCHURICHT.

VOL. II.

TABLE OF CONTENTS.

Vol. II.

PERIOD II.

German Life in Virginia During the 19th Century to the Beginning of the Spanish-American War.

Page

APPENDIX.

HERRMANN SCHURICHT. ✝

Herrmann Schuricht was born February 13th, 1831, at Pirna, Saxony. He early showed a great love for study and after due course of schooling he entered upon university life at Leipsig, when by the death of his father he was abruptly forced to terminate his studies and assume control of his father's business. In this he was not successful and after many reverses he came to America in 1859. At Richmond, Virginia, he published a daily newspaper, "Die Virginische Zeitung." When the Civil War broke out he left the city, a member of the "Richmond Blues," was made sergeant of the Ordnance Department of the Wise Legion, later promoted captain of a German volunteer company. After the war he returned to his native city and filled the position of principal of the "Pirna'er Handels-Schule" and a young ladies' academy. He gained a large fortune by a successful land speculation, which was subsequently lost by the failure of a bank. Thereupon, in 1874, he returned to the United States and for four years he was principal of a school at Newark, N. J., and later at Boston, Mass. Forced to give up teaching, on account of a serious throat and eye trouble, he engaged with L. Prang & Co. of Boston, educational book publishers, to represent them in the West. This position he filled until 1886; at that time he settled on his farm "Idlewild," near Cobham, Virginia, where he resided up to his death, May 27th, 1899, with only a brief interruption, when he assumed editorial charge of "Der Sueden," a German weekly published at Richmond.

Mr. Schuricht was author of many educational essays and books, correspondent of several papers in this country and abroad, a good teacher and an accomplished speaker and journalist. He was for many years president of the "National German-American Teachers' Association" and an honorary member of leading social, scientific and historical societies. With him the Germans of the United States have lost one of the most devoted and faithful advocates of their cause. An American and a Republican by heart and conviction he was ever active in the rights of his countrymen against a class of men who see in this nation nought but a colony of England. It was his aim, as a historian, to establish and perpetuate the claim for recognition of the merits of the vast mass of Germans, who helped to build up in time of peace and to defend in time of war this great land of their choice, — and as a teacher and writer furthermore to imbue upon their progeny and hold sacred that part of German character and life that would be most conducive to mould the growing nation. He was foremost and ever a German-American, free from all narrow-mindedness, of an amiable and ideal disposition, seeking to obviate all prejudice of factions in the one great task of building and fining a nation. He often met with disappointment, but he never wavered in his efforts to work the common good.

His last work, "The History of the German Element in Virginia," the second volume of which is herewith given to the public after the death of its author, will bear out proof of his struggle to establish a true record of German effort in Virginia, considered by many to have been an exclusively English settlement, — and it is to be hoped will instigate others to follow his example in other States.

PERIOD II.

German Life in Virginia During the 19th Century to the Beginning of the Spanish-American War.

CHAPTER XI.

Retrogression of the German Type During the First Three Decades.

> "With nations it is as with individuals: these have weak hours and those feeble periods."—*Jahn.*

THE German element of Virginia entered the new century much weakened. The Indian massacres, the long years of war, and the emigration to the West, had reduced it in number, and the anglicizing process had made rapid progress. During the War of Independence the relations of the two nationalities, the English and the German, had become more intimate, — the Germans had been obliged to adopt and use the English language, and after independence was gained, *they felt themselves as much Americans as the English descendants.* Immigration from Germany almost ceased when Napoleon I. involved the nations of the European continent into bloody wars, while that from Great Britain continued undiminished. The bitter feeling that the Anglo-Virginians entertained on account of the assistance the German allied troops had rendered the British armies in the War of Independence, the German citizens most erroneously thought to conquer by timid submission and by surrendering their national peculiarities. The majority of the German-Virginians were not embellished with feelings of national pride, or pious attachment to the Fatherland. National self-esteem, which makes a language imperishable, — that honors and retains the noble character and worthy habits of the ancestors, — the national pride that is the most sacred feeling of the stranger in a foreign land, — this the German-Virginians were wanting, although they had materially helped to raise Virginia to what it was by their worthy ancestral qualities: industry, perseverance, economy and love of liberty. They had forgotten that a German who looks with veneration upon his Fatherland, adheres to its customs and language, esteems the inheritance of his fathers, becomes a most desirable citizen, for his energy will benefit his new home, his habits will refine those around him, just like the scion on a wild stock.

Friedrich von Schiller, — bitterly commenting on the unworthy position the Germans held at the beginning of the new century as compared with other nations, — gathered new hope from the precious treasures of the German language, that expresses everything: "The profoundest and the most volatile, the genius, the soul — and which is full of sense." Only self-respect gives to the man manly vigor and secures to him, even far from his native land, recognition and influence. The firm adherence to the mother-tongue expresses this noble intention, but upon its surrender the mark of peculiarity, of self-confidence and self-dependence, is lost. The German poet Theodor Koerner expressed this sentiment as follows:

"Denn mit den fremden Worten auf der Zunge
Kommt auch der fremde Geist in unsere Brust, —
Und wie sich mancher, von dem Prunk geblendet,
Der angebor'nen heiligen Sprache schämt
Und lieber radebrechend seiner Zunge
Zum Spott des Fremden fremde Fesseln aufzwingt,—
So lernt er auch die deutsche Kraft verachten!"

The tie that binds the German-Virginians to this country will never be loosened by their pious attachment to the old Fatherland, — for being true to it, their patriotic devotion to America can all the more safely be relied on.

In Virginia the German clergy faithfully upheld the German tongue until about 1825. On May 28th, 1820, the German-Lutheran Tennessee Synod was organized and Reverends Jacob Zink, of Washington county, and Paul Henkel, of New-Market, Virginia, participated. It was resolved: *that all business and work should be transacted in German*, for reason that a conference in which both the German and English languages were used, the one or the other side would be dissatisfied. It was also deemed of the highest importance to use all possible diligence to acquaint the German children with all doctrines in faith and in the German language.[152]) But already on September 8th, 1826, the same Synod resolved that: "Both the German and English languages may be used in the proceedings of the Synod,"[153]) and this resolution was the first step, among the members of this influential body, towards the abolishment of German in their respective congregations.

The emigration of the German element to the "Far West" still continued, and the old mother colony lost many good and brave men. Colonel Luke Decker for instance is named with distinction in the history of Indiana.[154]) At the beginning of the 19th century he emigrated from western Virginia to southern Indiana, and in 1811, when the Indians threatened the white population of the new territory with annihilation, he was placed in command of part of the militia. In the decisive battle at Tippecanoe he helped to gain the victory and was badly wounded, — and the Legislature of the Territory meeting at Vincennes passed resolu-

---

152) "History of the Evang.-Luth. Tennessee Synod," by S. Henkel, D. D., p. 25. New-Market, Va., 1890.

153.) "History of the Evang.-Luth. Tennessee Synod," by S. Henkel, D. D., p. 29. New-Market, Va., 1890.

154.) "Geschichte des Deutschthums in Indiana," pp. 12 and 13, by Dr. W. A. Fritsch. Published by E. Steiger & Co., New York, 1896.

tions of thanks acknowledging his bravery. He died, loved and esteemed by his fellow-citizens, on his farm near "Decker's Station," which derived its name from this German-Virginian patriot.

The U. S. Census of 1890 states that the population of Virginia — East and West — amounted in 1800 to 880,200 inhabitants, of whom 41.52 per cent. were negroes. It is a low estimate to fix the number of the white population at about 514,000, and the German-Virginians at 85,600. To verify this estimate, be it remembered that Richmond, — although Tidewater Virginia had at the beginning of the 19th century fewer German inhabitants than the Valley or the Piedmont district, — numbered in 1830 in all 16,060 inhabitants, of whom 10,025 were whites, — inclusive of about 3000 of German descent, — which is almost one-third of the white population of the city.

The German Jewish element, which now forms a very considerable part of the German population of Virginia, and particularly of the city of Richmond, commenced to increase about 1820. With reference to the German Jewish population of the United States Hon. Simon Wolf says[155]): "The emigration of the German Jews remained altogether sporadic throughout the period of the Napoleonic wars, because of the almost insuperable obstacles which hindered their departure. The increase of the Jewish population in this country was thus limited mainly to the surplus of births over deaths, until some time after the close of the war of 1812. In the course of the reaction against the innovation of liberalism which ensued after 1820, the hardly gained political rights of the German Jews were gradually curtailed or entirely withdrawn, and at this time the Jews of the German maritime cities began to emigrate to the United States in increasing numbers." — This statement fully applies to and explains the causes of the Jewish immigration into Virginia.

Heinrich Foss, who sailed on the 13th of March, 1837,

155.) "The American Jew as Patriot, Soldier and Citizen," by Simon Wolf, pp. 67 and 68. Philadelphia, 1895.

from Bremerhafen to Norfolk, Va., was employed for six months on the James river canal, but he emigrated to the West and died at Cincinnati, Ohio, in 1879, an esteemed master-mason. He liked to speak about his travels through Virginia.[156])

On his way to Ohio he stopped at Lynchburg, Campbell county; Buchanan, Botetourt county; Staunton, Augusta county; Harrisonburg, Rockingham county; Woodstock and Strassburg, Shenandoah county; Winchester, Frederick county; Shepherdstown, Jefferson county, and Wheeling, Ohio county, and in all these towns he met with old German farmers who received him kindly. "*It was as like as if I was travelling in Germany*," Mr. Foss used to say.

This simple narrative of a reliable man characterizes the condition of the German-Virginians at that time. The old folks still retained their German character, but their descendants were more and more anglicized. Jahn's sentence, quoted at the head of this chapter, proved true with the German settlers in Virginia.

The dark clouds of that period are however dispersed by some bright sunlight sparks, that kindle the heart of the German-Virginian historian. In the year 1783 Rev. Adolph Nuessmann, of Mecklenburg county in North Carolina, wrote[157]): "From Georgia to Maryland there is no German printing office, and in North Carolina even no English one." It is therefore a matter of great satisfaction to every German-Virginian, that at New-Market, in the Shenandoah Valley in Virginia, or "Neu-Markt," as it was originally called, soon after the foundation of the Republic, a German printing office was established by a descendant of the first German clergyman in Virginia.[158]) He built the press with his own hands and undertook the publication of "German schoolbooks and religious works." This meritorious man was the Lutheran *Pastor Ambrosius Henkel*, of New-Market. In 1806 his

156.) "Der Deutsche Pionier," Vol. 11, p. 402. Cincinnati, Ohio, 1880.

157.) "Der Deutsché Pionier," Vol. 13, p. 316. Cincinnati, Ohio, 1880.

158.) "Der Süden," Vol. 1, No. 2, pp. 4 and 5. Richmond, Va., 1891.

printing office was in the hands of his son, *Solomon Henkel*, and an "ABC Book," for use in the German school at New-Market, — and probably the first schoolbook ever printed in Virginia, — was published, with lines of poetry and illustrations for each letter of the alphabet, cut in wood by Rev. Henkel himself. A second edition of this book appeared in 1819, of which a copy is in possession of Charles E. Loehr of Richmond. The title of the book was: "The little ABC Book or first lessons for beginners, with beautiful pictures and their names arranged in alphabetic order, to facilitate the spelling to children. — By Ambrosius Henkel, New-Market, Shenandoah county, Virginia; printed in Solomon Henkel's printing office, 1819." — The poetry to each letter is written in a German dialect almost like "Pennsylvania Dutch;" it is not very fastidious in expression, but adapted to the perceptive faculty of children, as for instance:

B.—Der Biber had im Damm sein Haus,
Bald is er drinn', bald ist er draus;
Da wohnt er drinn', so wie er's baut.
Oft man ihn fang't, nimmt ihm die Haut.

G.—Der Geier friszt mit Ernst und Muth,
Stinkt wohl das Fleisch doch schmeckts ihm gut,
Er hackt mit Kopf und Fuess hinein,
Und friszt es weg bis auf das Bein.

K.—Die beste Milch die giebt die Kuh,
Gieb nur den Kindern Mosch dazu,
Und auch ein gross Stueck Butterbrod,
So stirbt dir keins an Hungersnoth.

R.—Der Rabe riecht das Aas von fern,
Er kommt und friszt das Luder gern, —
Der Dramm schmeckt manchem auch so wohl,
Dass er sich saufet toll und voll.

The book closes with some morning and evening prayers, as:

"Nun will ich in die Schule geh'n
Und lernen wie ich soll,
Wird mir der liebe Gott beysteh'n
So lern ich alles wohl."

"Nun dieser Tag ist wieder hin,
Die fins'tre Nacht bricht ein,
Dass ich noch an dem Leben bin
Des soll ich dankbar sein."

In speaking of the printing-establishment at New-Market, Rev. G. D. Bernheim says[159]): "The Lutheran Church in America has had its publication boards and societies in abundance, which doubtless accomplished a good work, *but the oldest establishment of the kind is the one in New-Market, Virginia,* which dates its existence as far back at least as 1810, for the minutes of the North Carolina Synod were printed there at that time. It was established by the Henkel family and has continued under their management to this day."

One of the most prominent members of this illustrious family was Rev. Paulus Henkel, already mentioned. From a biographical sketch[160]) we copy the following: "He was truly a man for the times; vigorous in mind and body. He labored unceasingly, willingly and cheerfully, undergoing trials, hardships, and sacrifices *for good,* and *not* for *gain.*

"His parents were Jacob and Barbara Henkel, née Teters. He was born December 15, 1754, in Rowan county, North Carolina, near the present city of Salisbury, where he resided until 1760. The Indians becoming troublesome, the family removed to Loudoun county, Virginia; thence to Maryland; thence to Hampshire county, Virginia, where they remained not quite a year, having frequently to live in block-houses, for protection against the Indians. Then they moved to Mill Creek, Hardy county, Virginia, where the father of Paul Henkel died and was buried.

"At the age of about 22 Paul Henkel beginning to prepare for the ministry, placed himself under the instruction of Rev. Krug, pastor of the Evangelical Lutheran church,

---

159.) "History of the German Settlements and the Lutheran Church in the Carolinas," by Rev. G. D. Bernheim, pp. 445 and 446.

160.) "Biographical Sketch of Rev. Paul Henkel," compiled by his great-grandson Ambrose L. Henkel, New-Market, Va., 1890.

at Fredericktown, Maryland. After becoming proficient in German, Latin and Greek, and other studies, he was examined and licensed to preach by the Evangelical Lutheran Synod of Pennsylvania and adjacent States,—the only Lutheran Synod at that time in America. He located at New-Market, Virginia, and at once became an active, earnest, zealous minister, laboring in Shenandoah, Rockingham, Frederick, Madison, Culpepper, Pendleton, Botetourt, Wythe, and many other counties in Virginia.

"On June 6th, 1792, he was solemnly set apart for the office of pastor in Philadelphia, Pennsylvania, the ordination being performed by Rev. John Frederick Schmidt. He labored at New-Market for a while, and then located at Staunton, Virginia, where he remained three years, when he returned to New-Market, Virginia. In 1800, he felt it to be his duty to accept a call to his native home in Rowan county, North Carolina, in which and adjoining counties he successfully labored.

"In 1805, owing to the malarious condition of the country, he returned to New-Market, Virginia, and became an independent missionary. He did not desire wealth or fame, but strove to do good. He made tours on horse-back and "gig" through Virginia, Tennessee, Kentucky, Indiana, Ohio, North and South Carolina, preaching and organizing congregations, catechising and confirming the young, and giving words of comfort and cheer to all. He underwent sore trials and severe privations without faltering. He kept a faithful diary of all his labors, which to us, at the present day, seem almost incredible. He often endured hunger, thirst, fatigue, and loss of rest, excessive heat and cold—every hardship and discomfiture incident to sparsely settled sections and dangerous frontier life.

"When the war of 1812 came, he went to Point Pleasant, Mason county, Virginia, where he organized several congregations.

"In 1809 he published a work on 'Christian Baptism and the Lord's Supper,'—'Ueber die christliche Taufe und das

Abendmahl,' in German and afterwards in the English. He published a 'German Hymn-book' in 1810, then in 1816 another 'Hymn-book' in English, containing 476 hymns, many being of his own composition. In 1814 he published a German Catechism: 'Der christliche Catechismus, verfasst zum Unterricht der Jugend in der Erkenntniss der christlichen Religion; sammt Morgen- und Abend-Gebaete.' A second edition appeared in 1816, and soon after an 'English Catechism.'

"He was never idle, and though arduously engaged in traveling, preaching, catechising, and admonishing in private and public, he found time to write many books and letters. One of his books in rhyme: 'Gereimter Zeitvertreib,' (Pastime,) was a strong rebuke to fanaticism, superstition, corruption, and folly. It was full of sarcasm and created much friendly and unfriendly criticism. He was a man of indomitable energy in Church work, and his liberality was almost in excess of his means in such labors and works of charity. It is said, that more than a century ago he helped to fell the trees and build a 'log church' at New-Market, Virginia, his equally energetic wife cooking in an open field, in wash kettles, for the hardy men who came 'to the hewing and log-raising;' and that he made a trip with a one-horse cart to Philadelphia, three-hundred miles distant, for glass and a bell, which some friends in that city gave him for the church.

"His first sermon was preached in Pendleton county, Virginia, in 1781, and his last one in New-Market, Virginia, Oct. 9th, 1825, a month prior to his death—having been actively engaged in the ministry for 44 years."

In the year 1807 the first German newspaper in Virginia: "*Der Virginische Volksberichter und New-Marketer Wochenschrift*"—edited by Ambrosius Henkel, and printed and published by Solomon Henkel, appeared. For the head of the paper Rev. Henkel had prepared a wood-cut representing a mounted postilion sounding his bugle-horn, with the devise:

"Ich bring das Neu's!
So gut ich's weiss!"

This newspaper was however discontinued after the lapse of a few years, not finding the necessary support.

School-matters had been in a deplorable condition since the foundation of the colony. It was not until 1779,[161]) one hundred and seventy-two years after the settlement of Jamestown, that a bill providing for Public Education was introduced in the Assembly. It was framed by Thomas Jefferson, but it failed to pass, and not until 1797 did the main features of the bill become law. It was left to the option of the counties to enforce the act or not, and the number of the schools established is not given in any document. A second school-law was passed in 1818, but Gov. McDowell, in his message to the Legislature, Jan. 1843, said of the whole School-System, inaugurated under this law, "that after having existed for thirty years it gave only sixty days of tuition to one-half the 'indigent' children of the State *as its grand result*, and that it was therefore little more *than a costly and delusive nullity, which ought to be abolished, and another and better system adopted in its place.*" The census of 1840 states, that 58,787 white inhabitants of Virginia, over twenty-one years of age,—that is one-twelfth of the total white population of the State, could neither read nor write. However the Germans *had their parochial schools* since the time of Gov. Spotswood. In Richmond a Swiss or German established in the beginning of the century a large school, named after him: "Haller's Academy."[162]) It was an extensive establishment and located in a large and homely block of buildings on Carey street, near the head of the basin. Haller is represented as an adventurer of little learning, but he had judgment enough to enable him to select good teachers.

In 1825 the University of Virginia, at Charlottesville, which had been planned by Thomas Jefferson, and still retains the cosmopolitan and liberal character which he gave to it, was organized. It deserves special mention, that from

---

161.) "Report of the Commissioner of Education for 1876," p. 399. Washington, 1878.

162.) "Richmond in By-gone Days," p. 203, published by George M. West. Richmond, Va., 1856.

the very beginning the course of study embraced *German language and literature.* The first German professor on this State-institution was *Georg Blaettermann,*[163]) a native of Germany and a graduate of the University of Goettingen. At the time of his appointment he was professor of Philology at Oxford, England,—and he occupied his professorial chair at Charlottesville until 1840.. *He was the first teacher in America to introduce "comparative German-English instruction."*

Professor Dr. M. D. Learned, of the University of Pennsylvania, and formerly of Baltimore, Md., in his lecture delivered before the National German-American Teachers' Association at Cincinnati, O., on July 8th, 1898, bestowed the following brilliant testimonial on the German immigrants[164]): "The importance of the early German influence in America is still unappreciated by the Anglo-American writers of American history, the best accounts of it having been written either in the German language and thus made practically inaccessible to the Anglo-American public—and I blush to say it, to some of our most heralded Anglo-American historians—or if written in English, having been published more as special or local history, without being considered in its vital relations to the life of the American republic." The same impartial scholastic also stated: "The first epoch of German influence in America was followed, after the Napoleonic wars, by a new and vastly more significant period which has witnessed the revolution of American thought and education *by the touch of German culture.* The German influence this time came through three different channels: (1) through the Anglo-American students who from 1815 on finished their studies at German universities; (2) through the indirect influence of German philosophy, science, and letters by way of England; and (3) through Germans who brought the new stimulus direct after 1825. From the American students in Germany we received the

163.) "Das deutsche Element in den Ver. Staaten," p. 405, by Gustav Körner. Cincinnati, 1880.

164.) "Erziehungs-Blätter," 28. Jahrgang, Heft 12, Seite 3 und 4. Milwaukee, Wisc., 1898.

new impulse in American education. . . . . . The turn of the first quarter of the present century brought a new generation of Germans to American shores. Germans this time not only from the shop and fields, but Germans of thought and heroism, graduates from the universities, etc."

Among the German-Virginian clergy *Rev. Louis Frederick Eichelberger*[165]) was a prominent literary man. He was born in Frederick county Md., on the 25th of August 1803. At an early age he was placed in the school of Rev. Dr. Schaeffer at Frederick. Subsequently he was sent to Georgetown, D. C., where he attended the classical school of Dr. Carnahan, who afterward gained distinction as President of Princeton College. From Georgetown, Mr. Eichelberger went to Dickinson College, at Carlisle, Pa., where he graduated in 1826. From college he removed to the newly organized Theological Seminary at Gettysburg, and while a student Mr. Eichelberger was invited to become the pastor of the Lutheran church at Winchester, Va. In 1849 he was elected professor of Theology in the seminary at Lexington, S. C.; the honorary degree of Doctor of Divinity was conferred on him by Princeton College,—and resigning his professorship in 1858, he immediately returned to Winchester, Va., warmly welcomed by many ardent friends. In addition to his labors as teacher and preacher, Dr. Eichelberger was the editor and proprietor of a weekly paper, "The Virginian," at Winchester. He also edited and published from 1833–35 a monthly periodical known as "The Evangelical Lutheran Preacher and Pastoral Messenger," which presented sermons and occasional articles on doctrinal and practical subjects by leading ministers of the Lutheran Church. Drs. Schaeffer, Miller, Hazelius, Baugher, Strobel, Endress and the editor were among the principal writers. His great work was "The History of the Lutheran Church," which however was never published. The author of this history regrets not to have been able to examine this valuable manuscript which is in possession of the library of the Lutheran College at Salem, Roanoke county. It covers seven hundred large and closely written

165.) "Some Items of Lutheran Church History," by Rev. J. E. Bushnell. Roanoke, Va.

pages. While negotiating for the publication of his favorite work, Mr. Eichelberger died. Although all his publications are in English, they are inspired by a genuine German spirit.

Rev. Samuel Simon Schmucker, at New-Market, Va., wrote several theological works: "Kurz gefasste Geschichte der christlichen Kirche auf Grundlage der Busch'schen Werke," "Portraiture of Lutheranism," and "The American Lutheran Church, Historically, Doctrinally and Practically delineated." The son of this learned minister, Samuel Mosheim Schmucker, or "Smucker," as he styled his name, was not less productive. He wrote biographical and historical works. His most important composition: "History of the American Civil War," remained unfinished on account of his death in 1863.

Dr. Charles Porterfield Krauth,[166]) the most distinguished American advocate of the Lutheran faith, translated the "Augsburger Confession," and was the author of an important treatise contrasting the Romish and Evangelical Mass. He also wrote some religious articles in German.

Heinrich Boehm, in 1800, a journeying preacher of the Methodist Church, and previously a preacher of the "United Brethren in Christ," came to the Valley and preached the new dogma in German. His grandfather was a German-Swiss; his father, Martin Boehm, who was Bishop of the United Brethren, travelled with him. They presented the remarkable aspect of advocates of two different creeds, and yet lived in perfect harmony. The Germans of the Valley were much attracted by both of them; the United Brethren accepted much of the Methodist doctrine and may therefore properly be called "German Methodists." Church statistics of Virginia,[167]) dated 1870, enumerate 38 organizations with 7450 United Brethren, and say: "The population is of German origin where the German Reformed, Lutheran and United Brethren are found."

It has been stated that the Germans in Virginia did not

166.) "Virginia," a History of the People, by John Esten Cook, p. 494. Boston, 1884.

167.) "Virginia, a Geographical and Political Summary," p. 197; by the Board of Immigration. Richmond, Va., 1876.

take a very active part in State politics, and yet several German immigrants and descendants of same occupied very prominent positions in the Union, the State and the Army during the first decades of this century.

One of the most distinguished German-Virginians was *B. William Wirth.* His father immigrated from Switzerland to Maryland, and his mother was a native of Wuertemberg. He gained a high reputation as a lawyer and statesman, and in 1819 was appointed by President Monroe Attorney-General of the United States. He retained this important office for twelve years, to the end of the presidential term of John Quincy Adams.

Wirth had also a reputation as an author. In 1803 he wrote, "Letters of the British Spy" for the "Virginia Argus," published in Richmond. These letters created quite a sensation, but the author remained unknown for a long time. He criticized, in a satirical manner, Virginian social life and the customs and eccentricities of the people. These letters furnished much to interest and amuse the public, and much enlarged the subscription lists of the "Argus;" but when the author became known, he earned the hatred of many of his neighbors. — Wirth's "Sketches of the Life of Patrick Henry," merit great credit as one of the most popular biographies in American literature. In the beginning of the fourth decade he published a series of letters of political and social character in the "Alte und neue Welt," printed at Philadelphia, under the pseudonym of "Kahldorf." These letters were dated from Florida, where Mr. Wirth organized a German colony that afterwards declined. The following ludicrous anecdote is related by Kennedy in his "Life of Wirth." It happened in 1803, when Mr. Wirth was awaiting Colonel Gamble's sanction to his marriage with Miss Gamble.

"Colonel Gamble had occasion on a summer morning to visit his future son-in-law's office. It unluckily happened that Wirth had the night before brought some young friends there, and they had had a merry time of it, which so beguiled the hours that even now, at sunrise, they had not separated. The

Colonel opened the door, little expecting to find any company there at that hour. His eyes fell on the strangest group! There stood Wirth with the poker in his right hand, the sheet-iron blower on his left arm, which was thrust through the handle; on his head was a tin wash-basin, and as to the rest of his dress, — it was hot weather and the hero of this grotesque scene had dispensed with as much of his trappings as comfort might require, substituting for them a light wrapper, that greatly aided the theatrical effect. There he stood, in this whimsical caparison, reciting with great gesticulation Falstaff's onset on the thieves, his back to the door. The opening of it attracted the attention of all. We may imagine the queer look of the anxious probationer as Colonel Gamble, with grave and mannerly silence, bowed and withdrew, closing the door behind him without the exchange of a word."

Another memorable personage was *Albert Gallatin*, who came to Virginia in 1779. He was born in Geneva, (Genf) Switzerland, and was a pupil of the celebrated Johannes von Mueller. The Elector of Hessia, who was a schoolmate of Gallatin, offered him a position in his cabinet, which he declined to accept. He came to Richmond, a young man, entrusted with the recovery of some claims, and although he could with difficulty express himself in English, his talents were very soon discovered by Patrick Henry and others. He boarded in the house of Mrs. Allegre, to whose daughter he became attached, and he asked the mother to sanction his addresses. The old Virginian lady was quite wroth at his presumption and, seizing a spit, threatened to transfix and baste him if he dare aspire to her daughter's hand. Finally she relented, the marriage took place and the old lady lived to see her son-in-law highly honored. It is said that Mr. Gallatin consulted Mr. Marshall, afterwards Chief-Justice, about studying law, but was advised to give his attention to statesmanship and finance. The result proved his correct estimate of Mr. Gallatin's talents. In 1780 he joined the Continental Army, and after the war he accepted the professorship of modern languages at Harvard University. In the year 1793 he was elected a member of the U. S. Senate; appointed 1801, under Jefferson and Madison, U. S. Secretary of

Treasury; negotiated 1813 at Gent with Quincy Adams the peace with England; was ambassador to France and England from 1815 to 1823, and retired to private life in 1826. He published, "Memoir on the North-Eastern Boundary," New York, 1843, and "Synopsis of the Indian Tribes in North America." With Thomas Jefferson he vigorously opposed the "Federals," who aimed to give to the Republic a constitution after the British pattern and even inclined to change the confederacy of States to a constitutional monarchy. In the critical period of 1812 he framed the laws of taxation. He died August 12th, 1849, at Astoria, N. Y.

The Counties Gallatin in Kentucky and Illinois commemorate his name, and various townships and cities in New York, Mississippi, Tennessee and Missouri are named after him.

In the presidential election of 1824 a caucus was held and Mr. Gallatin nominated for Vice-President of the United States, — an honor which never again has been bestowed on a foreign-born citizen. But Mr. Gallatin withdrew.[168])

During his stay at Richmond, Va., he occupied a residence on a square between Leigh and Clay, and Seventh and Eighth streets. Death ended his distinguished career in New York city.

It is fairly probable that *Chief-Justice John Marshall* was of German descent, and that his name was originally spelled with "sch" instead of simply "sh." The fact that Mr. Marshall was born in the German settlement of Germantown, in Fauquier county, on the 24th of September, 1755, and that Dr. Louis Marschall,[169]) the first physician of Frankfort, Ky., and father of Humphrey Marshall, who anglicized his German name, came from Germantown, Va., too, speaks in favor of this conjecture. He was a general of the Colonial Army and the friend and biographer of George Washington. He married Miss Mary Willis Ambler, daughter of the Treasurer Jaquelin Ambler, in the year 1783, and he died in 1835. His residence

---

168.) "The North American Review," Vol. 131, No. 5, p. 406.

169.) "Compare Vol. I of this History, p. 159.

still stands in Richmond, on the street named in his honor, between Eighth and Ninth streets. Judge Marshall was a man of great merit, of unpretentious manner and true republican simplicity.

Daniel Sheffey of Staunton, Augusta county, was the son of German parents. He represented Virginia in Congress from 1809-17. Other German-Virginian members of Congress were *John Kerr* of Richmond, 1813–17, and *Isaac Leffler* from the Shenandoah Valley from 1827–29.[170]) The biography of Daniel Sheffey is given by Andreas Simon[171]) as follows:

"*Daniel Sheffey* was born in the year 1770, in Frederick, Md. His father, a German shoemaker, introduced his son into the secrets of his trade, but he did not care to give him a good school-education. Daniel However was desirous of learning and used his leisure time to study astronomy and mathematics, for which he possessed a particular fancy. When he was of age he wandered up the Valley to Augusta county, and from there to Ablesville, Wythe county, where he received employment as shoemaker. His originality and wittiness soon attracted general attention, and finally he quitted his trade and studied law with lawyer Alexander Smyth. When admitted to the bar, and having proved his talent in several complicated law suits, he removed to Staunton, Va. There he was very successful. Mr. John Randolph, the well known statesman, once opposed him before court, and satirically remarked: 'A shoemaker better remain at his bench,' whereupon Sheffey answered: 'Of course if you had been a shoemaker you would still be one.' Although Sheffey spoke the English language with a strikingly German accent, he was elected in 1805 to the Senate of Virginia, 1809 to Congress and again in 1823 to the Legislature of Virginia. He died at Staunton in 1830."

In 1812, during the second war of the Republic with Great Britain, *Major George Armistaedt* defended the harbor

170.) "Virginia and Virginians," by Dr. R. A. Brock. Richmond, Va., 1856.

171.) "Lord Fairfax in Virginien," von A. Simon in "Der Westen," June 12th, 1892. Chicago, Ills.

of Baltimore against the fleet under Admiral Cockburn. He was born April 10th, 1780, at New-Market, Va., where his ancestors had immigrated from Hessen-Darmstadt. Five of his brothers served in the army during the war of 1812, three with the regulars and two with the militia. In 1813 George Armistaedt was promoted to Major of the 3rd Artillery Regiment. He distinguished himself at the capture of Fort George at the mouth of the Niagara river, and after his brilliant defence of Fort Henry near Baltimore he was raised to the rank of Lieutenant-Colonel.

Walter Keith Armistead, a brother of the aforenamed, was born in 1785 and died in 1845 at Upperville, Va. He, like his brother, was a brave soldier. From 1808—1811 he distinguished himself as engineer and superintendent of the fortifications of Norfolk, Va., and was appointed Brigadier-General.

The Armistead family is held among the most prominent in the old mother State. The mother of President John Tyler belonged to it. She was a daughter of Robert Armistead, whose grandfather had immigrated from Hessen-Darmstadt. From a petition of Mrs. Letitia Tyler Semple, addressed to Hon. George G. West, U. S. Senator of Missouri, and dated Louisenheim, Washington, D. C., April 20th, 1897, we learn the interesting fact: that the Armstädt or Armistead were relatives of *four Presidents* of the United States. Mrs. Semple, the daughter of President Tyler and during his term "first lady of the land," writes: "James Monroe, William Henry Harrison, John Tyler and Benjamin Harrison are cousins, being related with the Armisteads and Tylers of Virginia."

In 1794 Joseph Ruffner, a member of the before mentioned Ruffner family and a Shenandoah farmer, bought the Dickinson survey of Kanawha. He made no haste to visit his purchase, relates Dr. W. H. Ruffner,[172]) but the next year, riding among the mountains in search of iron-ore, he

172.) "Historical Papers," No. 5, 1895, pp. 17—21. Washington and Lee University, Lexington, Va.

saw a salt spring. When he had considered the fatness of those river bottoms, along which he had ridden for thirty-six miles; when he looked at that clear, placid "river of the woods," alive with red-horse, white perch, buffalo and blue cats, something whispered, "It is good to be here." Joseph Ruffner bought the salt spring and a large tract of bottom land including the site of the present city of Charleston. He used the old fort for a residence and dying in 1803 he left the Dickinson survey, as it is commonly called, to his sons David and Joseph, who soon went to drilling in the rock to get a larger supply of salt water. Joseph, Jr., became discouraged and sold out to his brother David, whilst he went down the Ohio and began to farm on land which, in time, he sold out in town lots to accommodate the incoming population of the town of Cincinnati. David remained on the Kanawha and went on disclosing the vast treasures in coal and salt—or with his "churning in the ground," as his incredulous neighbors jeeringly called his operations. Meanwhile, however, he kept his farm a-going. He invented many devices for boring wells that continue to be approved. In November 1808 he struck a good supply of brine at forty four feet from the surface, and erected a large furnace, by means of which he promptly reduced the price of salt from five dollars a bushel to two dollars. When David died, Rev. Stuart Robinson, his pastor, wrote: "Colonel Ruffner was one of our first settlers; and by general acknowledgment has been our most useful citizen." He represented Kanawha in the Virginia Legislature in 1799, 1801 and 1802, 1804 and 1811. The Kanawha saltworks and the first coal mines, the chief industries of this district, were established by this energetic German-Virginian. Col. Ruffner died Feb. 1st, 1843.

Gen. Lewis Ruffner, the grandson of David Ruffner, occupied a high and enviable position as a business and public man. He was the first child born in what is now the capital of West Virginia, (Oct. 1st, 1797.) He received an excellent college education and then returned to Kanawha and taught school one year. In 1820 he commenced the manufacture of salt, built a furnace adapted to the use of coal for fuel, and in 1823 he took possession of the property and salt business of his father Henry Ruffner. In 1825 he was elected to the Legislature of Virginia, and was re-elected in 1826, and again in 1828, and during the same year he was appointed Justice of the Peace.

High praise is due to other German-Virginians for their meritorious labours in various directions. In 1809[173]) a number of gentlemen, interested in Agriculture, residing in Maryland, Virginia and the District of Columbia, organized the "Columbian Agricultural Society." As the germ of a national organization, embracing different States, and as the initiative of agricultural exhibitions, this society's operations are entitled to an honorable record, and were heartily endorsed by German farmers. At the second exhibition of the Society, held at Georgetown, eighteen premiums were offered for the best agricultural products and domestic manufactured goods, and to the German exhibitors William Steinberger of Shenandoah county, Va., and George M. Conradt of Frederickstown, Maryland, five premiums were awarded. The cattle exhibited by Mr. Steinberger attracted general notice, especially an extraordinary steer raised by him. This animal was believed to be the largest ever raised in Virginia. The steer was killed the next day at the slaughter-house of Mı. Krouse and weighed near two thousand pounds net beef.

In the year 1800 the population of Richmond was 5,300 white and colored inhabitants, and there were ten or twelve physicians. *Dr. Leiper* was esteemed as one of the favorite doctors. In his office W. H. Harrison, afterwards President of the United States, began the study of medicine. Contemporaries of Dr. Leiper were doctors *Warner* (Werner?) and *Wyman* (Wiemann?) whose names indicate their German origin. *W. F. Ast*, a Prussian by birth, established the *first* mutual Assurance Company against fire in Virginia; but in succession very extensive fires occurred in Norfolk, Richmond, Petersburg and Fredericksburg and the

---

173.) From an editorial article in the "Agricultural Museum," 1809, and the "U. S. Agricultural Report" of 1866.

first paid quota of premium was exhausted in a few years. When a second one was required, payment was refused in many cases and finally the company dissolved. *Joseph Darmstadt,* a Hessian, who came to this country as a sutler of the allied troops of Great Britain, established a business for country produce in Richmond. "He was a shrewd man," says the Chronicler,[174]) "and as the Valley beyond the Blue Ridge was settled by Germans, his knowledge of the language enabled him to attract the custom of the farmers, who drove their wagons to Richmond, laden with the products of the dairy, the mill, forest and the chase. The social disposition of Mr. Darmstadt brought him into society, even the best. His own entertainments were given daily. Almost all our citizens, in those days, went early to market to furnish their larders, and Mr. D. would have a large coffee pot before his fire-place, of the contents of which, prepared by himself, many of his friends, judges, lawyers, doctors and merchants, partook, whenever they were so inclined, particularly on wet and cold mornings; and here the chit-chat of the day was first heard and much news was circulated from this social house."

Another enterprising merchant of that time was *Joseph Marx.* The tobacco and tanners' trades were mostly in German hands, and so were the comparatively small number of inns throughout the State. The Chronicler of Richmond[175]) describes the primitive mode of transporting tobacco to market at the end of the last and the beginning of this century as follows: "The cask containing it was actually rolled to market on its own periphery, through mud and stream. A long wooden spike, driven into the centre of each end, and projecting a few inches beyond it, served for an axletree; a split sapling was fitted to it for shafts and extended in rear of the cask; they were there connected by a hickory withe; a few slabs were nailed to these, in front of the cask, forming a sort of foot board, or box, in which were stowed a middling or two of bacon, a bag of meal, a frying pan, a hoe, an axe, and a blanket

174.) "Richmond in By gone Days," pp. 110 and 111. Richmond, Va., 1856.

175.) "Richmond in By-gone Days," pp. 270—272. Richmond, Va., 1856.

for the bipeds; the whole covered to some height with fodder for the quadrupeds. If the distance to market was moderate, the hogshead was rolled on its hoops, which were stout and numerous; but if fifty to a hundred miles or more were to be overcome, rough felloes were spiked on at each end, or quarter of the cask, and these rude tires served to protect it from being worn through. The *tobacco roller*, as the driver, (often the owner) was called, sought no roof for shelter during his journey, sometimes of a week's duration and severe toil; but at nightfall he kindled a fire in the woods by the road side, baked a hoe cake, fried some bacon, fed his team, (I omitted to mention the bag of corn,) rolled his blanket around him and slept by the fire under the lee of his cask. When he reached the warehouse, his tobacco was inspected, a note or receipt expressing the weight, etc., was handed to him, and he then sallied forth into the streets in search of a purchaser; calling out as he entered a store, 'Mister, do you buy tobacco.' When he had found the right 'Mister,' and obtained his money and a few articles to carry to his 'old woman,' he strapped the blanket on one of his horses and rode home. These men generally travelled in small parties, and if the weather and roads were good, had a merry time of it; if bad, they assisted each other when obstacles occurred. The journey from beyond Roanoke, the only section of the State where German farmers cultivated tobacco, consumed ten days going and returning. Tobacco rollers are now an extinct species."

In the year 1788 "*The Amicable Society*" was formed in Richmond, with the benevolent object of relieving strangers and wayfarers in distress, for whom the law makes no provision. The list of members contains many German names, as: Wm. Schermer, J. Kemp, Joseph Darmstadt, J. Kerr, A. Leiper, Samuel Myers, Jos. Marx, S. Jacob, B. Brand, W. Bibber, G. H. Backus, W. W. Henning, J. Bosher and D. W. Walthall.

At the beginning of the century a place called the "Rock Landing," near the mouth of Shockoe creek at Richmond, was the resort for oyster boats and small crafts. On the occasion of a severe ice-freshet a great deposit of drift-wood, soil and sand formed a small island in James river. "A German[176]) named *Widewilt* procured a land warrant and located it on this new formed land, and to secure it against becoming a floating island, he drove stakes all around his slippery domain and wattled them so that future freshets might add further deposits; and thus 'Widewilt's Island' became a possession of some value as a fishery and sand-mart. The island remained above water longer than its owner did above ground; a similar accident to that which formed the island recurred and destroyed the work of its predecessor."— The courageous work of the German fisherman calls forth admiration and has surrounded his name with romance.[177])

In the year 1804 a German hunter *Bernard Wier* discovered in the magnesian limestone region of Augusta county, on the land of his countryman Aymand,[178]) the beautiful cave known as "Wier's Cave."

Immigration in the farming districts of the State had almost ceased, as has been mentioned, within the first decades of the nineteenth century. Only the country around Alexandria made an exception, as the farmers of that section found a ready sale for their farm products in the adjoining city of Washington. The farmers directed their attention mainly to fruit culture, market gardening and dairy farming. Dr. Julius Dienelt, of Alexandria, informed the author "that in the period of 1830–40 quite a number of Germans settled in the immediate vicinity of Alexandria, naming: Hartbauer, Hohenstein, Grillbortzer, Dietz, Petshold and others, and their descendants still own the land of their fathers, which has much increased in value."

The most convincing evidence of the importance, strength and propagation of the older German element in Virginia is furnished by the large number of German names in the lists of members of the "General Assembly of Virginia." From

176) "Richmond in By-gone Days," pp. 19 and 20. Richmond, Va., 1856.

177.) "Widewilt's versunkene Insel," Gedicht von H. Schuricht. "Der Süden," Vol. I, No. 10. Richmond, Va., 1891.

178.) "Virginia Almanac for 1816," Johnson & Warner. Richmond, Va.

the "Journals of the House of Delegates and of the Senate" the author obtained the following German names, not taking into consideration many doubtful ones like: Adam, Arnold, Baker, Christian, Cook, Fox, Friend, Hunter, Marshall, Martin, New, Thomas, Smith, Young, etc.

1777–1780: Starke, A. Hite, (Hampshire); W. Fleming, S. Hart, (Rockingham); Isaac Zane, (Shenandoah); S. Helm, George Skillering, (Botetourt); W. Drinkard, Th. Hite, (Berkeley).

1781–1783: Rucker, John Skinker, (King George): H. Fry, (Culpepper); Ch. Simms, (Fairfax); Thomas Helm, Francis Worman, Ebenezer Zane, (Ohio); J. Marks, J. Fry, (Albemarle); Th. Coleman, (Halifax).

1784–1786: W. Armistead, (New Kent); J. Reed (Pendleton); William Gerrard, (Stafford); J. Cropper, Wm. Gerrard, (Fayette); A. Hines, A. Stephan, (Berkeley); G. Stubblefield, (Spotsylvania); John Marr, R. Gregory, Gustavus Brown.

1787–1788: J. Turner, John Stringer, D. Fisher, B. Temple, (King William); John Broadhead, Joseph Swearinger, J. Trotter, Th. Kemp, (Princess Ann).

1790–1794: A. Waggoner, (Berkeley); Th. Edgar, Isaac Parsons, G. Stump, W. Nilms, A. D. Orr, Richard Hickman, (Clarke); Jacob Froman, (Mercer).

1795–1798: George Buckner, (Caroline); Th. Starke, (Hanover); Wm. Buckner, (Mathe); John Koontz, (Rockingham).

1805–1816: Daniel Sheffey, (Augusta); Noah Zane, (Ohio); Gorman Baker, (Cumberland); Wm. Starke, (Hanover); T. W. Swearinger, (Jefferson); Dr. Jos. De Graffenriedt, (Lunenburg).

1823–1828: L. T. Date, (Orange); George May, (Bath); F. G. L. Buhring, (Cabell); Jos. Holleman, (Isle of Wight); George Rust, (Loudoun); James Fisher, (Lunenburg); R. P. Fletcher, (Rockingham); Col. John Thom, (Fauquier); John Perringer, (Alleghany); Samuel Herdman, (Brooke); George Stillman, (Fluvanna); Ed. Sangeter, (Fairfax); Wm. Finks, (Madison); Dr. John Stanger, (White); John F. May, (Petersburg).

CHAPTER XII.

Revival of German Immigration and Life to 1860.

IN the fourth decade of the nineteenth century the German element of Virginia, particularly of Richmond, several country towns and the present State of West Virginia, received large additions of German immigrants. They came by way of New York, Philadelphia, Baltimore and New Orleans. Representing nearly all of the German States, yet they principally came from Hessia and Saxony—particularly from the city of Marburg in Hessia. Mr. Nolting, a merchant whose descendants still live in Richmond, imported by sailing vessel direct from Bremen to Rockets, now Fulton, Va., a large number of German laborers and artisans, who were employed in building the James river or Kanawha canal. Numerous German Hebrews settled in the various county seats of Virginia, where they established stores. Mr. Julius Straus, the present president of the Beth Ahaba congregation, reported on Nov. 6, 1898, in a brief sketch of the Jews of Richmond: [179])

"In the years 1837, 1838 and 1839 there arrived in this city from Bavaria several families which had been accustomed to the German mode of worship. In these years the Congregation Beth Shalome was the only Synagogue in Richmond, and the history of this congregation is, to some extent, the history of the Hebrews in Richmond. A minute-book, which perished in the flames of evacuation day, together with other valuable papers belonging to the synagogue, dated back to the year 1791, which is generally accepted as the date of organiza-

179.) "The Richmond Dispatch," November 6th, 1898, p. 3.

tion of this congregation following the Portuguese form, which was strange to the German immigrants. About the year 1840 some twenty German families were organized into a society for religious purposes, and held services at the residence of Mr. Myer Angle. Then more German settlers arrived in the city, and a synagogue was built on Marshall, near Sixth street, and in 1848 the present synagogue, Beth Ahaba, on Eleventh street, near Marshall, was dedicated."

Mr. Jacob Ezekiel, who has written a very interesting pamphlet, entitled "The Jews of Richmond," says: "The first place of worship of the Beth Shalome congregation was a room in a three-story brick building on the west side of Nineteenth, between Franklin and Grace streets, in which one of the members resided. The next place of worship was a small brick building, erected on the west side of Nineteenth street, in the rear of what was known as the Union Hotel, on the southwest corner of Main and Nineteenth streets.

"After some years a lot of ground was purchased from Dr. Adams, on the east side of Mayo, above Franklin street, on which a commodious synagogue was erected, in which the congregation worshipped for upwards of three quarters of a century. On account of the decrease of membership by death and removal from the city this synagogue was recently sold to another congregation, the K. K. Sir Moses Montefiore, and the remnant of the congregation of Beth Shalome have worshipped since then in Lee Camp Hall, on Broad street, near Seventh, and in 1898 this oldest Jewish congregation united with the congregation of Beth Ahaba.

"The reading desk of this once flourishing Beth Shalome congregation has been filled from time to time by prominent Hazanim, who afterward occupied honorable positions in the most prominent congregations in the United States, among whom were the following Revs. with German names: Isaac H. Judah, Abraham H. Cohen, Isaac Leeser, Solomon Jacobs, Julius Eckman, Henry S. Jacobs, George Jacobs."

The history of Beth Ahaba will follow further on.

Senator Wm. Lovenstein of Richmond, in his English oration at the "German Day," 1890[180]), mentioned the names of several Germans, who came to Richmond in 1835 and 1836, who are to be considered as pioneers of the later large immigration: B. Briel, C. Liewer, J. Knauf, J. Brauer, V. Hechler, Gottfr. Noelting, J. Rebman, Havermare, Mrs. P. Fahr, Georg Lentz, Mrs. G. Lentz, Mrs. H. A. Philips, Mrs. Kohlhausen, P. Kepler, P. Schafer, C. Weber, H. Kracke, Joseph Myers, Mrs. Joseph Myers, G. Wilhelm, A. Bodecker, Scherer. George Schoenberger, J. Doerflinger, Pitz, W. Ewerts, W. Miller, F. Wittemaier, Beck, O. A. Strecker, Stein, Kruesman, John Maybus, William Menzing, Myer Angle, Moses Waterman and Isaac Solomon.

Richmond, the capital of the State, now became the nucleus of German life in Virginia. Here the celebrations of German national events took place. The first *public festival* or "Volksfest," was celebrated in 1840, in honor of *Guttenberg*, [181]). It is to be deplored that no description of this festive event is left. On the 14th and 15th of September, 1857, a grand celebration in honor of General von Steuben: *Das Steubenfest*, was arranged. The entire affair was a triumph and every feature of it a success. The leaders in this festival, O. A. Strecker, Oswald Heinrich, Jul. Fischer, Weilbacher, Louis Rueger, Honneger, Marxhausen, Diacont, Meier, Morgenstern, Lehmann, Sturm, Schad, Harrold, and B. Hassel, hoped[182]), that it would demonstrate to their countrymen the strength of the German element and impart to them more national self-confidence, while on the other hand the Anglo-American fellow-citizens would better learn to understand and to respect German customs; and these expectations were realized. The German Rifle Company, Saengerbund, Krankenverein, Schiller-Loge, Theaterverein, Turnverein and citizens belonging to none of these organizations assembled about noon on the 14th Sep-

180.) "The Richmond Dispatch," p. 2, October 7th, 1890.

181.) "Das deutsche Element in den Ver. Staaten," Seite 404, von Gustav Körner. Cincinnati, 1880.

182.) "Virginische Zeitung," Sonntagsblatt des Anzeigers. Richmond, Va., September 14th, 1890.

tember, 1852, in the Capitol Square, on the north side of the Capitol, formed in procession and marched to Bellville Place. There the formal ceremonies: prayer, speeches, music and singing, the unveiling of Gen. Steuben's bust, moulded by Mr. Hubert, were followed by social gaiety and games for children arranged by the ladies. The best order prevailed.

Oswald Julius Heinrich delivered the German oration, which was highly enjoyed and applauded. We quote in his own words and language from his brilliant speech the following remarks:

"Hat nicht der Fleiss der Deutschen, wenn nicht in höherem Maasse, doch sicher zu gleichen Theilen, die Gauen des neuen Vaterlandes in blühende Auen verwandelt? Ist nicht das Verdienst der Deutschen um Kunst, Literatur und allgemeine Kenntnisse von allen Denen anerkannt, welchen beschränkter Nationalstolz ein freies Urtheil nicht verkümmert? Kämpften nicht zu allen Zeiten und in allen Ländern die Deutschen für die Sache der Freiheit und Unabhängigkeit, für Wahrheit und Licht? Und zeigen auch einige schwarze Blätter der Geschichte, dass vereinzelte Schaaren sich verleiten liessen, aus gemeiner Gewinnsucht sich zu Gegnern derselben zu machen, gingen sie nicht früher oder später, von ihrem Unrecht überzeugt, in den rechten Pfad zurück? Und mannen sich nicht noch jetzt die Deutschen um die flatternde Fahne derjenigen Partei, welche die Grundsätze der Väter der Republik zu den ihrigen macht und die Freiheit und Gleichheit Aller gegen freche Uebergriffe und Monopole zu schützen sucht?" u. s. w.

Heinrich was born on the 2d April, 1828, at Dresden, Saxony, studied architecture and mining at the academies of Dresden and Freiberg, Saxony[183]). Having participated in the revolution at Dresden in May, 1849, he was prosecuted and obliged to leave the land. In 1850 he came to America and worked as mason, carpenter, painter, teacher and engineer in Tennessee, South and North Carolina. In 1855 he moved

183.) Correspondence of the late Mr. Benno Heinrich (the brother of O. Heinrich.) Richmond, Va.

to Richmond, Va., and established himself as architect and teacher of mathematics and drawing. During the civil war Heinrich held a position in the Confederate mining office. Afterwards he was superintendent of the Lead Works at Austinville, Va., and still later of the Midlothian Coal Mines in Chesterfield county, Va. In 1878 he finally succeeded in obtaining an office fully complying to his wishes and eminent talents. Messrs. Cox Brothers' Co., proprietors of the coal mines at Drifton, Pa., invited him to organize a mining academy, and he remained the principal of it until February 4th, 1886, the day of his death. His corpse was cremated at New York and his ashes interred at Hollywood cemetery, Richmond, Va.

A similar success like the "Steuben Fest" was the "*Schillerfeier*," on November 10th, 1859. The entire German population of the city participated in honoring the favorite poet of all Germans: Friedrich von Schiller, at the 100th anniversary of his birthday. In order to make this celebration an impressive demonstration against the detestable "Knownothing movement" prevailing at the time, Schiller's centennial festival was celebrated in a glorious style.

The liberal era in Germany and Austria, from 1848 to 1850, had ended in revolutions and the victory of reaction. Many political fugitives emigrated to the United States, and the Republic received during that period a most desirable influx of emigrants from Germany. The refugees were men of high education and noble character; they had sacrificed their homes and positions in life for the unity and liberty of their beloved Fatherland; and such elements were well qualified to give a new impulse to German life in America, and to successfully advocate not to give up the mother language and the accomplishments and good habits of the native land. Virginia received her share of this valuable immigration, although the greater number stayed in the cities of the East or went to the "Far West."

There were, unfortunately, among these refugees a number of enthusiasts, who cherished the idea to germanize America, or to establish at least a German State in the Union. The number of these fanatics was *very small*, but their foolish agitation was the cause of great evil to the entire German element. Almost all German-Virginians were opposed to the movement, but the leaders of it selected the city of Wheeling, situated in the extreme north of Virginia before the division of the State, as the seat of a "*Congress of German Revolutionists*" to meet in September, 1852, and the Anglo-Americans attached to this convention more importance than it merited. *Only sixteen delegates* of nominally 1112 Revolutionary Associations (Revolutionsvereine) attended the so-called Congress; and most of them came from Eastern States. The participants were[184]): Dr. Conradin Homburg, of Indianapolis, Ind., formerly practicing medicine at Fredericksburg, Va., president; E. Schlaeger, of Boston, Mass., secretary; Leonard Roos, of Newark, N. J., R. Fischer, of Wheeling, Va., C. Strobel, Wheeling, Va., L. Meyer, Boston Masc., I. N. Winkle, Wheeling, Va., W. Rothacker, of London, A. Gerwig, Cincinnati, O., J. Mueller, Cleveland, O., E. Goepp, Philadelphia, Pa., W. Rosenthal, Philadelphia, Pa., Lorenz Kirchner, Troy, N. Y., G. Baczko, Albany, N. Y., J. Roth, Pittsburg, Pa., and C. Hoffmann, Pittsburg, Pa. These eccentric persons traced out a program for the foundation of an "*Universal Republic*" (Welt-Republik). They proposed to organize an Alliance of the Nations of the New and the Old World, (einen Voelkerbund der neuen und alten Welt), and to accomplish "*the annexation of Europe to America.*" The German-American newspapers treated the resolutions of the Wheeling Congress with ridicule and contempt, but the Anglo-American press pretended to see in the proceedings of the convention an insolent interference with the political affairs of this country. Thus the "Wheeling Congress" offered to the so called "natives" the welcome opportunity to false representations of the patriotic sentiment of the "foreigners," and particularly of the Germans. Another organization, "the Free German Society, (Freie Gemeinde), at Richmond," excited about 1850 suspicion and severe critique. The principles of radicals frightened the slaveholders and church-goers, although they include economic social and political questions which in our days have in part been realized or grown to importance.

184.) "Der deutsche Pionier," 8. Jahrgang, Seite 96. Cincinnati, Ohio.

Louis P. Hennighausen, in his interesting "Personal Reminiscences of the Political Life of the German-Americans in Baltimore during the decade of 1850-1860," reports[185]): The Free German Society in Richmond, Va., demanded: 1, Universal suffrage; 2, The election of all officers by the people; 3, The abolition of the Presidency; 4, The abolition of the Senates, so that all Legislatures shall consist of one branch only; 5, The right of the people to recall their representatives at their pleasure; 6, The right of the people to change the Constitution when they like; 7, All law-suits to be conducted without expense; 8, A department of the Government to be set up for the purpose of protecting immigration; 9, A reduced term for immigrants to acquire citizenship.—*Reform in the Foreign Relations of the Government:* 1, Abolition of all neutrality; 2, Intervention in favor of every people struggling for liberty.—*Reform in what relates to religion:* 1, A more perfect development of the principle of personal freedom and liberty of conscience; consequently, (a) abolition of laws for the observance of the Sabbath; (b) abolition of prayers in Congress; (c) abolition of oath upon the Bible; (d) repeal of laws enacting a religious test before taking an office. 2, Taxation of church property; 3, A prohibition of incorporations of all church property in the name of ecclesiastics.—*Reform in Social Conditions:* 1, Abolition of all land monopoly; 2, Ad valorum taxation of property; 3, Amelioration of the condition of the working class, (a) by lessening the time of work to eight hours for grown persons and to five hours for children; (b) by incorporation of Mechanics' Associations and Protective Societies; (c) by granting a preference to mechanics before all other creditors; (d) by establishing, at public expense, an asylum for superannuated mechanics without means. 4, Education of poor children by the State; 5, Taking possession of railroads by the State; 6, The promotion of education, (a) by the introduction of free schools, with the power of enforcing parents to send their children to school, and prohibition of all clerical influence; (b) by instruction in the German language; (c) by establishing a German University. 7, The

185.) Eleventh and Twelfth Annual Reports of the Society for the History of the Germans in Maryland," 1897—1898, pp. 5 and 6; and "Political Text Book and Clopadia," by W. W. Cesky, pp. 220, etc. Philadelphia, 1860.

supporting of the slave emancipation exertions of Cassius M. Clay by Congressional laws; 8, Abolition of the Christian system of punishment and introduction of the humane amelioration system; 9, Abolition of capital punishment.

The "Freie Gemeinde" was however only an *ephemeral organization*; its membership was only twenty-two, and it was looked upon by the majority of the Germans of Richmond with almost hostile sentiments. The participation in such a society was full of dangers in a slave State, and in spite of its insignificance it gave the nativists sustenance for their animosity.

The recollection of this association has almost died out and it was only possible after manifold query to obtain some reliable information about it from the contemporaries of its time [186]) still living in Richmond.

It was about 1850 when a certain Mr. Steinmetz came to Richmond and made energetic efforts to organize a "Freie Gemeinde." He was assisted by brewer Richter, of the Chimborazo Brewery, Mr. Kempe, Mr. A. Rick, two Mess. Teupel Mr. Steinlein, &c. Several meetings were held at Monticello Hotel, where Steinmetz addressed the members on the principles of Free-thinkers. A great deal of animosity was aroused, particularly among their countrymen, by the hoisting of a "red flag" over the meeting house, and this demonstration brought down on them the appellation of "Die Rothen," *i. e.*, "the Reds." In the early part of 1851 Steinmetz was advised to shake the dust of the city off his feet if he did not desire to be subjected to complications peculiarly disagreeable to himself, and he heeded the advice. With his disappearance the whole movement was wrecked.

Since the introduction of slavery the pro-slaverymen in Virginia had looked upon the Germans with hidden suspicion and antipathy, and now their animosity was shared by a very great portion of the entire English element, which made itself observable by paltry but inimical actions.

136.) Reminiscences furnished by Messrs. Louis Rueger, B. Hassel, C. R. M. Pohl and C. Wendlinger.

The success of the Germans in agricultural, industrial and commercial pursuits, and their love of the old Fatherland demonstrated by their great public festivals at Richmond, increased the ill-will of the Anglo-Virginians. The political, religious and social institutions of the United States, as: general and free elections, freedom of speech, printing, worship of God, public instruction, equal rights before court and in political and social competition, *all these very fundamental principles of republican life* were at that period in Virginia not carried out to the letter. The so-called natives knew very well that their German fellow-citizens, although silently and patiently suffering, fully recognized the state of oppression and that they longed to exercise their constitutional rights without restraint or fear of evil consequences to themselves. Some intimidated writers have glorified the good relations claimed by them to have existed between the Anglo- and German-Virginians at that period, but the historian has to *tell the truth* and not to gild dark clouds, and he must acknowledge that the Germans were politically and socially slighted. From 1854—56 the spiteful "*know-nothing movement*" prevailed, and the so-called "natives" threw off the mask and openly showed their animosity for the "foreigners." At first the Germans continued to silently bear all abuse and threat—some of them even forgot their self-respect and joined their enemies—and it was therefore the good luck of the oppressed that from among the Anglo-Virginians an eloquent and ardent defender pleaded their cause. *Henry A. Wise*, afterwards Governor of the State and General in the Confederate army, in an open letter and many speeches during the memorable Electoral campaign of 1854, defended the rights of the abused foreigners and foiled the knownothing movement. At that time Governor Wise erected to himself a monument in the hearts of all German-Virginians that can never wither, *and he in truth made the relations between the English and the Germans in Virginia more harmonious and beneficial,* although the rivalry between the two nationalities continued for some time, as may be illustrated by the following incident:

On July 26th, 1856, the following appeal was published in the Richmonder Anzeiger:

AWAKE GERMANS!

The City Council, elected to protect the welfare and rights of the citizens, having resolved, on the 21st inst., to pay to each uniformed military company an annual allowance of 50 dollars—but upon motion of Mr. Gretter: with the exception of the German Rifle Company—all German citizens of Richmond and all who have taken their intention papers, are hereby invited to attend, on Monday next, July 28th, at eight o'clock, P. M.,

A GENERAL MASS-MEETING

at the St. Johannes Church, on Fifth street,

to discuss the following questions:

1. Is the City Council justified to ignore the rights of citizens and to expend the public funds with partiality?

2. Is the City Council entitled to tax the German citizens at equal rates as other citizens, without granting them equal privileges?

3. Is the City Council authorized to grant German citizens and taxpayers fewer benefits of public funds than citizens of other nationality?

4. And is the action of the City Council of the 21st inst. not to be termed an act of impudence and insult to the German Rifle Company, and also an offence against the Constitution of the country, and an outrage to the whole German population of the State of Virginia?

Every German who values the rights of citizens and German honor is expected to attend the meeting!

SEVERAL CITIZENS."

The author of this appeal was Mr. C. R. M. Pohle, and about 200 Germans attended the meeting in the German church. Mr. B. Hassel called the assembly to order and was appointed chairman, while Mr. J. Reinhardt was chosen secretary. Messrs. Pohle, Gronwald, Rev. Hoyer, Rick and others criticized the action of the City Council in the strongest terms, and *blamed it to be partial and to provoke discord and hatred among the citizens.* Finally resolutions were adopted and afterwards published in the leading English city papers: the "Enquirer," "Examiner" and "Dispatch," which neither lacked plainness nor energy; but the expected result did not follow. The City Council justified its action by a most deplorable incident that happened at a target shooting on a picnic place called the "Hermitage." Although the shooting was arranged by the German Rifles, this military company had nothing to do with the occurrence. A young German butcher, who was no member of the company, had indulged in too much spirits and become quarrelsome. He insulted and attacked a corporal of the Rifle Company, who finally shot and wounded his offender fatally, so that he died in the hospital during the night. The corporal disappeared and was never heard of again; all German citizens of Richmond lamented the sad event, but no one considered the Company in any way responsible. The City Council took a contrary view. However, the German Rifle Company kept up its organization without the aid of public money, and at a later time, when the Civil War broke out and the Governor called on the citizens to defend the State, the members of the ill-treated company shouldered their rifles and took the field under the command of Capt. Florence Miller.

C. R. M. Pohle, who was the chief arranger of the above described mass-meeting, is a man of German sentiment and of ideal disposition. He was born on April 17th, 1821, at Delitsch, Prussia. He came to America in 1844, and lived in New York until 1849. At New York he accepted an engagement as actor in Palm's Opera House, a German theatre under the management of Mr. Schwan, and he gained the esteem of the public[187]), In 1849 until 1852 he was a musician of the U. S. Navy Band, and afterwards he removed to Richmond, Va., where he received the appointment of Pro-Sector of the anatomical department of the Richmond Medical College. With a particular liking he filled the position of Drum-Major of the First Virginia Militia Regiment, and accompanied it in the war[188]). Pohle also tried himself as author. He wrote two dramas: "Der Blitz" and "Maria, oder Leidenschaft und Liebe," and also many German poems, published in 1855 by B. Hassell, Richmond, Va. These pub-

187.) "New-York Staatszeitung," August 13th, 1845.

188.) "War History of the old First Virginia Infantry Regiment," by Charles T. Loehr. Richmond, Va., 1884.

lications were much criticized as being deficient in form and sometimes objectionable in expression, but they are not without poetical merit and full of devotional German patriotism. Mr. Pohle was for years solicitor of the "Virginia Staats Gazette;" he died an inmate of the Soldiers' Home at Richmond.

German newspapers, published in Richmond, have been already repeatedly mentioned, and now their history shall be supplemented.

In the year 1853 B. Hassel, a native of Cassel, Hessia, a compositor by occupation, founded the "Richmond Anzeiger." Many years Mr. Hassel had to compete with serious difficulties to keep up his paper; at times he combined the functions of editor, compositor, printer and distributor, and to the present time his wife and children have faithfully assisted him in his toilsome work. The perseverance of Mr. Hassel deserves great credit, and the "Anzeiger" has to-day the honor to be the second oldest of all the existing Richmond newspapers.

About the year 1858 Rev. Hoyer, pastor of the German Evangelical St. Johannes church, published the "Beobachter," a German weekly. The paper was well edited, but insufficiently supported, and existed but a short time.

In the beginning of 1859 Hermann Schuricht, the author of this history, came to Richmond and started with Henry Schott, born in Marburg, in Hessia, the daily "Virginische Zeitung" and a comic Sunday paper, "Die Wespe." These publications were favorably received by the public, but unfortunately the Civil War broke out soon after and injured the enterprise. In January, 1860, the proprietors accepted the proposition of the owners of the "Richmond Enquirer" to consolidate the "Virginische Zeitung" with their widely circulated paper. Henry Schott remained in charge of the German printing department and H. Schuricht continued as German editor. The "Enquirer" appeared hereafter until the war opened in April, 1860, its outer pages printed in German and the inner in English, edited by O. Jennings Wise, son of Governor Wise, and Col. N. Tyler. Editor Schuricht had stipulated, however, that he should not be obliged to write in favor of slavery, and that all contributions of the English editors to the German part of the paper were to be signed by them. After the close of the war Mr. Hassel undertook to publish the "Virginische Zeitung" as Sunday edition of the "Anzeiger," and it is so continued to the present day.

Several German-Virginians were contributors to these German Richmond newspapers, like: *G. A. Peple,* whose biographical sketch follows in chapter 13, and who for some time, towards the close of the war, edited the "Richmond Anzeiger." *Hugo Plaut* furnished the "Virginische Zeitung" with pretty poems. He was a native of Hessia and kept a trimming store on Main street. At the beginning of the Civil War he joined the Wise Legion, was afterward a manufacturer in New York city, and died in 1895. *Wilhelm H. Lotz,* born at Marburg, in Hessia, contributed several articles on technical questions to the "Virginische Zeitung." He died in 1894 at Chicago.

The "Virginische Staatszeitung" was published at Wheeling, before the separation of West Virginia.

A modest German citizen of Richmond also deserves mention, having joined in the intellectual endeavors of that period and who may, by comparison, properly be called: "the Hans Sachs of Virginia."—*Gottfried Lange,* born March 20th, 1809, at Erfurt, Prussia, was like the "Meistersinger of Nuremberg," a shoemaker and a poet. He came to Richmond in 1837 and worked for some time as a common laborer on the James river canal. After saving some money, he established himself as shoemaker, also pruned vines and finally opened a wine and beer saloon. Lange took great interest in public affairs, and in 1841 he prompted the organization of the "Deutsche Krankengesellschaft zu Richmond," which, in his presence, celebrated its fiftieth anniversary on Oct. 19th, 1891. A song that Lange had composed at the time of the founding of the society, was printed and distributed at the festival. He also participated in the organization of the St. Johannes church and was esteemed by all who knew him. He died in 1893.

Among the physicians of Richmond *Dr. M. Rust* took a prominent place, and several of his medical publications were highly commended.

Karl Minnigerode, doctor of theology and rector of the St. Paul Episcopal church, was another German much esteemed in Anglo- and German-American circles[189]). He was born August 6th, 1814, at Arensberg, in Westphalia, and studied jurisprudence at the university of Giesen. He then became an active member of the German "Burschenschaft" and took part in politics and the distribution of revolutionary publications. After several years of imprisonment he determined to emigrate, and on Dec. 1st, 1839, he came to America. He first went to Philadelphia as teacher of ancient languages and soon attracted the attention of Anglo-American scientific men. At that time he took part with enthusiasm in the cultural endeavors of his countrymen and at the "Guttenberg Celebration" at Philadelphia he was the German orator. In 1842 he followed a call to the professorship of classical literature on "William and Mary College," at Williamsburg, Va., and from that time forward the former German revolutionist adopted the cause of the Virginian slave-holders. In 1844 he joined the Episcopal church, which from the beginning of the colony had aimed to rule and to suppress all other creeds, and in 1848 he exchanged the professorship with the pulpit. His estrangement from his countrymen became more and more apparent, although occasionally, when requested, he performed nuptial and other ceremonies in German. His countrymen regretted that a man of such antecedent, eminent talent and knowledge disregarded them, when by his influence he might have assisted the German element to develop its importance and merit. During the War of Secession Rev. Minnigerode was the friend and confessor of Jefferson Davis, President of the Confederate States, and after the capture and imprisonment of Mr. Davis at Fortress Monroe, Rev. Minnigerode obtained permission to visit the fallen statesman and to afford him his ecclesiastical consolation. Rev. Minni-

189.) Compare "Das deutsche Element in den Ver. Staaten," von G. Koerner. Cincinnati, Ohio, 1880.

gerode has been severely blamed by northern writers on account of this action, but it honors him not to have deserted his friend in the hour of need. In the presence of an officer and the guard he repeatedly administered the sacrament to the ex-president in his prison. Some religious publications in English originated from Dr. Minnigerode's pen. Dr. Minnigerode died in 1894.

In 1844 another German scholar *Maximilian Schele de Vere* was appointed Professor of modern languages and literature at the University of Virginia, Charlottesville, Va. After the death of Professor George Blaettermann, before mentioned, Dr. Med. Karl Kreutzer, a native of Saxony, had occupied the professorship, and he was succeeded by Dr. Max. Schele de Vere. The "Richmond Times" of June 14th, 1894, says in an editorial: "His career has been one of singular honor to himself and the institution with which his name is linked, and his services of learning, especially in the science of comparative philology, have been of very high order." He was born in 1820 in Pommerania. Maximilian Schele de Vere received an excellent college education; subsequently he visited the universities of Bonn and Berlin, and thanks to his commanding talents and favorable social position, he was very early a "Regierungs-Referendar" in the Prussian civil service and an attaché to the embassy at St. Petersburg. The sudden death of his father deprived the family of his large official income, and as the above two offices were "unpaid," he was compelled to abandon the career so hopefully begun. In 1842, at the age of twenty-two, he emigrated to the United States, and at once engaged in literary pursuits. He edited for some time "Die alte und neue Welt," published in Philadelphia. In 1843 he took an active part in the foundation of the "Deutsche Einwanderungs-Gesellschaft zu Philadelphia," and following an invitation of Dr. R. Wesselhoeft, he removed to Boston, where he established himself a teacher of modern languages and literature. His labors were noticed with approval and he soon secured the friendship of several learned men of influence. In the summer of 1844 Schele de Vere travelled through the States of the Union to extend his knowledge of the country and its people, and upon his return to Boston was handed a call to be professor of modern languages at the University of Virginia, which he accepted. During the War of Secession Prof. Schele de Vere served for some time as an officer in the Confederate Army, and was afterwards appointed Commissioner to the various German States by the Confederate Government. Peace re-established, Professor Schele de Vere re-occupied his place at the University, and in 1894 he celebrated the fiftieth anniversary of his affiliation to the University of Virginia. At this occasion the German-American Society of Virginia, at Richmond, conferred on him, as a mark of esteem, the honorary membership of the society. The professor was known as a productive author. The "Deutsche Pionier" and "Rattermann's Deutsch-Amerik. Magazin" of 1886 contain many valuable contributions written by him, and in 1891 Prof. Schele de Vere was one of the contributors of "Der Sueden," published in Richmond. Of his numerous English writings must be mentioned: Comparative Philology, Studies in English, Americanism, Leaves from the Book of Nature, The Myths of the Rhine, illustrated by Doré (edition de luxe, Scribner's Sons), Leaves from the Book of Nature, republished by Blackwood, London, The Romance of American History, Modern Magic, Problematic Characters, From Night to Light, The Hohensteins, (the last three publications are translations from Spielhagen), Wonders of the Deep, The Great Empress, Glimpses of Europe in 1848, etc. He also published several articles in the "Southern Literary Messenger," "Scribner's Magazine" and "Harper's Monthly."

Professor Schele de Vere was the recipient of acknowledgments by German and American scientific corporations. The University of Greifswald bestowed on him the degree of doctor of philosophy, and that of Berlin that of doctor of jurisprudence. He was also tendered several honorable positions by highly renowned academies, but he declined all for reason of his attachment to Virginia. He died in 1897 at Washington.

During the middle of this century the German language was more and more supplanted by the English, particularly in all the country towns and villages. This is especially true of the German parishes. Besides at Richmond, only in the Lutheran churches at Charlottesville, Va., Wheeling and Martinsburg, W. Va., and in a few communities of Dunkards in Botetourt and Rappahannock counties, preaching in German was continued.

Rev. Socrates Henkel, since 1850 in charge of the Evangelical Lutheran church at New-Market, Va., in his "History of the Evangelical Lutheran Synod of Tennessee,"[190]) names the following Virginian Lutheran churches of German origin, omitting however some we have mentioned in Volume I, chapters 5 and 6, that did not belong to the Tennessee Synod:

Shenandoah county.—Emmanuel, New-Market; Mt. Zion, Solomon's; St. Mary's, (Pine) Powder Springs; St. Paul's, St. Jacob's; Zion, St. Matthew's, St. Stephen's, St. David's, Mt. Calvary, Morning Star, Orkney Springs.

Rockingham county.—Bithany, (St. Jacob's), McGaheysville; Trinity, St. Peter's, Rader; St. John's, Bethel; Phanuels, Philipps.

Augusta county.—Bethlehem, St. Paul's; Keinadt's or Koiner's, 12 miles from Staunton; St. John's, Waynesboro.

Madison county.—Mt. Nebo.

Prince William county.—Bethel.

Page county.—St. Paul's, St. William's, (Fairview); Grace, Mt. Calvary, Morning Star, St. Mark's, Cedar Point, Hawksbill, Luray, Alma, Stony Man.

Wythe county.—Valley church.

Washington county.—Church in the Fork.

Roanoke county.—Salem.

He states that Lutheran churches also exist or existed in the counties of Mason, Smyth, Frederick, Botetourt, Cul-

---

190.) "History of the Evangelical Lutheran Tennessee Synod," by Socrates Henkel, D.D., page 270 and elsewhere. New-Market, Va., 1890.

pepper, Montgomery, and in West Virginia in Shepherdstown, Jefferson county, Zion; Mill Creek church, in Hardy county, and Probst church, in Pendleton county.

From Rev. A. Phillippi's interesting paper to the Lutheran Pastors' Association of Wythe county, published in "Wytheville Dispatch" of April 9th, 1897, we gather the following historical facts: "After the death of Rev. George Flohr, before mentioned, the Rev. Jacob Sherer took charge of St. John's church, near Wytheville, Va., until 1836. His successor was Rev. John T. Tabler. The four years during which Rev. Tabler was pastor was a very critical time in the life and history of the congregation. It was the time of the introduction and use of the English language in place of the German. In 1841 to 1854 Revs. J. J. Greever and J. A. Brown jointly took charge of the congregation, and from 1854 to 1862 Rev. J. A. Brown continued on in the pastorate. He was followed by Revs. Wm. D. Roedel and E. H. McDonald, and in 1866 by Rev. Alex. Phillippi. The old constitution, adopted in 1804, but lost sight of in the transition of the congregation in the use of the English in place of the German language in its public services, was hunted up, translated into English, revised in a few points and re-adopted amidst general and great rejoicing. Thus the congregation has preserved its German character to this day. Rev. Phillippi was succeeded by Rev. S. S. Rahn and Rev. Paul Sieg. The beautiful, stately Trinity church in Wytheville, and also St. Mark's and St. Luke's, are now holding honorable places among the working and growing churches of the Lutheran Synod of Southwest Virginia."

The oldest German Christian community in Richmond, which has never ceased to use the German language, is the *Lutheran St. Johannis church.* On Christmas day, 1844, the first divine service was celebrated by Rev. Hoyer in the old church, corner Jackson and Fifth streets. The old church was a plain brick building, and the basement was used as school-room. Unfortunately the pastor was not the right guardian of so sacred an office. He was a highly educated man and an excellent orator, but too fond of strong drink, and consequently he gave serious cause for disappointment.

In 1852 another Lutheran Evangelical community, the "*Betlehemgemeinde*," was organized in the Capital. Reverends Schmogrow and Gross were the first pastors, and a good school was connected with the church, situated corner of Clay and Sixth streets.

Until 1849 only one Catholic church existed in Richmond, but at that time many German Catholics settled in the city and they rented a dwelling house on Marshall street, where they were organized in community by Rev. Father Braun. The following year Rev. Braun was superseded by Father Palhauber, and soon after the German parishioners bought the property on corner of Marshall and Fourth streets, where they built the *St. Mary's* (*St. Marien*) *German Catholic church*. The successor of Father Palhauber was Father Polk, under whose administration the community enlarged and prospered. He was followed by Rev. Mayer, a man of science and a member of the St. Benedict's Order. A flourishing parochial school and a classical high-school for boys and girls were organized by the last-named reverend and conducted by brethren and sisters of St. Benedict's Order.

Ahead of all in forming a German community in Richmond, as already mentioned, were the German Hebrews. As early as 1840 they founded the synagogue *Beth Ahaba* and elected M. G. Michelbacher rabbi. Moses Millhiser deserves the greatest credit for his devotion as president of this community, — exclusively composed of Germans and German-Virginians.

The Statutes of Virginia say[191]): "The *Lutherans* are numerous in portions of the Valley where the original population was of German origin. The *German Reformed Church* is found in the same localities, as is also the *United Brethren*, which, from resemblances, may be called the *German Methodist Church*."

The same official document gives the census returns in

191.) "Virginia," by the Board of Immigration and by Authority of Law, page 198. Richmond, Va., 1876.

Virginia of the following religious denominations in 1860: *Lutherans,* 69 churches, 24,675 members; *German Reformed Church,* 12 churches, 4,000 members; and in the year 1870 the *United Brethren* 38 churches and 7,450 members. These figures embraced some English congregations, but the great majority was originally undoubtedly German. The German element is also largely represented in the Methodist-Episcopal, the Baptist, Protestant-Episcopal, Roman-Catholic and Moravian orders. The Lutherans have two institutions of learning of advanced and higher grades: the Roanoke College, located at Salem, Roanoke county, and the Staunton Female Seminary at Staunton, Augusta county. The foundation of German parochial schools of elementary and higher grades, as for instance at Harper's Ferry, New-Market and Richmond, deserves acknowledgment, as the public education in the State was very deficient. The census of 1840 revealed the startling fact that there were in the commonwealth 58,747 white persons above the age of twenty years who could not read or write, being one-twelfth of the entire white population; and in 1850 the illiterate white adults numbered 77,005, besides 490,865 slaves living in ignorance. Governor McDowell (1843), always a friend of eduation, sought to advance its more general diffusion under the patronage of the State; "that every child in Virginia should be able to read for himself the confession of his faith and the constitution of his country." But he failed to carry out his wishes.

In 1840 the number of children in the State in attendance on the State schools was only 27,598, one-fifth of all the white children between eight and fifteen years of age.[192]) The other four-fifths were being educated by the more popular neighborhood, field, private and denominational methods, or — *not schooled at all.*

In the years 1859 to 1860 a German Israelite, whom the author knew personally, but whose name he cannot remem-

---

192.) Educational Report, 1895—96, page 274.

ber, established a "Commercial College" (Handelsschule) in Richmond.

The Medical Profession was at that time well represented by Germans, and particularly in the capital city by Doctors M. A. Rust, Wilhelm Grebe, Garwenzel, Th. Boldemann and Deutsch, and by the druggists O. A. Strecker, Julius Fischer, H. Bodecker, L. Wagner, J. Kindervater and Zaeckrissen, who, although a Swede by birth, associated with the Germans.

The development of the "Fine Arts" in Virginia had not yet passed the childhood state, but the little there was, was principally cultivated by the Germans. Music and the instruction in music rested in German hands. In Richmond Frederick and Karl Seibert from Ziegenhain in Hessia and ...... Woller from Johann-Georgenstadt in Saxony were known as organists and piano-teachers. The first claim of artist among the musicians of Richmond is due to Charles W. Thilow of Leipzig, Saxony; he is a master of the cello. Other musicians of good repute were John Kussnich, Otto Mueller, John Baier and others. The landscape painter Baier, probably a Saxon, was the first to paint the most beautiful scenery and places in Virginia. These were lithographed and published as the "Album of Virginia" in Berlin and Dresden. Baier died an inmate of the lunatic asylum "Sonnenstein," Pirna, Kingdom of Saxony.— The largest lithographic establishment in the State was conducted by Hoyer & Ludwig.[193])

The Germans were no less distinguished in architecture, engineering and mining. *Oswald Heinrich* was already spoken of as mining engineer. By him was drawn the *first Geological Map of Virginia. Captain von Buchholz*, a native of Wuertemberg, designed the *first accurate topographical map* of the State by order of Governor Henry A. Wise. Among the architects of Virginia *Captain Albert Leibrock* ranks very high. He was born January 11th, 1827, at St. Johann,

193.) During the period of the "Southern Confederacy" Hoyer & Ludwig printed the Confederate notes, bonds, etc.

Rhein-Provinz, and studied at the Polytechnic School at Karlsruhe. In 1850 he came to Richmond. The most important of his works are the Miller Labor School of Albemarle and the Custom House and Mozart Academy at Richmond. At the beginning of the Civil War he organized a German infantry company. He died at Richmond on his 59th birthday in 1886.[194]) Karl Seibert, previously mentioned as pianist, was also a talented architect.

Horticulture was at that time hardly known in Virginia and the city of Richmond possessed only one small Public Park: the "Capitol Square;" but this park was in charge of the German horticulturist *E. G. Eggeling*, afterwards assistant park-commissioner in St. Louis, Mo., and during the Confederate period steward at the Jefferson Davis mansion.

In the development of industry and commerce the Germans have also taken a prominent part. In the manufacture, sale and export of Virginia's great staple: tobacco, the Germans have been leaders almost from the time of the settlement of the Colony. Several wholesale houses of Bremen sent their representatives to Richmond and the export of tobacco increased considerably the first half of the present century. Sailing vessels from Bremen and Hamburg anchored at Rockets and thousands of hogsheads were shipped to Europe. Sometimes six or eight German vessels were seen at a time in Richmond harbor. The Austro-Hungarian government entrusted German tobacco houses in Richmond (E. W. de Voss & Co. and F. W. Hanewinkel & Co.) with the purchase of its supplies, and the French, Italian and Portuguese governments also transacted most of their tobacco purchases through German-Virginian firms. At *Lynchburg* the German houses: Holt, Schaefer & Co., Guhling & Co., John Katz, etc., and at *Petersburg:* H. Noltenius and Ferd. Schwenk & Co. controlled the trade. E. P. Whitlock in Richmond, of German descent, became well known as manufacturer of "Old Virginia Cheroots," etc.[195])

194.) Correspondence of Oscar Cranz, Jr., son-in law of Capt. Leibrock. Richmond, Va.

195.) Correspondence of Christ. Droste, with L. Borchers & Co., Austrian Consulate, Richmond, Va.

The wholesale and retail trade in dress-goods was and is almost entirely in the hands of German Israelites. Many watchmakers, jewelers, milliners, dealers in musical instruments, artists' materials, frames and pictures, stationers and book-binders, tailors, shoemakers, hat and cap makers, furriers, dealers in coal and wood, building materials, paints, china and glassware, furniture manufacturers, tin and sheet-iron workers, grocers, bakers, butchers, wine and liquor dealers, coopers, etc., were Germans, and in any mechanical trade or workshop intelligent German artisans were to be found. Two breweries existed in Richmond before 1860: *Eduard Euker's* and the Chimberazo Hill Brewery of *Morris & Richter*, brewing lager-beer, and also one brewery making weiss-beer. A peculiar and unsuccessful undertaking was the construction of a *floating mill*, at the foot of James river falls, by *Siege Brothers* in the beginning of the sixth decade. Much money was sacrificed in the enterprise. The mill was twice destroyed before completed, first by high water and the second time by an incendiary.

In Volume I, Chapter I, it has been stated that the production of wine in Virginia was believed to be practicable and that the planting of vineyards had been already encouraged by the London Company at the earliest time of the Colony. The expectations were not realized, but the London Society persevered in its endeavors and in 1758 proposed the following premium for the wine itself[196]): "As producing wines in our American colonies will be of great advantage to those colonies, and also to this kingdom, it is proposed to give to that planter in any of our said colonies who shall first produce within seven years of the date hereof from his own plantation five tons of white or red wine, made of grapes the produce of these colonies only, and such as in the opinion of competent judges, appointed by the society in London, shall be deemed deserving the reward — not less than one ton thereof to be imported at London — one hundred pounds." In 1762 the society announced: "A premium of two hun-

---

196.) "History of the Agriculture of the United States," by Ben Perley Poore, Agricultural Report for 1866, pp. 509—510. Washington, D. C.

dred pounds will be given for the greatest number, not less than five hundred, of the plants of the vines which produce these sorts of wines now consumed in Great Britain;" and this offer was raised in 1765 to two hundred and fifty pounds. Again the results did not correspond to the expectations. The memoirs of the society, published in 1769, say: "The first account of the success of the premiums for wines was in 1763, when Mr. Castor sent a dozen bottles of two kinds of wines from grapes which grew in vineyards of his own planting in Virginia. The one of these kinds was the product of vines brought from Europe, the other of the American wild vines. They were both approved as good wines and the society gave its gold medal to Mr. Carter." Probably Mr. Carter lived in Albemarle county and planted his vineyard on "Carter's Mountain" with the assistance of the grape-growers from the Palatinate, who were settled in the adjacent Madison county. These vineyards however never prospered and towards the close of the century[197]) Thomas Jefferson imported French vines — and Italian and Swiss vintagers — and planted quite extensively about Carter's Mountain, near his beloved Monticello. This too was a failure, for the European vines did not stand the climate. It was not until in the fifties of this century that the native Virginian vines — Catawba and Norton — were discovered and disseminated largely by Germans in Ohio and Missouri, that grape-culture at last succeeded in Virginia. In the environs of Richmond several Germans planted the Norton vine and manufactured red wine of excellent quality, but sufficient only to supply the home demand. Thus this new industry was finally started and has prospered ever since.

One of the brightest features of German life in Richmond that is less conspicuous, but exerted an exceedingly beneficial influence, was the social intercourse of the German inhabitants and the sensible and convivial spirit with which they enjoyed themselves. It has been already described how they celebrated historical events. There is a peculiar charm about their popular festivals, but above all the introduction

---

197.) "Albemarle," by Prof. W. H. Seamon, p. 52. Charlottesville, Va., 1888.

of the German Christmas-tree into America is worthy of comment. The happy disposition of the Germans, that touches the heart, has worn off the sharp edges of American everyday life, and their sincere and beneficent influence has finally secured harmonious relations between the Anglo-Saxon and the German settlers of Virginia, that were endangered by the spiteful know-nothing movement. The Germans of Virginia were peaceable, industrious citizens; they enjoyed considerable wealth and they contributed their share to the administration of the commonwealth. Their isolation in political affairs had at least one good effect: a most intimate consistence among themselves. There was, before 1860, no other city in the Union where the Germans lived in better harmony.

A publication: "Virginien," by C. A. Geyer, Meissen and Leipzig, 1849, states: "Richmond has 24,000 inhabitants, whereof 5,100 are Germans," and in 1860 the city had 37,900 inhabitants, whereof 23,625 were whites, and 7,000 of these Germans. The balance of the population was made up by 2,576 free negroes and 11,699 slaves. The German element of the city therefore represented nineteen per cent. of the whole and nearly thirty per cent. of the white population.

The German social associations were mentioned before, but it is desirable to add a few words about the predominant ones: the vocal musical association *Virginia*, the *Theatrical Society* and the *Social Turnverein.*

The "*Gesangverein*" was organized July 1st, 1852, by O. Cranz, Sr., H. C. G. Timmermann, E. Behrend, B. Krausse, A. Schad, M. Mielke, C. Rittershaus, G. Koenig, F. Lehmkuhl, J. Keppler, D. Weimer, H. von Groening, F. Dollinger and C. Emminger, its first president. The following were the presidents of the society: A. Gipperich, O. Cranz, Dr. W. Grebe, H. Boehmer and J. C. Fischer. The "Virginia" soon took part in the singing festivals at Philadelphia, Baltimore and New York. It flourished especially from 1857 to 1860 under the leadership of Fred. Seibert. The meetings and festivals took place in the hall of the New Market Hotel and in that very close locality harmless joy, pleasure and enthusiasm frequently reigned. Vocal and instrumental productions and theatrical performances were generally followed by dancing. Even comedies of local character, especially written up by members of the society, (G. Peple and H. Schuricht), were performed on the stage.

The "*Theaterverein*" assembled in Schad's Hall, Broad street, between 6th and 7th, and the performances were much admired and well attended. The leading personages and actors of the association were Mr. and Mrs. Hassel, C. Boettcher, Heinrich, Lehne, I. Hirsch, Mrs. Reith and Mrs. Doell.

The "*Social Turnverein*" had the largest membership; its meetings, concerts, balls, etc., were held in Steinlein's Monticello Hall, opposite Schad's Hall. The most ardent gymnasts and social managers were Ed. Kempe, H. Schott, O. Camman, H. Koppel, etc.

Thus Richmond had three German amateur theatres. The great majority of the members of the above spoken of societies were born Germans and at festive occasions German was almost exclusively spoken.

In the fall of 1860 the author of this book agitated the organization of a *Technical Society* (Gewerbeverein), and published in his paper, the "Virginische Zeitung," an invitation to meet at Schad's Hall. The meeting was well attended; H. L. Wiegand, a Saxon, presided, and the proposed society was formed. Only a few weeks later the first gun was fired at Fort Sumter, — the Civil War commenced, and the movement was swallowed up by the wild waves of general excitement.

Some other German associations like the "*German Society for the Relief of the Sick*" (Krankenunterstützungsverein), present president Valentine A. Halbleib, and the "*Schiller Lodge*" (Odd Fellows), aimed at charitable and social objects.

The news of the prosperity and the pleasant social life that the Germans in Virginia led, spread to their countrymen settled in the northern States and also to the old Fatherland,

and induced emigration to the old mother State of the Union. A large number of German Pennsylvanian farmers emigrated with their families about 1830 from western Pennsylvania to West Virginia, and they all prospered, raising principally cattle for the eastern markets. It is also reported that in the year 1845[198]) about one hundred and twenty families from northern States settled in Fairfax county and purchased 24,000 acres of land at a cost of about $180,000. Among these settlers were several Germans and by their industry and skill they made money on the crops they raised. Within a few years the value of their land increased from twenty-five to one hundred per cent. There were about fifteen million acres of available land in the State — West Virginia not included — uncultivated or thrown out of any regular rotation of crops, and all could be bought very cheap. In Germany attention was called to the low-priced Virginia farms. The well-known "Augsburger Allgemeine Zeitung" for instance said in 1848: "Virginia, which is about twice as large as the kingdom of Bavaria, is only inhabited by 1,300,000 people, of whom 400,000 are slaves. For several reasons she now desires to attract white settlers, — she recognizes the rapid growth of the western States, — that the comparatively rough Wisconsin is developing in a fabulous manner and that Ohio is outrivalling her mother State. Virginia however possesses a better climate than either of these States and other most favorable conditions, as several millions saleable acres of good soil, the best harbors on the Atlantic coast, numerous navigable rivers and excellent railroads. On James river good land is sold for four dollars an acre, and some settlers have gained within a few months double the amount of the purchase price by clearing the woods and selling the timber." The German Zeitung furthermore reports: "That some years ago it had been projected in Wuertemberg to settle Suavians in the mountain region of Virginia near the 'springs,'" and it expressed regret that this plan was not carried out.

Endeavors were made about 1850 to colonize artisans, miners and farmers from Saxony in western Virginia. A pamphlet

198.) "U. S. Agricultural Report for the year 1864," p. 20. Washington, D. C.

entitled: "Virginien, physiko-geographische und statistische Beschreibung," — by C. A. Geyer, president of the emigration society at Meissen, Saxony, — with a colored map, was published at Meissen and Leipzig to induce Saxons to settle in West Virginia. The descriptions of the land, people, institutions and advantages of Virginia are pretty reliable. The names of the German-Virginians who advocated this enterprise, are of interest: A. W. Nolting, Richmond; Dr. A. O. Strecker, Richmond; H. Sheffey, Augusta county; Friedrich A. Mayo, Richmond; Fleischmann, Monroe county; Dehar, Parkersburg, W. Va.; W. F. Deakins, Preston county; H. Brown, Kanawha county; John B. Shrerer, Buchanan, Lewis county; John Sharff, Leetown, Berkeley county, and L. Ruffner, Kanawha county; — and also the statement that a German colony prospered in Dodridge county. A similar publication: "Forty years in Virginia, or emigrate to West Virginia," by Friedrich A. Mayo of Richmond, a native of Oederan, Saxony, was printed 1850 in Meissen, Saxony. Mr. Mayo, whose office was situated at the northern corner of the Exchange Hotel, Richmond, Va., relates in his little book his observations in Virginia during a stay of forty years without exaggeration, and he reports: that an Immigration Society was organized in Richmond to cooperate with the Emigration Society in Meissen, Saxony. He also states that the engineer Ernst Kurth, born at Koelln near Meissen, and residing in Richmond, had been authorized to give his countrymen all information they might ask about Virginia; that he had been employed upon the recommendation of Dr. Cabell by the Society for the Construction of Railways in Virginia and that the plan of the Danville railroad bridge across the James river near Richmond and other architectural works were drawn by Mr. Kurth. No visible traces however are left of any noteworthy results of this Saxon-Virginian colonization enterprise.

Loudoun county received several newcomers from Germany and they all did well. Commodore Maury states as an example[199]): Godfrey Schellhorn of Saxe-Coburg came to this county (Loudoun) in 1851 with his wife and a flour-barrel for

199.) "Physical Survey of Virginia," by M. F. Maury, p. 93. N. V. Randolph, Richmond, Va., 1878.

a trunk; he had nothing. He and she were striving, industrious people and lived scantily. He now, in 1878, owns a house worth $1,200 and a farm of ninety-four acres that cost $2,812; on this he owes $1,000. He is a pretty good stone mason. Grape-vines planted by him are also bearing.

German farmers settled in Middle Virginia and the Tidewater belt during the period of 1840 to 1860. There were many gardeners among them and being saving, skilful and industrious they rarely failed to enrich themselves. The United States Agricultural Commission[200]) gives for example among the names of successful farmers in Southhampton county the following German: Alfred Ricks, J. D. Massenburg and Dr. C. Bowers. Col. S. B. French of Whitby, Chesterfield county, says in a report: "Gardening vegetables pays handsomely. Perhaps there is but one wealthier man in this county than a German, who, when I first came into the county twenty-eight years ago (about 1850), was a gardener on the Fall Plantation (man on wages). He made his fortune gardening."

Several other experiments were made about 1850 to establish German settlements in Virginia, but unfortunately most of the enterprisers were selfish, unscrupulous or incapable men. One von Schulenburg attempted to settle a large number of Tyrolians in Lunenburg county, and a Saxon named Meisner aimed to induce Saxons to purchase land near Lewisburg in Greenbrier county; but both projects failed. Another grand plan to establish a German colony near Parkersburg, now in West Virginia, had the same unhappy fate; but prosperous German settlements were founded at "New Hessen" and "Helvetia," in what is now West Virginia, and German Hungarians and Poles bought land in Henrico county, Va., and built up the village "Hungary." In 1860 two German Israelites[201]) came to Richmond and secured land in Norfolk county, south of Portsmouth, on the Elizabeth river, for the foundation of a new town to be named "Virginia City." They advertised in the German and English newspapers and distributed a litho-

---

200.) U. S. Agricultural Report of 1851.

201.) "Virginische Zeitung," Richmond, Va., December 1860.

graphed plan of the projected town; but the speculation failed on account of the outbreak of the Civil War.

The total number of Germans and their descendants in Virginia at the end of the sixth decade is not absolutely ascertained. I. G. Rosengarten says[202]) in "Freiheit und Sklaverei unter dem Sternenbanner, oder Land und Leute in Amerika," by Theodore Griesinger, Stuttgart, 1862: "I find the statement that in Virginia were 250,000 of German birth and descent at the time of the Rebellion." — General G. Tochman, who in 1867 was appointed by the Virginian Governor "Agent for European Immigration," and who had the best opportunities for gathering information, stated in an article, "Der Staat Virginien"[203]): "The population of Virginia in 1860 consisted of 1,047,299 whites, 58,042 free colored, 490,865 slaves and 112 Indians, or 1,596,318 in all. Among the white inhabitants there were 35,058 foreigners, (adopted citizens), or 5,490 English and Scotch, 10,512 Germans, 16,501 Irish, 517 French, etc." — The German immigration amounted therefore to *one third* of the foreign population[204]) and was second in rank. Adding to it the posterity of the large German immigration since 1714, the estimate of Griesinger of the numerical strength of the German element in Virginia: to represent *the fourth part of the total white population of the State,* appears creditable. The large number of German names of members of the Legislature during the period of 1830 to 1860[205]) is also proof of the strength of the German element and of its distribution over the entire State.

1831-1834: Samuel Coffman, (Shenandoah); Wm. Armistead, Wm. D. Simms, (Halifax); Harman Hiner (Pendleton); Vincent Witcher, (Pittsylvania); Wm. P. Zinn, (Preston); John Keller, (Washington); J. Helms, (Floyd); J. J. Moorman, A. Waterman, (Rockingham.)

202.) "The German Soldier in the Wars of the U. S.," p. 191. Phila., Pa., 1890.

203.) "Virginische Staatszeitung," No. 17. Richmond, Va., January 25, 1868.

204.) "Virginia," by the Board of Immigration and by authority of Law, page 178. Richmond, Va., 1876.

205.) "Journals of the House of Delegates and of the Senate of Va. State Library, Richmond, Va.

1836: F. G. Buhring, (Cabell); T. H. Stegar, (Floyd); Major S. Wagener, (Mason); J. Conrad, (Rockingham); Abr. Rinker, (Shenandoah); Col. Edw. Lucas, (Berkeley.)

1838: Th. Shanks, (Botetourt); W. Castleman, (Clark); Edw. Lucas, jr., (Jefferson); H. E. Fisher, (Mason); Alexander Newman, (Marshall.)

1839: Edm. Broadus, (Culpeper); W. Hoffman, (Lewis); Alfred Leyburn, Ch. P. Dorman, (Rockbridge.)

1840: Wm. Lucas, (Morgan and Berkeley); Rob. Y. Conrad, (Frederick); Jos. Hannah, (Botetourt); C. G. Coleman, (Charles city.)

1846: Henry Bedinger, (Frederick); John D. Stringer, (Harrison); K. Martz, (Rockingham.)

1850–1851: W. A. Buckner, (Caroline); R. R. Flemming, (Halifax); W. Stump, (Hampshire); J. R. Heuser, (King and Queen); F. Warman, (Monongalia); H. Sturm, (Randolph); J. Horner, (Fauquier.)

1852–53: H. W. Sheffey, (Augusta); Albert G. Reger, (Upshur); W. Heveler, (Highland); M. D. Newman, (Madison); Andr. Keyser, (Page); J. Wellman (Wayne); S. Carpenter, (Alleghany); J. M. Newkirk, (Berkeley.)

1856: Wm. Bush, (Charles city); P. J. Eggborn, (Culpeper); J. M. Holman, (Fluvanna); J. L. Kemper, (Madison); J. Lantz, (Monongalia); J. Paul, (Ohio); M. Spitler, (Page); A. J. Bowman, (Wood); F. H. Mayo, (Botetourt.)

1860: Ferd. Wm. Coleman, (Caroline); F. G. L. Bouhring, (Cabell); M. R. Kaufman, (Frederick); J. S. Hoffman, (Harrison); W. W. Flemming, (Highland); Gust. A. Myers, (Richmond); W. M. Seibert, (Shenandoah); Arthur J. Boreman, (Wood), and many more doubtful names.

Among the members of the U. S. Congress we meet with the following names of German sound:

1841: Joseph Holleman (Isle of Wight), and 1860 Alex. R. Boteler (Loudoun). In 1863 Mr. Boteler was a member of the Congress of the Confederate States.

The number of German delegates was probably much larger, for the author had not the opportunity to examine all lists. The fact deserves notice that since 1777 the great majority of the counties of eastern and western Virginia were represented by German-Virginians in the Legislature.

The political horizon clouded at the end of the sixth decade; the slavery question had become more complicated by the conflicting opinions concerning the Territories. The North claimed all the Territories "as free States" and the South asked the right of ingress and protection of its slave-property in half of them. Furthermore "the free-trade interests of the Southern States" were seriously threatened by "the protective policy of the North," and in this question the German-Virginians agreed fully with their Anglo-American fellow-citizens. The merchants of the North reaped advantage from the South; they shared in the profits of every pound of cotton, tobacco or sugar which the southern planter raised. The northern manufacturer had the advantage of this great market, and the Germans recognized that the industrial and commercial interests of the North, protected from foreign competition by a high tariff, made every inhabitant of the South pay tribute to him on almost every article he purchased. The ills thus inflicted upon the southern people the Germans desired should be corrected.

The "Fugitive Slave Law" intensified the hostile feeling between the two sections of the Country and led to the passage of the "Personal Liberty Bills" in several of the free States. Finally in 1859 *John Brown* invaded Virginia with twenty-one followers to revolutionize and liberate the negro slaves, thereby endangering the life and property of the whites. All inhabitants of the State — those of German origin included — felt alarmed and asked: "Where will it lead to, if the hatred and the wild passions of the uncultivated negroes become unfettered? Shall we be exposed to similar horrors like the French in St. Domingo in 1791?" The dangers may have been overestimated, but the safety of the white population was certainly threatened. John Brown seized upon the United States Arsenal at Harper's Ferry, but was soon overpowered and hanged as a traitor. The wild design of John Brown aroused the southern feeling and the fanatics among the pro-slavery party represented his act as significant of the sentiments of the whole North. No doubt well meaning, people in the North looked upon John Brown's deed as meritorious and humane, while many southern men, *no less noble-minded and feeling for the oppressed negroes, condemned it as madness.* Different surroundings and circumstances influence the opinions of men and produce different views of events and their consequences. The worst of it was that the hope *to abolish Slavery by legislative action,* vanished. Not only the German-Virginians, but also many Anglo-Americans were opposed to Slavery and anticipated that it would be the rock upon which the Union would split.

Thomas Jefferson, Virginia's noble son, proposed as early as 1776 a scheme of gradual emancipation, which was approved by the Convention framing the Constitution of Virginia.

The prevailing ideas entertained by him (Jefferson) and most of the leading statesmen at the time of the formation of the U. S. Constitution have been acknowledged in a speech at Savannah, Georgia, March 21st, 1861, by Alexander H. Stevens, at that time the Vice-President of the Confederacy.[206]) He said: "They were of the opinion that the enslavement of the African was in violation of the laws of nature; that it was wrong in principle, socially, morally and politically. This idea, though not incorporated in the Constitution, was the prevailing idea at the time."

From 1820 to 1830 there were movements in Virginia, Tennessee, Kentucky and Maryland for the gradual emancipation of their slaves. In Virginia the movement had nearly succeeded, *when it was the aggression of the northern abolition-*

206.) McPherson's "Political History of the Rebellion," 1860—1864, p. 103.

ists which arrested it in all these States. The German-Lutheran reverends in convention at St. James, Green county, Tennessee, *unanimously* resolved as early as 1822: "*That Slavery is to be regarded as a great evil in our land, and we desire the Government, if it be possible, to devise some way by which this evil can be removed.*" The Synod also advised every minister to admonish every master to treat his slaves properly.[207]) Rev. Paul Henkel was one of the Virginian delegates, and this resolution was probably the first move in that direction in the South on part of the Germans.

Dr. Henry Ruffner, a German-Virginian and president of the Washington and Lee University situated in Lexington, Va., also made *a most remarkable protest against the institution of Slavery* that defied the unanimity of sentiment that prevailed among the Anglo-Virginians before the Civil War. What was known as "*The Ruffner Pamphlet,*" advocating the gradual abolition of Slavery, was published in 1847 and excited much controversy.

Dr. Henry Ruffner was born in what is now Page county in the year 1790 on the old homestead of the Ruffner family and reared in Kanawha county. He was a pupil at the Lewisburg Academy, a graduate of Washington College (now Washington and Lee University) and a student of theology. Ordained as minister in 1818, he organized the First Presbyterian Church of Charleston, Kanawha, in 1819; accepted a professorship in Washington College in 1819, was made president in 1836 and resigned in 1848.

Henry Ruffner was a profound scholar and a writer of ability. His most elaborate book entitled: "The Father of the Desert," and his novel: "Judith Bensadeli" first appeared in the "Southern Literary Messenger." He spent the last years of his life in Kanawha county and is there buried. He died in 1861.

In fact all representative Virginians and thoughtful southern men generally since Washington and Jefferson entertained

---

207.) "History of the Evangelical Lutheran Tennessee Synod," by Socrates Henkel, D.D., p. 52. New-Market, Va., 1890.

similar views upon Slavery. Even Robert E. Lee, afterwards Commanding General of the Army of Northern Virginia, expressed these views very clearly in a letter addressed to Mrs. Lee, written December 1856. He said: "In this enlightened age there are few, I believe, but will acknowledge *that Slavery as an institution is a moral and political evil in any country.* It is useless to expatiate on its disadvantages. I think it however a greater evil to the white than to the black race, and while my feelings are strongly interested in behalf of the latter, my sympathies are stronger for the former. The blacks are immeasurably better off here than in Africa, morally, socially and physically. The painful discipline they are undergoing is necessary for their instruction as a race, and, I hope, will prepare and lead them to better things. How long their subjection may be necessary is known and ordered by a wise and merciful Providence. Their emancipation will sooner result from a mild and melting influence than the storms and contests of fiery controversy. This influence, though slow, is sure." — This letter shows that General Lee was an advocate of negro-emancipation. He favored however, like the German-Virginians, to see it abolished *in a lawful and peaceable manner*, and he was opposed to endangering the Union by a rash action. He once declared: "Both sides forget that we are all Americans;" and at another time he said: "If I owned the four million slaves, I would give them all for the Union!"

Unfortunately in February 1831 an unforeseen event: *an insurrection of negroes in Southampton county*[208]), excited the people of Virginia and induced even a German-Virginian member of the Legislature, Mr. Goode of Mecklenburg, to oppose "*the proposed emancipation of the slaves by some gradual scheme.*" The blacks in that section largely outnumbered the whites; there were no large towns in that region, only scattered here and there villages and hamlets. There was no arsenal for arms and ammunition nearer than Richmond, and no means of defence other than fancy fowling pieces for gentlemen's sport. The old Virginians of that day had no pistols under their pil-

---

208.) Compare "Historical Papers No. 5, 1895, of the Washington and Lee University, Lexington, Va.," pp. 77 to 97.

lows; in many cases no bars to their doors; no police making their rounds about the negro quarters in the dead hours of night, — the master sleeping among his slaves in peaceful security. There was indeed scarce any hindrance to prevent savage deeds of cruelty. Nat Turner, a slave on the plantation of a Mr. Travis of Southampton, was the leader in the insurrection, silently working upon the superstitions of the negroes about him and waiting for some supernatural sound or sight to call him to act. In February 1831 there came an eclipse of the sun, and accepting this as the long looked-for signal, he selected four of his immediate associates and on the morning of the 22d of August, while it was yet dark, crept into the house of his master with his band and in a few minutes killed five members of the family in their beds. They then hurried on, murdering all the whites they found, gaining recruits as they went to the number of fifty or sixty, all mounted on the horses and armed with the guns, swords, axes and clubs they had stolen from the houses of the dead. They were now a bloodthirsty gang. Early the next day the news of the wholesale massacre spread far and wide; squads of men and militia companies hastily gathered and the bloody mutiny was soon quelled, but not until the negroes had gone a distance of twenty miles and killed sixty-one white citizens. On the 11th of November Nat Turner was executed. But death put no extinguisher upon the excitement created by this rebellion of slaves. A suspicion that a Nat Turner might be in every colored family; that the same bloody deed might be acted over at any time and in any place, gained ground; — the husband would look to his weapon and the mother would shudder and weep over her cradle! It is not positively known how many German farmers were among the victims, but some documents show the following names of German sound: Mrs. T. Reese, Mrs. Turner, Mr. Levi Waller, a schoolmaster, his wife and ten children, etc. Naturally the Germans felt greatly alarmed and with few exceptions they advocated: *that the evil, that is, the institution of Slavery, be removed by legislative means.* They claimed that Slavery had ultimately to come to an end in the one way or the other, because it was impossible to reconcile the slave to his fate.

However the split between the North and the South became more and more evident, — not on account of Slavery alone, but for various reasons previously mentioned, — and when in 1860 Abraham Lincoln of Illinois, the candidate of the Republican party, was elected to the Presidency, the southern fanatic leaders regarded it as a menace to Slavery and advocated the doctrines of State rights and Secession. On December 20th, 1860, the people of South Carolina declared the connection with the Union abolished. The great majority of the Virginians *did not agree with this rash measure* and received it with distrust. Only the pro-slavery men and those doubtful elements that speculate on the ruin of others and seek to realize their selfish designs by the overthrow of law and order, applauded and praised the revolutionary Palmetto State. The German-Virginians particularly did not at that time believe in the outbreak of war, *but expected that some compromise would be agreed upon* and that Virginia would not separate from the Union. This trust was so firm with them that at the close of 1860 they still enjoyed life in their peculiar harmless manner. They celebrated a joyful Christmas and on New Year's Eve the "Gesangverein" at Richmond arranged an animated "Sylvesterfeier," for which occasion H. Schuricht had composed a dramatic scene, "Der Jahreswechsel."

CHAPTER XIII.

THE CIVIL WAR AND THE GERMAN-VIRGINIANS.

IN the beginning of 1861 the outlook for the future rapidly darkened; affairs steadily drifted towards hostilities between the North and the South, and finally the German-Virginians after a long struggle were drawn into the whirlpool of popular excitement. In the western part of the State they belonged in large numbers to the "Union Party," but in Middle and Southern Virginia the great majority sympathized with the South, whose constitutional rights they considered threatened. With all their devotion to the Union and pride of American citizenship, they felt in duty bound towards the State where they had become domiciled. Only a small number of Germans avowed the principles and programme of the Republican party and recommended *unconditional submission* to the Federal Government; but at this period of the great crisis *not one German-Virginian* — American or foreign born — was in favor of Secession. All German citizens in the State heartily endorsed a resolution of the Legislature to call a "Peace Congress" in order to avoid civil war. The Peace Congress assembled in Washington, D. C., on the 9th of February, 1861, and Ex-President John Tyler presided; but every proposal looking to a peaceful settlement was rejected by the extremists. Meanwhile the revolutionary example of South Carolina had been followed by Mississippi, Florida, Alabama, Georgia, Louisiana and Texas. These seceded States formed on February 4th a new union under the title of "*the Confederate States of America*." They organized an army to oppose intruders and seized forts, navy-yards and arsenals. This Southern Revolution would yet have remained hopeless of success and never would have resulted in a long and bloody war without the assistance of the Border States. Efforts at conciliation on part of the North might have averted the conflict, but the pleadings of the peaceable Border States were in vain. Rev. R. C. Cave[209]) very rightly said in his oration at the unveiling of the Confederate soldiers' and sailors' monument at Richmond on May 30th, 1894, with reference to Virginia and the other Border States:

"Not as a passion-swept mob rising in mad rebellion against constituted authority, but as an intelligent and orderly people, acting in accordance with due forms of law and within the limit of what they believed to be their constitutional right, the men of the South withdrew from the Union in which they had lived for three-fourths of a century, and the welfare and glory of which they had ever been foremost in promoting. States which had been hesitating on the ground of expediency and hoping for a peaceable adjustment of issues, wheeled into line with the States which had already seceded. Virginia, mother of States and statesmen and warriors, who had given away an empire for the public good, whose pen had written the Declaration of Independence, whose sword had flashed in front of the American army in the War for Independence, and whose wisdom and patriotism had been chiefly instrumental in giving the Country the Constitution of the Union, — Virginia, foreseeing that her bosom would become the theatre of war with its attendant horrors, nobly chose to suffer."

In justice to the memory of the Confederate dead, the distinguished orator protested at this occasion also against the aspersion *that they fought to uphold and perpetuate the Institution of Slavery.* He remarked: "Slavery was a *heritage* handed down to the South from a time *when the moral consciousness of mankind regarded it as a right,* — a time when even the pious sons of New England were slave-owners and deterred by no conscientious scruples from plying the *slave-trade* with proverbial Yankee enterprise. It became a peculiarly Southern Institu-

---

209.) "The Memorial Oration," by Rev. R. C. Cave of St. Louis, Mo., the "Weekly Times," p. 3, Richmond, Va., May 31st, 1894.

tion, not because the rights of others were dearer to the northern than to the southern heart, but because the condition of soil and climate made negro-labor *unprofitable in the northern States and led the northern slave-owner to sell his slaves down South.*"

These arguments are based on history!

We are not yet sufficiently removed from the strife to do impartial justice to the motives of its authors. Those who have not felt the bitterness of the then existing conditions ought not to judge the whites of the South too harshly. Let it be remembered that in no time or clime have the Caucasians ever consented to live with an inferior race *save as rulers.* To the present day the British in India, the French in Guiana, Madagascar and Tonking, the Dutch, Portuguese and Germans in Africa, the Spaniards in what is now left of their once extensive colonial possessions, and our own forefathers on this continent have abundantly demonstrated that the white man will not be governed by uncivilized races. Sentimentalists may deplore this spirit, but all sober thinkers must recognize the fact as an irreversible one.

Secession was a sudden movement on part of the Cotton States, but Virginia and the other Border States hesitated to approve and to join the Confederacy and they continued their efforts to effect a compromise. In fact it was at that time the common expectation of all thoughtful citizens, and particularly of the Germans, — North and South, — that there would be "*no coercion*" and "*no war.*"

Mr. Lincoln had become President of the United States on the 4th of March, 1861. The inaugural address of the President was very considerate and conservative. He renewed the declaration he had made in previous speeches: *that he had no intention to interfere with the Institution of Slavery in the States where it existed.* "I shall take care," said he, "that the laws of the Union shall be faithfully executed in all the States. In doing this there need be no bloodshed or violence, and there shall be none unless it is forced upon the National Authority."

But these truly moderate words were received by the fanatic leaders in the South as a declaration of war. Mr. Lincoln's promise, *not to interfere with Slavery where it existed*, did not satisfy them. Eight days after Mr. Lincoln's inauguration two southern commissaries called on him and applied for a *peaceable separation* of the southern States from the Union, demanding the evacuation of Fort Sumter in South Carolina and Fort Pickens in Florida. These demands he could not but refuse,—and the fall of the iron dice of war had to decide.

In the northern States there were two leading parties; one demanded an energetic action against the seceded States; they proclaimed that the Union was *an inseparable whole*, an American State, that secession was revolution and revolution equal to civil war. This party called itself "*Republican*," and its adherents were called "*Abolitionists*." Another powerful party was the "*Northern Democracy*" and "no coercion" was its watchword. Upon this party rested the hopes of the Germans in Virginia and of all friends of peace and unity, and some of the most influential newspapers of the North supported it. The "New York Tribune" opposed all measures to force seceding States to remain in the Union, and voices like this influenced many German-Virginians to declare in favor of a peaceable secession.

In the South the politicians were also divided into two parties: the "*Secessionists*" or *defendants of* "*State Rights*," who claimed that every State was a political unit and was entitled to enter into a Confederation of States as well as to withdraw therefrom, and the "*Union Men*," who persisted to uphold the Union of States. The first named did not give time to the latter to get organized; the demand to join the seceded States was urged, — even the personal safety of the Union men became endangered and many, being alarmed, left their southern homes fugitives.

About this time the German citizens of Richmond held a very well attended mass-meeting at Steinlein's Monticello Hall to consider what steps could be taken to secure peace. H. L. Wigand, an acknowledged Union man, was in the chair, and among the speakers was Captain O. Jennings Wise, son of Ex-Governor Wise[210]), who addressed the meeting in German. But no course was agreed upon, *as the majority considered it the duty of every adopted citizen to submit to the will of the people and to sacrifice their life and fortune, if necessary, in defence of the State.*

A very marked change was now taking place among the citizens. The Union party lost many adherents; the cry "to secede" found more supporters and the German-Virginians also yielded to the general current. *But they never embraced the southern cause in order to protect the interests of slaveholders; there were no pro-slavery men among the Germans except a few Hebrews; but they were ready to defend the political and commercial independence of the States.* Time was a great leveler of opinions as well as author of mighty issues in those days.

The Germans in the southern States have been harshly criticized by northern fanatics, and among them by many of their countrymen in the North, for taking up arms in defence of the South. It will readily be granted by every German-Virginian that these northern critics were aiming to carry out the noble design of emancipating the slaves, but they ignored the Constitution of Rights, interest and safety of the white population in the South. The northern accusers were carried astray by passion, *inclined to sacrifice a cultured part of the southern people* to the terrorism of an uneducated and inferior race; and the Germans felt the wrong that the North, *having sold its slaves to the South,* attempted to compel the southern slaveholders to free their negroes without compensation.

Suddenly the news reached Virginia: Fort Sumter has capitulated to the Confederate forces under General Beauregard on the 13th of April, 1861, — and the effect of this event was electrical. Virginia (April 17th), Arkansas, North Carolina

---

210.) O. Jennings Wise, Captain of the Richmond Light Infantry Blues and killed at the battle on Roanoke Island, had studied jurisprudence at the University at Goettingen in Germany and was for some time Attache to the U. S. Legation at Berlin, Prussia.

and Tennessee, which had hesitated, now joined the Confederacy. President Lincoln called for seventy-five thousand troops on April 15th and on April 19th a regiment of Massachusetts troops, passing through Baltimore for the defence of Washington, was attacked. So the first blood was shed, but no one guessed at the time of the terror and the loss which were to follow.

With reference to the Secession of Virginia a remark of the historian Edward A. Pollard may here be repeated. Pollard says[211]): "Virginia did not secede in the circumstances or sense in which the Cotton States had separated themselves from the Union. She did not leave the Union with delusive prospects of peace to comfort and sustain her. She did not secede in the sense in which separation from the Union was the primary object of secession. Her act of secession was subordinate; her separation from the Union was necessary and became a painful formality which could not be dispensed with."

Virginia troops now seized the United States Arsenal at Harper's Ferry (April 18th) and the Navy Yard at Norfolk (April 21st.) All over the South the enthusiasm was spreading; the rich and the poor were alike eager to enter the army. Army and navy officers of the United States, natives of the South, resigned their charges and joined the Confederate service; and the majority of the German-Virginians within the present State limits entered military organizations.

It can be asserted that all the recently immigrated Germans, embracing the Confederate cause, did so with throbbing hearts, and in most cases only under the pressure of compulsory circumstances; but whether voluntarily or not, they have fulfilled their duty in the defence of the State with never faltering true German bravery.

About the middle of April, 1861, a "Legion of mounted men for border service" was organized by Col. Angus W. McDonald, Sr., of Winchester and among the captains of the com-

---

211.) "The Second Year of the War," by Edw. A. Pollard, pp. 45—46. West & Johnston, Richmond, Va., 1863,

mand were the following descendants of German pioneers: S. W. Myers, Shands, Jordan, Miller and Sheetz.[212]) With special pride every Virginian speaks of the "Stonewall Brigade" and this heroic command *was mostly composed of descendants of German settlers in the Shenandoah valley.* Nearly every other section of the State furnished German-Virginians to the army; there was hardly a company without some German members, but the largest number came from Richmond, where several entirely German companies were formed. The old "German Rifle Company," organized on the 1st of March, 1850, was attached to the First Virginia Infantry Regiment as Company "K." Charles T. Loehr, Sergeant of Company D of said regiment, gives the following names[213]):

Florence Miller, Captain, resigned 1861.
F. W. Hagemeier, Capt. after Capt. Miller's resignation.
C. Baumann, Lieutenant (first year.)
H. Linkhauer, Lieutenant.
F. W. E. Lohmann, Lieutenant, resigned 1861.
Herman Paul, Lieutenant.
Wm. Pfaff, Lieutenant.
George F. Deckman, Sergeant.
H. T. Elsasser, Sergeant.
Gerhard Haake, Sergeant.
Fred. Hebring, Sergeant.
C. E. Gronwald, Quartermaster Sergeant.
Henry Burkhard, Corporal.
Aug. Weidenhahn, Corporal.

Julian Alluisi
Charles Arzberger
B. Bergmeier
Adam Bitzel
G. Blenker
Julius Blenker
John W. Bornickel
L. Botzen
John Braw
C. Brissacher
R. Brunner
C. Buchenan
H. Buchenan
W. E. Crec

212.) "The Second Year of the War," by Edw. A. Pollard, p. 50. Richmond, Va., 1863.

213.) "War History of the Old First Virginia Infantry Regiment," by Charles T. Loehr. Richmond, 1884.

C. W. Creedins
D. DeBar
C. P. Degenhart
Adam Diacont
Ph. Diacont
Wolfgang Diacont
John T. Dick
Joseph Dilger
Henry Dubel
John Emmenhauser
Aug. Fahrenbruch
John Fink
H. Fleckenstein
Joseph Gehring
L. Gelnhausen
J. W. Gentry
F. J. Gerhardt
George Gersdorf
George Glass
E. Grossman
Fred. Gutbier
G. Habermehl
Fred. Hach
John Hach
H. Haderman
H. Heinemann
J. L. Helwick
E. Herzog
A. Hoch
J. P. Hoffman
Andrew Hatke
George Koch
F. Lauterbach
F. Lehmkul
Ch. Lindner
P. Lucke
Tobias Merkel
Felix Meyer
Jos. Nagelmann
David Nolte
Henry Nolte
Herman Nolte
Jos. Ocker
Martin Oeters
George W. Paul
Wm. H. Paul
L. Peters
L. Raymann
P. Reidt
Rob. Richter
Jos. Rick
John Rodins
J. A. Rommel
S. Shapdock
— Smith
Ph. Staab
M. Stadelhofer
Chr. Stephan
G. Tolker
John Viereck
Jacob Wachter
John Wagner
A. Werner
J. Winter

Sergeant Charles T. Loehr mentions in his valuable book also the following officers with German names: Capt. F. B. Shaffer of Company F; Capt. W. E. Tysinger of Company H; Lieutenant F. M. Mann of Company B; Lieutenant M. Seagles of Company C and one hundred and two non-commissioned German-Virginian officers and privates, — all belonging to the First Regiment.

A new German Company, "The Marion Rifles," was mustered into service on May 1st, 1861, and ordered to the Peninsula on the 24th of the same month. The muster-roll[214]) contains the following names:

Alb. Leibrock, Captain.
Aug. Schad, 1st Lieutenant.
Heinrich Schnaebele, 2nd Lieutenant.
Edw. Euker, "
Jul. Fischer, "

Ed. Bell
Heinr. Beckman
Aug. Braun
Chr. B. Braun
Fr. Bierschenk
H. Buckelman
Geo. Blantz
Phil. Briel
W. Doell
Fr. Dill
Ad. Drescher
Charles Euker
Wm. Eggeling
Chr. Eshernbusch
E. Fillman
A. Frank
Aug. F. Fiedler
Aug. Faulhaber
H. Grimmel
Chr. A. Hennighausen
A. v. Halem
E. v. Halem
H. v. Halem
Chas. Haase
Wm. Heidmueller
G. Hassenohr
Coleman Hecht
John Hauk
A. Heuers
Theo. Krone
J. Johnson
J. Keppler
G. Klein
Chr. Krebs
Herm. Kroedel
John Kolbe
W. Kempf
H. Lehman
E. Lieberman
W. Linz
Ed. Lies
L. Merkel
O. Meister
John Miller
H. Miller
R. Mear
John Marxhausen
D. Nenzel
— Nopwitz
Fr. Otto
G. Paul
Chas. Pflugfelder

214.) The author is obliged to Lieut. Chr. A. Hennighausen of Richmond for furnishing this list. Lieut. Hennighausen was a member of the "Marion Rifle Company."

Louis Reinhardt
C. Roeth
H. Reidt
G. Runge
C. Rungwitz
Fr. Ries
Ph. Stecker
Fr. Schneider
H. Schneider
Fr. Saeger
John Sevin
Jac. Schwartz
Valentin Schwartz
J. Schmidt
H. Schuerman
Ch. Siemens
B. Siemon
— Taunbold
J. Teske
R. Tiele
E. Wacker
J. Walter
L. Wuertemberger
Ch. Wagner
Ch. Volk

Company H, 19th Regiment Virginia Militia, was first organized as follows[215]):

Karl Siebert, Captain.

L. Friedlaender
M. Schaaf
H. Rosenstein
Ch. Funk
P. Kraus
C. Stephan
L. Nachman
Fred. Scheiderer
Ed. Senf
Jul. Wohlgemuth
H. Heineman
R. Morgenstern
Leopold Rind
L. Stein
Herm. Broedel
J. Gessinghausen
Jos. Stump
M. Hurge
J. Reinhardt
Chr. Heise
F. Martin
Anton Kretzmar
S. Bolz
H. Winten
Mich. Hanna
Jos. Adelsdorfer
Jac. Heiss
A. Fuchs
T. Singer
C. Calbe
E. Asmus
C. L. Miller
J. Merkel
Fred. Englert
Otto Huber
H. Rabe
Dietrich Euker
A. Drescher

215.) Reported by Lieut. Ch. A. Hennighausen, Richmond, Va.

Ph. Rapp
M. Stahl
F. Wollcher
A. Huebner
Constantin Hirt
C. H. Northheim
W. Kellner
G. Wolff
J. Minnis
F. Seibert
Chr. S. Schmidt
Ch. Gardewein
J. Weckerly
Geo. Zander
H. Hahn
— Bernstein
F. Reine
Aug. Israels
Ph. Staub
Lorenz Welzenberg

In October 1863 Company H was reorganized as "German Home Guard," serving in the field and guarding the prisons until April 3d, 1865. The roll gives the following names[216]):

C. Baumann, Captain.
G. Runge, 1st Lieutenant.
Von der Hoehl, 2nd Lieut.
Ch. A. Hennighausen, do., Jr.
C. F. Fischer, Sergeant.
V. Schwartz, "
W. Schotchky, "
J. Dinkel, "
F. Clevesahl, Corporal.
L. Morris, "
R. Senf, "
F. Holle, "
E. Albers, "
G. Aichele "

M. Bottigheimer,
E. Boehme
R. v. Bueren
S. Bolz
Ph. Briel
Ch. Braun
W. Becker
N. Becker
F. Busshaus
C. Berndt
W. Behle
G. Dietrich
W. Doell
Ch. Emmenhauser
— Ehmig
J. Feldner
C. Feldner
W. Flegenheimer
A. Frank
W. Finke

216.) Reported by Lieut. Ch. A. Hennighausen, Richmond, Va.

A. Frick
A. Frommhagen
B. Fischer
A. Feldheimer
B. Gottlieb
L. Goepphardt
— Goyer
Chas. Haase
Chr. Heise
H. Holzhauer
Chr. Holzbach
P. Huebner
R. Heusler
W. H. Heinz
E. Herzog
J. Hauser
M. Hentze
A. Hopp
G. Hirsch
P. Keil
N. Kestner
H. Koppel
H. Knorr
W. Krug
A. Kolbe
E. Kuh
F. Lemggut
N. Lieberman
H. Meier
C. Mueller
C. Meister
P. Martin
W. Miller
G. Mueller
J. Meier
R. Merkel
N. Nussbaum
J. Nagelsman
G. D. Obitz
L. Peter
H. Propst
L. Rammstedt
A. Ruppert
J. V. Reif
Chas. Schmidt
P. Sorg
B. Schaaf
J. Schumacher
Jac. Schneider
John Schneider
Ch. Schoenleber
F. Schulte
Ph. Staab
L. Stern
Ph. Stecker
A. Spies
Ch. Siemens
Ch. Schoenborn
A. Schmidt
A. Schmus
J. Steinman
R. Thiele
Ch. Wiemer
G. Wolff
L. Welsenberger
R. Werne
L. Wagener
J. Wolfram
L. Walter
F. Witte
— Weiner
Jac. Wolff
W. Zimmerman

Towards the end of the year 1863 the condition of his health had obliged the author of this history to resign as 1st Lieutenant of Comp. D, 14th Virginia Cavalry, C. S. A., but by request of Governor W. Smith of Virginia he organized a German company for home defence: Comp. M, 19th Virginia Militia. The Company was composed as follows[217]):

Herrmann Schuricht, Captain.
Friedr. Seibert, 1st Lieut.
J. Kindervater, 2nd Lieut.
Henry Wenzel, Orderly Sergt.
G. F. Paul, 1st Sergt.
H. Grimmel, 2nd Sergt.
P. Ruhl, 3d Sergt.
F. Schneider, 4th Sergt.
G. A. Krieger, 1st Corporal.
Georg Klein, 2nd "
G. Koenig, 3d "
P. Rosmary, 4th "

E. F. Baetjer
— Beck
C. Bernstein
L. Binda
Ch. Brown
C. Buckenthal
E. Crehen
H. Demler
C. W. Dow
O. Ericson
— Feldner
G. Freitenstein
Emil Fischer
J. Fritz
E. A. Flemhardt
L. Gallmeyer
J. C. Ganter
J. Grom
— Grote
H. Gundlach
J. Guggenheimer
Ch. Haas
H. Klein
D. Klein
A. Krezmarcz
Wilh. Loeffler
B. Momonthy
J. D. Nauk
H. Rodenkirchen
— Robert
Henry Schott
D. Schoenfeldt
C. Schulze
Julius Schultz
John J. Spilling
Chs. Spott

217.) From a "muster-roll" in possession of the author.

M. Stoll
C. W. Thilow
F. Verspohl
F. Warnicke
H. Wenton
John Werner
J. Wittman

Capt. J. Herbig, formerly a Lieutenant in the Bavarian army, recruited a German "Infirmary or Sanitary Company," but the muster-roll of this troop is lost.

Several German-Virginians occupied very prominent positions in the Confederate army, as:

James L. Kemper, Brig. General of Pickett's Division.

Louis A. Armistead, do

D. C. Kemper, Brig. General Confederate Artillery.

J. N. Adenbousch, Col. of 2nd Virginia Infantry, Stonewall Brigade.

D. A. Weisiger, Col. of 12th Va. Inf. Regiment, Mahon's Brigade.

John S. Hoffman, Col. of 31st Va. Inf. Regiment, Smith's Brigade.

— Neff, Col. of 33d Va. Inf. Regiment.

— Harper, and later J. H. S. Funk, Col. of 5th Va. Inf. Regiment, Stonewall Brigade.

Capt. Buckner, commanding 44th Va. Inf. Regiment, Jones' Brigade.

Col. Harman, of 52nd Va. Inf. Regmt., Gen. Stonewall Jackson's Corps.

Col. Rust, of Gen. Stonewall Jackson's Corps.

V. D. Groner, Col. of 61st Va. Inf. Regmt., Mahone's Brigade.

Maj. John Harman, Chief Quartermaster of Stonewall Brigade.

— Sheetz, Capt. of Independent Troop of Horse, Gen. Jackson's Corps.

Capts. Schumaker and Carpenter, commanding batteries, Gen. Stonewall Jackson's Corps.

Heros von Borke, Col. and Chief of Staff of Gen. Stuart's Cavalry Corps.

Captain — Schubert, Engineer Officer in General Rob't E. Lee's staff.

Gustav Adolph Schwarzmann, Colonel and Adjutant-General of Gen. Albert Pike.

G. A. Peple, Major and Professor at Conf. Navy School.

E. von Buchholz, Captain of Ordinance, Wise Legion.

Dr. Max Roemer, Major of Wise Legion.

— Tucker, Captain and Aide-de-Camp of Gen. Fitzhugh Lee.

— von Massow, Aide-de-Camp of Gen. Mosby; and although not a native of Germany or Virginia, but of German descent.

Carl Friedrich Henningsen, Brig. General and second in command of Wise Legion.

The following biographies of these officers include all reliable information that could be procured.

James Lawson Kemper, whose family history has been given in Vol. I, Chapter 4, studied law. In the year 1847 President Polk appointed him Captain of Volunteers, and he took part with honor in the Mexican War. After his return he represented his native county in the Legislature, and the Virginia Convention appointed him Colonel of the 7th Virginia Infantry Regmt. after the secession of the State. He was commissioned Brig. General after the battle of Williamsburg, May 5th, 1862, and fought with distinction in many bloody engagements. On the second day of the battle of Gettysburg Pickett's division had its grand day of honor and death, and Gen. Kemper was one of the victims of the struggle; he was carried from the field badly wounded. On May 1st, 1864, he was appointed Major-General and placed in command of the forces for the defence of Richmond. The army of Northern Virginia having surrendered at Appomattox Court House, General Kemper returned to his law office in Madison county and issued a farewell address to his old brigade. "It is the most painful duty of my life," he said in that paper, "to sever the relations which for three years have harmoniously united us; which have carried us together through memorable and fiery trials, and have bound you to my heart with ties stronger than hooks of steel." From 1873–'78 Gen. Kemper was Governor of the State, and then he retired with his family to Orange Court House, honored and loved by his fellow citizens. He died in 1895.

Gen. David A. Weisiger, a veteran of two wars, the hero of the battle of the Crater and a successful business man, was born Dec. 23d, 1818, at "The Grove," the ancestral home in Chesterfield county. His paternal grandfather was Samuel Weisiger, who came from Germany of a family prominent for military achievements; he was a relative of Colonel William Smith, of Revolutionary fame, and of the ancient Mayo family of Richmond. He was partner in the firm Rowlett, Weisiger & Tanner, at Petersburg, when the Mexican War began, and soon became second lieutenant of Company E, First Regiment of Virginia Volunteers. While in Mexico Weisiger was appointed adjutant of his regiment, and he made a proud record during the war. On his return home he connected himself again with the commission business, and when the Civil War commenced he enlisted at once, was elected Major of the Fourth Virginia Battalion organized at Petersburg, and promoted Colonel of the Twelfth Virginia. After the battle of the Crater, July 30th, 1864, in which he commanded Mahone's Brigade, of which the Twelfth Regiment was a part, he was commissioned Brigadier-General. Gen. Weisiger was one of the most gallant officers of the Confederate army, of great dash and approved courage. He commanded his regiment and also his brigade in many of the leading battles and was wounded several times. After the war he entered in Richmond in business and died there February 22nd, 1899.

General Louis A. Armistead was born at Newbern, N. C., on the 18th of February, 1817. In 1839 he was commissioned an officer in the U. S. Army. He distinguished himself in the Mexican War, and at the time Virginia seceded he entered the Confederate service. Gen. Armistead commanded a brigade of Pickett's famous division, was mortally wounded at Gettysburg and died a prisoner of war. His personal courage was of the truest temper. He descended of a German family, which has previously been mentioned with distinction, and has always enjoyed high esteem in Virginia.

General D. C. Kemper, a cousin of Gov. Kemper, was in charge of artillery. He resides now at Alexandria, Va.

Col. J. N. Adenbousch commanded the second regiment of Virginia Volunteers from September 16th, 1862, accredited to the immortal "Stonewall Brigade." He was a descendant of a German settler in the Shenandoah valley.

Capt. — Sheetz was only a comely youth, says Gen. Dabney in his "Life of Lieut.-General Jackson," when he left his father's farm to join the army. However, very soon he showed himself a man of no common mark. Collecting a company of youths like himself in the valleys of Hampshire, he had armed them wholly from the spoils of the enemy, and without any other military knowledge than the intuitions of his own good sense, had drilled and organized them into an efficient body. He speedily became a famous partisan and scout, the terror of the invaders and the right hand of Colonel Ashby. Sheetz was ever next the enemy; if pursuing, in command of the advanced guard; or if retreating, closing the rear; and Gen. Stonewall Jackson had learned to rely implicitly upon his intelligence; for his courage, enterprise, sobriety of mind and honesty assured the authenticity of all his reports. He was killed May 23d, 1862, in a skirmish near Buckton, between Front Royal and Strasbourg.

Col. Heros von Borke, born in Silesia, was a Prussian cavalry officer. At the beginning of the Civil War he took furlough, came to America, offered his services to the Confederate Government and was attached to Gen. J. E. B. Stuart's staff. He was a thorough soldier, and as a model officer soon became the friend and advisor of his brave General. The position of Chief of Staff of Gen. Stuart, with rank of Lieut.-Colonel was conferred on him. In an engagement near Upperville, Fauquier county, Aug. 19th, 1863, v. Borke was shot through the windpipe, and while still convalescent his friend and general was mortally wounded at Yellow Tavern, Hannover county. General Stuart on his death bed wished the promotion of v. Borke to his successorship, but the Confederate Government did not comply to the desire of the dying hero. The Congress of the Confederate States however voted resolutions of thanks for Col. v. Borke's services, acknowledging his military talents and bravery.

The author met von Borke at that time in the Spottswood Hotel in Richmond, and he received the impression that the wounded Colonel was not yet qualified to endure the exposures, hardships and excitement incident to the position as Commander of the Cavalry Corps of the Army of Northern Virginia. Von Borke returned to Germany and served as Major of Dragoons (die Schwed'schen Dragoner) in the war of 1866, but his old wound forced him soon after to retire. In 1886 he revisited Virginia and was received with due honors. "His once robust constitution appeared much affected by the ball he still carried in his right lung, but his jovial, impulsive, warm-hearted nature had not forsaken him"[218]). During his stay at Richmond his sword, which he had brought from his Fatherland to Virginia, and worn when a Confederate officer, was returned to him. Von Borke presented this relic to the State and the Legislature accepted it with the following resolution:

> "Resolved by the General Assembly: That the State of Virginia, appreciating the high manly qualities and virtues of Lieut.-Colonel Heros von Borke, accept the sword, and hereby directs the Secretary of the Commonwealth to place it among the relics preserved in the Public Library."

Von Borke published in German and English a book: "Zwei Jahre im Sattel," a description of his military life as a Confederate officer, and lately he wrote in conjunction with Major Scheibert: "The Great Cavalry Battle near Brandy Station."

Captain — Scheibert[219]), of the Prussian Engineers, detailed by his government as an observer, but taking an active part as a combatant, was attached to Gen. Robert E. Lee's headquarters. His interest in the southern cause did not end with the war; on returning to Germany, where he was appointed Major in the Prussian Engineers, he corresponded with the editor of the "Southern Historical Society's Papers," and he wrote a book:

218.) "Southern Bivouac Magazine," p. 515. Louisville, Ky., February 1886.

219.) "The German Soldier in the Wars of the United States," by J. G. Rosengarten, pp. 179 and 180. Philadelphia, Pa., 1890.

"Sieben Monate in den Rebellen-Staaten," published in Stettin in 1868, characterized by its southern tone. In 1883 Major Scheibert published a German translation of Allan's: "History of the Valley Campaign;" and in a letter of October 13th, 1881, dated Hirschberg, Silesia, Prussia, he says that he has translated and printed in German: Early's "Gettysburg," Stuart's and Lee's "Report," Hubbard's "Chancellorville," Patton's "Jackson," McClellan's "Jeb Stuart," Stuart's "Gettysburg," and biographies of Lee, Jackson, Stuart and Mosby. His "Buergerkrieg in den Vereinigten Staaten" has been translated into the French and Spanish.

Colonel Gustav Adolph Schwarzmann[220]) was born at Stuttgart, Wuertemberg, March 17th, 1815, and received a thorough and complete education. A young man of eighteen he came to Baltimore and received a situation as clerk in a commercial house. At the time of the Seminole War, 1835–'42, he enlisted in the U. S. Army and owing to his superior education he was soon promoted to a lieutenantship of the 4th Artillery Regiment. Schwarzmann was wounded several times and after the close of the war he was appointed superintendent of the U. S. Arsenal at Fayetteville, N. C., and later on to a position in the General Postoffice at Washington city. Sympathizing with the South he went to Richmond at the beginning of the Civil War, and he was at once appointed to the General Postoffice of the Confederacy; but this civil service was not what he longed for, and he soon joined the Confederate army. He was commissioned Colonel and Adjutant-General to Gen. Albert Pike; participated in numerous engagements and battles and again distinguished himself by his bravery. After the termination of the war Colonel Schwarzmann went to Baltimore and established himself as notary-public. His many friends in Richmond tried in vain to induce him to take up his abode there. A serious disease of the eyes, a result of exposures during the war, darkened the remainder of his life, and after twelve years of suffering he died on the 20th of February, 1882.

Col. David Lewis Ruffner, son of Dr. Henry Ruffner, was

220.) From "Der Deutsche Correspondent," February 22nd, 1882. Baltimore, Md.

born in Lexington, Va., and was a graduate of Washington College, now the Washington and Lee University. He was in the Confederate army as Captain of "Kanawha Riflemen" until he received an injury and was placed in the Quartermaster's department of Gen. Williams' Brigade, and later on staff duty in the field. He was commissioned Colonel Aide de Camp by Gov. Jackson of West Virginia in 1881.

G. A. Peple was born at Henry-Chapelle, in the "Rhine-provinz," Kingdom of Prussia, in 1828, and received a normal school education to fit him for the profession of teacher. After his graduation a predilection for the mechanic arts induced him to visit the polytechnical schools at Geneva and Vevay in Switzerland. About 1850 he emigrated to America, where he for years engaged in educational pursuits and was favorably known as a successful teacher. In 1859 he came to Richmond, Va., and during the Civil War he acted at first as topographical engineer, later as Commissary Sergeant at Buchanan, Botetourt county, and finally he received the appointment as professor of history and modern languages at the Confederate Marine School on board the school-ship "Patrick Henry," stationed in the harbor at Rockets, Richmond, Va. In this position he ranked as "acting master" or "Major of the army." Towards the close of the war he also edited for some time the "Richmond Anzeiger," which the Confederate government had purchased, and after the conclusion of peace he took charge of the "Cotton and Woolen Mills" at Manchester, opposite Richmond, Va. Thus he turned his pedagogical and technical education to good account. G. A. Peple was up to his death, October 24th, 1895, the superintendent of the above named mills. He took an active part in the political and German social life of Richmond, and for a long time he was the stirring spirit among his countrymen. He composed a pretty comedy entitled: "Frau Lipps," which was enacted on the stage of the Virginia Gesangverein at Richmond, and upon several occasions he delivered the official festive oration. As a member of the Board of Education at Manchester he gained general admiration for his talents as an organizer and by his pedagogical experience.

Captain E. von Buchholz, a native of the Kingdom of Wuertemberg, was the son of the chief ranger von Buchholz and served as cavalry and artillery officer in the Royal army. About 1850 he emigrated with his family to America, located first in Washington, D. C., and afterwards removed to Richmond, Va. Gov. Henry A. Wise, recognizing his capacity, engaged him to survey the State and to draw an accurate topographical map of the same. In the fall of 1859 a hostile invasion of Virginia, known as "John Brown's Raid," occurred at Harper's Ferry, and Capt. von Buchholz accompanied Gov. Wise to Jefferson county as a member of his staff. At the breaking out of the Civil War Ex-Governor Gen. Henry A. Wise was ordered to Kanawha valley in West Virginia and von Buchholz was commissioned to organize the artillery of his brigade. Soon after he was placed in charge of the Ordinance stores of the brigade and in the spring of 1862 was again transferred to the Virginia Ordinance Department at Richmond. After the end of the war there were no funds in the State treasury for the completion of the survey of Virginia and its map, and Capt. Buchholz went to San Francisco as superintendent of a factory for the manufacture of explosives. There he died in 1892.

Major Max Roemer, who claimed to be a German-Hungarian, belonged to the Wise Legion during its western campaign. After the war he settled in St. Louis, Mo., where he is practicing as a well-to-do physician.

Capt. — Tucker was born in Holstein, the son of Jewish parents. Some months before the war broke out he came from Memphis, Tenn., to Richmond, and when hostilities commenced he joined Capt. Caskey's Cavalry Company, which was attached to the Wise Legion. At Gauley Bridge Sergt. Tucker was detailed as messenger to headquarters and shared the tent with the writer. The opinion of all his superiors and companions in arms was an unanimous approval of his ability and courage. He was a splendid horseman and very ambitious. For some time Capt. Tucker was in command of a company of cavalry, and during the Pennsylvania campaign in 1863 he was one of Gen. Fitzhugh Lee's aides. At a very lively engagement at

Shepperdstown, Va., the author met Capt. Tucker for the last time and admired his boldness and sangfroid in the midst of the fight.

Von Massow was a Prussian cavalry officer and came to Richmond in 1861 to enter the Confederate service from eager desire for war. Not successful in securing a commission he joined Gen. Mosly's independent troop and acted as one of his aides. At a skirmish near Upperville, Va., he was shot through the breast and left on the field for dead. Von Massow recovered, returned to Germany and in 1866 fought as Lieut. of Dragoons under Gen. Vogel von Falkenstein.

Carl Friedrich Henningson, one of the most picturesque figures, an excellent soldier and well-known military author, was born in England, of German parents (from Hanover) in 1816. He received a superior German education, spoke several languages and was a highly gifted man and amiable companion. But he was inclined to seek adventures and for that reason never enjoyed a quiet and prosperous life. A lad of hardly sixteen years of age he volunteered in the army of the Carlists in Spain. For his gallantry he was appointed Captain of the body-guard of Don Carlos. Afterwards he rose to the position of Colonel of cavalry and received the decoration of the order of St. Ferdinand. After his return home he wrote a "History of the Spanish War," which secured him the favor and protection of Wellington and Soult. In 1842 he went to Russia and took part in the Circassian War, and his publication: "Recollections of Russia," created quite a sensation. In 1849 he joined the Hungarian army. He delineated the plan of campaign, which was confirmed by Gen. Guyon, and he received the appointment of military governor of Komorn. After the downfall of the Hungarian Revolution Col. Henningson embarked for America, where he worked jointly with Kossuth for the Hungarian cause and also engaged in literary work. Some of his publications of this period are: "The Twelve Months Campaign under Zamalacarregen;" "The White Slave," a novel, "Eastern Europe Sixty Years Ago," a novel, and "Analogies and Contrasts." At the beginning of the "Filibuster War" in Nicaragua he took command of the invading force and defended "Granada" heroically with about 300 against 4,000 men. He repulsed the besieging army several times, and on the 24th of November, 1859, cut his way to the sea-coast through the overwhelming forces of his enemies. He burnt Granada before evacuating it and erected a spear on its ruins to which he nailed a placard bearing the inscription: "Aqui fué Granada," that is: "here stood Granada." At the outbreak of the Civil War he accepted the position of military adviser to Gen. Henry A. Wise, and was appointed second in command of the Wise Legion. After the battle on Roanoke island Gen. Henningson commanded at Curritue bridge the fragments of the legion and there the author acted for a few days as his adjutant. Gen. Henningson did not find proper opportunity to display his military genius during the War of Secession. The cause was that Gen. Wise was no favorite of President Davis and his legion was constantly ordered to untenable or lost positions. Referring to Mr. Davis' partiality Ed. A. Pollard says: "No man was ever more sovereign in his likes and dislikes"[221]).

General V. D. Groner, of Norfolk, and Gen. A. L. Long, of Charlottsville, who are said to be descendants of German families, are also named with distinction. There was another officer in the Confederate army who must be numbered with the German element: *Count B. Estván*; but the German-Virginians would gladly disclaim all relation to him. The so-called "Count" came to Richmond some years before the Confederate episode. Estván lived there upon the earnings of his two ladies, his wife and his sister-in-law, who gave lessons and were acknowledged to be very highly educated. He himself was a very good-looking jovial man and knew how to perform the part of an upright Austrian country nobleman to perfection. When the Civil War commenced he pretended to have recruited in North Carolina a regiment of Lancers and was authorized to draw from the Ordinance Department the necessary equipage. He took all accoutrements received: saddles, bridles, blankets, etc., to North Carolina, sold the articles

221.) "The Second Year of the War," by Edw. A. Pollard, p. 302. Richmond, Va., 1863.

at any price and disappeared. Estván went to Washington city in full uniform of a Confederate Colonel and claimed to have deserted in sympathy with the Union. He was received with distinction, introduced to President Lincoln and the best society of the Union capital. From Washington he went to England and Germany, and assisted by his ladies, wrote a book: "Kriegsbilder aus Amerika," first published in English at London and later in German by F. A. Brockhaus, Leipzig, 1864. Finally Estván ventured to revisit his old Fatherland, Austria, and at Vienna he was arrested and prosecuted as a criminal.

In the Union army were many Germans and also some German-Virginians. Gen. Robert E. Lee gave these German soldiers in the Union army a very brilliant testimonial. At the time when the southern cause was rapidly falling away he angrily exclaimed: "Take out the Dutch and we will whip the Yankees easily."

Gen. Jacob Ammen[222]), distinguished during the rebellion, was a native of Virginia, a graduate of West Point in 1831, had resigned to engage in teaching and engineering, and when the war broke out he re-entered the service as Colonel of the 24th Ohio; later as Brigadier-General he served with great bravery in the West.

Gen. Hugo Dilger, born in Baden, enjoyed the reputation of one of the boldest officers of the Northern army. During the war he learned to know and admire the Shenandoah valley and its German population, and after the close of the hostilities he concluded to live among the "Sesesh." He purchased a farm near Front Royal and is a very popular man among his Virginian neighbors.

Gen. Lewis Ruffner, of Charleston, Kanawha county, before mentioned, participated in the establishment of the separation of West Virginia. Against the wishes of most of his relatives [223]) and many of his warmest personal friends he declared for

---

222.) "The German Soldier in the Wars of the U. S," by J. G. Rosengarten, p. 166. Philadelphia, 1890.

223.) "Historical Papers, No. 5, 1895, Washington and Lee University, Lexington, Va.," pp. 21—23.

the Union and stood for it with the courage of inflexible conviction. He was twice elected as a member of the Legislature of West Virginia. In 1863 he was one of the delegates to the Wheeling Convention, which framed a constitution for the new State, and in the same year he was appointed by the Legislature a Major-General of militia for the State. He was also about that time tendered the position of Colonel of a regiment in the Federal army, which he declined on account of the large business interests he represented and which were continually in peril. His public life closed with the war and he died in 1883 at his home.

The contents of these biographies have run in advance of the historical reports given and we return to the events in the first year of the war.

On May 20th, 1861, the seat of the Confederate Government was transferred from Montgomery, Alabama, to Richmond, and on the 29th of the same month President Jefferson Davis was received in the new capital. The face of the city at once became altered, — it was overrun by wild fanatics, speculative adventurers, office seekers, gamblers and discreditable women,—the respectable inhabitants soon retired, alarmed and disgusted, from publicity. In the beginning of the war the Confederate armies had been victorious, but victory was followed by disaster; the enthusiasm and valor of the people cooled down and the volunteer soldiers felt desirous to return home. The exigency was very critical and the government was forced to resort to conscription. In April and again in September, 1862, acts of conscription were passed by Congress and generally cheerfully acquiesced in. New disasters on the Mississippi frontier, the evacuation of Norfolk, Va., and the destruction of the "Virginia" or "Merrimac," caused great distress and public alarm in the old mother State. The destruction of the "Merrimac" left the James river and Richmond almost unprotected, and there appeared unmistakable signs of the intention of the Confederate Government to remove to some safer place than the capital of the Old Dominion. The sound of the guns of the Federal gunboats at Drewry's Bluff and the thunder of the cannons during the battles around

Richmond were heard in the streets of the city. Many prepared to leave and there were cries of treason and disloyalty. The foreign born inhabitants and especially such that kept away from the army were objects of suspicion and all possible influence was urged to force them into service. The Germans in Richmond who were not citizens and therefore claimed exemption from military duty were in a difficult situation. No powerful German Empire then existed to protect and shield them, only the "Free City of Bremen" was represented in Richmond by a Consul appointed to take care of her commercial interests. To this Consul, Edw. W. de Voss, all those alarmed and suspected Germans hastened to seek protection. Upon oath that they had not obtained American citizenship and paying a fee of one dollar they received a certificate worded as follows:

Consulate of the Free City of Bremen,,Richmond, Va.

I, — E. W. de Voss, Consul of the free City of Bremen, declare and certify that the bearer, ———, has taken oath that he is a native of ———, Germany, and that he has never taken the oath of allegiance to the United States or the Confederate States of America, or to any other foreign nation.

Given under my hand and seal of office, ——

Edw. W. de Voss, Consul.

For some time these certificates were respected by the Confederate police and military authorities, but they also intensified the ill-feeling towards the foreigners.

The close of the summer of 1862 found the soil of Virginia again almost cleared of the invading enemy, who had been defeated around Richmond, at Cedar mountain, at Manassas and in Kentucky. These victories and the battle of Sharpsburg or Antietam had cost great loss of life. Maryland and Kentucky failed to come to the support of the Confederate armies. Disastrous events followed then in the Southwest: the defeat of Corinth, the capture of Galveston, etc., and on the 22nd of September, 1862, President Lincoln issued his proclamation of the *Emancipation of the Slaves.* The scarcity of all supplies, the enormous prices and the depreciation of the

Confederate currency seriously added to the calamities and disheartened the people. In fact the depreciation of the Confederate currency did more to demoralize the South than anything else. The advance in prices was enhanced by greedy speculation. Although it was no secret that *southern planters* were eager to smuggle and sell cotton, sugar and tobacco to the North, the animosity of the natives *accused the German Jews and foreign adventurers* to speculate on the misfortunes of the South. However the truth was occasionally acknowledged. Edw. A. Pollard for instance says in his book[224]), written at the time: "Whatever diminution of spirit there may have been in the South since the commencement of the struggle it has been on the part of those pretentious classes of the wealthy, who in peace were at once the most zealous 'secessionists' and the best customers of the Yankees, and who now in war are naturally the sneaks and tools of the enemy. The cotton and sugar planters of the extreme South who prior to the war were loudest for secession, were at the same time known to buy every article of their consumption in Yankee markets and to cherish an ambition of shining in the society of northern hotels. It is not surprising that many of these affected patriots have found congenial occupation in this war in planting in co-partnership with the enemy or in smuggling cotton into his lines." This criticism certainly is to some extent too severe in its general form of expression. The devotion of the southern people to their cause is too well known to be discredited, but it is equally unjust to accuse the Jews and foreigners without distinction to have been corrupt and unpatriotic. The large number of Germans who served in the southern army and dared their lives on the battle fields are strong proof against such spiteful accusation.

"In the South, during the dark and trying days of the Confederacy," says Hon. Simon Wolf, Washington city[225]), "the Jewish citizens of that section displayed to the full their devotion to the cause which they held at heart. The Jewish South-

224.) "The Second Year of the War," by Edw. A. Pollard, p. 303. Richmond, Va., 1863.

225.) "The American Jew as Patriot, Soldier and Citizen," by Simon Wolf, p. 429. Philadelphia, Pa.

erners were as zealous in their efforts as were their neighbors all about them, and however mistaken was their contention they adhered to it tenaciously. A Jew, it is said, fired the first gun against Fort Sumter, and another Jew gave the last shelter to the fleeing President and Cabinet of the fallen Confederacy."

It cannot be disputed that Jews have been foremost among the foreign-born population of Virginia in advocating the secession-movement, — being interested in the "Negro trade." The largest auction-house in Richmond for the sale of slaves was owned by a Jew. Although slaves were considered a necessity by the planters and slave property being legitimate, the Negro-trader was looked upon with contempt, and therefore it reflected to a disadvantage on the Jews that several of them were engaged in this detested trade. However, the cheerful alacrity with which they entered the Confederate service in the hour of need, is evidence of their devotion to the southern cause. In a number of southern Jewish families all the male members able to bear arms were enrolled in the southern army. In Virginia three brothers: Leopold, Samson and Solomon Levy enlisted, and the last-named died of wounds received in battle.

Hon. Simon Wolf gives in his interesting history: "The American Jew as Patriot, Soldier and Citizen," *the following German-Virginian names of Jewish officers and soldiers in the Confederate army:*

Adler, Henry, Company E, 1st and 14th Inf. Regmt.
Abrams, Isaac, Company G, 1st Inf. Regmt.
Angle, Meyer, Company D, 12th Inf. Regmt.
Angle, M., Company E, 46th Inf. Regmt.
Angle, B., Company —, 46th Inf. Regmt.
Angle, Joseph, Company E, 59th Inf. Regmt.
Adler, A., Company A, 1st Artillery.
Bear, Alexander, Lieutenant and subsequently, Surgeon Company D, 4th Infantry.
Bacharach, M.
Bacarach S.
Baach, Siegmund, Longstreet's Corps.
Baach, Seligman, do.

Baach, Solomon H, Longstreet's Corps.
Bernheim, Samuel, Sergt.-Major, City Battalion.
Cohen, Jacob, Company B, 12th Infantry.
Cohen, David, Richmond Hussars.
Cohen, M., do.
Dogen, Samuel, Company A, 19th Infantry.
Dreyfus, Leon, Company A, 10th Cavalry.
Deichs, Wm., Norfolk Blues.
Ezekiel, E. M., Company A, 1st Infantry.
Ezekiel, Joseph K., Company B, 46th Infantry.
Eiseman, Louis, Wise's Brigade.
Ezekiel, Jacob, 1st Militia.
Ezekiel, Moses, Lieutenant of Cadets Va. Institute.
Frankenthal, Simon, Company B, 46th Infantry.
Friedenwald, Isaac, " A, 53d "
Friedland, A., Richmond Light Inf. Blues.
Goldstein, B., Company E, 46th Infantry.
Guggenheim, Simon, Company E, 46th Infantry.
Gunst, Michael, " E, 46th "
Goldstein, J., " E, 46th "
Gunst, Henry, " E, — Cavalry.
Gersberg, Henry.
Hirschberg, Joseph, " A, 1st Infantry.
Hutzler, Siegmund L., " A, 1st "
Hexter, Simon, " E, 1st "
Hessburg, Julius, 3d "
Heilbroner, Henry, " H, 27th "
Hesser, S., " E, 46th "
Hirsch, Herman, " A, 1st Cavalry.
Hessburg, M., "
Isaacs, Abrh., " E, 46th Infantry.
Kuh, E. L., " H, 8th "
Kull, M. E., " A, 12th "
Kadden, A., " A, 10th Cavalry.
Kalten, Aaron, Wise's Legion.
Lichtenstein, Isidore, Company H, 1st Infantry.
Lowenstein, William, Richmond Light Infantry Blues.
Levy, Lewis, Company A, 12th Infantry.
Lowenstein, Isidore, " A, 12th "

Lorsch, Henry, Company A, 19th Infantry.

Levy, Ezekiel, " E, 46th "

Levy, Isaac J., " E, 46th "

Levy, Alexander H., " E, 46th "

Levy, Alexander, Lieutenant, Staff of General Magruder.

Levy, Joseph, Company E, 46th Infantry.

Levy, Emanuel G., " E, 46th "

Levy, Leopold, } brothers. " G, 1st Cavalry.

Levy, Sampson, } " G, 1st "

Levy, Solomon, } 23d Infantry.

Levy, E., Captain, Richmond Light Infantry Blues.

Lichtenstein, K., 19th Reserves.

Lowenstein, I., Richmond Grays.

Literman, Simeon, Young's Battery.

Myers, Wm., Company A, 1st Infantry.

Myers, Marks, 12th "

Myer, Max, " B, 12th "

Middledorfer, Chas, " E, 12th "

Myers, A., " — 17th "

Myers, Solomon, " — 18th "

Moses, J. C., " E, 46th "

Myers, C., " E, 46th "

Myers, Lewis, " — 46th "

Myers, Herman, " — 1st Cavalry.

Myers, Benjamin, " C, Wise's Legion.

Middledorfer, Max, Fayette Artillery.

Newman, Joseph, Company K, 20th Infantry.

Newman, Isaac, 46th "

Newman, Jacob, 59th "

Obermayer, H., 2nd "

Oethenger, David, Company B, 18th "

Oberndorfer, B., Young's Battery.

Plaut, Hugo, Sergeant on General Henry A. Wise's Staff.

Rosenberg, M., Company G, 6th Infantry.

Rosenfeld, Simon, " A, 12th "

Reinach, A. S., " B, 12th "

Reinach, Isidore, " B, 12th "

Rosenheim, Henry, " E, 46th "

Rosenberg, Michael, Norfolk Blues Infantry.

Reinach, M., Petersburg Grays.
Seldner, Isaac, Lieutenant, 6th Infantry.
Schwartz, –, 17th Infantry.
Semon, Jacob S., Company E, 46th Infantry.
Schoenthal, Joseph, Company E, 46th Infantry.
Strauss, David, 7th Cavalry.
Simon, Isaac, Richmond Hussars.
Simon, Nathan, Richmond Hussars.
Smith, Henry, Otoy's Battery.
Seligman, H., Petersburg Grays.
Triesdorfer, G., Company B, 14th Infantry.
Tucker, — Lieutenant, Caskey's Riders.
Unstadter, M., Company A, 6th Infantry.
Whitlock, P., " A, 12th "
Wilzinsky, L., " H, 12th "
Wolf, W. M., Lieutenant 25th Infantry.
Wasseman, Levy, Company E, 46th Infantry.
Wamback, Leopold, Norfolk Blues Infantry, and several uncertain names.

The losses of the Confederate armies had to be repaired in some way and the conscription laws were now carried out with extreme rigor. The Confederate government took the police authority from the State of Virginia and appointed *Gen. J. Winder "provost marshall of Virginia."*

He originated from Baltimore, had been a Colonel in the Union army and was promoted by the Confederate government to the rank of Brigadier-General. It probably was his intention and orders to enforce the law and to guard the safety of the city, but he did so in an almost savage manner. He organized a secret police force of men, who for the most part ought rather to have been put under police control, and a detestable system of espionage and denunciation was inaugurated. A reign of terror began in Richmond. Arrests upon the charge of political disloyalty or secret connection with the enemy were daily occurrences. Several respectable German citizens who were known to have opposed secession—like H. L. Wiegand—were imprisoned in the ill-famed "Castle Thunder," and frequently had to wait there several months before the charge against them was investigated. Armed patrols marched the streets of Richmond and arrested anyone who had no passport of Gen. Winder to show. If the prisoner could not give other satisfactory legitimation he was sent to the army.

However an Englishman, a correspondent of the "Cornhill Magazine," contrasting the rival capitals, sketched Gen. Winder rather favorably as follows[226]): "Gen. Winder, the provost marshall, every sojourner in the city knows full well. Gen. Butler would rejoice in the possession of so vigilant an officer. While Washington is overrun with the intriguing and the disappointed, Richmond has ears for every whisper, and there can come no stranger to the city whose movements are not watched and his mission understood. To Gen. Winder the whole government of the city is entrusted. Offenders are marched singly before the provost; he sits absolute and imperturbable, erect, prompt and positive. He has small searching eyes, a beaked nose and white bristly hair, which suggests the unapproachable porcupine. He adopts a harsh voice with prisoners of war and with his justice may blend just a little retaliation; for his brother has long been shut up in Fort Warren by Federal gaolers."

Not any less embarrassing was the situation of foreigners or foreign-born citizens in other cities and towns, but particularly of those living isolated in the country. Bands of masked and armed men harassed foreigners and tried to compel them to leave the country.

The depot agent at Trevillians, Louisa county, Mr. Hancock, related to the author the following incident, sounding almost like a romance:

"Some years before the war a German and his wife, relatives of the Rueger and Loehr families in Richmond, settled at Trevillian and opened a store. The industrious couple prospered and thereby they awakened the envy of several less successful neighbors. After the outbreak of hostilities they were by these persons accused to be "Abolitionists" and to

226.) "The Record," p. 42, July 16th, 1863, publ. by West & Johnston, Richmond, Va.

have sold merchandise to negroes, thereby offending against the Virginia code. In consequence of these incitements a band of masked men on horseback, headed by one of the spiteful neighbors, approached their house in nighttime and ordered them: "to leave the country within three days or their house would be burnt." In the third following night the horsemen reappeared to carry out their threat, but the brave wife of the German stood at the door of her dwelling armed with a gun and told them that she would shoot anyone who dared to destroy her husband's property. The disguised men hesitated and held a short consultation, and finally they turned their backs to the house and disappeared in the darkness. The German storekeeper and his wife, in dread of further molestations hereafter, removed to Richmond until the reestablishment of peace and order. Although successful in their undertakings in the city, they returned to Trevillians and reopened their store. Their son and the daughter of the leader of their assailants visited the same little country school, became attached to each other and after years they were married. At present the son of the German and the daughter of the "Ku-Klux" are a happy couple and the proprietors of a much enlarged storehouse."

In spite of distrust and sufferings the Germans, and even those who seriously regretted the separation from the Union, competed with the Anglo-Americans in the endurance of severe trials. The long war had entangled by its consequences all the different parties; all had finally but one material interest and entertained but one hope: victory and peace. Defeat appeared to every inhabitant of Virginia, suffering most of all the Confederate States and liable to undergo dreadful hardships in case of being vanquished, as identical with ruin.

This sentiment, especially felt by the descendants of the German pioneers, is closely shown in "Virginia!" a battle song, composed by Mrs. C. J. M. Jordan[227]). The song closes:

227.) "War Songs of the South," p. 216, Richmond, Va., West & Johnston, 1862.

"Hark, hark! o'er mountain, vale and glen
The distant thunders rattle;
The foe, the foe is at our door,
Up, brothers, to the battle!
He comes, — above our native hills
His flaunting banners wave;—
Up, brothers, to a Victor's palm
Or to a Freeman's grave.

CHORUS:

Up, noble Queen, the brave, the free,
Thou'ld bow thee to none other;
God will thy shield and buckler be,
Virginia, oh, my mother!"

There was now one great danger threatening the Confederacy. The army suffered heavy losses sustained and *by absentees.* Already in 1862 Gen. (Stonewall) Jackson complained about the absence of officers and men from the ranks without leave[228]). One of his brigades reported at that time twelve hundred absentees. This state of affairs naturally began to disgust the men doing faithful service, the armies grew feeble and in a great measure disorganized.

The death of Gen. Jackson on May 10th, 1863, was also very discouraging to the soldiers as well as to all the people. The entire South was in mourning and the Germans looked upon this sad event as the foreshadow of subjugation.

"Other countries and ages," said R. L. Dabney[229]), may have witnessed such a national sorrow, but the men of this generation never saw so profound and universal grief as that which throbbed in the heart of the Confederate people at the death of Jackson. Men were everywhere speculating with solemn anxiety upon the meaning of his death. They asked themselves: "has God taken the good man away from the evil to come?"

The fall of Vicksburg and the result of the battle of Gettysburg in the beginning of July, 1863, were fatal and

---

228 and 229.) "Life and Campaigns of Lieutenant General (Stonewall) Jackson," pp. 683—684 and 726—727, by R. L. Dabney.

considered as a reverse in the general fortunes of the contest. The news of these disasters reached Richmond on the same day and despair took the place of the hope of an early peace. Dissatisfaction, distrust, want of discipline and desertion steadily increased.

The author is still in possession of a diary he kept in those days, and an extract from it may find room here to illustrate the low spirit prevalent in the army.

"Near Brandy Station, Va., August 5th, 1863.—After our victorious fight of yesterday we passed the night in readiness to march. Everyone tied the bridle of his horse to his wrist and laid down in the grass. Now we are ordered to relieve the picket line on Miller's Hill, near Brandy Station, and I remain in command of Companies D and H, (14th Va. Cavalry). My wounded men from yesterday are doing well and are to be taken to Culpeper. Men and horses suffer for want of rations and I am almost broken down by rendering constant service. The dispositions from headquarters of our brigade frequently appear to be rash and thoughtless. Want of military knowledge and experience cause the troops many useless exertions and hardships and create therefore much complaint. Desertion is increasing, every night the gaps in our reduced brigade are widened. Yesterday the first desertion occurred from our regiment, hitherto honorably exempted. Unfortunately even officers listen, ignoring duty and honor, to the peevish conversation of their men about the capitulation of Vicksburg, our retreat from Maryland, our gloomy prospects, etc., and likewise to quite unconcealed provocations to desert the army. Such indifference is almost equal to sanctioning treason, and such occurrences are very alarming. It is true that the deserters do not join the enemy, but hide in the woods and mountains near their homes, but every one of them reduces our number and leaves a vacancy in his company which cannot be filled."

The Governor of Virginia now ordered 8,000 militia under arms for home defence and in order to relieve the regulars from guarding the prisoners. All foreigners still exempted from service were called upon to join. The Confederate government also organized a Brigade of Officials and Mechanics, employed in the offices and workshops, for like purposes. The Virginian forces were placed under command of Governor Gen. W. Smith and the Confederate brigade in charge of Gen. C. Lee. The 19th Regiment of Va. Reserved Forces was chiefly composed of foreigners: Germans (Companies H and M), Frenchmen, Italians, etc. Very soon these forces were also ordered to the field about Richmond, but the members enjoyed the privilege of following their occupation if not on duty and to draw rations from the government magazine for their families at government prices. This permission was the more valuable as all supplies commanded enormous prices, for instance: One barrel flour, $300 to $600; one dozen eggs, $10; one glass whisky $5; one cigar, $5; board per month, $450–$500; a furnished room per month, $100–$125, etc. However the above mentioned measure to strengthen the army was ruinous, it demonstrated: *that the South was exhausted.* One Richmond regiment of the Confederate brigade under Gen. C. Lee was called with harsh sarcasm the: "Silver Grays," the men being aged and with gray sprinkled hair. By these desperate circumstances the North was much encouraged and the Union armies were at the same time heavily reinforced. The Federal Government gave the order *to employ all liberated slaves* to work on fortifications or to be enrolled in separate regiments. In the beginning of 1864 the Northern armies numbered about 500,000 men and 65,000 negro troops, and the United States Navy was very strong. The Confederacy had only 150,000 to 200,000 soldiers left and the best part of the Southern Navy was captured by Admiral Farragut on August 5th, 1864, in the Bay of Mobile. Disaster followed disaster, many important places were taken by the Union army and on November 12th Gen. Sherman commenced his famous march through Georgia to the Atlantic coast, cutting the Confederacy in two, while Gen. Grant with his mighty army of the Potomac obliged Gen. Lee to fall back upon Richmond, bravely contesting foot by foot the advance on the capital of the Confederate States. Lee defeated Grant once more at Cold Harbor, a few miles from the city, and Grant transferred his army to the south side of James river and besieged Petersburg. Gen. Early, after an unsuccessful invasion of Maryland, was obliged to give up the Shenandoah valley to Gen. Sheridan. Sherman invaded the Carolinas and Wilmington, N. C., was captured. *The Confederates could no longer offer effectual resistance;* they were losing their strongholds one after the other, and the end of the bloody drama was drawing near. On the other side the reelection of Lincoln to the presidency of the United States and the call for 300,000 men to strengthen the Union armies, increased the confidence and determination of the North to finally overwhelm the South.

The Confederate government, impressed by the imminent danger of the situation, in March, 1865, *resolved to arm the slaves,* but this last hope failed. Fate outran the realization of this scheme. After several bloody battles around Petersburg, Gen. Lee was obliged to evacuate Petersburg and Richmond, still hoping to be able to force his way through the lines of the Union army and to unite with Gen. Johnson in North Carolina. But the odds surrounding him were too great. Not conquered but overwhelmed, he surrendered April 9th, 1865, near Appomattox Court House with the remnant of the army of Northern Virginia, numbering only 28,355 men, and the other Confederate Generals, Johnson, Dick Taylor and Kirby Smith soon followed his example.

The evacuation of Richmond was accompanied by circumstances that deprived many German citizens of all they owned and for the moment placed them in a desperate position; but by diligent labor they quickly succeeded to regain prosperity and wealth.

On Sunday forenoon, April 2nd, President Davis, while attending Divine service at St. Paul's Church, received a message from Gen. Robert E. Lee, informing him: "that he could no longer hold Petersburg and Richmond." The news of the impending evacuation spread like wild fire and the streets were soon filled with fugitives. The night came, but no one rested. The militia companies received orders to maintain quiet and order, but only few members of these organizations responded. About midnight several hundred barrels of whisky and brandy were rolled into the streets and emptied. A number of stragglers from the Confederate army and negro-lurkers possessed themselves of part of the intoxicating contents, and from that moment law and order were disregarded. Gen. Ewell, before leaving the city, gave order to set fire to the Confederate storehouses, and very soon the conflagration was beyond control. Everything was in confusion; there were not sufficient means of transportation to save the endangered property. Plunderers and thieves were at work, taking advantage of the calamity, and for some time it seemed as if the whole city would be destroyed. The terror of the scene was increased by the explosions of ammunition in the Confederate magazines and the blowing up of the gunboats. But early the next morning the U. S. *Gen. Gottfried Weitzel*, born November 1st, 1835, at Winzlen, Rhineprovince, Germany, took possession of the doomed city and at once restored order. Energetic measures were taken by his command to subdue the conflagration and save the endangered property. Col. Benjamin S. Ewell says:

"To the credit of this officer, Gen. Weitzel, it ought to be known that when his command, consisting of two divisions, one white, the other colored troops, the latter being in front, approached the city, he changed the order of his march and put the white soldiers in front when he saw the fire, as being less likely to commit excesses, and being more skilled and experienced in extinguishing fires."

Nearly all the cities and towns throughout Virginia can tell a story of sufferings; only those occupied by the Union forces soon after the outbreak of hostilities made an exception *Alexandria*[230]) received at the beginning of the war a large influx of Germans and a very busy time began. Musical and singing societies were organized, and although there were many adventurers and tramps among the new comers the majority was made up of able and useful men. Even a German newspaper: "*Der Spassvogel*," was started, but the publisher was a queer fellow and his paper enjoyed only a short existence. A social club: "Die Eintracht," was founded and it owned its

230.) "Correspondence of Dr, Julius Dienelt, Alexandria, Va., April 3d, 1892.

club-building, bar and restaurant. The club rooms were opened every evening and twice a week dances and stage performances took place. All branches of business prospered, in short it was a time still cherished in the memory of the few survivors. At that time too an effort was made to organize a German church, and the endeavor was supported by Rev. Butler, chaplain of the House of Representatives at Washington. The intention was to have an English sermon in the forenoon and a German one in the evening, but for want of concord the project failed. However, the religious spirit was live amid the German Israelites and they erected a pretty and large synagogue on the principal street of the city. Rev. Loewensohn, a highly educated and noble-spirited man, was elected rabbi, and under his leadership the first German school was established in Alexandria, attended by children of every faith. Before closing this important chapter the names of some German-Virginians who occupied conspicuous Confederate offices must be mentioned.

Christoph Gustav Memminger[231]), born at Mergentheim in Wuertemberg, came to Charleston, S. C., in 1806, when a little boy. His parents died soon after and he was taken to the Orphan Asylum. His talents awakened the sympathy of Governor Bennet, who took him into his family and enabled him to study law at the University of South Carolina. In 1822 Memminger graduated and in 1825 he was admitted to the bar. He married Governor Bennet's daughter and soon became a prominent figure in political and financial circles. He was a member of the State Legislature from 1836 to 1860, and took great interest in the organization of public schools at Charleston. In 1860 he was appointed Treasurer of South Carolina and elected to the first Confederate Congress. In February, 1861, President Davis called on him to be Secretary of Treasury. He accepted and removed to Richmond, Va. Mr. Memminger has been severely criticized for endorsing the illimitable issues of treasury notes. Edw. A. Pollard for instance accused him of "ignorance"[232]), but contradicting himself says: "When

231.) "Das deutsche Element in den Ver. Staaten," von Gustav Koerner. Cincinnati, Ohio, 1880.

232.) "The Second Year of the War," by Edw. A. Pollard, p. 303 Richmond, Va., 1863.

gold was quoted (at the close of 1862) in New York at twenty-five per cent. premium, it was selling in Richmond at nine hundred per cent. premium. Such have been the results of the financial wisdom of the Confederacy, *dictated by the President.*" In June 1864 Mr. Memminger resigned this sorrowful position and after the close of the war he returned to Charleston to practice there as attorney. He died on the 7th of March, 1888.

The list of members of the Confederate States Congress presents the following German-Virginian names[233]):

Ch. M. Conrad, born in Winchester, Va., 2nd district of Louisiana.

C. C. Herbert, born in Winchester, Va., 2nd district of Texas.

John Goode, Liberty, Bedford Co., Va., 6th district of Virginia.

A. R. Boteler, Shepherdstown, Jefferson Co., Va., 10th district of Virginia.

Samuel A. Miller, Shenandoah Co., Va., 14th district of Virginia.

233.) "The Record," p. 241, by West & Johnston, Richmond, Va, December 10th, 1863.

CHAPTER XIV.

THE NEW STATE, WEST VIRGINIA.

GERMANS, and especially Pennsylvania-Germans, largely participated in the settlement of the western mountain region of Virginia, now known as "West Virginia," the "Little Mountain State," or "the Daughter of the Old Dominion." Portions of West Virginia adjoining the Ohio, Potomac, Kanawha and New river show to this day many traces of an early German immigiation, reinforced at the close of the last century by the numerous colonization of German prisoners of war. It has already been stated that Gen. Washington valued the Germans as desirable colonists, and donated in 1770 by the English government with 10,000 acres of land south of the Ohio, and by purchase the owner of large estates on the Kanawha and Greenbrier rivers, he intended to colonize these with German settlers. The realization of his plan was delayed by the Revolutionary War; but after its close he invited the German prisoners of war to stay in the New World, and a very large number of them accepted his favorable proposal and built their cabins in Greenbrier, Pocahontas, Nicholas, Fayette and Kanawha counties.

The very first German immigration to the wild and romantic valleys of the Alleghanies occurred about the middle of the last century. The oppression of the English High Church and large land owners had driven them from their homesteads in Pennsylvania and Eastern Virginia. Separated from the civilized world, exposed to the attacks of the treacherous Indians, they became a hardy, independent and even rough people. In the first part of this history it is stated that the counties Hardy and Pendleton were settled by a part of the early German immigration to the Shenandoah valley, and part of the following reports has also been previously mentioned. In what is now Jefferson county, Robert Harper, a German, located in 1734, and his name is given in Harper's Ferry. Jacob Hite founded *Legtown* and Thomas Shepherd became the founder of *Mecklenburg*, now *Shepherdstown*. In Berkeley county the Waggeners and Faulkners, who distinguished themselves during the French and Indian War and the War of Independence, counted to the pioneer settlers. The two brothers Andrew and Edward Waggener came from Culpeper to Berkeley in 1750 and settled at *Bunker's Hill*, and later on General Adam Stephan (Stephens) and Colonel W. Darke also made Berkeley their home. With the first white inhabitants of Morgan county Thomas Hite, van Swearinger and others are numbered, and still more numerous were the German pioneers in Hampshire county. Among the founders of *Watson Town* in 1787 were Jacob Hoover, V. Swisher, R. Bumgardner, Isaac Zahn and other Germans. Dnring the French and Indian War the German settlers of this section had to fight for their homes and families. Bowers and Furman were killed and H. Newkirk wounded. In Pendleton county the horrible massacre at *Fort Seybert* by the Indians in May 1758 tells of the early settlement of Germans. Among the first white inhabitants of Pocahontas county were Peter Lightner, H. Harper, W. Hartman and J. Wolfenbarger, the Jordans, Tallmans, etc. The name "Knapp's Creek" reminds of the German pioneers. In 1754 David Tygar and Files came to Randolph county. The nationality of these pioneers is not known, but in 1790, on the land of Jacob Westfall, the county-seat *Beverly* was laid out and the Germans J. Westfall, Th. Phillips, H. Rosecrouts and V. Stalmaker were appointed trustees. Tucker county was settled by Germans in 1776, but all pioneer colonists were murdered by the savages. In 1758 Thomas Decker was the first white man who entered the territory of Preston and Monongalia counties. He established a settlement on *Decker's creek*, but he and his comrades were also slain by the Delaware and Mingoe Indians. The same evil fate in 1779 befell another German settlement on *Dunkart's creek.* At the time when the county of Preston was formed by a division of Monongalia, the following Germans were among the first county officers: F. Hara, W. Sigler, Jacob Funk, etc. The counties Grant, Mineral, Marion, Harrison, Barbour, Lewis, Upshur, Webster, Braxton, Gilmor, Ritchie, Doddridge, Taylor, Tyler, Pleasants, Calhoun, Rean, Logan, Mason, Putnam, Cabell, Wayne, Lincoln, Wyoming, McDowell, Mercer, Raleigh and Boone are of later creation and are but little populated, but in all of them the German element is more or less represented. The historian V. A. Lewis relates as a remarkable circumstance: "A Mr. Gordon, an American-German, had had by two wives twenty-eight children." — *Weston* or formerly *Flesherville,* the county-seat of Lewis county, was laid out on the land of David Stringer; the same land had in 1784 belonged to Henry Flesher. *Hacker's creek* also derives its name from a German settler. The German element of *Wirt county* can boast of several well-known men, as: A. G. Stringer, first County Clerk; W. E. Lockhart, Commissioner in Chancery; Arthur L. Boreman, first Governor of the new State and later U. S. Senator; John G. Stringer, State Attorney, etc. In the counties Wetzel, Marshall, Ohio, Brook and Hancock, forming a long and narrow strip of land, the so-called "Panhandle," and which are situated between Pennsylvania and Ohio, the first attempts at a settlement were principally made by Germans. William Boner came to Burke county in 1774, Moses Decker about 1787, etc., but the settlements in Brooke and Hancock counties suffered heavily from the savages, and the last white men killed by the Indians in that part of the Panhandle were the Germans Captain von Buskirk and John Decker. No less endangered were the lives of the German colonists in Ohio county and their courageous tenacity deserves exemplary credit. — *West Liberty* was established by legislative enactment November 29th, 1787, on the lands of R. Foreman and others, and in 1793 *Wheeling* was first laid out in town lots by Colonel Ebenezer Zane.—Marshall county, formerly part of the county of Ohio, was first settled in 1769 by John Wetzel and family, who were soon followed by the Siverts and Earlywines. In 1777 Nathan Master (Meister),

James and Jonathan Riggs found homes within the limits of Marshall county. During the struggles with the Indians Captain Foreman (1777), Captain John Baker (1778), and Colonel Beeler (1780) fought with distinction; they and their men and also the Tusch family were slain by the savages. The counties Wood, Jackson and Mason near the Ohio river also owe their present flourishing condition to German diligence. The German Christopher Gist or Geist, whom the historian of West Virginia, V. A. Lewis, erroneously represents to have been an Englishman, was in 1750 by order of the Ohio Land Company the first explorer of this region. George Washington, George Muse, Andrew Waggener and others were donated by the English government with extensive land tracts in Mason county in recognition of their eminent services during the French and Indian War, and they desired, as has been previously mentioned, to draw German farmers to their estates. Traces of an early German immigration are found to this day in the counties of Kanawha, Fayette, Greenbrier, Sumers, Monroe and Nicholas. With the first white men who reached this part of the country came the Hugharts, Rader, Moss, Hyde, Carpenter or Zimmermann, Strickland, etc., and the last victims of Indian treachery were a German family by name of Straud (Stroud) as previously stated, who lived near the junction of Gauley and Kanawha rivers, respectively the Gauley and New river.

With the enlarged settlement of the country the manners of the mountaineers were gradually refined, but they retained their independent and energetic character. Within the first half of the present century the Germans participated in several demonstrations against *the infringement on vital interests and fair claims of Western Virginia* on part of the State government and against *the unequal representation* of the two great sections of the State — the West and the East — in the General Assembly. The unjust representation gave to the East virtual sovereignty and rendered the western section almost powerless in all matters of State legislation.

224.) "History of West Virginia," by Virgil A. Lewis, pp. 320—321. Philadelphia, Pa., 1889.

"In the Assembly in 1820[234]) the former had one hundred and twenty-four members, while the latter had but eighty. The result was that the East secured to itself nearly everything in the character of internal improvements. The public buildings, with a single exception, the 'Western Lunatic Asylum at Staunton,' were all east of the Blue Ridge. But that which produced the greatest dissatisfaction and caused deepest displeasure was the restriction of the right of suffrage. Its exercise depended on a property qualification and was restricted exclusively to the freeholders of the State. The doctrine: 'that all men are born free and independent,' was declared in the first clause of the 'Bill of Rights,' but while it was claimed to be true in theory, it was declared to be dangerous in application.

The system of taxation[235]) *was also unequal*, discriminating against the free mountain section, taxing lightly those interests which the West did not possess, while expensive internal improvements, adding greatly to real property values, were only undertaken in the East. Railroads of greatest feasibility and utility, surveyed and brought into notice by public-spirited individuals, were procrastinated and killed by the same determination to override the interests of this region.

The eminent value of this country was intentionally or unintentionally ignored by the oligarchy of the southeast of Virginia. For the variety and fertility of its soil, mineral and forest resources, abundant waterpower, numerous mineral springs possessed of sanitive character, a delightful and healthful climate, etc., invited immigration, but the slave-owners of the East feared the influx of an intelligent and progressive population, as is generally concentrated in industrial districts, and they endeavored *to reduce to a minimum the means of communication and traffic*, like railroads, canals and good roads, necessary to the development of the rich resources of Western Virginia. Before the War of Secession the road sys-

235.) "West Virginia," by J. R. Dodge, U. S. Agricultural Report, 1863, page 45. Washington, 1863.

tem of West Virginia consisted only of the stage-road from Guyandotte and Charlestown, by way of Gauley Bridge and White Sulphur Springs, to Jackson River Depot, now Clifton Forge, which was at that time the terminus of the Virginia Central Railroad, now the Chesapeake and Ohio Railroad, and of the turnpike route from Parkersburg to Staunton and Winchester. The Baltimore and Ohio Railroad was the only railroad that touched West Virginia. Thus the interests of East and West Virginia seriously conflicted; but the most potent cause of the ill-feeling between the two sections was *the institution of Slavery.* Statistical reports estimate the number of slaves in the West, as stated previously, at seven per cent. of the entire population, and in the East at more than fifty per cent. Especially in the northern counties of the present State of West Virginia slavery and slave-labor were discredited. Free labor was valued more profitable and honorable than servile, yielding more comely social results and sweeter moral fruit, and more successfully advancing the national well-being and the progress of intellect. The Germans of the lower Shenandoah valley in the counties of Jefferson, Berkeley, Morgan, Hampshire, Hardy and Pendleton and of the "Panhandle" joined in these humane aspirations. They were in constant commercial and social intercourse with the people of the adjoining northern colonies or free States, and it is but natural that they adopted their views and manners.

"It was evident," says Virgil A. Lewis,[236]) "that a redress of grievances never could be secured under the existing constitution, and as early as 1815 the question of a constitutional convention to revise that instrument began to be agitated."

In 1828 the people's vote was taken in regard to the call of a convention and the proposition was carried by 21,896 assenting against 16,646 dissenting votes, showing that even in the East many voters recognized the necessity of reforms. In 1829 and again in 1850 conventions were held at Richmond to revise the constitution in favor of West Virginia, but none of the re-

236.) "History of Virginia," by Virgil A. Lewis, p. 322. Philadelphia, Pa., 1889.

forms sought were secured in 1829. Among the members of the convention of 1850 several western delegates bear German names. A redress of many grievances was secured; the right of suffrage was extended, taxation rendered more equitable and the basis of representation so remodeled as to secure to the West greater equality in the halls of legislature. But the Civil War again created disharmony between the two sections; the East favored secession, while the West remained faithful to the Union.

On May 13th, 1861, or twenty-four days after the Richmond convention had passed the ordinance of Secession, the delegates of twenty-five western counties assembled at Wheeling and declared unqualified opposition to Secession and that in the event of the ratification of the ordinance of Secession by the people the counties represented *would separate from the eastern part of the State and form a government of their own,* and a general convention should meet on June 11th at Wheeling.

A list of the members of the "First Wheeling Convention" contains the following German names:

Hancock county. — Wm. B. Freeman, J. L. Freeman, R. Breneman, Sam. Freeman.

Brooke county. — Adam Kuhn, Joseph Gist, John G. Jacob.

Ohio county. — J. R. Stefel, G. L. Cramner, A. F. Ross, John Stiner, J. M. Bickel, J. Paull, John C. Hoffman, Jacob Berger, J. C. Orr.

Marshall county. — H. C. Kemple, Dr. Marshman, J. W. Boner, Ch. Snediker, J. S. Riggs, Alex. Kemple.

Wetzel county. — A. W. Lauck, B. T. Bowers, Geo. W. Bier, W. D. Welker.

Tyler county. — W. B. Kerr.

Harrison county. — S. S. Fleming, Felix S. Sturm.

Pleasants county. — R. A. Cramer.

Wood county. — S. L. A. Burche, W. Vroman, J. Burche, Peter Dils, H. Rider.

Monongalia. — L. Kramer, H. Deering, E. D. Fogle, J. D. Hess, Ch. H. Burgess, J. T. M. Bly, J. Miller.

Preston county. — D. A. Letzinger, W. B. Zinn.

Jackson county. — A. Flesher, G. Leonard.

Marion county. — J. Holman, John Chisler.

Mason county. — W. E. Wetzel, L. Harpold, W. W. Harper, Wm. Harpold, Sam. Yeager, Ch. H. Bumgarten, Ch. B. Waggener.

Wirt county. — H. Neuman.

Hampshire county. — George W. Sheets, G. W. Rizer.

Berkeley county. — J. S. Bowers.

Roane county. — I. C. Stump.

and many others of doubtful origin like Smith, Young, Winters, Conrad, Brown, King, Fish, Hunter, Baker, Snyder, Cook, Walker, Marshall, etc. Wm. B. Zinn of Preston county was made temporary president and Ch. B. Waggener was one of the secretaries.

On the 23d of May the vote on the ordinance of Secession was taken and while the eastern portion of Virginia was almost unanimously in favor of Secession, in the western counties of the 44,000 votes cast 40,000 *were against the ordinance.*

On the 4th of June the delegates to the "Second Wheeling Convention" were chosen and assembled with the senators and representatives elected in May at the general election to membership of the General Assembly of Virginia on June 11th at Wheeling. The German element was again largely represented in this memorable assemblage in which forty counties of the old mother State took action. The convention resolved[237]): "We, the delegates here assembled in convention to devise such measures and take such action as the safety and welfare of the loyal citizens of Virginia may demand, have maturely considered the premises, and viewing with great concern the deplorable condition to which this once happy commonwealth must be reduced unless some regular adequate measure is speedily adopted, and appealing to the Supreme Ruler of the universe for the rectitude of our intentions, do hereby, in the name and

237.) Compare "A Declaration of the People of Virginia represented in Convention at the City of Wheeling, Thursday, June 13th, 1861."

on behalf of the good people of Virginia, solemnly declare that the preservation of their dearest rights and liberties, and their security in person and property, imperatively demand the reorganization of the Government of the Commonwealth, and that all the acts of said convention (that is, the Richmond convention which passed the ordinance of Secession) and executive tending to separate this Commonwealth from the United States, or to levy and carry on war against them, are without authority and void; and that the offices of all who adhere to said convention and executive, whether legislative, executive or judicial, are vacated."

Thus the Wheeling convention had proclaimed an interregnum in the State government and already the following day began the work of reorganization. Arthur J. Boreman of Wood county was president of the convention and G. L. Cramner secretary. The new government of Virginia was acknowledged by the United States authorities as the legal government of Virginia. On the first day of July the General Assembly organized at Wheeling and elected senators and representatives to the National Congress at Washington, who were admitted to seats in the respective houses.

"Having reorganized the government[238]) and elected a chief executive officer, Francis H. Pierpont of Marion county, Governor of Virginia, and provided for the election of all other officers, civil and military, the labors of the convention were evidently drawing to a close. Nothing had been done that appeared to directly inaugurate the popular movement for the formation of a new State. In reality however the true theory had been adopted and the only legitimate mode of arriving at the most desirable result had been conceived and acted upon by the convention. If the government, thus restored, was acknowledged by the Federal authorities as the only government in Virginia, then the legislative branch of it could give its assent to the formation of a new State, as provided for by the Constitution of the United States." August 6th, 1861, the convention reassembled at Wheeling and adopted an ordinance *to provide for the formation of a new State,* and on the 24th of October the

238.) J. H. Hagan's First West Virginia Report, p. 63.

people of the respective counties sanctioned this resolution. On the 26th of November a Constitutional Convention assembled again at Wheeling, the first capital of the new State, to frame the first Constitution of West Virginia. The following German names are among those of the delegates who performed this important labor: R. W. Lauck of Wetzel county, Rob't Hager of Borne, Henry Dering of Monongalia, Harmon Sinsel of Taylor, J. A. Dille of Preston, G. W. Sheets of Hampshire, Louis Ruffner of Kanawha, etc. On the 3d day of May, 1862, the Constitution was confirmed by a general vote of the people, and on the 9th of the same month a State convention assembled at Parkersburg elected the German-Virginian Arthur L. Boreman Governor of West Virginia, while Governor Pierpont of Virginia moved the archives of the restored government to Alexandria, which continued to be the rallying centre of Unionism in Virginia until the 25th of May, 1865, when the Pierpont government removed to Richmond.

In the meanwhile Federal and Confederate armies had entered the mountain region of Old Virginia and on the 7th of July, 1861, the first blood was shed in the battle at Scary creek. General Henry A. Wise, in command of the Confederate forces sent into the Kanawha valley, was victorious in this first engagement, but the Federals under General Cox being in strong force, the Confederates were in danger of being cut off and retreated to Meadow Bluff, north of Lewisburg, Greenbrier county. "The disaster at Rich mountain, the surrender of Pegram's force, and the retreat northward of Garnett's army," says A. Pollard,[239]) "had withdrawn all support from the right flank and indeed from the rear of General Wise."

The campaign of the Confederate troops in West Virginia, thus quite unsuccessful, the Legislature of Old Virginia on the 13th of May, 1862, proposed to acknowledge the formation of the new State of West Virginia, *but only within the jurisdiction of Virginia*. The waves of the conflict rolled over this attempt to bring about a reconciliation, and on December 31st, 1862, President Lincoln confirmed the resolution of the United States

239.) "The Lost Cause," by Edw. A. Pollard, p. 169. New York, 1866.

Congress *to admit West Virginia as a State in the Union*, with fifty counties of 24,000 square miles and 376,688 inhabitants.

There was a feeling of relief among the friends of the Union as from an irksome and heavy burden in the separation from the Old Dominion, the influence of which had long rested like a nightmare upon the western section; but there were still many adherents to the old Government in the new State. The Germans and German descendants were mostly Union men. For instance, in Preston county the German citizens demonstrated and agitated already in January 1861 against the secession movement.[240]) "A county convention appointed a committee of which S. W. Snider, J. Wolf, I. Startzman, G. Hildenberger, Ch. Bischoff, etc., were members, and elected delegates to the 'People's Convention,' to assemble at Richmond, Va., the 13th of February, 1861. On the same day about 150 citizens of the German settlement met, electing Ch. Hooton chairman and G. H. Schaffer secretary, and the meeting passed resolutions disapproving the course of the extreme southern States and deprecating the doctrine of secession. Other meetings were held at the Gladesville schoolhouse and at Pleasant Valley church; patriotic songs were sung and even the women expressed their attachment to the Union."

When the crisis came and war broke out, the German descendants promptly responded to the call for troops to join the Federal army. Preston county for example showed on its muster-rolls the German names of the following officers: Sam'l Snyder, Lieutenant-Colonel of the 16th West Virginia Regiment; Captain W. M. Paul, 15th West Virginia Regiment; Captain M. M. Snyder, 17th West Virginia Regiment; Captain D. A. Letzinger, 3d Regiment West Virginia Cavalry; Captain J. S. Hyde, 3d Regiment West Virginia Infantry; Captain W. A. Falkenstine, joined 3d Maryland Volunteers; Jacob Stemple, Major of Militia; Captain Peter Zinn, etc. The number of Germans from West Virginia on the Confederate side was comparatively small. The census of 1860, which does not consider the older German immigration, but simply anglicizes it, num-

240.) "History of Preston county, W. Va.," by S. T. Wiley, p. 96, Kingswood, W. Va., 1882.

bers the German population of the new State at 10,512 and states: that 869 engaged in the war. However these figures *are much too low.* According to the report of the Adjutant-General of the State for the year 1865 it appears, that West Virginia furnished in all 36,530 troops to the Federal army, and in proportion to the strength of the German element — Germans and their descendants — it must at least have supplied one-third, or 12,200 men. No official data exist to show the number, that went from West Virginia into the Confederate army. The historian Virgil A. Lewis[241]) estimates the number at about 7,000, and the author, who was an officer of General Jenkin's Cavalry Brigade, which was principally recruited in West Virginia, from his observations would appraise the Germans and German descendants among them at not more than 3,000—4,000. Of Confederate officers from West Virginia and of German descent Colonel J. S. Witcher, 3d Virginia Cavalry; Captain Wm. H. Haffner, Company E, Edgar's Battalion; Captain Wm. Keiter, who commanded a Tennessee Artillery Company; Lieutenant Hawer, Company D, 14th Virginia Cavalry; Chaplain Brillkart, 8th Virginia Cavalry; Lieutenant Henry A. Wolf, 3d Virginia Cavalry, and Captain Peter Carpenter are known. "Shriver (Schreiber?) Greys," a handful of exiles from Wheeling, only thirty strong, are mentioned in Confederate reports as a gallant band.[242])

During the late war the German districts of the new State had chiefly suffered, especially the lower Shenandoah valley and the counties on Greenbrier, New and Kanawha rivers, but by the energy and industry of the population they soon regained their former wealth. The development of West Virginia since its separation from Old Virginia is surprising and is a conciliating moment of the dismemberment of the Mother-State of the Union. Astonishing activity has characterized the construction of railroads; the Monongahela and Kanawha rivers were made navigable for steamboats; a thorough and stringent law was enacted relative to the construction and working of

---

241.) "History of West Virginia," by Virgil A. Lewis, p. 423. Philadelphia, 1889.

242.) "The Life of Stonewall Jackson," by a Virginian, p. 78. Ayres & Wade, Richmond, Va., 1863.

roads; the hidden treasures of the earth: coal, iron, lead, copper, silver, antimony, nickel, borax, soda, alum, salt, lime, petroleum, etc., have been mined and developed; the mineral springs of remarkable variety and of high reputation are rapidly attaining celebrity among the most noted and elegant watering places of the northern States and even of the Old World; agriculture and rural enterprise, fruit growing, wine making, dairying, and the production of wool are progressive and the value of real estate is constantly advancing. In consequence of the last named progress many German farmers have gained great wealth. Before, during and after the late war several Germans have been entrusted with surveying the land and with exploring and analyzing the mineral resources. The first topographical map of the two Virginias was drawn, as already mentioned, by order of Gov. Henry A. Wise, by Capt. v. Buchholtz, a native of Wuertemberg and a resident of Richmond; Oswald Heinrich, a Saxon, explored the mineral wealth of the Alleghanies by order of the Confederate government and he has drawn the first geological map of West and East Virginia; General L. Ruffner, a member of the well known Ruffner family originating from the kingdom of Hannover, was the superintendent of the celebrated Kanawha Salines,—and Dr. Heinrich Froehling, chemist of Richmond, collected and analyzed samples of ore, etc.

Among the names of the high officials of the new State, as was already stated, are several German ones, like: Arthur I. Boreman, Governor from 1863—1869; Daniel Polsley, Congressman, Judge and Lieutenant-Governor, born at Palatine, Marion county, Va., and of German descent[243]), and H. A. G. Ziegler, State School Superintendent from 1869—1870.

Previous to 1861 the public education was as much neglected in West Virginia as in East Virginia, but already in 1872 of 170,035 boys and girls of school age 85,765 were enrolled in 2,479 public schools, and in 1882—1883 the total enrollment amounted to 155,544. The German language was taught in almost every high-school and college.

246.) "Prominent Men of West Virginia," p. 231.

Another evidence of the important part the Germans have had in the settlement and development of West Virginia is furnished by the following names of counties, cities, villages, rivers, etc.: *Wetzel county*, named after the Indian hunter Ludwig Wetzel; *Wirt county*, after the lawyer and statesman B. W. Wirt; and in the counties: *Barbour:* Hackersville, Huffman, Burnersville, Galls; *Berkeley:* Martinsburg, Gerrards Town, Flaggs, Darkesville; *Boone:* Coon's (Kuhn's) Mills, Hager; *Braxton:* German, Cutlip's (Gottlieb's); *Brooke:* Steubenville, Herrmann Creek, Bowman; *Fayette:* Ansted, Nuttalburg, Leblong, Crickmer, Deitz, Frederick; *Gilmer:* DeKalb, Tanners; *Greenbrier:* Frankford, Hughart, Lewisburg; *Grant:* Lahmansville, Keyser, Kerms, Kelterman, Jordan's Run; *Hampshire:* Frankfort, Hainesville, Ruckman; *Hardy:* Moorfield (formerly Mohrfeld, Doman, Baker's Run; *Harrison:* Hessville, Hacker's Creek; *Jackson:* Wiseburg, New Geneva, Muse's Bottom, Lockhart's, Fisher's Point; *Jefferson:* Shepherdstown (formerly Mecklenburg), Harper's Ferry, Charlestown, Snyder's Mills, Lectown (founded by Jacob Hite); *Kanawha:* Winifreds, Sissonville, Copenhaver's Mills, Jordan; *Lewis:* Freemansburg, Berlin, Hacker's Creek, Fink's Creek; *Logan:* Burch; *Marion:* Palatine, Metz, Meyers, Sturm's Mill; *Marshall:* Becler's Station; *Mason:* Cologne, Grimm's Landing; *Mercer:* Duhring; *Mineral:* Frankfort, Hartmonsville, Schelle, Keysertown; *McDowell:* Jaeger; *Monongalia:* Statler's Run, Decker's Creek; *Monroe:* Lindside, Peterstown; *Morgan:* Unger's Store, Statler's Cross Road; *Nicholas:* Kessler's Cross Lanes; *Ohio:* Wheeling, Zane's Island; *Pendleton:* Macksville, Fort Seybert, Kline's Cross Roads; *Pleasants:* Schultz; *Preston:* Kyer's Run, Newburg Town, Gussman, Amblersburg, and also founded. by Germans: Kingwood, Franklin and Fellowsville; *Putnam:* Carpenter's; *Pocahontas:* Knapp's Creek; *Raleigh:* Launa; *Randolph:* Helvetia; *Ritchie:* Rusk; *Roane:* Linden, Schilling, Harper's District; *Summers:* Mohlers, Barger's Springs, Foss; *Taylor:* Westermans, Fetterman Town, Astor, Forman's Ford; *Tucker:* Hannah's Ville; *Upshur:* Hinklesville, Hinkle's Mill, Tallmansville, Lorentz, Peck's Run; *Wayne:* Krout's Creek; *Webster:* Hacker's Valley, Stroud's Knob, Boughman's; *Wetzel:* Lowman, Steinersville, Cline's Mill; *Wirt:* Shertzville;

Wood: Luebeck, Vienna, Boreman, Lockhart's Run; *Wyoming:* Saulsville. — Many other places settled by Germans or with their aid bear English names, and also in some counties not mentioned above the German element is strongly represented, as for instance the St. Clara Colony in Doodridge county.

Wheeling in Ohio county has the largest German population of the West-Virginian cities. The U. S. Census of 1890 numbers the total population of Wheeling at 34,552, and the German element at 9,612. Ohio county, in which Wheeling is located, is in a high state of cultivation and among its farming population are many Germans. The grapevine has been cultivated by them with gratifying results. On the island at Wheeling, known as "Zane's Island" and owned by the descendants of the original German owner, the pioneer of that name planted a large vineyard. C. L. Zane, one of the proprietors, claims[244]) an average product of 500 (?) gallons of wine to the acre. In Wheeling itself, which was first laid out in town-lots by Colonel Ebenezer Zane in 1793, many of the leading manufacturers and merchants are of German nationality. German churches, schools, societies, lodges and several German newspapers have been founded in that city. Education has always had ardent supporters among the German citizens. The liberal and humane tendency of progressive pedagogical science possesses many warm advocates in their circles. When in 1837 a "German Convention" at Pittsburgh, Pa., discussed the means for the maintenance of German customs and language, Virginia was represented by Andreas Schwarz of Wheeling. He was one of the vice-presidents of the convention and took a prominent part in the foundation of the first American Independent *Teachers' Seminary* at Philipsburg, Pa.[245])

After the separation of West Virginia an excellent public school system was established and an important concession was made to the Germans of Wheeling by the organization of a

244.) "U. S. Agricultural Report of 1833," p. 60. Washington, 1863.

245.) Compare "Geschichte der deutschen Schulbestrebungen in Amerika," von H. Schuricht, Seite 41—42 und 47—48, Leipzig, 1884, und "Deutsches Magazin," von H. A. Rattermann, Seite 594—613. Cincinnati, Ohio, 1866.

"*German Department in the Public Schools of the city.*" Six teachers for instruction in German were appointed,[246]) and in 1875 the German classes numbered 482 pupils, besides several German private and parochial schools with about 300 pupils. This concession to the German element was made in recognition of their patriotism displayed during the struggle for the independence of West Virginia and the war against the Confederacy. The German citizens of Wheeling organized an entirely German company, "First West Virginia Artillery," under the command of Captain Fuerst, which joined the Union forces. But in 1877 knownothing intrigues succeeded in limiting the instruction in German to the higher classes of the public schools, and consequently the list of the enrollment of the German department was reduced to 166 pupils. In the Spring of 1865 a German Educational Society for mutual instruction in educational matters was formed by Prof. C. A. Schaefer, superintendent of the German department, and everything indicated a sound spirit for the cultivation of mind among the German inhabitants. The culture of music rested, like in other American cities, almost exclusively in German hands. A lady vocalist of eminent talent lived in Wheeling about 1860: Louise Gubert, born 1837 in Philadelphia of German parents[247]); but her sonorous melodious voice and efficiency never benefitted the great world. She was content as music teacher at the De Chantal Seminary. Celebrated artists, composers and managers repeatedly tried to secure her talent to publicity; Max Strakosch offered her fifty thousand dollars for a concert tour of six months, and Rubinstein was put in ecstasy by her truly phenomenal voice; but nothing could induce her to resign her conventual privacy.

During the stirring time of war Johann G. Eberhard[248]) was chosen Pastor of the free Protestant church, which he administered until 1867. He was editor of the "Protestantische Familienblatt," the author of "Onkel Biesebrecht's deutsch-

---

246.) "U. S. Report of Commissioner of Education for 1871," p. 366. Washington, D. C., 1872.

247.) "Der deutsche Pionier," 14. Jahrgang, Seite 259–261. Cincinnati, Ohio.

248.) "Deutsch in Amerika," by Dr. G. A. Zimmermann, p. 229. Chicago, 1894.

amerik. Volkserzählungen" and published a number of pretty poems.

Only once, as mentioned previously, a small number of German fanatics, who dreamed of Germanizing America, endangered the friendly relations of the Anglo and German elements of the city. In September 1852 a "Congress of German Revolutionists" assembled at Wheeling[249]) and issued a program for the formation of a "Universal Republic." The attendance was very small, only sixteen delegates participating, of whom only three were German inhabitants of Wheeling; but this so-called Congress created an angry feeling among the Anglo-Americans, exciting suspicions, and gave, as stated before, an impulse to the unjust and hateful knownothing movement which disturbed the harmony of Virginia from 1854 to 1856.

Next to Wheeling, Martinsburg in Berkeley county and Parkersburg in Wood county have many German inhabitants. The influence of the German element of *Parkersburg* is demonstrated by the appointment of Prof. W. M. Strauss to the office of superintendent of the public schools.[250]) *Martinsburg* was made a town by legislative enactment in October 1778, on the lands of a German: General Adam Stephan, anglicized to Stephen or Stevens, and its first inhabitants were Pennsylvania-Germans, Germans and Dutch. At present [251]) the German element amounts to about one-fourth of the population, numbering in 1880 in round figures 8000 inhabitants. The descendants of several of the German pioneers are still residents of the town, as the families Seibert, Noll, Rentsch, Kuschwa, Doll, Diefendoerfer, Schaefer, Klein, Schmal (now Small), Bentz, Martin, Blessing, Homrich, Schobe, etc. Most of them are farmers, but some of them are engaged in commercial and industrial pursuits and all are esteemed as good citizens.

Shortly after the foundation of Martinsburg a Lutheran

249.) "Das deutsche Element in den Ver. Staaten," von Gustav Koerner, Seite 122. Cincinnati, Ohio, 1880.

250.) "U. S. Educational Report of 1888—1889," Vol. I, p. 274.

251.) Correspondence of Mr. C. P. Matthaei at Martinsburg, W. Va.

and Reformed church were built, but the divine service was conducted in English. The first German church was erected in 1858 by the influence of Rev. Cast, a native of Baden; but during the late war it was burned down (1863.) After the war Rev. Prof. Gehrhardt of Lebanon, Pa., became pastor of the German community and he was also elected superintendent of the public schools. In the year 1868 a German private school, a Turnverein and a German lodge were organized, but at present they only have a bare existence.

Charlestown, the county-seat of Jefferson county, gained historic fame by the execution of John Brown; it is also one of the early German settlements in Shenandoah valley. A native of Germany, Mr. Gustav Braun, was for years, up to 1897, Mayor of the town.

Charleston, in Kanawha county, now the capital of West Virginia, has 7,500 inhabitants and several of its prominent merchants and manufacturers are Germans.

The new State of West Virginia has rapidly increased in population and wealth. In 1870 the population amounted to 442,014 inhabitants, in 1880 to 618,457 and in 1890 to 762,794, and the German immigration can claim to have added largely to this progress.

CHAPTER XV.

German Immigration and Rural Life in Virginia After the War.

MORE than a quarter of a century has elapsed since the army of Northern Virginia grounded their arms at Appomattox Court House and the soldiers returned to the plough and harrow to restitute the devastated land. The progress of building up the waste places however has been slow. During the war farming was brought to a partial standstill and for some years thereafter it was in a state of extreme depression. The determination and physical endurance of the planters and the former slave-owners appeared seriously broken; only in those sections of the State which were settled by Germans, especially the Valley, the farmers went to work with renewed energy and enterprise. The Anglo-American land-owners, disheartened and in a state of dejection, were almost helpless. Burdened with debt, without money to pay wages or taxes, their houses, farm implements and stock reduced or demolished; unaccustomed to work and also too proud to sell a part of their large estates in order to procure the necessary means for repairs and improvements, no progress in tilling the soil was made and their fields and meadows turned into a state of wilderness. Very singular circumstances resulted. The formerly wealthy slave- and land-owners were drifting into poverty, the amount of unpaid taxes was increased to exorbitant amounts, and finally the large estates of many were sued by the executive officers and offered at public sale. Very frequently no purchaser able to pay appeared, and consequently the indebted estates were left in the hands of the old owner. The lands were then taxed to the utmost capacity of production and their fertility was rapidly exhausted, for the soil was not fertilized, but scantily tilled; there was no change of seed and the same crops were grown successively year after year. The forests were laid waste without consideration, but only in order to make money for the most urgent needs. Similar uncongenial conditions existed among the small Anglo-American farmers. Slavery always and everywhere degrades labor; this degradation is positive in the South. The small white farmers have adopted during the time of slavery the example of the rich planters: to look upon manual labor *as disgracing a "white gentleman."* They are possessed of presumption which strongly contrasts with their poverty and their want of learning. The wife of a neighbor of the author once complained to a lady-relation of his: "You cannot imagine how poor we are!" — "Why," replied the lady, "you have three grown daughters and four strong boys able to work, who can hire out. Female and male help are much in demand and high wages are offered."—"How can you propose that we shall become servants," she was interrupted by one of the daughters, "if we should work for other people, *we would no more be received in society.*" —This occurrence illustrates the notions prevalent among this class of Virginian farmers. The "society" of which the girl spoke, consists of people just as presumptuous and as poor and ignorant as herself; people who are even called by the negroes with disregard: "poor white trash."—Labor for a fair remuneration, whether mental or physical, should be the glory of all Virginians, as it is among the German-Virginians. There is true dignity in labor, especially in the tilling of the soil; there is also success in labor, as is demonstrated by many German-Virginian farms; but it has been distasteful to the Anglo-Virginian element and considered degrading by them. The result has been violation of wise economy and the State has been retarded in its progress. Another peculiar symptom is, that after the war many of the old masters became the debtors of their former slaves. They frequently lacked the ready money to pay the labor of the blacks; the claims of the latter accumulated and finally the negro received in payment a tract of land or some cattle. In this way negroes came to be the present neighbors of their former masters.

It would however be unjust to hold the Virginian people alone responsible that the wealth and prosperity of the State are slowly augmenting. After the war the Virginians, with but few exceptions, were zealous to reestablish good relations with the victorious Union. The fourteenth Amendment to the Constitution of the United States, abolishing slavery and giving citizen-rights to all persons born in the Republic, was ratified by the required majority, and General Grant, who was sent to Virginia to investigate the feeling of the people toward the Union Government, stated in his report: "That the inhabitants had submitted to the results of the late war and that the two chief differences — secession and emancipation of the slaves — had been definitely disposed of." The North did not however assist, as had been hoped, to heal the bleeding wounds and to make the southern land again a source of national wealth.

"When the Confederacy fell," says Edw. Ingle in his book, "Southern Sidelights," "the whites of the South were relieved of an enormous incubus — slavery — but were at the same time deprived of the means to turn the relief to their immediate advantage. The blacks had freedom without the capacity to undertake the responsibility of freedom, and presently were, through partisan politics, surrounded by influences that would, for a generation at least, stand in the way of their development."

The Northerners boast of the forbearance and clemency towards the conquered "rebels," but on the other hand it cannot be denied, that the Government at Washington has with partiality considered the Eastern and Western lands and that the South was the neglected drudge of the Union. If a proportionate share of the enormous sums which have been spent to develop the Northwest had been invested in the South; if the spirit of enterprise, which constructed a network of railroads in the unpopulated prairies, would have been induced to restore and enlarge the roads of travel and traffic in the Southern States; and if efforts had been made to direct the stream of an industrious and wealthy immigration to the South as well as to the West, the traces of imperfect negro labor and poor tillage and of all the devastations of the war would have disappeared years ago. Beladen Virginia was left to herself; she could not make liberal venture to attract immigration of intelligent white laborers. In 1866 the Legislature passed an act to encourage and increase immigration to Virginia; a Board of Immigration was organized and General G. Tochmann and Mr. B. Barbour were appointed agents of immigration to Germany and England, *but without any obligation on the part of the State to pay the expenses.* Only insignificant results could be expected of such illiberal policy. Colonel Frank Schaller [252]) was authorized by General Tochmann to travel to Germany and to visit first his native State of Saxony, to draw immigrants to the Old Dominion. But the success was very trifling. However full credit must be given General Tochmann for his endeavors and good will. He was a native of Poland and had participated in the campaigns of 1830 and 1831 as major in the Polish army. During the period of 1832 to 1834 Tochmann was vice-president of the Polish Revolutionary Committee at Avignon in France, and in 1837 he came to America and visited the principal cities to awake sympathy for his suppressed fatherland. In 1845 he was admitted to the bar as a lawyer and since 1852 he settled in Virginia, where he lived and associated principally with the Germans. Henry G. Miller of Richmond was his secretary. After the failure as agent of immigration he left the State in disgust.

During the summer of 1868 Rev. I. A. Reichenbach came to Richmond, Va., with the intention to organize German colonies in the South. On July 21st a public meeting was arranged in front of the City Hall to hear the propositions of the pastor, and a committee was elected to examine his plan. The committee consisted of the following highly respected citizens: Peple, Hoffbauer, Tiedemann, Gimmi, Leybrock, Dr. Strecker and Dr. Grebe. But the project was soon abandoned for want of confidence in the propositions and the person of the reverend.

German settlements promising good results were started in the counties Chesterfield, Prince George, Louisa, Lunenburg and Mecklenburg. Wm. Grossmann of Petersburg, Va., a native

252.) "Virginische Staatszeitung," January 25th, 1868. B. Hassel, Richmond, Va.

of Silesia, and in the old country professor at a German college, but now real-estate agent, has done very much to develop the German settlement at Port Walthall in Dinwiddie county, near the city of Petersburg. In Chesterfield county at Granite Station, not far from the city of Manchester, is a prosperous settlement of German Catholics. In Lunenburg[253]) Ch. Rickers and O. Jansen from Schleswig-Holstein and A. and G. Petzold from Saxony are successful farmers, and the same may be said of E. Williams (Wilhelm?) of Prussia, in Prince George county. In the southwestern part of Louisa county in 1868 two German villages, Frederickshall and Buckner, stations on the C. & O. R. R., were started by Heselenius, Frosh, Mauker, Lieb, Goering, Stolz, Schrader, Lorey and others. Some of these settlers have removed to other parts of the country, but the majority still remain and are doing well. In the northwestern corner of the same county the author purchased in 1886 a farm and planted a large vineyard, known as "Idlewild Vineyards." The reports of the State Commissioner of Agriculture mention, that in 1888 to 1892 several Pennsylvania-Germans came to Botetourt. Into Albemarle and Orange Germans immigrated from Illinois, Wisconsin, Dakota, Nebraska and Ohio; in Prince George a number of Germans from Russia and Bohemia purchased farms, and in Goochland many families from the northeastern States, and among them some Germans, settled since the war and are well pleased. Other official documents show that the counties Henry, Norfolk, Warwick, Roanoke, Alleghany and Taxwell increased in population from 126 to 195 per cent. and that a large number of the newcomers are Germans. The old German settlements on Opequan, Shenandoah, Rapidan, Rappahannock, Dan, New and Roanoke rivers also received some additions from the Northeast and direct from Germany. The status of Virginia for the year 1870 says (page 178): "Of the foreign population of Virginia Ireland furnished nearly one-half, *Germany one-third*, England one-sixth and Scotland one-twentieth. Over 49 per cent. of the foreign-born population were found in tidewater, where they are located in the seaport cities. Over 29 per cent. lived in the middle country and nearly 8 per cent. in Piedmont, while the Valley had over 11 per cent."

253.) Correspondence of Mr. Wm. Groszmann, Petersburg, Va.

During the last two decades there was a slight increase in immigration, owing to efforts made by some of the railroad companies. They had pamphlets printed explaining the advantages in Virginia for capital and labor, and these papers were liberally distributed. The conclusion had gained ground that it be better to seek immigrants from other States of the Union, especially from the Northwest, rather than to repeat the efforts to invite a stream of promiscuous population from abroad, — and immigration from the northwestern States has actually set in. The German element being very strong in the West, it is also well represented among these newcomers. All of these are desirous to escape the rigorous winters of the inhospitable western climate; to get nearer to the markets and to again enjoy society and those home-like comforts which charm life and which are wanting upon the borders of civilization. Immigrants going to the cities and into some professional or mercantile occupation did not succeed, on an average, as well as those engaged in farming. The statistics show that something like 90 per cent. of all those who go into mercantile pursuits in the United States either become bankrupt or have to make arrangements with their creditors, while of the remaining 10 per cent. not more than half succeed in making more than a bare living.[254])

Among the number of successful merchants in Virginia the Germans are largely represented. Virginia is also a good field for German medical men speaking the English language. German musicians are predominating and German mechanics are much in demand; but surest of success, we repeat, are those engaging in farming. They at least secure a good livelihood; they produce on their farms sufficient of nearly all the necessaries of life and many of its luxuries, and above all the farmer *if not rich, is at least independent.* It is surprising that the direct immigration of farmers from Germany is not taking larger proportions. The settler will find in Virginia a lovely climate, neither too hot in summer nor too cold in winter, for regular work all the year round. Its proximity to the ocean on the

254) "Virginia;" a Synopsis published by the State Board of Agriculture, p. 81, Richmond, Va., 1889.

East and the range of mountains on the West modify the climate and make it most healthful, enjoyable and suited for outdoor life. The farms, and in many cases with dwellings and outhouses, can be bought at very low prices and will, with intelligent working and proper manuring, produce as good crops as anywhere else. The taxes on the lands are light and the produce can be sold readily. Why then does the great mass of Germans seek the far West in preference to Virginia? At the annual meeting of the State Board of Agriculture on October 31st, 1888, the Committee on Immigration made the following statement in its report[255]): "Virginia needs population; it needs more good men, women and children. It has thousands of acres of broad, fertile, unoccupied lands awaiting the tiller's toil; it has thousands of acres of timber awaiting the woodman's axe and thousands of veins of most valuable ore and coal, only awaiting capital." — In fact every Virginian asserts: "What we want is good working people." But in truth it is not foreign labor, but *foreign money* they are looking for; and the selfish and unkind tendency is felt and keeps immigrants and especially the sensitive Germans away. A correspondence in "Der Sueden,"[256]) written by a highly respected German citizen of Charlottesville, Va., gives a good illustration of this assertion. The correspondent wrote: "It is easily explained why Virginians give preference to English immigration. In the period from 1870 to 1876 a large number of Englishmen came to Albemarle, Orange and Nelson counties and bought farms. Most of these newcomers were young gentlemen from London and other large cities in England and possessed little or no experience in farming. They generally paid one-third cash of the price of their lands and, anticipating large profits, they agreed to settle the balance in one, two or three years. They invested the balance in costly improvements on their farms and when the restitute payments became due, there was in many cases no money on hand, and the former owners were well pleased to foreclose the indebted property; for they received their farms back with costly improvements made upon them

255) "Der Sueden," Jahrgang I, p. 60, No. 6. Richmond, Va., Feb. 8th, 1891.

256.) "Virginia," a Synopsis published by the State Board of Agriculture, p. 111. Richmond, Va., 1889.

and gained besides the money already paid. With few exceptions the unfortunate Englishmen returned to England, while the German settlers, who came at the same time, still remain here and have paid for and improved their farms. The former had come with the idea to lead the life of English country gentlemen, but the latter were determined to work and persevere. The sales made to the English thus proved more profitable to the Virginians than those made to Germans, whom they envy on account of their success." — The opinion expressed in this correspondence appears severe, but is correct. However a new era is at hand and it brings a change of people and conditions. The old Virginian planters, who would rather starve than sell an acre of their neglected and indebted lands to a hard-working foreigner, are gradually dying out and their heirs are less determined not to part with some of their surplus lands. Besides, the example given by the foreigners already settled in the State, is now stimulating the native element to renewed efforts and revives their dormant energy.

There are other causes that impede German immigration and particularly that of German laborers. Since the first settlement of the colony tobacco has been considered one of the staples of Virginia, but the Germans have not become acquainted to any extent with its cultivation here. This is a surprising fact, as the German farmers in other countries — in southern Germany and in the German colonies in Africa — are very successful in its growth, and as the export of Virginian leaf principally rests in German hands. There is but one explanation for the small part they take in cultivating the plant and that is, that formerly the work in the tobacco-fields was exclusively done by negro slaves, and that the Germans did not desire to concur with them; while at the present time farm labor is scarce and wages much too high compared with the prices of farm products, tobacco included. The competition of the former slaves is the main cause in keeping white laborers at a distance, combined with the methods of the planters to treat them as they do their colored hands. We are not disposed to be placed on the same level as negroes, to be fed like them on corn-bread and bacon and to work for low negro-wages. These are the reasons given by white laboring men for their antipathy towards the South. The negroes know very well that the farmers depend on their labor, and it pleases them to let the white folks feel *that they are now independent, free citizens, who can work or be lazy, just as they like.* Very frequently the farmers are left deserted when help is most needed; the crops cannot be gathered in time and consequently suffer a partial or complete loss. "The negro is gregarious,"[257]) says the standing committee of the State Board of Agriculture, "and prefers gang work on a railroad, or as a stevedore, or in a tobacco factory, rather than the quiet, monotonous labor of the farm." This unreliability of the colored farm-hands explains why at present the German farmers do not grow tobacco, and at the same time why the German immigration is not as numerous as desired.

Grape culture is most successfully carried on by Germans. In the vicinity of Charlottesville and Cobham, Albemarle and Louisa counties; near Front Royal in Warren county; near Afton in Nelson county; at Haymarket in Prince William county; around Richmond in Henrico county and also in the counties Fairfax, Madison, Goochland, Appomattox, Brunswick, Greenville, Hanover, Lunenburg, Middlesex, Spottsylvania and Surrey vineyards have been planted by Germans or with the aid of German vintagers who are experienced in viticulture. The first large and prosperous vineyard was planted at the suggestion of an old Swiss, Sol. Seiler, in 1866 at Pen Park near Charlottesville by Wilhelm Hotopp.[258]) Mr. Hotopp was born at Celle in Hannover and came to America when a boy of eighteen years. He was for years a successful manufacturer in New Jersey, settled in Virginia after the conclusion of the Civil War and purchased the farm "Pen Park" near Charlottesville, once owned by the well-known statesman B. William Wirth. There he planted his vineyard, and after years of prosperity he died May 4th, 1898.

257.) "Report of the State Board of Agriculture of Va,," p. 135. Rich., Va., 1838,

258.) "Albemarle," by W. H. Scamon, p. 55, Charlottesville, Va,, 1888,

Several Germans, who had settled in Albemarle, eagerly grasping for something more remunerative than corn, oats or tobacco, planted vineyards, and Englishmen and Americans followed soon after. In 1888 about three thousand acres had already been planted in Albemarle county. In the fall of 1870 Mr. Hotopp began to make his grapes into wine — red and white, — and finding a ready sale, some other growers in the vicinity of Charlottesville in 1873 resolved on cooperation and formed the "Monticello Wine Company" under the successful management of Mr. Adolph Russow, a native of Holstein. Other German establishments are: F. Peters' Mill Parks Wine Company at Haymarket, Prince William county; Idlewild Vineyards of H. Schuricht & Son, near Cobham in Louisa county, and Fritz Baier, Nelson county. Their wines are of the very best.

In fact the Germans are known to be successful in every branch of farming. They are excellent stock raisers; the German dairies are remarkable for their neatness, and their gardens and orchards are kept clean of weeds and in model order.

At a mass-meeting of prominent farmers and truckers at Norfolk, Va., on February 21st, 1889, for the purpose of securing a sub-experimental station for Eastern Virginia[259]), a committee of eighteen was elected and among them we meet with the following German names: J. A. Whetsel (Wetzel?) James Wagner, C. Miller, Walter Jordan, A. C. Herbert, etc. And only lately the present Governor, J. H. Tyler, has paid a flattering compliment to the German-Virginian farmers of the Valley by the appointment of Mr. George W. Koiner of Augusta county to be Commissioner of Agriculture. To a "Dispatch" reporter[260]) the Governor remarked:

"I do not think I could have gone to a more appropriate section of the State for a Commissioner of Agriculture than the Great Valley of Virginia and the county of Au-

259.) Report of the State Board of Agriculture of Va., p. 39. Richmond, Va., 1888

260.) "Weekly Dispatch," Richmond, Va., Dec. 6th, 1898.

gusta. I have been on the splendidly-tilled farm of Mr. Koiner. I was farmer enough to see he knew his business. He will get all the practical good possible out of the department."

George W. Koiner, a member of the well-known Koiner family, is a little upwards of forty years of age — a live, energetic, up-to-date farmer. He represented Augusta county in the House of Delegates for two terms.

Absalom Koiner of Fisherville, Augusta county, is another member of the distinguished Koiner family. He was for several years a member of the State Board of Agriculture and in 1888 president of this body.[261])

Dr. W. H. Ruffner, the first State Superintendent of Public Education in Virginia, wrote to the author of this history, referring especially to the Germans in the Valley: "There are and have been a great many interesting and some important characters among the Germans of Shenandoah and Rockingham, and much worthy of notice in their way. They are certainly the thriftiest people now in Virginia and they are the leaders in popular education. They have in fact a great future before them."

In the neighborhood of Richmond the farms of the late Major Lewis Ginter and C. L. Miller are known as model stock farms.

In conclusion it may be said, that the frugal and industrious German farmer may today prosper here as well as did the German pioneer who settled in Virginia a century and a half ago.

261.) "Report of the State Board of Agriculture," pp. 1 and 5, Richmond, Va., 1888.

CHAPTER XVI.

THE GERMAN CITIZENS OF RICHMOND AFTER THE WAR.

THE German population of Richmond was already previous to the war the nucleus of the entire German element of the State, and it has ever since retained the leadership. After the fall of the Confederacy the German merchants and mechanics were in a state of numbness, the first effect of forlorn hopes and destructive blows. Many had lost all and momentarily despaired of future prosperity, but very soon they roused themselves and by diligence, enterprise and perseverance they gained new wealth. They lost no time in repining, but addressed themselves immediately to the work of rebuilding upon the ruins, and in their success made a record that is unparalleled. The task before them was a herculean one, but they accomplished it in an incredibly short time. Several of those who left Virginia at the outbreak of hostilities returned. After the great victories of the German armies in Austria and France in 1866, 1870 and 1871; upon the establishment of the North German Confederation, and most of all by the foundation of the powerful German Empire, the Germans and German-Virginians were inspired with feelings of self-consciousness and pride and with an admiration of their people and Fatherland heretofore unknown. This feeling of national self-respect soon found expression in a more active participation in political affairs. However this newly aroused enthusiastic admiration of the dear old Fatherland possessed nothing anti-American, but on the contrary instigated only to advance the condition of Virginia with truly German loyalty and piety.

The devotion of the Germans to the State was manifest during the struggle for readmission to the Union. The Republican party desired to control the vote of Virginia with the militia, the apparatus of the State government, and the vote of the freed men, and for this purpose they tried to impede the right of election of the white democratic citizens. In other words, the question was put: "If the intelligence and wealth. or the organized carpet-bagger and African ignorance should control the State?" and the German voters held the decisive vote.

No doubt this was cause for anxiety; the unequal distribution of illiterates throughout the Union might be a source of national peril. The following table, compiled from the census of 1870, will sufficiently disclose this fact:

Voting population of the United States . . .	7,623,000
" " " former slave States .	2,775,000
Illiterate male adults in United States . . .	1,580,000
" " former slave States . .	1,123,000
Per cent. illiterate voters in U. S. to entire vote,	20
" " " slave States . . .	45
" " " States not slave . .	9
" " " South Carolina . .	59
Illiterate voters in Southern States (white) . .	304,000
" " " " (colored) .	819,000

This table will make apparent that forty-five per cent. of the voters of the Southern States were unable to read their ballots and that the illiterate vote involved great danger. It threatened the white population of the South with an unbearable terrorism of ignorance.

The majority of the German citizens of Richmond counted to the moderate Democrats. They had accepted the final result of the war and faithfully submitted to the laws of the Union. Their leader was Prof. G. A. Peple. A comparatively small number of Germans was connected with the Republicans and their leader was Hermann L. Wiegand.

On June 5th, 1868, a *German mass-meeting* was held at Dueringer's Park to discuss the new Constitution of the State and the elections on hand. Prof. Peple addressed the assemblage and several resolutions were adopted, condemning *the military rule since 1864 and the unlimited favors bestowed on the negro element.* Although *not one in the large assembly was an advocate of slavery, it was resolved:*

"We are proud to be of German descent and we reject with indignation as an insult to be placed on equal political and social footing with the negroes just extracted from the mire of slavery. We consider it as sacrificing the nation, to force the white population of the South under the rule of a half-civilized and inferior race."

This resolution was *unanimously* adopted; even the German Republicans voted for it. All of them adhered to the opinion of the "Declaration of Independence," which is the Magna Charta of American liberty, stating: "That all men are created equal; that they are endowed by the Creator with certain inalienable rights; that among these are life, liberty and pursuit of happiness." But they considered *as a crime against civilization* to expose them to the danger of negro rule and they predicted that negro suffrage would break down American reverence for the ballot-box and lead to bribery and fraud in conducting elections. This peril was also recognized by Anglo-Americans and even by leaders of the Republican party. It was clearly apparent to the mind of General Grant, when he recommended: "to exclude all illiterates from the right of suffrage by constitutional amendment." President Hayes also revealed his conviction of the danger in several of his messages to Congress.

The result of the elections in 1868 was, in consequence of the German vote, a decided victory for the democratic candidates. Mr. Lovenstein was elected member of the Legislature, — after Prof. Peple had declined to be a candidate, — and until his death he represented the district either in the House of Delegates or in the Senate. The Germans also voted against the Clause 4, Sect. 1, Art. 3, and against Sect.

6, Art. 3, "test oath" or "iron oath," as it was called, by which those should be deprived of the right to vote, who had served in the Confederate army, or who had in any way, *even only by business transactions*, been connected with the Confederate government.

The German citizens of Richmond again took a very active part in the elections of 1870. Two Germans were candidates for the office of Commissioner of Revenue: Isaac Hutzler and Julius Fischer, and the latter was elected by a majority of twenty-five votes. A. Bodecker represented the city in the Legislature and within the last twenty-five years the following German-Virginians were members of the Board of Aldermen and City Council: Laube, Lohman, Louis Wagner, A. Bodecker, Eduard Euker, H. Metzger, F. Brauer, C. E. Brauer, G. Klein, Christian Zimmer, Chris. Thon, O. Grasser, H. Bodecker, Spangenberg, Lauer, Strauss, Charles H. Philips, S. L. Bloomberg, Jos. Wallerstein, Wm. Zimmermann and F. C. Ebel. In 1894 Ch. Philips was chosen city treasurer and he was reelected without opposition in 1897.

The Germans and German descendants have also greatly assisted in the establishment and administration of the public schools. The good results of these efforts are shown by the fact, that in 1860, before the outbreak of the war, the total number of pupils in all the schools of the State was only 67,024,[262]) but in 1895—1896 the pupils enrolled in the public schools alone had increased to 360,133.[263]) *Dr. Wm. H. Ruffner* was elected the first State Superintendent of Public Instruction in 1870 and he continued in this important office for twelve years. In reply to an inquiry of the author in regard to his descent, he answered: "I take pleasure in saying that my father was of pure German stock, though American born.[264]) And his son, A. H. Ruffner, wrote: "The first Ruffner ancestor who came to America, is

262.) International Exhibition 1876, by Francis A. Walker, p 90. J. B. Lippincott & Co., Phila., 1878.

263.) Report of the Commissioner of Education, 1895—1896, Vol. I, p. lxi. Washington, 1897.

264.) Correspondence of Dr. W. H. Ruffner, Lexington, Va., October 2, 1890.

said by our family history to have been the son of a German baron, who lived in Hanover, Germany. He came to Virginia about one hundred and fifty years ago and owned a large tract of land on the Hawksbill creek near Luray. Father is the author of the Virginia School Law. Geology is now his profession. He is the son of Dr. Henry Ruffner, for many years President of Washington and Lee University in Lexington. Father has always taken great interest in Germans and Germany, so much so that his family often laughs and tells him, that he shows himself a true son of the Fatherland."[265]) Dr. W. H. Ruffner was born at Lexington and received his excellent scientific education at Washington and Lee University. He afterwards studied theology at the Union and Princeton Seminary and for some years officiated as preacher in Philadelphia. Dr. Ruffner wrote several essays on social and political questions and after 1870 devoted himself to education. By numerous lectures and articles published in the newspapers he materially aided to arouse the interest of the public for public instruction. Dr. Ruffner was editor of the "Educational Journal of Virginia" and associate editor of the "New England Journal of Education." The Ruffner family certainly numbers among the most prominent of the State. We copy from the U. S. Educational Report of 1895—1896, Vol. I, page 270, the following right creditable, well deserved and highly interesting statements:

"While this college (the Washington and Lee University) never contributed to the cause of popular education, yet through its president, Dr. Henry Ruffner, it made *a most remarkable protest against the institution of slavery*, that defied the unanimity of sentiment that prevailed before the Civil War. His son, Dr. William H. Ruffner, was the first State Superintendent of Education of Virginia; still *the most notable southern educator* of late enlisted in the cause of the people's school, the Horace Mann of the South."

The introduction of German instruction into the public schools of Richmond has repeatedly been agitated, but not suc-

265.) Correspondence of A. H. Ruffner, Lexington, Va., October 3, 1890.

cessfully. German is only taught in the High School, but not in the Grammar or lower grades. The German press of Richmond has repeatedly urged its introduction in the lower grades, where it would benefit the mass of the pupils. An excellent article published in "Der Richmond Patriot," July 23d, 1869, entitled "The Public Schools and the Germans," (Die öffentlichen Schulen und die Deutschen), and signed Dr. A. S. B., deserves special comment. In the fall of 1886 the author of this history lectured in "Saengerhall" under the auspices of the Gesangverein "Virginia," and advocated the support of the National German-American Teachers' Seminary at Milwaukee, Wisconsin, recommending also the organization of an *Educational Association*, the aim of which should be the introduction of German instruction into the public schools; the support of German private and parochial schools and the establishment of German Kindergartens. "The more you do to keep alive the German spirit, the more inviting our State will be to German immigrants; they will feel at home where their native tongue is spoken," he argued.[266]) A committee composed of Hermann Schmidt, Henry Wenzel, G. A. Peple, H. C. Boschen, H. L. Wiegand, R. Wendenburg and B. Heinrich was appointed and authorized to take action, but nothing was achieved.

Again, in his oration at the German-Day celebration, 1896, the same orator advocated[267]): "Not to cultivate unfair German notions, but to enable German parents to educate their children with the assistance of the mother tongue, which they naturally command better than any other idiom; that they may become intelligent and faithful Americans! For this noble aim we must not cease to demand: that the German language be taught in our public schools wherever the German element is sufficiently numerous to justify this measure, as for instance in our Richmond. Our Anglo-American fellow-citizens must take into consideration *how helpless their wives would be* in their educational task, if left to influence the mind and heart of their children only through the medium of a foreign language."

266.) "Virginische Staats Gazette," Richmond, Va., Dec. 22, 1886

267.) "The Times," Richmond, Va., September 16, 1896.

German church life has prospered in the city of Richmond during the last three decades, and the statement of the New York historian, Anton Eickhoff[268]): "In the German church in Richmond the English language is used," is unfounded. There are also, instead of one German church, two Protestant and one Catholic church, and also a synagogue of German Israelites in the city; and the statutes of the *German Evangelical St. Johannis Community* expressly state:

"§ 5. In all the regular divine services on Sundays and holidays, in the meetings of the community and the presbitery, in all records and the parish register, the German language *shall be exclusively used.*"[269])

Reverend Hoyer, previously mentioned in Chapter XII, was succeeded in office as pastor of this congregation by Reverends Schwarz, Blenner, W. Ide, Dr. Carl Scholz, Eduard Huber, R. A. John and, since 1886, Dr. Paul L. Menzel. During the pastorate of Rev. Huber the new church building corner Eighth and Marshall streets was erected and the community joined the German Evangelical Synod of North America. About three hundred families are embraced in this community. A school was established and children of all creeds admitted. During tne pastorate of Rev. John a pretty schoolhouse was built on Eighth street, between Broad and Marshall. The number of pupils exceeded one hundred, and a German teacher, assisted by two lady associates, was employed; but in 1888, on account of ill-luck with the teachers and discord among the members of the community, the school was discontinued. In place of it a Saturday school, principally for tuition in German and singing, was instituted, which is attended by about sixty pupils, instructed by the pastor. A Sunday School is also connected with the church and is frequented by about three hundred pupils. An association of the ladies of the church, the "Frauen-Verein," has contributed large sums of money for charitable purposes and about twelve thousand dollars for expenses of the parish and the payment of building debts. Another association

268.) "In der Neuen Heimath," von A. Eickhoff, p. 203. New York, 1884.

269.) Statuten der Deutschen St. Johannis Gemeinde zu Richmond, 1889.

of young ladies, "Der Tabea Verein," has like purposes for its object and its contributions have amounted to about four thousand dollars. The reestablishment of the day school is not altogether abandoned. § 69 of the statutes of 1889 says: "to maintain and to cultivate the German language and German customs, to educate the youths to become respectable members of the community and to make secure thereby its continued existence, a day school shall be kept if possible." A great honor was conferred upon this community and its pastor in 1898. The Emperor of Germany invited the Evangelical Synod of North America to designate one of its members to participate in the consecration of the Protestant church (Erlöser-Kirche) at Jerusalem, as his Majesty's guest. The Synod elected Dr. Paul L. Menzel delegate.

The German Evangelical Lutheran Bethlehem Community has also prospered. The Reverends L. Lochmer and F. Dreyer officiated within the last decades and at present Rev. C. I. Oelschlager is pastor. The new church building, Sixth street near Clay, was finished in 1868 and the old church adjoining the new building was converted into a schoolhouse. Previous to the opening of the public schools the enrollment was from eighty to one hundred pupils, but since then it has decreased to thirty or forty. The instruction is given by the pastor and a lady teacher. In 1889 a Sunday school was organized, which is visited by eighty or ninety pupils. A ladies' association (Frauen-Verein) has contributed large sums for charitable works and the support of the parish, and in conjunction with the community at large it furnishes the means for the theological and pedagogical education of one of the members' sons of the community. Two pastors and two teachers educated at the expense of the association and church are already in office. *Rev. Christian Jonathan Oelschlager*, the present pastor, is a German-American. His parents came from Wuertemberg and he was born 1849 in Pennsylvania; he graduated at Columbus, Ohio, and holds his present office since 1883.

St. Mary's (Marien) German Catholic Community, to which nearly all the German Catholics of Richmond and the adjoining counties belong, numbers[270]) 225 families with a total membership of 1200. To these are to be added eight families at Buckner's Station, Louisa county, who have a pretty chapel of their own and are visited every month by one of the fathers of St. Mary's church. *Rev. Willibald Baumgartner*, a native of Bavaria, is the Pastor Prior. The following schools are connected with St. Mary's church: Boys' Highschool, Rev. F. Edward Meyer, O. S. B. Principal, 16 pupils; Boys' Parish School, I. Section, Prof. C. F. Mutter, teacher, 33 pupils; II. Section, 40 pupils; Girls' Parish School, I. Section, 58 pupils; II. Section, 22 pupils; Girls' Highschool, 120 pupils. The schools for girls are managed by sisters of St. Mary's Benedictine Institute under the supervision of the pastor. Another school connected with St. Mary's church is kept in Chesterfield county, near Granite Station. A lady teacher is in charge of it and the pupils number twenty. The total enrollment of the various schools amounted at the close of 1890 to 309. The pupils, assisted by an excellent choir under the leadership of Prof. Mutter, perform the ecclesiastical singing in German, English and Latin. The following German Catholic societies are also connected with the church:[271])

St. Joseph's Beneficent Society (Unterstützungs-Verein) 101 members.

St. Benedict's Society (Unterstützungs-Verein) 60 members.

St. Mary's Social and Beneficent Society, 102 members.

St. Anna Ladies' Society (Frauenverein) 210 members.

Society of the Living Rosary (Verein des lebendigen Rosenkranzes) 225 members.

St. Mary's Sodality for Young Men and Ladies, 240 members.

Society for the Poor of St. Mary's church.

The voluntary subscription is very liberal and is dispensed among the poor by the officials of the society. St. Mary's church, Priory and school buildings are located corner Fourth and E. Marshall streets.

270.) "Der Sueden," I, No. 3, p. 10, January 1891. Richmond, Va.

271.) "Der Sueden," I, No. 5, p. 11, February 1891. Richmond, Va.

The Beth Ahaba Synagogue, Eleventh street between Marshall and Clay, is one of the prettiest buildings in the city. The membership is constantly increasing. The Rabbis who succeeded Rev. M. G. Michelbacher, already mentioned, are Wechsler, Dettelheim, Hoffmann, Dr. Abraham Harris, born in England by German parents, and at present Ed. N. Calish. Moses Millhiser was president of this German-Jewish community ever since its organization to his death in 1892, and Hon. Wm. Lovenstein was for years its secretary. The present officers are: Julius Strauss, president; Charles Hutzler, vice-president; Henry S. Hutzler, secretary; L. Z. Morris, treasurer; Isaac Held, financial secretary; Greentree, sexton. Board of Managers: Messrs. E. Gerst, Isaac Strauss, E. Bottigheimer, I. Thalhimer, E. Raab, and Sol. Bloomberg. With the synagogue is connected "*The Society of the Home for the Enfeebled by Age and for the Sick*," which has over 300 members. Henry S. Hutzler is president of this charitable institution. The "*Hebrew Benevolent Association of Richmond*" elected the following officers: President, S. Stern; Vice-President, B. Jacob; Secretary, H. E. Hirshberg; Treasurer, Harry Marks. The "*Congregation Keneseth Israel*," Rev. Dr. L. Harfeld, Rabbi, elected the following officers: President, Harris Jacob; Vice-President, P. Hirshberg; Secretary, H. E. Hirshberg; Treasurer, M. Meyer. The congregation of "Beth Shalome" has lately combined with "Beth Ahaba."

The *Protestant Episcopal Church Home*, 517 North Fourth street, was the gift of the late German Consul Friedr. W. Hahnewinkel and can therefore be termed a German foundation. It is a retreat for gentlewomen,[272]) those ladies in Virginia destitute of friends and fortune and unable to support themselves; but it is designed for members of the Episcopal Church exclusively. It is presided over by the bishop, but no German-Virginian is at present in the Board of Managers.

Scientific and artistic efforts had until the middle of the nineteenth century not attained a very prominent degree in Virginia; however the Anglo- and German-American citizens

---

272.) "The Richmond Dispatch," January 1, 1898.

of Richmond have always participated in every attempt to promote them. The *Richmond Microscopical Society*, chartered in 1880, consisted entirely of Germans. The founders were Dr. Wm. A. Weissiger of Manchester, Rev. Ed. Huber and G. A. Peple. Membership was limited to active workers with the microscope. Regular meetings were held the first Friday of each month and the society had a reference library and subscribed to microscopical journals. Meetings were held at Dr. Henry Froehling's office, corner of Twelfth and Cary streets. Members had the use of Dr. Froehling's chemical laboratory for research. In 1889 Dr. H. Froehling was president, G. A. Peple secretary, Thomas Christian treasurer and Dr. Wm. Grebe librarian.[273]) Dr. Henry Froehling is analytical and consulting chemist for the Chesapeake & Ohio railroad, R. & A. and M. & O. Central railroad and Banking Co. of Georgia. Dr. M. A. Burt, who by accident was killed at his residence on March 20th, 1890, was vice-president of the Richmond Medical and Surgical Society; and the German-Virginian Dr. C. L. Cudlipp (according to his own explanation this name was derived from Gottlieb) was secretary. Another German-Virginian, Dr. W. T. Oppenheimer, is president of the Board of Health and professor at the Richmond Medical College. The "*Jeffersonian Literary and Social Circle*," owning a library of 1250 volumes, and the "*Mercantile Club*," with elegant reading rooms, are composed mostly of German-Virginian Hebrews, and their object is the cultivation of social and literary relations. L. Hutzler, J. S. Levy, Charles Hutzler, M. S. Block, Myer Heller, D. Mitteldorfer, Wm. Lovenstein, E. Raab, F. S. Myers, Wm. Heller, Moses May, Sol. Sycle, Israel I. and Jacob I. Cohen, N. Ezekiel, M. Rosenbaum, J. Thalheimer, L. and Joseph Wallerstein, W. and J. Gans, H. S. Binswanger, Ch. Strauss and others are among the leading men and former presidents of the clubs. The literary activity of the Germans reawakened after Richmond rose out of the ashes of the evacuation fire in 1865. The "*Richmond Anzeiger*" was the only German newspaper that survived the terrors of the war, but it did not satisfy all liberal Germans and consequently a new German weekly, "*Der Richmond Patriot*," was published.

273.) Richmond Directory, p. 26. 1889—1890.

The paper was well edited and the management rested in the hands of Isaac Hutzler and Wm. Lovenstein. On July 20th, 1870, the "Patriot" was transferred to the "*Virginia Deutsche Publishing Co.*," which had started on April 11th, 1870. The daily "*Virginia Staats Gazette*" continues to this day. Editors of the "Gazette" were in succession: Paul Ketterlinus, Jacob Rosenfeld, Heinrich Pein, (born at Altona, Holstein, died at Richmond June 7th, 1886), and Moritz Friedrich Richter, (born at Grossschoenau near Leipzig, Saxony.) In 1890, after the successful celebration of the first "German Day," the *German News Company of Virginia* was organized: G. A. Peple, president; Christian Droste, secretary; Joseph Wallerstein, vice-president, and Hermann Schmidt, Fritz Sitterding, Carl Ruehrmund, H. G. Miller, directors. Herrmann Schuricht of Louisa county was chosen editor of a new German weekly, "*Der Sueden.*" The principal object of the promoters of this paper was to secure through a large circulation in the United States as well as in Germany and wherever the German tongue is spoken, the influx of German settlers into Virginia and the other southern States. To make "Der Sueden" instructive as well as attractive, its columns were filled with descriptions of all the features of German-American life in the southern States, the topics of the day discussed, the different branches of agriculture, commerce, science, art and literature represented, and the cooperation of eminent professional men and well known distinguished writers was secured. The first number appeared on January 4th, 1891, and the paper was very favorably spoken of by the leading German and English journals of the Union; but in October 1891 Mr. Schuricht resigned the editorship on account of his impaired health. Mr. B. Hassel was elected his successor and a few weeks later the News Co. sold "Der Sueden" to the publishers of the "Staats Gazette," who still continue it as their Sunday publication, but changed in shape and contents. Of the originals written by German-Virginians and published in "Der Sueden" during the time of its independent appearance are to be mentioned: Novels and poems by Christian Droste under the nom-de-plume of "R. Helge;" educational and popular articles by Prof. G. A. Peple; poems and two novels by H. Schuricht, and by the same author: "Pedagogical Letters to a German-American Mother." Dr. William Grebe wrote different articles for English papers on medical questions and he also translated and published in 1893 in English: "Gesunde und kranke Nerven," by Dr. Freiherr R. von Kraft-Ebings.

Several German-Virginian artists have gained well-merited recognition. The sculptor *Edward V. Valentine*, who is said to be of German descent and a pupil of Professor Aelquoit Kiss of Berlin, enjoys a national reputation. His exhibition gallery, 801 E. Leigh street, is open to visitors from 10 to 11 o'clock on Saturdays, but strangers are usually admitted on other days upon presenting their cards. Besides his recumbent statue of General Lee at Lexington, Va., Mr. Valentine produced other important art works, among them the Stonewall Jackson statue at Lexington and the Jefferson statue in the court of the Jefferson Hotel at Richmond. The sculptor's brother, the late Mann S. Valentine, left a bequest of $125,000 for a permanent Museum and Library under the name: "The Valentine Museum." The purposes of the museum are: to preserve the relics illustrative of the civilization of Virginia and the United States, from the discovery of America to the present time, and more especially to secure from destruction portraits, manuscripts, etc., the products of southern labor; to preserve the archaeological remains of Virginia and the South, and so arrange them as to show the habits and customs among the aborigines; to acquire, classify and exhibit the natural products, botanical and mineral, of Virginia, for the purpose of developing further knowledge of the State's resources among Virginians and prospectors; to acquire collections exhibiting raw materials, and the processes of manufacture of the same into finished products; to acquire and classify specimens of art and its allied industries in order that students may derive practical benefit from them; to acquire a complete reference library on the above subjects and to make this library of practical value to earnest investigators. The treasures of the Valentine Museum are known in all the leading scientific circles throughout America and Europe, and they are housed in a beautiful old Virginia home corner of Eleventh and Clay streets. The very large number of valuable and interesting German manuscripts, autographs, books and engravings is really surprising. The most notable and rare collections were thrown open to the public on November 21st, 1898, and will for ever commemorate the name of Valentine.

Moses Ezekiel, a native of Richmond, Va., and of German-Jewish extraction, sculptured in Rome "The Statue of Religious Liberty," exhibited and much admired at the Centennial Celebration, 1876. It is in the form of a group of statuary in Carrara marble. An eminent and thoughtful foreigner, a statesman of world-wide fame, passing through Fairmount Park (Philadelphia Exhibition Grounds), earnestly gazed at the marble group and exclaimed: "If the Centennial Exhibition of 1876 resulted in this work of art and nothing else, the American people should be satisfied. I, the subject of a monarch, salute the nation that makes this creation possible."[274)]

Caspar Buberl, a native of Eger in Bohemia, now a resident of New York City, has only temporarily resided in Virginia but his name is inseparably connected with some of Virginia's proudest monuments. He came to America forty years ago, aged twenty-two. Since his arrival in this country he has been an active, busy man and has executed many decorative pieces of sculpture North and South. The sculptor, in a letter dated May 1894, says: "My last piece of modelling, *the Confederate for the Richmond Soldiers' and Sailors' Monument*, will, I hope, be liked by the public, as I did this work with a feeling of thanks for all the kindness I have received from the generous people of the South." Mr. Buberl has modelled this monument and also the *A. P. Hill* monument and the *Howitzer* monument, both at Richmond, after designs by Mr. W. S. Sheppard. The bronze statue of *the Confederate Soldier* at Alexandria, Va., is another piece of his work.

Alfred H. Raynal, an engineer of superior qualifications and talent, and highly regarded, was superintendent of the Richmond Locomotive and Machine Works. In 1891 he retired from office and accepted a position in New Jersey.

274.) "The American Jew as Patriot, Soldier and Citizen," by Simon Wolf, pp. 65 and 63. Philadelphia, 1895.

The most important lithographing establishment in Richmond is the well known firm of *A. Hoehn & Co.* on Bank street.

Of German architects and builders *Capt. Leibrock* and *Carl Seibert* have already been mentioned. The last named built the new St. Johannis church. *Fritz Sitterding,* a very enterprising and successful business man, has built many churches and residences in all parts of the State. The large Exhibition Building, with its ingenious roof-work, but now taken down, was erected by him. *Carl Ruehrmund* is another excellent architect and draughtsman. His biography follows later.

It is also a matter of pride with the Germans of Richmond, that many of the principal buildings there, are from designs of German architects; that the plan of the new and magnificent City Hall was drawn by a German architect, Myer of Detroit, Mich., and that the designs of the Masonic Temple are also the work of a German.

Friedrich Roeth is spoken of in the local papers of 1870 as a superior fresco painter, and it is a matter of regret, that the son of the late A. Hottes, who had studied at the art schools of Muenchen and was looked upon as a very promising talent, died soon after his return to Richmond.

Music was again cultivated by the German citizens of Richmond after the thunder of the cannon around its hills had ceased. In speaking hereafter of the public festivals of the Germans, occasion will be found, to point to the charming effects of music and its inspiring influence, and it is therefore sufficient for the present to name the various organizations devoted to its culture.

The "*Gesangverein Virginia*" survived the war and gained reputation by the performances of the operas "Stradella," April 15th and 19th, and "Der Freischuetz," April 16th and 20th, 1875. These performances were universally appreciated and were *the first rendering of opera by home talent* in the South. The society was from that time on very popular and the whole city showed its interest for it at the celebration of the 25th and 40th anniversaries of its foundation on September 24th, 1877 and July 1st, 1892. At the 25th anniversary "*Saengerhall*" was dedicated and for the occasion a poem, "Weihe-Gesang" (Dedication Song) by G. A. Peple, set to music by the musical leader *C. L. Siegel*, was sung. In honor of the 40th anniversary H. Schuricht composed and dedicated a festive play, "Huldigung dem deutschen Liede."

In 1870 two other similar societies were formed: the "*Germania Maennerchor*," ..... Krause, leader, and "*Richmond Philharmonic Association*." On April 20th, 1876, the "*Richmond Mozart Association*" was organized and received the hearty support of the wealthy Germans. E. A. Hoen and Samuel Hirsch were members of the board of directors, while *Prof. Jacob Reinhard* was for several seasons the musical leader. German ladies and gentlemen took active part in the performances.

The *Arion Society of Richmond*, a singing society for the promotion of vocal musical study, was organized June 17th, 1887; Joseph W. Laube, president, and Jacob Reinhard, director. It was not a German society, but listed many members of German descent.

The *Richmond Musical Protective Society* was organized January 1st, 1886, and consists of professional musicians only. Its membership numbers 38. Its objects are social intercourse, interchange of views on all things pertaining to the musical profession and the protection of its interests generally. To its members counted: H. F. Laube, John Baseler, John Reintz, J. T. Pulling, C. B. Baseler, G. A. Thilow, J. C. Reinhardt, Richard Wagener, A. J. Leiss, Jacob Beier, Geo. Voelker and H. J. Tremer. These names indicate that the society was composed chiefly of Germans.

There are several German lodges in the city and others in which the German element is heavily represented. On September 13th, 1870, the *Germania Lodge of Knights of Pythias*, previously mentioned, was established by Ch. T. Loehr, Otto Morgenstern, J. Hutzler, A. Blenner, F. Fischer, O. F. Cammann,

C. Dunker, L. Gimmi, H. Metzger, G. Habermehl, I. Marxhausen, L. Michel and G. W. Robinson.[275]) After an existence of twenty-four years the lodge numbered about two hundred members and the total receipts amounted to about $16,000, of which sum more than $9,000 have been paid for benefits, funerals and endowments. Several of the *Hebrew orders* have a decided German character and to their most prominent members are counted: M. Hepburg, Ch. Hutzler, Julius Strauss, H. S. Hutzler, W. Lovenstein, L. Hexter, A. Levy, M. C. Block, H. Fisher, C. Goldenberg, J. Baer, J. Hirschberg, I. Held, A. Cohen, N. Nachman, E. Bettingheimer, J. Thalheimer, P. Hellstern, A. Gunst, S. Binswanger, W. Flegenheimer, M. J. Rosendorf, M. Kaufman, M. Myer, J. Lewit, E. A. Ezekiel, M. Cohen, E. Solomonsky, E. Ullmann, etc.

The German military organizations were dissolved at the end of the Civil War and since that time no entirely German company has been formed. However the *Stuart Horse Guard* is almost a German troop. It was commanded until October 1892 by Captain Carl Euker, afterwards Colonel of the First Virginia Cavalry Regiment, and his successor in command of the Company was Captain Edward Euker, his nephew. Chas. Euker, Jr., the son of Colonel Euker, was elected one of the lieutenants. Other Germans or German descendants have held high positions in other military corporations, like Captain Chas. Gasser of Company D, First Virginia Volunteers, Captain Chas. H. Philips and Lieutenant Werne, Lieutenant Armin Heinrich of Richmond Light Infantry Blues; Lieutenant-Colonel Stern, Inspector-General; Captain P. T. Conrad, Quartermaster of First Virginia Regiment; Lieutenant H. D. Messler of Company B; Captain A. A. Spitzer, Adjutant-General of Grand Camp Confederate Veterans; Dr. R. B. Stover, Surgeon-General of the same Camp; Charles T. Loehr, Commander of Picket's Camp Confederate Veterans, and Captain John Trusheim of the Petersburg Artillery.

It is further proof of the influence and respect the Germans of Richmond enjoy, that foreign States have appointed

---

275.) Nebengesetze und Ordensregeln der Germania Loge. Printed by Va. Staats Gazette, Richmond, 1889.

several of them their commercial representatives. *Friedrich Hanewinkel, Heinrich Boehmer* and *Adolph Osterloh* officiated as *Consuls of the German Empire,* respectively of the North German Confederacy; *Emil O Nolting, Belgian Consul, Charles L. Ludwig,* Consul of the *United Kingdoms of Norway and Sweden,* and *Louis Borchers,* succeeded A. Osterloh, Consul of the *Austrian Empire.*

In the development of industry and commerce the Germans have taken active part. In *the manufacture, purchase and export of tobacco,* Virginia's great staple, they are still much engaged. After the restoration of peace the export of tobacco underwent a great change. Steamers took the place of the sailing craft, so that for many years gone by no merchant ship has sailed from Rockets with a full cargo to the rivers Weser and Elbe. All tobacco is at the present time shipped by railroad to Baltimore or New York and forwarded from there by steamer. The purchases for the Austro-Hungarian Government have been made by the German firms of Fr. Wm. Hanewinkel & Sons, H. Boehmer, Osterloh & Co., A. Osterloh & Co., and L. Borchers & Co. These firms have also supplied most of the demand of the French, Italian and Portuguese Governments, and the German tobacco houses: Schaer, Koetter & Co., E. O. Nolting & Co., Nolting & Koetter, E. R. Victor & Co., and Williams & Rehling, have successfully participated in this export. Major Lewis Ginter, of German descent, one of the most meritorious men of Richmond, was partner of the firm of Allen & Ginter, manufacturers of tobacco and cigarettes. The firm has been changed to Allen & Ginter Branch of the American Tobacco Company.

In 1891 a *very valuable invention* was made by Prof. G. A. Peple for the drying and assorting of leaf tobacco, to dispense with steam and impure air. The invention is now the property of "The Mayo Tobacco Drying and Ordering Company," of which G. A. Peple was up to his death vice-president. The apparatus has been adopted by the American Tobacco Company and by other large tobacco houses.

Major Lewis Ginter, above named, was born in New York.

His great grandfather had emigrated from Germany and settled there. When a young man he came to Richmond and at the outbreak of the Civil War he joined the Confederate forces and was promoted to the rank of major. After the war Major Ginter went North, but a few years later he returned to Richmond and engaged in the tobacco trade with astonishing success. He was the first to use the light colored tobacco of Virginia and North Carolina in place of Turkish tobacco for the manufacture of cigarettes. The firm of Allen & Ginter gained a widespread reputation under his management, and finally Major Ginter accepted the presidency of the Allen & Ginter Branch of the American Tobacco Company. Important as were the business talents of Major Ginter to the interest of the city, of still greater value was the delight he took in the beauty of nature, his desire to beautify by all manner of improvements the picturesque environs of Richmond and to further in this way the prosperity of the city. West of the Capital, where the Confederates had thrown up earthworks on sandy hills, Maj.Ginter purchased large tracts of land, built elegant avenues and boulevards, laid out parks and invested much money to secure a beautiful landscape. The city of Richmond is greatly indebted to the sense of beauty, the enterprise and the noble spirit of this German-Virginian. No man could have made better use of the wealth he gained by diligence and intelligence. Greatly beloved by all Richmond, he died October 2nd, 1897.

In the period of 1889—1890 Ashton Starke, another German descendant, was president of the Virginia State Agricultural and Mechanical Society.

German business men engaged in the management of banks, insurance companies and building associations. The cedar works and several other manufacturing interests are controlled by Germans and their descendants. Two large breweries, *The Richmond Brewery* of Kersten and von Rosenegk, now *Rosenegk's Brewing Company*, and the *Peter Stumpf Brewing Company*, Peter Stumpf late president, are in successful operation since 1891, after *Euker's Brewery*, Edw. Euker, proprietor, and the *James River Brewery* of Baier, Juengling & Betz had been discontinued. In all branches of the wholesale and retail trade the Germans are engaged. The sale of dress-goods is almost the exclusive domain of the German Israelite citizens. The sole furrier of importance in the South is Charles Haase. German artisans are employed with preference in all the various factories.

CHAPTER XVII.

The Celebration of German Public Festivals in Richmond and Biographies of German-Virginian Prominent Citizens.

THE historical facts mentioned in previous chapters show that the Germans have contributed very materially to the wealth and progress of the city of Richmond and the entire State. They have helped in a great measure to bear the burden and expenses of the community and commonwealth. It is asserted that the German-Virginian population of Richmond pays about *one-third* of the whole amount of the city's taxes.

More and still better than by anything else, the true moral value and influence of the German-Virginian element and its love and admiration for the native land and people of the forefathers, are illustrated by their *public festivals*.

On the 14th of September, 1869, the German associations celebrated the *Centennial Anniversary* of the eminent German naturalist, philosopher and explorer, *Alexander von Humboldt*. The German societies: Schiller Lodge, Gesangverein Virginia, Turnverein, the Druids, the Redmen, and the Society for the Relief of the Sick, with banners floating, formed in procession in front of the City Hall under the direction of their marshalls: Charles Klein, Carl Euker, Christian Unkel, A. Blenner, Otto Camman and H. Dabble. They paraded the principal streets to the theatre, where a large number of ladies and gentlemen had already assembled. The stage was handsomely decorated and after the orchestra had performed an overture the curtain was drawn and the singing societies, under the leadership of C. L. Siegel, sang Mohr's grand hymn. Next followed the unveiling of a fine plaster bust of Humboldt, cast by E. Valentine. Surrounding the bust, globes, maps, telescopes and other emblems of science were scattered. Dr. Boldeman recited a prologue, followed by Prof. G. A. Peple, the German orator of the day; Patrick Henry Aylett delivered the English oration. The speakers were heartily applauded and the singing societies intonated the "German Song of Victory," by F. Abt. Resolutions were read and adopted, which had been prepared especially in acknowledgment of the anticipated large participation and the hearty sympathy of the Anglo-American citizens by a committee composed of G. A. Peple, Herman Koppel, Alors Rick, A. Osterloh, G. Klein, Otto Meister, Ch. Simmons, Hermann Boschen, H. Burchard, H. Diebel, H. Willers, A. Blenner, Christ. Meckel, Henry Demler, F. Thomas, F. Laube and F. Dush.

Although the American population had *not* taken part in honoring the memory of the great explorer and writer of the American continent in such measure as had been expected, yet the resolutions were unanimously adopted.[276]) The proceedings were closed by a "Volksfest" at Hattorf's Garden. The houses and business places of the Germans generally were decorated with flowers and evergreens, and the Stars and Stripes and the emblem of the North German Confederation waved from many of them.

A few months previous to the Humboldt Centennial Celebration, and as a kind of continuation of the great "*Singing Festival*" at Baltimore, Md., several singing societies of New York city visited Richmond as the guests of the Gesangverein Virginia.[277]) They were members of "Socialer Maennerchor," "Teutonia" and "Liederkranz," and on July 16th, 1869, a grand concert of the combined visiting and home societies was given at the Richmond Theatre. Hon. George Chahoon and Prof. G. A. Peple welcomed the New York singers in short but appro-

---

276.) "The Daily State Journal" of Sept. 14, 1869, Vol. I, No. 275. Richmond, Va.
277.) "Richmond Patriot," July 23, 1869. Richmond, Va.

priate speeches. On the next day the visitors were shown the city and its environs and on July 18th a picnic at Hattorf's Garden closed the festivities.

Another "*Singing Festival*"[278]) of still more elaborate character was arranged September 28th to 30th, 1873. The following societies took part: "Germania Maennerchor," Baltimore, Md., "Maennerchor," Philadelphia, Pa., "Saengerbund," Washington, D. C., "Gesangverein Virginia," "Germania Maennerchor," and "Richmond Philharmonic Association," Richmond, Va. A grand concert, assisted by *Kessnick's* double orchestra, under the leadership of Prof. Carl Lenschow, at Assembly Hall, excited the admiration of a large audience. It was followed by a "Commers" at Monticello Hall, where Prof. Peple, Mr. Wolf of Washington and Oswald Heinrich of Richmond delivered addresses. I. H. Pein recited a poem, "Gruss an die Saenger," composed by him. On September 30th the festival closed with a picnic at the Fair Grounds, where several mass choirs were chanted.

A deep and proud feeling came to the heart of every German Virginian, when the news of the brilliant victories of the German armies in France reached America. On August 13th, 1870, an appeal was published to meet on the evening of August 15th at Monticello Hall, in order to make arrangements for the collection of funds for the relief of the wounded German soldiers. This appeal was signed by Carl Seibert, secretary, and the highest enthusiasm prevailed at the meeting. It was largely attended and a "*Deutscher patriotischer Unterstuetzungsverein,*" (German Patriotic Beneficial Society) was organized. A committee was elected for the collection of money, consisting of Eduard Euker, J. E. Fischer, William Euker, W. Wild, C. L. Siegel, G. Klein, Dr. Boldeman, Louis Euker, Dr. Grebe, H. Schmidt, M. Millhiser, S. M. Rosenbaum, G. Hoffbauer, A. Osterloh, J. Kobbe, I. Preskauer, Dr. Strecker and H. Metzger, and already in the beginning of September one thousand, one hundred dollars could be forwarded to the Consul-

278.) "Täglicher Anzeiger," Sept. 30, 1873. Richmond, Va.

General of Germany at New York. The *young German-Virginian ladies of Richmond* also evinced enthusiastic sympathy with the glory of the old Fatherland. On September 10th, 1870, Miss Emma Grebe (now Mrs. Cordes) president; Miss Marie Thilow (now Mrs. Rehling) secretary; Miss Pauline Lybrock, treasurer, and Mr. Heinrich Phillips, assistant secretary, issued another appeal to the Germans of Richmond to furnish money, to be given for the support of the children of German soldiers killed in battle or who died in the hospitals. A "Fair" was arranged by the patriotic young ladies, and they were delighted to be enabled to forward through Consul Hanewinkel three hundred and twenty-seven dollars, the proceeds, to the Consul-General, Mr. Johannes Roesing at New York.

The *sons of the city of Marburg* in Hessia, residing in Richmond, collected among themselves about three hundred and fifty dollars as a contribution to the erection of a "Siegesthurm" in the neighborhood of their native city, and they also shipped a nicely polished quarter-stone of Richmond granite for the same monumental structure. Finally, on March 13th, 1871, a grand "*Friedensfeier*" was arranged. George Klein acted as president and the festive committee was composed of Carl Seibert, I. Rosenfeld, H. G. Miller, Wm. Graeser, R. Senf, H. Domler, A. Blenner and E. Kempe. Paul Ketterlinus, editor of the Virginia Staats Gazette, delivered the festive oration from the portico of the City Hall. The torches borne in the procession were then thrown on a pile and burnt while "Die Wacht am Rhein" was sung. Houses and residences of Germans were everywhere decorated and illumined, and at the banquet at Monticello Hall Consul Hanewinkel, Consul Boehmer and Prof. G. A. Peple addressed the partakers.

In 1881 the Germans of Richmond participated in the "Yorktown Centennial." Mr. G. L. Siegel composed a festive march for the occasion. Although Germany had not been the ally of the American colonies during the War of Independence like France, yet it had furnished them several men who rendered very important services. Prominent among those German partisans was General von Steuben, — and his descendants, living in Germany, participated in the centennial festivities as the

"Guests of the United States." The representatives of the Steuben family were: Colonel Arndt v. Steuben, Captain Fritz v. Steuben, Captain Eugen v. Steuben, Lieutenant Cuno v. Steuben, Lieutenant Berndt v. Steuben, Lieutenant Anton v. Steuben and the royal high forester Richard v. Steuben. They were invited by their countrymen to Richmond to attend a "Commers at Saengerhall" arranged in their honor. A grand parade marched through the principal streets of the city and several artistically decorated floats of historical character presented its leading feature.

However the most successful of all festivals arranged by the German citizens of Richmond were the celebrations of "German Day" on October 6th, 1890; September 23rd, 1891; September 15th, 1893; October 3rd, 1894; September 12th, 1895, and in 1896 and 1897. The enthusiasm displayed by the citizens of German birth or descent on these occasions was almost unexampled, while an interest hardly less great was shown by the public in general. The newspapers, English as well as German, contained full descriptions of the proceedings. In 1890 and 1891 the "Richmond Dispatch"[279]) printed the German oration and the prologue not only in English, but also in German, while in 1893 the "Richmond Times" published H. Schuricht's "Festive Play" in the original, and in 1896 and 1897 the orations of H. Schuricht, von Rosenegk, Dr. Menzel and Dr. Calish.

The last-named paper, with reference to the first German Day, said[280]): "These proceedings were such as to inspire our citizens of German blood not only with a warmer attachment to the land from which they originally sprung, but also with a keener devotion to the adopted soil in which they are now so deeply rooted. The excellent influence of such a celebration was clearly illustrated at every point in its course, and that influence will long survive in the Community." — The "Richmonder Anzeiger" of October 7th, 1890, had printed in large

---

279.) "The Richmond Dispatch," No. 12,231, pp. 1, 2 and 4. Richmond, October 7th, 1890.

280.) "The Times," No. 2486, p. 2. Richmond, Va., October 7th, 1890.

letters at the head of its report of the first "German Day": "Great Success! 8000 participants! The grandest German festival ever held in this city!" — The celebration of 1891 was fully as well attended. The visitors at the festival grounds were estimated at from 8—10,000.

The officers of the *First German Day* were Alfred von N. Rosenegk, president; Hon. Wm. Lovenstein, first vice-president; H. G. Miller, second vice-president; Wm. Felthauss, third vice-president; F. C. Ebel, fourth vice-president; Carl Ruehrmund, first secretary; C. T. Loehr, second secretary; and W. H. Zimmermann, treasurer. A committee of ladies, of which Mrs. B. Hassel was president, assisted in the arrangements for decoration of the hall of the Exposition Building, and also arranged and managed the plays for the children about the grounds. The officers of the "*Young German-Americans*" were C. F. Kohler, president; John C. Seibert, first vice-president; A. H. Felthaus, second vice-president; W. P. Klein, third vice-president; George C. Ditrich, Jr., and A. Vonderlehr, secretaries; and H. Schott, treasurer. Mr. C. F. Kohler acted as chief-marshall and his assistants were J. C. Seibert, P. W. Klein, Henry Schött, Tony Felthaus and G. C. Ditrich, Jr.

The day was opened with the parade of the Young German-Americans, which took place at 9.20 o'clock in the morning. Long before the time to start a large crowd had collected in front of Saenger Hall, where the procession was to form. This building, as well as many residences, was beautifully decorated with a profusion of flags and streamers, bearing the American and German colors, and every window was filled with ladies and girls who were to follow the parade in carriages. The scene was an inspiring one and calculated to arouse to enthusiasm the most staid individual. At the head of the column rode ten mounted policemen. Next followed Chief-Marshall Kohler and Grand Chief-Marshall von Rosenegk with their aides. All of the marshalls of the young Germans wore soft white felt hats and sashes, bearing the German and American colors. The aides of Grand Chief-Marshall Rosenegk were clothed in black suits, silk hats and regalia, and also wore sashes with the American and Teutonic colors. Several of the horsemen, who were all finely mounted, bore the flags of both nations. Behind the marshalls followed several young men, who were also mounted, and a squad of twenty-two policemen on foot. Next came Voelker's Band, followed by seventy young Germans, employees of the Richmond Locomotive and Machine Works. Behind these came the young German-Americans, who numbered about three hundred. They carried at their head a handsome white satin banner with the name of their organization printed upon it in gold letters. This was presented by the German ladies of the city. Their uniforms were very pretty and elicited general admiration. Carriages containing the ladies followed in the rear and ended the procession. Along the entire route the sidewalks were filled with people, Broad street from Seventh to First being impassable for a short time. The beauty of the procession was enhanced by the magnificent horses ridden by the Germans.

At twelve o'clock the formal ceremonies were opened in the large main building of the Exposition Grounds. On the platform were seated Governor Phil. McKinney, Mayor J. Taylor Ellyson, Members of Congress, the Board of Aldermen and the City Council, Judges, Rev. Menzel, many other distinguished invited guests, the orators of the day: H. Schuricht and Wm. Lovenstein, the Committee members, members of the Gesangverein Virginia and the Chorus. In front of the platform a space was reserved for the five music bands and below this the front row of seats was occupied by the oldest German citizens, among whom were: M. Kaiser, G. Albrecht, John Lintz, W. Graser, J. C. Lange, J. J. Kuhr, C. Reitz, S. Boltz, C. Wendlinger, F. Krainzler, A. Bensal and John Does. There were about two thousand chairs occupied by the ladies; the aisles and galleries were also filled.

After the overture Mr. J. J. Spilling, chairman of the Reception Committee, introduced President A. von N. Rosenegk of the *German-American Association* of Richmond, who welcomed the vast assemblage. Next a selected choir of mixed voices, composed of members of the "Virginia" and a large number of ladies, rendered the "Festive Song," composed by Prof. E. L. Ide, and then Rev. Paul L. Menzel offered the prayer. Next the

Soldier's Home Band played the "Bridal Rose" overture, and then followed the German and English orations, being replete with valuable historical information and breathing a fervent spirit of patriotism and devotion to the Fatherland and the Union. The orators were frequently interrupted by applause and they were, together with Mr. von Rosenegk, Rev. Menzel and Mr. Siegel, the recipients of beautiful floral tributes. Mr. Schuricht was the special recipient of a beautifully worked banner by Miss Emma L. Brimmer, as a token of remembrance of the occasion. After the execution of several musical selections, Governor P. McKinney and Mayor Ellyson were introduced, who in appropriate terms complimented the Germans of Richmond upon their loyalty, patriotism and love for their native land, and the success of the festival. At the conclusion of the set programme German hospitality was lavishly manifested and the rest of the day was given over to amusements until the grand torchlight procession for the evening was formed.

The climax of scenic effect and enthusiasm was reached, when, after dark, the grand torchlight procession formed in line. The streets were thronged with spectators. Housetops, windows, telegraph poles, lamp-posts, etc., were considered advantageous points for look-out. At the corner of Eighth and Broad streets a large bonfire of the torches was made and amid a grand pyrotechnic display "Die Wacht am Rhein" and the "Star Spangled Banner" were sung by a chorus of thousands, and with an intensity of feeling never before exceeded.

The festival closed with a "Commers" at Saenger Hall, which was attended by the Governor and the Mayor of the city. This first celebration of "German Day" in Richmond proudly deserves the adjective "glorious," and the author has given it such a detailed description because, in his opinion, it illustrates the sentiment and influential strength of the German element in the city. It has also left some useful traces. On January 12th, 1891, the "*German-American Association of Virginia*" (Die Deutsch-Amerikanische Gesellschaft von Virginien) was organized, to further German immigration into the State, to aid settlers with advice and also pecuniarily, and to cultivate German customs. About three hundred persons joined the Association and the officers elected were: A. von N. Rosenegk, president; H. T. Miller, F. C. Ebel, Joseph Wallerstein and H. Mittendorfer, vice-presidents; Carl Ruehrmund, secretary; Ch. T. Loehr, financial secretary; C. Wippermann, treasurer; and W. Flegenheimer, J. Strauss, F. Tholl, Hermann Schmidt, Theo. Moecker, J. C. Seibert and F. W. Wagner, directors.

The Association soon gained acknowledgment by the leading Anglo-American citizens. On October 17th, 1894, an "Immigration Convention" assembled at Richmond and the German-American Society was invited to be represented by delegates. Rev. Dr. Paul Menzel, as chairman of the delegation, addressed the convention on[281]): "The class of immigrants most desired and the sections or countries abroad from which it is most desirable to secure them," and his remarks received universal approval.

In March 1891 a branch of this society, "*The Young Men of the German-American Association*," was formed and the following officers were chosen: Fred. Koehler, president; J. C. Seibert, H. Bromme, A. Felthaus, vice-presidents; Geo. C. Dietrich, Jr., secretary; E. H. Metzger, financial secretary; H. Schott, treasurer; A. Dietz, C. Guenther, H. Metzger and H. F. Grimmel, directors. The "German Day" also indirectly prompted the establishment of the "*Teutonia Club;*" Carl Ruehrmund, president; C. Burgdorf, secretary; F. C. Ebel, treasurer; and also of the "*Alert Social Club*" of young German-Virginians.

The *second* "*German Day*" and the "*Theodor Koerner Centennial Celebration*" on September 23rd, 1891, was inaugurated on the eve of the 22nd by an imposing torchlight procession. The programme for the occasion was as follows: Parade of the Young Men's German-American Association to the Exposition grounds, including the German-American pupils of the public schools; at 12 o'clock the celebration of the 100th Anniversary of Koerner's Birthday at the large music hall, followed by plays and dancing. The "Koerner Actus"

281.) In print by A. E. Strauss Printing Company, Richmond, Va.

opened with a musical overture. The rear of the platform had been transformed into a stage[282]), in front of which and to the right the invited guests and members of committees and to the left the singers were placed. Vice-President Miller and President von Rosenegk welcomed the large audience and bespoke the twofold character of the celebration, and they were succeeded by Hon. Mayor Ellyson, who illustrated the qualifications of Germans as citizens. The speakers were heartily cheered and then the Singers, led by Prof. E. L. Ide, under accompaniment of the orchestra, intonated with grand effect Theodor Koerner's "Prayer during battle," (Gebet während der Schlacht.) As soon as the applause had subsided, Christian Droste stepped to the front and delivered an excellent biographical speech of the youthful German poet and martyr-hero and happily succeeded to excite the due admiration for the patriotism and talent of Theodor Koerner. The Virginia Gesangverein next sang Koerner's "Schwertlied;" then Judge Flournoy made some eloquent complimentary remarks, followed by the culminating point in the ceremonies. H. Schuricht took the stand in front of the curtain and recited a "Prologue" composed by him,—the curtain was raised and amid a group of beautiful exotic plants, on a high pedestal, the fine plaster bust of the poet, cast by a true friend of the Germans, Mr. Fr. Moynihan, of this city, was exposed to view. In front of the pedestal and on the steps leading up to it knelt "Clio," the Muse of History, the hand raised, engraving on the marble the name of Theodor Koerner, and from the left side "Germania" approached the bust, a laurel wreath in her hands, to decorate the poet's brow. Clio was personified by Miss Lizzie Euker, now Mrs. Dr. Meyer, and Germania by Miss Maria Menzel. When Mr. Schuricht concluded his poetical explication of the tableau, the Singers intonated the "German Song" or "Das deutsche Lied." The tableau, the prologue and the singing were received with rapturous delight.

This closed the proceedings in Music Hall, and the rest of the day was spent in mirth and gayety. The German News Company had published a Fest-Blatt of "Der Sueden."

282.) "Der Sueden," Vol. 1, No. 39, pp. 12 and 13. Richmond, Va., Sept. 27, 1891.

In 1892 the observance of the "*German Day*" was confined to an all-day picnic at Blandon Park. The attendance was a large and devoted one.

In 1893 the celebration of "*German Day*" was arranged by the junior association, in which the senior society participated. It took place on September 14th and was a pronounced success.

Long before 10 o'clock, the hour fixed for the starting of the parade, the German-Americans began to flock to Saenger Hall, their usual rendezvous, while President von Rosenegk assembled the members of his organization at the corner of Sixth and Grace streets, from where they joined the column of the parade. A carriage followed, containing "Germania," (Miss L. Wolff), "Columbia," (Miss M. Senf), and "Virginia," (Miss E. Schumann.) The rear was brought up by about thirty aides on horseback.

The procession started shortly after 10 o'clock in the following order: Squad of police; chief-marshall and aides; President von Rosenegk and aides; Blue's Band; Young Men's German-American Association; German Pleasure Club; other organizations; Social Home Band; members on horseback; members in carriages and children in wagons.

Immediately after arrival the grounds were turned over to the children, who indulged in all sorts of games and out-door sports. At 2 o'clock in the afternoon all the visitors repaired to the large music hall, which had been tastefully decorated. The Blue's Band opened this part of the .proceedings with the march "Wien bleibt Wien," followed by a festive performance or "Festspiel," entitled "Der deutsche Tag im Jahre 1893," composed and dedicated by Herrmann Schuricht of Louisa county, whereupon the entire audience sang "Die Wacht am Rhein."

A. von N. Rosenegk, president of the German-American Association, next delivered an address of welcome. The music played the Oriental Overture and a chorus of eighty children from St. Mary's Parochial School sang "Ich habe mich ergeben." Prof. C. F. Mutter conducted the singing, while the music played the accompaniment under direction of Rev. P. Gregory, S. O. B.

H. G. Miller, orator of the day, was then introduced and delivered an oration on the subject "Objects and Purposes of the German-American Association."

The fifth Celebration[283]) in Richmond of "German Day," October 3rd, 1894, which was held at Saenger Hall, proved no exception to the rule: that whatever the German-Americans of the community undertake they do well and with genuine enthusiasm. The day was generally observed as a holiday by the German population.

The festivities commenced at 2 P. M. under the auspices of the German-American Association, the officers of which were as follows: A. von N. Rosenegk, president; H. C. Miller, first vice-president; Joseph Wallerstein, second vice-president; E. A. Stumpf, third vice-president; Carl Ruehrmund, fourth vice-president; T. Moeker, recording secretary; Ch. T. Loehr, financial secretary; C. Wippermann, treasurer; directors: J. F. Kohler, Peter Stumpf, A. Pohlig, E. Kersten, C. Dunker and M. F. Richter.

The celebration opened with an entertainment for children in the garden of Saenger Hall. The City School Board had ordered that all German pupils in the public schools be given a half-holiday in order that they might participate in the celebration. The grounds had been tastefully decorated and the little ones were quick to crowd them. A happier, healthier set of children were never gotten together.

At eight in the evening, when the second part of the programme commenced, Saenger Hall was packed almost to suffocation; most of the audience were ladies. The programme opened with an overture by the orchestra; song, St. Mary's Church Choir; addresses by the President and C. Ruehrmund, chairman of the Executive Committee; chorus, Gesangverein

---

283.) From "The State," October 3, 1894, and "The Richmond Dispatch," October 4, 1894.

"Virginia;" speeches by invited guests, including Mayor Taylor's address; song, "What is the German Fatherland?" by the German-American Association's chorus; and the reading of a letter from Prof. Schele de Vere, at this time the only honorary member of the Association, acknowledging the compliment of his election. Then followed a comedy performance, and a ball and banquet concluded the entertainment.

On April 1st, 1895, *the 80th anniversary of Prince Bismarck's birthday* was celebrated in Saenger Hall under the auspices of the German-American Society of Virginia. Almost every German of Richmond city participated in the "Commers." Enthusiastic speeches were delivered by President von Rosenegk and A. Osterloh, Consul of Germany, and the entire large assemblage, arising from their seats, sang a "Festival Song" composed by Herrmann Schuricht.

The elaborate celebration of *the sixth German Day*, September 12th, 1895, consisted in parade, oratory and song. The "Times" gave the following description:

According to instructions, those who desired to participate in the parade on horseback or in carriages, assembled soon after 9 o'clock on Broad street or thereabouts and half an hour later the aides of the President A. von N. Rosenegk reported at headquarters. Everything worked smoothly and promptly at the minute fixed for the starting of the parade, for the bell at the Second Police station house had hardly struck 10, when Mr. A. von N. Rosenegk, the president, asked his aides to fall in line on Marshall street between Seventh and Eighth streets. This was done at once, and the parade started a few minutes later from the corner of Seventh and Broad streets.

The following is the order in which the participants in the big parade marched:

Marshal J. H. Blumelinck, Charles Gasser, W. Schmidt.

President A. von N. Rosenegk.

Aides of the president and color-bearers on horseback, in dark clothes, white neckties, white gloves and silk hats. Aides: H. G. Miller, W. H. Zimmermann, E. Kersten, Louis Euker, C. C.

Thon, J. H. Middendorf, Jos. W. Bliley, B. Wittkamp, H. L. Hutzler, R. B. Felthaus, M. R. Fritosche, O. L. Brauer, Marx Gunst, H. Graser, T. Schwanne, Aug. Boehling, Aug. Stille, C. Werner, William Rueger. Color-bearers: H. Kramer, H. Janning, Charles Battige.

Blues' Band.

Marshals, Charles E. Loeffler and Joseph Stumpf.

Members on horseback.

St. Mary's Home Band.

Captain Chas. Hara and members of the Germania Pleasure Club, dressed in the old German costume, on horseback, acting as escort to the float.

A magnificently decorated float, arranged by Mr. M. Lindner. Upon a throne in the centre, and under a large canopy were seated Columbia, represented by Mrs. Charles Gasser, and Germania, represented by Miss R. Weinbrunn, both appropriately and handsomely dressed. Behind each was stationed a page, and in front a herald, with trumpet. The float was drawn by six magnificently caparisoned horses, each led by a gentleman in continental uniform, and on each side of the float marched six gentlemen in old German costumes and halberds.

The float was ten by sixteen feet, with a large canopy six by nine feet, and was by far the handsomest masterpiece in the line of decoration ever exhibited in this city. Heavy drapery was placed around the bottom of the float, intermingled with shields of satin and silk flags, bearing the American and German colors, while a variety of satin banners ornamented the top. The canopy was curtained in red, heavily draped with a tinsel finish.

Festoons of evergreen were stretched from the bronze cornerposts of the float to the canopy, and besides there were other floral decorations in large number. The canopy was tipped off by a large brass eagle.

Then followed a large number of carriages, with ladies and gentlemen of various organizations.

The procession moved down Broad to Nineteenth, down Nineteenth to Main, up Main to Sixth, up Sixth to Broad, and up Broad street to the Exposition Grounds.

As soon as the grounds of Richmond College were passed President A. von N. Rosenegk lined up his aides on the south side of Broad street to have the parade pass them in review. Subsequently they brought up the rear, and about fifteen minutes later everybody found accommodation within the gates of the Exposition Grounds.

Shortly before 2 o'clock the Music Hall began to fill with people, who were anxious to listen to the singing and the speeches that had been announced. The ladies were nearly all dressed in light summer costumes, and the sight was certainly a beautiful one to behold. Notwithstanding the excessive heat the hall was completely filled during the progress of the proceedings, and a good many others remained on the outside. Take it all in all, there must have been fully 4000 people present during the celebration.

In the centre of the back part of the big platform a dais had been erected on which were seated Germania and Columbia, the former represented by Miss Weinbrunn and the latter by Mrs. Charles Gasser. Miss Weinbrunn wore a heavy white satin dress with red tunique and black trimmings and the German eagle embroidered in gold on the front of the corsage. In her hair she wore a wreath of laurel and oak leaves. Mrs. Gasser also wore a white satin dress with blue tunique, in which the stars, representing the various States of the Union, were interwoven. The bodice of the dress was trimmed with red silk, and on her head Mrs. Gasser wore a silk cap in the national colors. In front of Germania and Columbia sat the two pages, Johnny Krause, dressed in a pink suit and blue mantel, and Bernard Schott, dressed in pale blue. Between the pages little Anthony Schwane, Jr., found his seat, who was dressed in the uniform of a lieutenant of infantry of the German army. The orators of the day were Messrs. von Rosenegk, Ch. H. Phillips and William H. Zimmermann.

In September 1896 and 1897 the *seventh and eighth celebrations of German Day* were arranged in a similar manner in the new large Auditorium on Exhibition Grounds. Herrmann Schuricht, A. von N. Rosenegk, Rev. Dr. Paul L. Menzel and

Rev. Dr. Eduard B. Calish delivered the principal festive orations. The assemblages again attained considerable proportions. The main part of the gatherings was composed of sons and daughters of the Fatherland, but many native-born Americans participated and all mingled together in a brotherly unity, which in itself proved the fraternal feeling existing between them.

In the beginning of 1898 the meritorious president of the German-American Association of Virginia, A. von N. Rosenegk, resigned and Carl Ruehrmund was elected in his place. Under the supervision of the last-named the *ninth celebration of German Day* took place on October 6th, 1898, in Saenger Hall. During the afternoon a Juvenile Festival (Kinderfest) was happily carried out and at night the official part of the celebration consisted in a concert, an address by President C. Ruehrmund, a theatrical performance and dancing.

No doubt the celebrations of "German Day" have successfully served to keep alive in Virginia the individuality, feeling and thought, — the entire *soul* of the German element — combined with the true spirit of American institutions.

On August 9th, 1898, *memorial services in honor of Prince Bismarck*, "the artificer of the German Empire," were held at Saenger Hall under the auspices of the Gesangverein Virginia. The hall was full when the meeting was called to order, a few minutes after 9 o'clock, by Mr. Henry G. Miller, chairman of the committee which had arranged it. On the stage were a number of well-known Germans of the city, including Mr. Miller, Mr. A. von N. Rosenegk, Rev. Dr. Paul L. Menzel, the orator of the evening, and others. The decorations of the hall and stage were simple and tasteful, consisting of potted plants and combinations of German and American colors.

After prayer by Rev. Dr. Menzel, Mr. Miller presented Mr. A. von N. Rosenegk, the president of the society, who came forward and delivered a short address. In his speech he called attention to the following occurrence:

"Several years ago, as you know, the German-American

Ladies' Aid Society was organized. They opened two wards in the Virginia Hospital. The ladies wrote to Prince Bismarck, requesting the permission to use his name for the male ward, and received the following highly honored reply over his autograph:

An

Frau ANNA VON NICKISCH ROSENEGK

Richmond, Va.,

Virginia Hospital,

Corner Clay and Eleventh Streets,

U. S.

Friedrichsruh, den 18. Mai 1895.

Die Benennung der in dem Virginia-Hospital neu erbauten Abtheilung nach meinem Namen ist für mich eine ehrenvolle Auszeichnung.

V. BISMARCK.

Mr. von Rosenegk continued: "The letter is framed and placed in the Virginia Hospital, and we here present will show the love and esteem we cherish, and express the sorrow we feel, by drafting resolutions of sympathy and transmitting them to his family."

These resolutions were presented by Mr. Miller and adopted, and after the singing of "Spielmann's Testament" by the Gesangverein chorus, the brilliant memorial address by Dr. Paul L. Menzel followed, which was the chief feature of the evening. Hereupon the meeting adjourned.

The German ladies of the city, ever alive to the interests of human sufferers, have organized in 1895, as previously mentioned, a "*German-American Ladies' Aid Association of the Virginia Hospital,*" of which Mrs. W. Rehling is President; Mrs. A. von Rosenegk, First Vice-President; Mrs. C. Oehlschlager, Second Vice-President; Mrs. Bertha Haase, Third Vice-President; Mrs. Adam Feitig, Fourth Vice-President; Mrs. C. Kindervater, Fifth Vice-President; Miss Emma Grimmel, Financial Secretary; Miss Catharine Phillips, Recording Secretary, and Mrs. Chas. H. Phillips, Treasurer.

On the 30th of May, 1895, the "Times" published for the benefit of the Hospital a large "Woman's Edition," to which Herrmann Schuricht, of Louisa county, and Mr. Wermuth, of Berlin, Commissioner of the German Empire to the World's Fair at Chicago, were the contributors of German articles.

In the early part of 1897 a "Gemischter Chor" of fifty ladies and gentlemen was organized under the leadership of the gifted professor Carl F. Mutter, cantor of St. Mary's Church and musical director of the Gesangverein Virginia. On December 2nd, 1897, this newly started chorus for the first time arranged a public concert, which was a decided success.

On May 9th, 189[illegible], the German ladies of Richmond demonstrated again their appreciation of the cultivation of vocal music *by the gift of a magnificent flag* to the Gesangverein Virginia. Miss Helene Brauer delivered the gift in representation of the following ladies: Mrs. Wm. H. Zimmermann, C. W. Thilow, John Steinbrecher, F. C. Ebel, C. E. Loeffler, E. A. Stumpf and Misses Helene Brauer, A. Wenzel, Bertha Haase, Gussie Bromm and Rosa Schumacher.

To complete these reports of the German Festivals the biographies of some of the leading men may be added.

Alfred von N. Rosenegk[284]) is a son of a colonel of the German army, whose full name he bears. His mother was also of noble blood, a Miss Sophie von Kleist. The father still lives in Eberswald, near Berlin, Germany. Mr. von Rosenegk was born in Stettin in Germany November 21st, 1852, and went in 1862, when only ten years of age, to the Military Academy in Potsdam and Berlin, where he remained until 1870, when he was promoted as subordinate officer to the army, to serve in the Franco-Prussian war, which ended in 1871. During the progress of the war he gained the rank of officer, which distinction

284.) From the 'Richmond Dispatch," October 5th, 1890.

he retained until 1875, when he severed his connection with the German army and immigrated to this country, previously however having been joined with Miss Anna Weisser in the holy bonds of matrimony. During the first five years of their life in this country the two had to struggle hard for existence, as neither could master the English language. In 1880 he engaged in the hardware business, beginning with a very subordinate position, from which he was gradually promoted, and in 1885 he accepted a call from the Bergner & Engel Brewing Company of Philadelphia as manager for the Richmond depot. In 1891 von Rosenegk associated with Mr. Emil Kersten. They established the well-known Richmond Brewery, which was changed in 1892 into a stock company under the new firm "Rosenegk's Brewing Company." It has also been Mr. von Rosenegk's fortune, through his courteous manners, to gain the love, esteem and respect to the highest degree not only of his German friends and countrymen, but of a vast number of our worthy American citizens.

Mr. von Rosenegk is a member of Schiller Lodge of Independent Order of Odd Fellows, Germania Lodge, Knights of Pythias, Gesangverein Virginia, Benevolent Protective Order of Elks, Iron Hall and Fraternal Legion, and among their members he is very popular and highly respected. The German Day movement was greatly due to his effort and gained reality through his untiring labors. He was the president of the German-American Association for eight years and is at present the president of the Gesangverein Virginia.

Rev. Dr. Paul L. Menzel, the scholarly pastor of St. John's German Evangelical Church, was born March 5th, 1839, at Lausanne, Switzerland. He is the oldest son of Rev. C. W. Menzel. Until 1850 he remained with his parents in St. Hippolyte, in the south of France. Then a boy he went to Germany, studied the German language and spent ten and one-half years in different institutions, colleges and universities, where he prepared for the ministry. After passing his examinations, he accepted a professorship in the College of Niesky, Silesia. On August 29th, 1868, he was ordained a minister of the Gospel by Bishop E. Reichel of Saxony, and subsequently served at different places. In '74 he came over to America and held for six years the position of German pastor in the two churches in Dansville and Reikinsville, in Western New York. In 1879 he joined the German Evangelical Synod of N. America. Since 1883 he has been the secretary of the Atlantic District of this organization and in 1894 he was elected president. In 1880 he accepted the pastorate of the German Protestant Church of Albany, N. Y., and by his effort helped to erect the new building which was dedicated in May 1882. Since February 1886 Mr. Menzel has been pastor of St. John's Evangelical Church in Richmond. In 1894 the Washington and Lee University of Lexington, Va., conferred on him the honorary degree of Doctor of Divinity.

State Senator William Lovenstein, of Richmond, was born October 8th, 1840, at Laurel, formerly known as Hungary Station, Henrico county, about eight miles from Richmond city. In addition to a good common school education, he spent two years at an academy in New York city. Returning from school he entered mercantile business, in which he engaged until the beginning of the war. Upon outbreak of hostilities he immediately left for the front with the Richmond Light Infantry Blues, of which he was a member, and saw active service before he attained majority. Mr. Lovenstein remained uninterruptedly with his company until captured by some of Burnside's troops at Roanoke Island. At the conclusion of the war he reengaged in business. When the State was readmitted into the Union in 1869, he was elected, though only twenty-nine years of age, to represent Richmond in the House of Delegates. He was reelected four successive times, serving in that branch ten years in all, during which time he was upon the most important committees.

In 1881 Mr. Lovenstein was elected to the State Senate and in 1897, the time of his death, he was serving his fourth consecutive term of four years. Governor Lee appointed Mr. Lovenstein a member of the board of the Female Normal School, (an institution which to a great degree owes its existence to his efforts.) For years he has been a member of the City School

Board; past-master of Fraternal (formerly Française) Lodge No. 53, A. F. and A. M.; grand secretary and supreme representative of the Royal Arcanum; past-regent and secretary of Virginia Council No. 26; past-president of District Grand Lodge No. 3 and Rimmon Lodge No. 68, I. O. B. B.; a member of the Board of Trustees and secretary of the congregation of Beth Ahaba. He was chosen president of the Grand Convention of the B'nai B'rith at the session of that body in Richmond in June 1890. Senator Lovenstein's chief business occupation was that of cashier of the Richmond Perpetual Building, Loan and Trust Company.

Carl Ruehrmund, the son of Rev. F. W. Ruehrmund, was born September 22nd, 1855, at Berlin, the Capital city of the Kingdom of Prussia. He visited the "Louisenstädtische Real-Schule," where he graduated in 1874. After four years' study at the "Architectural Academy" at Berlin, and having served his term in the Prussian army, he was employed as assistant architect by the government surveyor of buildings (Baurath) Orth, and later on in the architectural department of the Royal Railroad System. The prospects of promotion in the government service being gloomy, Ruehrmund resolved to try his luck abroad, and after spending some time in Scotland and England, he came to America in 1881. Having worked in various architectural offices, he was engaged in 1884 by the Government to superintend the rebuilding of the custom-house and post-office at Richmond, Va., and after finishing this work he entered in 1887 into private practice. Among numerous public and private edifices which he erected may be mentioned: the St. Mark's Lutheran and the Calvary Baptist churches at Roanoke, Va.; the Hoge Memorial Church; the storehouse of Cohen Brothers; Third Police Station; the Henrico Court House; the cattle-yard at Richmond, and the hospital of the State Lunatic Asylum.

Carl Ruehrmund enjoys among his German fellow-citizens the reputation of being a warm and zealous advocate of all German cultural and social efforts, and they bestowed on him many honorary offices. He was elected president of the "Teutonic Club," secretary and vice-president of the "German-American

Association of Virginia," and now he holds the presidency of this the most important German society in the State.

Heinrich Georg Miller is one of the most active and persevering leaders of the German element in Richmond. He was born September 26th, 1834, at Lauterbach in Hesse-Darmstadt, and after completing his school-education selected horticulture for his vocation. In 1857 Mr. Miller emigrated to America and was first employed as gardener in Baltimore, Md., and finally came to Richmond in 1861. In the year 1866 Gen. Tochmann was appointed agent of European immigration and Mr. Miller was made his assistant. He has continued since that time in the public service and occupied for the last twenty-five years the position of assistant gas-inspector at Richmond, and at present he holds the position of bill-clerk in the department. He has for years been president of the church wardens of the St. John's German Evangelical Church, was president of the Gesangverein Virginia and is president of the German-American Association of Virginia. During the war Mr. Miller served in a cavalry troop, commanded by Captain Wm. English. The troop was assigned to local defence, but it took part in the engagements at Drewery's Bluff and around Petersburg.

G. L. Siegel was born April 12th, 1838, at Kirchheim, Bolanden, Bavaria, and died at Richmond January 4th, 1893. When a boy thirteen years of age he came with his parents to New York and studied music, for which he showed great talent. Desirous to see the world, he accepted different engagements with circus and minstrel troups and travelled with them over the entire United States and in Canada. In 1856 he participated in the Walker campaign in Nicaragua and then took service on a U. S. man-of-war and visited other parts of the globe. At the beginning of the Civil War he lived at Charleston, S. C., and enlisted in the 14th South Carolina Infantry Regiment of General Maxey Greggs' Brigade. He remained with this command throughout the war, from the bombardment of Fort Sumter to the surrender at Appomattox, and he fought in many battles. After the war Mr. Siegel remained in Richmond, married a daughter of John H. Boschen and established a shoe-store. He was very successful in his business, but his love for music did not allow his mind to rest quietly. What he has done to advance musical art in Richmond from 1870 to 1885 and as leader of the Gesangverein Virginia, is gratefully remembered and appreciated by his German fellow-citizens. G. L. Siegel was an artist born, but an adverse fate prevented him from making full use of his great talent.

Hermann Schmidt, the brother-in-law of Siegel, was born on March 11th, 1838, at Vlotho on the river Weser and came to America in 1860. He was the first German to select Richmond as a place of residence after the close of the war. In 1865 he established a grocery business. Being indefatigable in his efforts, a thoroughly educated German merchant and of great enterprise, the business rapidly prospered. With the same energy he displayed in his business, he supported every effort to improve the welfare of ill-fated Richmond. The Germans of Richmond soon recognized the nobleness of his intentions and organizing talents, and in all their undertakings he was a certain leader. He was a member of the church and school board of the St. Johannis Church; president of the German Relief Society; president of the Virginia Building and Loan Company, and director of the Gesangverein Virginia, of the German-American Society of Virginia and of the German News Company of Virginia, etc. The Transparent Ice Company was founded by him. He died in 1894 and his death was deeply mourned by his German and American fellow-citizens.

William H. Zimmermann is another prominent and representative German-American of Richmond, born in the city of Marburg, Germany, in 1845. He came to this country in 1860, and after a short stoppage at Rochester, N. Y., Baltimore, and Louisville, Ky., he made his home in Richmond. At the beginning of the late war he enlisted in the Confederate ranks, but being then only a boy of fifteen years, he was not sent to the front, and did military duty in and about this city. At the close of the war he engaged in the fur business in this city, and in 1875 gave his undivided attention to the restaurant and hotel business.

For many years he has been closely identified, not only

with the German-American interests in this city, but he has always proven himself a public-spirited citizen, and in all undertakings that tended to be of benefit to this city, his name could be found among those on top of the list. He is a prominent and influential member of the German-American Association, of the Gesangverein Virginia and many other organizations. In the year 1893 it was chiefly by his efforts that the German-American voters of Richmond rallied at Saenger Hall and organized the German-American Democratic Club, which very soon made its power and influence felt among the rest of the residents. His countrymen appreciated the interest in public affairs manifested by Mr. Zimmermann, and elected him a member of the City Council and president of the Democratic club, which offices he has held in an efficient and dignified manner.

Charles T. Loehr was born August 8th, 1842, at Altona, Westphalia, and came to Richmond in 1853 when a boy. He is a highly esteemed, self-made man. During the war he was sergeant in Company D, First Virginia Infantry Regiment, and his name has become widely known by his excellent publication: "War History of the old First Virginia Infantry Regiment, Army of Northern Virginia, Richmond 1884." Charles T. Loehr is at present notary public, local manager of the Virginia Fire and Marine Insurance Company and secretary and treasurer of the Virginia Building and Loan Association. Of the many honorary offices conferred on him, those of First Commander of Pickett's Camp Confederate Veterans, Grand Master of the Knights of Pythias of Virginia, treasurer of Hines Memorial Hall and finance secretary of the German-American Association of Virginia may be mentioned.

Rev. P. Willibald Baumgartner, O.S.B., pastor of St Mary's Catholic Church, was born May 5th, 1853, at Wolfratshausen. He received a thorough education in school at his native place, the Latin school of the Holland Institute and the Royal Ludwig's College at Munich. He writes: "From childhood I entertained a predilection for study and the Church, and it was my cherished desire to go to America and to work there among my German countrymen." In the year 1871 he emigrated and went to St. Vincents to join the order of St. Benedictus. He studied philosophy for two years and theology for three years and on April 23rd, 1878, he received the consecration to priesthood. Soon after, on May 1st, Rev. Baumgartner was designated assistant of Rev. P. Renno Hegele at Saint Mary's Church, Richmond, Va., and since 1884 he is the highly esteemed pastor of the German Catholics of the diocese Richmond. He is a true sympathizer and ardent supporter of the charitable and civilizing endeavors of his countrymen.

Joseph Wallerstein, the second vice-president of the German-American Association, is a native of Blacksburg, Va. When six years old, he came to Richmond with his parents, and has been living here ever since. Early in his youth he started out in the produce business and has followed that vocation up to the present day. He has been for the last ten years a member of the Travellers' Protective Association, which was organized in 1882, and is now the vice-president of the national organization. He has also for some time been the chairman of the Railroad Committee of the local organization.

Mr. Wallerstein is also a member of numerous other German-American organizations, and his activity and effective influence in the Common Council for the past few years has been too well noticed by all who pay attention to the affairs of this city as to be especially mentioned in this connection.

Christian Droste was born in Bremen, Germany, on March 8th, 1862. He received a thorough education, served an apprenticeship in a mercantile house in his native city and soon distinguished himself by his diligence and ability. He exhibited also a marked love for literature. Intellectual labor is his delight. In the beginning of 1887 he emigrated to America, arrived at Richmond, Va., on February 1st and was employed by L. Borchers & Co., leaf tobacco merchants. Chr. Droste soon advanced to the position of bookkeeper, and Mr. Louis Borchers, Consul of Austria-Hungary, made him secretary of his consulate. In 1891 he participated in the organization and management of the German News Company of Virginia and in the publication of the German weekly: "Der Sueden," contributing novels and poems under the nom-de-plume of "R. Helge." His oration at the "Theodor Koerner Anniversary" also merits credit.

Carl Wippermann holds the important position of Treasurer of the German-American Association, and has for years administered the financial affairs of the organization in a wise and economical manner. He was born in April, 1855, in Westphalia, Prussia, where he received his first school education. Later on he entered the gymnasium at Herford, and served as a volunteer in the Fifteenth and Ninety-third Regiments, Infantry of the German army. At the expiration of his term he was discharged with the rank and qualification of a commissioned officer.

Mr. Wippermann learned the mercantile business at Magdeburg, Prussia, in a most thorough manner under the direct supervision of an uncle, in whose establishment he remained until 1877, when he came to Richmond to accept the position of book-keeper with Mr. Hermann Schmidt, a brother of his former employer. He has been the book-keeper of the firm for a number of years, and is now its manager.

Nearly every German-American organization has the name of Mr. Wippermann on its roll of members, and he is also engaged in a number of business enterprises. He is one of the most prominent members of the Gesangverein Virginia, and is vice-president of the Virginia Building and Loan Association.

When the German-American Association was formed about seven years ago, Mr. Wippermann was among its original members, and when Mr. William H. Zimmermann resigned the position of treasurer of the organization, Mr. Wippermann was elected to succeed him, and has been in charge of the financial affairs of the association ever since.

Ferdinand Charles Ebel was born January 4th, 1858, at Frederick, Md., and received a thorough school education in a private German-American school at Baltimore and after the removal of his parents to Richmond in 1869 at the German-English school of the St. Johannes German Lutheran Church. At the age of fifteen years he entered his father's business to learn the tailor trade and in 1885 he became a partner in the paternal firm. Mr. F. C. Ebel took great interest in all affairs of public utility and rendered his hearty support to all endeavors for the preservation of German nature and culture to coming generations. He is one of the most popular men among his German-American and Anglo-American fellow-citizens, and he held the honorary positions of secretary and vice-president in the Gesangverein Virginia and of vice-president of the German-American Association of Virginia since its organization. In the year 1895 he was elected a member of the City Council and his services are highly appreciated.

Charles H. Phillips, the financial secretary of the German-American Association, was born in Richmond on March 29th, 1859. Mr. Phillips, though born in this country, has taken an active part in all the large entertainments given by the German-Americans in this city. Soon after completing his education, he began a course at the Old Dominion Business College.

While still a young man he began to take an active interest in the political affairs of the city. He served for some time on the Democratic City Committee, and in 1888 he was chosen to fill an unexpired term in the Board of Aldermen. There he soon worked to the front, and his abilities being recognized, he was made a member of the Board of Police Commissioners, under the regime of which board the police force of Richmond has been raised to the highest possible standard. In 1894 he became a candidate for the office of City Treasurer, and though there were in the field several other candidates, he was the successful applicant, leading the field by a good, clear majority.

In his youth Mr. Phillips began his business career in the store of his father, where he remained until the business was discontinued. Later he was associated with the firm of Phillips & Stein, and when that firm was burned out, he entered the employ of the Richmond China Company.

Mr. Phillips is a member of nearly every German-American organization in existence in this city. He was president of the Gesangverein Virginia and is one of those men who fully deserve the thanks of all German-Americans for the great interest which he has at all times taken in affairs they were most concerned in. He has also recently come into prominence as a military man, having been appointed on the staff of the First Regiment as commissary, with the rank of captain.

Rev. Edward N. Calisch was born in the city of Toledo, Ohio, on June 23rd, 1865. When he was six years old his father moved to Chicago, just four weeks before the great fire of 1871 in that city. The family lost everything they had in that fierce conflagration, hardly even saving the clothes on their back. The mother with her two boys went back to Toledo for a year, while the father endeavored to found a home for them. In that effort he laid the foundation of disease which carried him off four years later. His death left the family destitute. Edward and his brother went to work, the former, at the age of ten years, securing a position with the firm of Mandel Bros. After a year of work, place was obtained for him in the Jewish Orphan Asylum at Cleveland, Ohio, at which institution he remained three years, and winning a scholarship in the Hebrew Union College at Cincinnati, he entered the latter institution September 1879, whence eight years later he graduated as rabbi. He graduated the same year from the University of Cincinnati. His first official charge was in Peoria, Ills., where he remained four years. Then he was called in September 1891 to his present position as rabbi of the Beth Ahaba Synagogue at Richmond, Va. Rev. Calisch is a most eloquent orator and he has gained for himself the greatest respect of both Americans and Germans of all creeds.

Julius Straus was born in the city of Richmond on the 4th day of May 1843. His parents came from Bavaria in 1837 and he received his first instruction from the Rev. M. J. Michelbacher. At the age of ten years young Straus was sent for two years to a boarding school in New York and then attended the higher schools in his native city. His talents turning into a commercial channel, he went into his father's business and continued therein until the Civil War. After the conclusion of war he reembarked in business. He entered the insurance business in 1869 and is now engaged therein nearly thirty years. For four years he served in the City Council and in the year 1887 he was appointed a member of the Board of Directors of the Central State Hospital at Petersburg, Va. Julius Straus always took a firm stand. He interested himself in the affairs of the German-American Association of Virginia and was also conspicuous in the celebration of "German Day" at Richmond. He has been for thirty years a member of the Grand Lodge of Masons and is on several important standing committees; is Past President of the Independent Order B'nai B'rith, District No. 5; Past Chancellor of Knights of Pythias; Past Exalted Ruler of the B. and P. O. Elks, and has served for twenty-five years on the Board of Managers of the congregation "Beth Ahaba" at Richmond, of which he is now the president.

There are many other zealous German-Virginians, but the limit of space forbids further personal mention.

Many of the German societies have been spoken of in the foregoing descriptions of the public festivals and it remains only to name a few more in order to complete the report about the German social and public life in Richmond during the last decades.

The "*German Relief Society*" (Deutscher Unterstuetzungs-Verein) was to some extent the forerunner of the German-American Association. H. Schmidt and Henry Miller were the founders and managers of the society, which offered good advice and assistance to German immigrants. Several German settlers have received pecuniary help by this benevolent association, who are now well-to-do farmers in the neighborhood of Richmond, and many mechanics have been temporarily assisted by it when out of employment. The society numbered in its time about three hundred members.

Gymnastics (Turnen) has not prospered in Richmond since the war. The "*Social Turnverein*" had outlived the critical time of that event, but its existence had been seriously shaken by measures of the Confederate police, and it did not regain its former prosperity and popularity after the conclusion of peace. A humorous occurrence recalls those hateful times of persecution. During the third year of the war the papers and minutes of the Turnverein were suddenly seized by order of the provost-marshall, and being written in German a translation was ordered and undertaken by an unqualified man. In order to give to a very talkative member of the society a witty reprimand, the secretary had recorded: "H . . . talked tin" (H . . . schwatzte Blech), which means, he spoke nonsense; but the versed translator worded it: "H . . . talked about sheet-iron." The discussion of the Turnverein about "*sheet-iron*" was considered by the police decidedly suspicious, and poor H . . . was arrested and locked up in "Castle Thunder." Such ill-treatment, ridiculous as it was, caused many members to resign, and after some years of lingering existence the society was dissolved. However the desire to practice the gymnastic art, physically and intellectually, did not die out, and on February 1st, 1885,[285]) the "*Richmond unabhaengige* (*independent*) *Turnverein*" was organized. About seventy members joined the new association and the number of pupils (boys and girls) amounted to about fifty. A very handsome hall, Turnhalle, was equipped and the officers elected were: J. J. Spilling, first speaker; H. C. Boschen, second speaker; Theo. Moeker, first secretary; Max Lindner, second secretary; Oscar Pflamm, first Turnwart; Wm. Gehrmann, second Turnwart; J. A. Moll, treasurer, and C. Hassel, Zeugwart. But the young German-Virginians were not inclined to submit to the rules of strict discipline and regular attendance of the exercises, and so the praiseworthy undertaking was discontinued after one year's effort. This laudable enterprise had the good effect, that the Americans learned to appreciate gymnastic exercise, and the Young Mens' Christian Association established a very beautiful gymnasium.

285.) Constitution des Richmond unabhaengigen Turnvereins. Printed by Virginia Staats-Gazette, 1885.

In 1893 the Germans of Richmond resolved to regain political influence and to secure a proportionate representation in the administration of the city's affairs. They organized a "*German Democratic Club*" and elected an energetic man—Wm. Zimmermann—to the presidency. The result of this step was apparent in the next election. All the nominees made efforts to win the confidence and support of the German voters. They were invited to address the club, to explain their programme and to give assurance that the interests of all classes of the population would be regarded by them without partiality and preference. One of the resulting effects was the election of Charles Phillips for city treasurer.

CHAPTER XVIII.

German Life in Various Other Cities and Towns of Virginia.

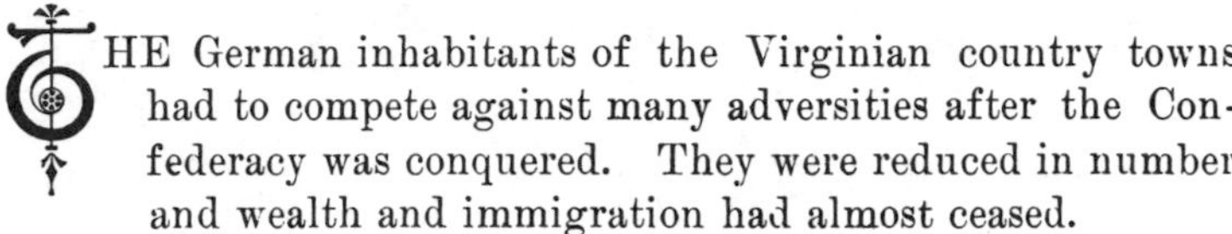

HE German inhabitants of the Virginian country towns had to compete against many adversities after the Confederacy was conquered. They were reduced in number and wealth and immigration had almost ceased.

Alexandria had prospered during the time the Union army was concentrated around it, but when the troops were withdrawn commerce and industrial life came to a standstill. The former inhabitants returned poor and disheartened[286]), the country all around was devastated and the northern business men left for other cities. Of the Germans who had settled in the city during war time, finally only a handful remained, and the German societies were discontinued for want of means and members. All had to struggle for daily existence and years passed by before confidence in a prosperous future was restored. It was in 1868 when Friedrich Pfaff, Adolph Diedel, W. Bauer, Brill, West, Mumm, Wenzel and others united to build a German-Lutheran church and school and invited Rev. J. R. Bischof to become the pastor; but the permanent organization of a community was not accomplished until 1884, although a church had been built. It was a wooden structure about sixty feet deep and forty feet wide, with a steeple and bell donated by the well known brewer Robert Portner. One day, when the church was in course of erection, Mr. Portner happened to pass by and he asked the architect to show him the plan. He was surprised

286.) Correspondence of Dr. Julius Dienelt, Alexandria, Va.

that no steeple had been projected and inquired for the reason. "The community is small and poor," explained the architect, "and they have not got the means." "Well," argued Mr. Portner, "without a steeple it will be no church. Draw a plan for one, bell included, and I will pay the costs." Nearby a dwelling-house for the pastor was built, which contains also the necessary school rooms, and between the two buildings is a shady playground for the pupils. The present pastor, Rev. Johann Schroy, was installed in office in 1884. The church and school registers show eighty-seven church members and thirty-five pupils. The Germans of Alexandria are known to be loyal citizens and several of them have held public offices. Geo. A. Mushbach was a member of the House of Delegates from 1878 to 1879 and at present is a member of the Senate of Virginia. Mr. Ch. Bendheim is the present representative in the House of Delegates. Robert Portner, Isaac Eichberg and Louis Kraft were members of the City Council, and the present Mayor of the city is Hon. Henry Strauss.

In 1854 *Dr. Julius Dienelt*, to whom the author is indebted for these items, settled in Alexandria as dentist. He also gave lessons for some years in the Military Academy and his hobby are literary labors. Dr. Dienelt translated: "Wieland's Oberon" and wrote several novels and poems in German. His festive poem, composed for the occasion of the unveiling of the Confederate monument May 24th, 1889, will always touch a patriot's heart. In 1891 Dr. Dienelt was a contributor to "Der Sueden."

The German element in the old German settlement, the city of *Fredericksburg*, is less prominent. The city suffered very much during the War of Secession and it is now the only place in Virginia which has gone backward in population and wealth. In 1860 Fredericksburg had 5,023 inhabitants, but the census of 1890 gives only 4,528. Among the German inhabitants Mr. John D. Elder, the distinguished artist, deserves especial mention. He died in February 1895. Mr. Elder was educated at Duesseldorf, Germany, under Leitz, and some of his most celebrated paintings — "The Battle of the Crater," the "Bust of Shylock," "After Appomattox," and portraits of

Lee, Jackson, Davis, Johnson, etc., were owned by General Mahone and Mr. Joseph Bryan. He was an exhibitor at art exhibitions in Germany and in this country, and won many prizes, and in his peculiar line was considered the peer of any artist in America.

Petersburg, which also suffered heavily in the various campaigns around Richmond, has quickly regained its ante-bellum prosperity. In 1860 it had 18,266 inhabitants and in 1890 it figured 22,680. Every visitor to the city will be astonished by the large number of German firms, as for instance, H. Noltinius and F. Schwenck & Co., tobacconists; M. Levy, pianist; W. Tappey, machine works; J. Liebert, wines and liquors; A. Rosenstock, M. Cohen, M. Sual and J. Eigenbrunn, dress goods; W. Grossmann, real estate; M. Mendel, toys, etc. The wealth of the German citizens is shown by the fact that they pay about one-fifth of the city and other taxes. In 1876 a "German Club" was organized, of which Mr. Tappey, A. S. Reinach and J. Rosenfield were the officers. Efforts were made to establish a German church and school; the city generously donated the grounds and a church and school house were actually built. But disharmony caused the abandonment of the laudable undertaking. In 1895 a German-Evangelic community was organized at Walthall's near Petersburg and is administered by Rev. Dr. Menzel of the St. Johannis church at Richmond. More unity prevailed among the German Israelites of Petersburg, who erected the synagogue "Rodof Sholem," at the head of which the rabbi Rev. J. Kaiser officiates. Mr. H. Nultinius deserves especial credit as the promoter of German music. On the first day of May 1890 the "German Society of Petersburg" was organized to promote immigration. E. Gieland was elected president and F. W. Leimburger was his next successor. Several members of the society formed a "Gesang-Section" and practiced vocal music, particularly German "Volkslieder."[287])

Norfolk, celebrated as one of the finest harbors on the Atlantic coast, and for the excellence and quantity of oysters and fish brought to its market, is rapidly growing in population and

---

237.) The author is obliged to Mr. W. Grossmann for this information.

importance. In 1820 its population numbered 8,478; before the war it had 14,620 inhabitants and according to the last census its population is now over 35,000. The German element is not as conspicuous as in Richmond, but in commerce and manufacture it takes a prominent part. In the summer of 1891 a correspondent of the "Richmond Times" named the following leading German firms: R. P. Voigt, Loewenburg & Hecht, Hecht & Herschler, Hamburger & Bro., Obendorfer & Co., Frey Bros., A. Myers & Co., Mayer & Co., Pinner & Derring, A. J. Kerns, Norfolk-Portsmouth German Building Association, etc. The "Norfolk Journal of Commerce" published in October 1888 a history and statistic of Norfolk and Portsmouth, naming the following German-Virginians as members of the "Common Council" and city officials: J. Adelsdorf, R. I. Borman, A. P. Thom, W. M. Hannah, S. Marx, Th. B. Rowland, Jos. A. Rolland, E. M. Baum, Dr. W. A. Thom, J. A. Brimmer, Jos. W, P. Veith, J. W. Blick, J. J. Kuling, etc. This list is evidence that the German-Virginian element in Norfolk is respected and influential. Gen. W. D. Groner, of German descent, previously mentioned, was appointed Commissary of Virginia at the World's Fair held at Chicago, Ills.

Portsmouth, the sister town of Norfolk, on the west bank of Elizabeth river, opposite Norfolk, numbered in 1870 10,492 inhabitants and now it has a population of about 14,000, of which many are Germans or of German lineage. Especially among the mechanics and the truck-farmers about the city, as well as in Norfolk, Princess Ann and Nansemond counties, German-Virginians are numerous.

Newport News, a creation of the Chesapeake and Ohio Railroad Company, promises to become one of the most important harbors on the Atlantic coast, being accessible at all seasons of the year to vessels of the heaviest tonnage. Within a few years it has grown to a flourishing city of about 7,000 inhabitants, of whom about one hundred families are Germans, mostly German Jews, and several of the leading business houses are conducted by them. However the German language is spoken very little by these people, being Germans only in name.[288])

288.) Correspondence of Walther Hoffmann, Clerk of Chesapeake and Ohio Railroad Office at Newport News, Va.

In *Farmville* and the entire Prince Edward county the number of Germans is small, but they enjoy the reputation of good, industrious people. There are about twelve German farmers[289]) in the county and some German Hebrews have stores in Farmville and in the country. A Lutheran reverend lives near the Danville railroad and has built on his farm a small church and schoolhouse. From time to time the German farmers assemble there for divine service and the worthy pastor gives instruction to their children. Dr. W. W. H. Thackton has kindly furnished the author the following characteristic information.[290]) "About 1815 Captain John Stephan came to Prince Edward county and built his home at the small village "Kingsville," about one mile from Prince Edward courthouse, now Farmville. Captain Stephan was a pleasant and intelligent man, full of wit and well known in Virginia and other southern States, being the owner of a very popular "Wayside house of entertainment for travellers," situated on the great stage-road from Washington to Middle Georgia. Many distinguished southern statesmen made it a rule to stop on their trips to and from the Capital of the United States at Captain Stephan's or Stevens, as they called him. John C. Calhoun and Wm. C. Preston from South Carolina, Crawford and Barrian from Georgia, and many others frequently enjoyed his gay conversation. Captain Stephan attained the age of eighty-five years and being childless, he invited a nephew from Germany to come over to him, and he inherited the property. The old gentleman died loved and esteemed by his neighbors and numerous friends, and his remains rest in the churchyard of Sidney College Church."

Danville is one of the chief tobacco marts of the State and is a growing city. In 1825 its population amounted only to 1,355, in 1870 to 3,464 and in 1890 to 10,305. Many of the early settlers of Pittsylvania county and of all the counties along the North Carolina line were Germans and German Swiss, as has been already stated, and since the war some thrifty settlements have been made by Germans and English along the line of the Richmond and Danville railroad. Danville itself

289.) Correspondence of C. Zimmermann, at Farmville, Va.

290.) Correspondence of Dr. W. W. H. Thackton, Farmville, Va.

has a fair number of German citizens; most of them are well-to-do merchants and mechanics.

Bristol, on the Tennessee line, *Wytheville*, the county-seat of Wythe, *Newbern*, *Christiansburg*, *Fincastle* in Botetourt, and *Lexington*, the seat of the Washington and Lee University, and the Virginia Military Institute in Rockbridge county, — all these towns have a good sprinkling of German population.

Roanoke, in Roanoke county, deserves special mention, being one of the most prosperous places in the Valley. Within a few years it has grown from a small village to a town of about 20,000 inhabitants, of whom the German element forms a very respectable part. A German brewery exists and several other large factories and firms are owned or managed by Germans.

Salem, the county-seat of Roanoke county, was formerly an exclusively German-Lutheran settlement, bnt situated in the heart of the "Iron District," it is now becoming an important centre of trade and manufacturing interests. At Salem is located the "Roanoke College," a Lutheran institution. Though one of the youngest colleges, it is one of the most flourishing.[291])

Lynchburg, situated on the banks of the James river in Campbell county, had in 1860 a population of only 6,853, which has increased to more than 20,000. It is largely engaged in the manufacture of tobacco and the most important firms are German, like: Holt, Schaefer & Co., Seeling & Co., John Katz, Jr., etc.[292]) Mr. Schaefer is president of the Lynchburg sugar factory. One of the largest dry-goods houses in the South is that of Guggenheimer. The number of German citizens however is small. An evidence of German life in Lynchburg is, that a publication, "War Songs of the South," edited by "Bohemian," correspondent of the "Richmond Dispatch," and published by West & Johnston, Richmond, Va., 1862, was printed by C. A. Shaffter at Lynchburg, whose name surely is German.

290.) "Virginia," a geographical and political summary, by the Board of Immigration. Page 213.

291.) Correspondence of Mr. C. Droste, Richmond, Va.

In 1892 E. Gieland, formerly of Petersburg, Va., organized a small German school for instruction in German and singing.[292])

Staunton, Harrisonburg, Woodstock, Front Royal, Strassburg, Berryville, Leesburgh, New Market and *Winchester*, all situated in the Shenandoah Valley, are justly termed, as has been stated before, of German origin. After the late war a few newcomers of the same nationality located there. The Lutherans have the "Staunton Female Seminary" at Staunton, and at Winchester exists, besides a Lutheran and a United Brethren church, also a German Reformed church.[293])

A widespread distinction among the descendants of the German settlers in the Valley was gained by *Harrison Holt Riddleberger*. He was born October 2nd, 1844, at Edinburg, Shenandoah county. At the early age of seventeen years he entered the Confederate army and was promoted to a lieutenancy and later on to the rank of captain. After the return of peace he studied law and domiciled himself as lawyer at Woodstock. In 1866 Riddleberger was elected State's Attorney and later on a member of the legislature for three successive terms. In 1875 he was made a member of the "State Committee," in 1876 and 1880 a presidential elector and from 1883 to 1889 a "Readjuster," a member of the U. S. Senate. Since 1870 he edited three Virginian newspapers. Riddleberger possessed great force as an orator and politician; he was a most violent opponent of General Mahone, the leader of the Republican party in Virginia, and made himself commendably known in the movement for settling the State-debts accumulated during the Civil War. The respective arrangements resolved upon by his suggestions to the Legislature of Virginia are known as "the Riddleberger Compromise." His prospects were certainly very bright, but his unfortunate passion for intoxicating drinks ruined his career and caused his early death on January 24th, 1890.

General John E. Roller of Harrisonburg is another German-

292.) Correspondence of Mr. Emil Gieland, Lynchburg, Va.

293. Compare "Winchester, the Metropolis of the Valley," by Hancock, Laughlin & Co.

Virginian of renown. He is an ardent admirer of the merits of the German pioneers in Old Virginia and now engaged in writing their history, which will no doubt furnish further proof of their exertions in promoting the growth and prosperity of Virginia as a colony and as a State.

Charlottesville, the county-seat of Albemarle and the seat of the University of Virginia, had in 1870 a population of 2,838 and at present it is estimated to be about 7,000. The German element is now not as large there as before the war, but the commerce of the town is still prominently in German hands. The wine-making industry flourishes in Charlottesville and its neighborhood. Mr. Hotopp's and the Monticello Wine Company, in charge of Mr. A. Russow, are the two largest establishments. Both firms have been awarded various exposition medals. Leterman Bros. are the leading clothing house in this part of the State. The German Israelites have for years had a synagogue, "Beth Israel," and there is also a German Lutheran church, of which Rev. J. L. Craemer was pastor, while afterwards Rev. J. A. Schroy of Alexandria administrated the pastorate. At present a German-American is pastor and he is endeavoring to anglicize his German community. A German school does not exist at Charlottesville or at any other place in Albemarle, but the German language and literature have been part of the courses of study at the University since its foundation. German is also taught at the celebrated "Miller Manual Labor School of Albemarle."[294]) Within the last decade several German-Virginians held public offices in the city and county.

Manchester is making rapid progress. Against 2,793 inhabitants in 1860, it now has to show a population of 10 to 11,000, and the population of the immediate suburbs is estimated at 3,000.[295]) A great number of Germans live in the city; most of these are mechanics and wage-workers employed in Richmond. Manchester and Richmond are really but one

294.) German instruction is given at all colleges and highschools in Virginia, the Washington and Lee University at Lexington included.

295.) The "Richmond Dispatch," p. 2. April 18, 1891.

city, being connected by several bridges spanning the James river and by electric and horse-car lines. After the war its people were of course impoverished, and though it escaped such a disaster as the conflagration, that burned the greater portion of the business quarter of Richmond, the latter by reason of its becoming early after the cessation of hostilities the money centre of the State, absorbed much of its trade. These conditions however were only temporary. Manchester has within herself the factors of recuperation and an independent progress in certain directions, and these were not slow in asserting themselves. She had the situation, the water-power, the railroad connections, the climate, the tributary territory and the will to make herself a city, and they were all converged to that consummation with substantial and gratifying results. The German inhabitants have naturally profited by all these advantages and are doing well.

It would require the space of a much larger volume to point out all the localities in the State where the German element is represented and forms a valuable addition to the Anglo-American population. German storekeepers are to be found all over the country in Culpeper, Warrenton, Gordonsville, Orange county, Louisa, Leesburg, New Market and many other minor towns. The author could not visit all parts of Virginia to personally collect information, and on the other hand he found it very difficult to induce people settled there to furnish him with reliable information by letter. But to give further evidence of the importance and influence of the German-Americans in Virginia, he presents a list of the German-Virginian delegates to the General Assembly and the U. S. Congress during the period from 1860 to 1893, a list of school officials from 1872 to 1896 and a list of the localities with German names throughout the State. To the latter the English names of such cities, towns and villages are added which are known to be of German origin.

List of German-Virginian Delegates to the General Assembly of Virginia and the U. S. Congress.[296])

Sam. A. Coffmann,	Rockingham Co.,	Member House of Delegates
David W. Berlin,	Upshur "	" " "
David M. Shriver,	Ohio Co.,	Member of the Senate of Va.
J. A. Nighbart,	Boone County,	Member House of Delegates
Benj. R. Linkous,	Fayette "	" "
G. W. Rust,	Page "	" "
A. J. Deyerle,	Roanoke "	" "
A. K. Trout,	Augusta "	" Senate of Va.
Geo. B. Keezell,	Rockingham County,	" "
George H. Peck,	Giles "	" "
Dr. L. F. Woltz,	Carroll County,	Member House of Delegates
F. Stearns,	Henrico "	" "
H. Peck,	Montgomery County	" "
H. B. Harnsberger,	Rockingham "	" "
J. B. Straver,	Shenandoah "	" "
M. Hanger	Augusta "	" "
A. B. Lightner,	" "	" "
Paul Lightner,	Bath "	" "
Henry W. Keyser,	Page "	" "
James P. Critz.	Patrick "	" "
Wm. Lovenstein,	Richmond City,	Member House of Delegates now Senator.
A. Bodecker,	"	Member House of Delegates
H. H. Riddleberger,	Shenandoah County,	Member House of Delegates and U. S. Senator.
J. H. von Auken,	Sussex County,	Member House of Delegates
Geo. A. Mushbach,	Alexandria City,	Member House of Delegates and now Senator.

296.) From the "Journal of the House of Delegates and the Senate of Virginia," and the "Illustrated Southern Almanac," J. L. Hill Printing Co., Richmond, Va., 1898.

D. F. May,	City of Petersburg,	Member House of Delegates and now Senator.
Sam. Burger,	Botetourt County,	“
P. B. Starke,	Brunswick “	“
Wm. A. Reese,	Greenville “	“
H. Conrad,	Frederick “	“
J. J. Deyer,	Southhampton County,	“
Ph. Herring,	Rockingham “	“
J. D. Honaker,	Bland “	“
Sam. E. Leybrock,	Pulasky “	“
H. W. Daingerfield,	Essex County,	“
J. V. Herring,	Chesterfield County,	“
G. C. Huffman,	Craig “	“
D. Riner,	Montgomery “	“
J. E. Sanger,	Rockingham “	“
L. D. Starke,	Norfolk City,	“
Ch. Bendheim,	Alexandria County,	“
George W. Koiner,	Augusta “	“
Alexander B. Lightner,	Augusta “	“
John C. Utz,	Madison “	“
J. W. Churchman,	Augusta County,	Member House of Delegates
A. L. Winter,	Bedfort “	“ “
K. B. Stoner,	Botetourt “	“ “
T. C. Pilcher,	Fauquier “	“ “
S. T. Turner,	Floyd and Franklin “	“ “
E. C. Jordan,	Frederick and Winchester “	“ “
C. G. Kizer,	Norfolk City,	“ “
M. Switzer,	Rockingham County,	“ “
J. M. Bauserman,	Shenandoah “	“ “

List of School Officials.

The list of school officials from 1872 to 1896 shows the following German names of county and city superintendents in Virginia and West Virginia.[297])

George M. Peck, Hampton, Elizabeth County, Virginia.
Dr. C. M. Stigleman, Floyd C. H., Floyd County, "
W. H. Gold, Winchester, Frederick " "
James P. Beck, Pearisburgh, Giles " "
Henry C. Coleman, South Boston, Halifax " "
Addison Borst, Fredericksburgh, King George and Stafford Counties, Virginia.
George H. Kendrick, Point Truth, Scott County, Virginia.
John W. Wildman, Leesburgh, Loudoun " "
S. B. Grose, Clay C. H., Clay County, West Virginia.
E. F. Vossler, Grant C. H., Grant County, "
John S. Kern, Nicholas C. H., Nicholas County, "
Wm. A. Newman, Knob Fork, Wetzel " "
R. Workman, Mouth Short Creek, Boone " "
C. P. Wirgman, Romney, Hampshire " "
J. C. Lininger, Winfield, Putnam " "
Jos. S. Loose, Harrisonburg, Rockingham " Virginia.
George J. Kayser, Hamlin, Lincoln " West Virginia.
John A. Bock, Farmington, Marion " "
M. H. Bittinger, Indian Creek, Monroe " "
George Buck, Berkeley Springs, Morgan " "
A. Workman, Falls of Twelve Pale, Wayne " "
C. L. Broadus, Roxalana, Roane " "
Richard L. Carne, Alexandria, Alexandria " Virginia.
W. W. Wysor, Newbern, Pulaski " "
Joseph Phipps, Osborn's Gap, Wise " "
John Hess, Duffield, Jefferson " West Virginia.
W. M. Wirt, Dallas, Marshall " "
A. B. Phipps, Princeton, Mercer " "

297.) U. S. Reports of the Commissioner of Education from 1872 to 1896.

W. A. Blankenship, Chesterfield	"	Virginia.
J. A. Holtzman, Jeffersonton, Culpeper	"	"
E. C. Glass, Lynchburgh, Campbell	"	"
W. M. Straus, Parkersburgh, Wood	"	West Virginia.
K. Kemper, Alexandria, Alexandria	"	Virginia.
John U. Bader, Staunton, Augusta	"	"
B. Rust, Roanoke, Roanoke	"	"

These school reports contain a still larger number of doubtful names and they give evidence of the active part German-Virginians are taking in public education.

List of Localities and Post Offices with German Names.

Counties.

Accomac.—Hoffman's Wharf, Mappburg, Wagram, Keller P.O., Horntown.

Albemarle.—Shadwell, Hotopp's Rapids, Blenheim P. O.

Alexandria.—Fort Myer.

Alleghany. Keyser's Mines, Selma, Stacks.

Amherst.—Jordan.

Amelia.—Smack's Creek, Ammon P. O.

Appomattox.—Karl P. O.

Augusta.—Koiner's Store P. O., Sangerville, Fishersville, Weyer's Cave Station, Croberger's Siding, Stover's Shop P. O., Shaffer's.

Bedford,—Coleman's Falls P. O., Emaus P. O., Marrville, Nininger P. O.

Botetourt.—Amsterdam, Coyner's Spring, Kyle, Obenshain P.O., Strom P. O., Tinker's Knob.

Brunswick.—Alps, Walthall's Store P. O., Ordsburg P. O., Thomasburg, Turner, Harper's Home.

Buchanan.--Schack's Mill P. O.

Buckingham.—Hardwicksville, Curdville.

Campbell.—Rustburg, Rosenberger Mine, Heald's, Reusen's P.O.

Caroline.—Shumansville, Knopf P. O.

Carroll.—Lambsburg, Woltz's P. O., Dutchman's Branch, Nester P. O., Peck P. O., Piper's Gap.

Charlotte.—Reese's P. O.

Chesterfield.—Port Walthall, Granite, Ettrick's P. O., Hallsburg, Frank's Branch.

Clarke.—Castleman's River and Ferry, Singer's Glen, Meyerhoefer's Store P. O., Berryville.

Craig.—Huffman's P. O., Kyle's, Simmonsville, Layman P. O.

Culpeper.—Stevensburg, Hedgeman's River, Freeman's Ford, Waylandsburg.

Cumberland.—Colemansville.

Dinwiddie.—Burgess P. O., Waldemar.

Dickinson.—Freeling P. O.

Fairfax.—Vienna, Franconia, Lewinsville, Springman P. O., Wiehle P. O., Germantown, Shueter's Hill.

Fauquier.—Germantown, Linden, Bristersburg.

Floyd.—Ultizer's Ford, Huffville.

Fluvanna.—Stillman P. O., Bullenger's Creek.

Franklin.—Helm's P. O., Sontag, Hickman, Holland's, Prillaman's, Wirtz P. O., Naff's P. O., Germantown.

Frederick.—Winchester, Kernstown, Stephensburg (formerly Stephansburg), Front Royal, Foreman's Creek, Sydner's Gap, Rosenberger P. O., Siler P. O., Hinckle P.O., Jordan's Springs.

Giles.—Lurich.

Grayson.—Clem's Branch, Redman's P. O.

Goochland.—Vinetaville P. O.

Greene.—Ruckersville, Wetsel's P. O.

Hanover.—Hanover.

Henrico.—Dutch Gap, Hungary, Carl's Neck.

Henry.—Waller's, Koger's, Irisburg.

Highland.—Wier.

Isle of Wight.—Smithfield, Auguste.

King and Queen.—Walden's P. O., Truhart.

King George.—Comorn, Spillman's, Weedonville.

King William.—Frazer's Ferry.

Lee.—Fritz P. O.

Loudoun.—Middleburg, Snickersville, Leesburg, Snicker's Gap, Lovettsville.

Louisa.—Frederickshall, Buckner Station, Bumpass, Arminius Coppermine.

Lunenburg.—Lunenburg Court House (now Lewistown), Meherrin, Kinderwood, Kunath P. O., Lochleven P. O.

Madison.—Criglersville, Froyman's Mills, Fisher's Gap.

Middlesex.—Conrad's Mill P. O.

Montgomery.—Blacksburg (formerly Schwarzburg), Christiansburg, Langhorn's P. O., Riner's P. O., Flagg P. O., Vickers.

Nansemond.—Holland.

Nelson.—Hartwicksville, Roseland, Faber's Station.

New Kent.—Bock P. O.

Norfolk.—Tanner's Creek, Bower's Hill, Rodman.

Northampton.—Franktown, Burgess' Store, Cohn's Wharf.

Northumberland.—Lottsburg.

Nottoway.—Drauker's P. O.

Orange.—Germanna Mills, Falknerland, Mugler.

Page.—Marksville, Rust Siding, Ruffner's Cave, Audenried, Printz and Strickler's Mines, Kountz, Brand.

Patrick.—Mack's Gap, Critz P. O.

Pittsylvania.—Berger's Store.

Powhatan.—Tucker's Creek.

Princess Ann.—Kempsville.

Pulaski.—Newbern, (formerly Neu Bern), Honaker Iron Bank, Altoona, Schooler Station, Mack's and Strouble's C'k's.

Rappahannock.—Hollandsburg, Jordan's River.

Roanoke.—Salem, Singer, Deyerle's Station, Gish's.

Rockbridge.—Lexington, Tinker's Creek, Kerr's Creek, Brownsburg, Barger, Locher's Siding, Rapp's Mills, Goshen Pass, Engleman P. O., Zack P. O., Appold's, Zollman P. O.

Rockingham.—Keezletown (formerly Kieselstadt), Rushville, Harrisonburg, Falk's Run, Chrisman, Singer's Glen, Frieden's, Brock's Gap, Seller's, Meyerhoefer's P. O., Chrisman.

Russel.—Honaker Station, Heyter's Gap.

Scott.—Welchburg, Speer's Ferry, De Kalb District.

Shenandoah.—Strassburg, Woodstock (formerly Müllerstown), Maurertown, Saumsville, Hamburg, New Market (formerly Neu Market), Fisher's Hill, Getz P. O., Lantz Mills, Hepner's P. O., Edenburg, Bowman's.

Smith.—Holstein Mills, Grosse's P. O.

Southampton.—Berlin, Jerusalem, Bower's, Vicksville.

Spotsylvania.—Fredericksburg, Brokenburg, Brockville, Hardenburg, Beck's Landing, Thornburg, Twyman's P.O.

Stafford.—Fosterville, Germanna Ford, Musselman.

Sussex.—Coman's Well, Belsche's, Freeman's.

Tazewell.—Tannersville, Shrader's P. O., Adria, Steeleburg.

Warren.—Front Royal, Linden.

Washington.—Mangel's Spring, Hyter's Gap.

Westmoreland.—Hague, Templeman's X Road, Horner's P. O., Tucker's Hill.

Wise.—Lipp's District, Berge's Gap, Banner.

Wythe.—Umbarger's, Stearn's, Simmerman's Mineral Lands, Witheville, Cragger's Bank.

CONCLUSION.

In the beginning of 1898 the United States were involved in war with Spain, but the author abstains from recording this very important event and the part the German-Virginians have taken in it. The time has not yet arrived to form a safe and impartial opinion of the causes and consequences of this conflict and the victories won by our Army and Navy. This book is designed to illustrate firmly established facts: the advantages Virginia offers to immigration and particularly the efforts, genius and perseverance with which the German population has enlarged year by year the elements of its vitality and prosperity, although frequently subject to adverse conditions. Virginia,—in wealth and importance once at the head of all the States,—appears destined to advance again with the assistance of a new and numerous immigration from the German Fatherland to the front rank of this glorious Union. The soil of the old mother-state is so diversified, its climate so delightful, the range of crops so great, the working season so long, water-power so abundant, its mineral resources are so rich and farm-lands so cheap, that a future may be predicted of a rapid improvement of its population, agriculture, industries, commerce and all that includes prominence and happiness of a country.

APPENDIX.

List of Anglicized German Names in Virginia.

Adler	to Eagle.
Armstaedt	" Armistead and Armsteed.
Baer	" Bear.
Bauer	" Bowers.
Baumann	" Bowman and Baughman.
Becker	" Baker.
Beier	" Byer and Byers.
Berger	" Barger.
Betz	" Bates.
Bieler	" Beeler.
Blume	" Bloom.
Blumenberg	" Bloomberg.
Boscher	" Bosher.
Brauer	" Brauer and Brewer.
Braun	" Brown.
Breitkopf	" Broadhead.
Brockhauss	" Brookhouse.
Buehring	" Bouhring.
Buerger	" Burger.
Busch	" Bush.
Christmann	" Chrisman.
Clemenz	" Clements and Clemons.
Engel	" Angle and Angel.
Erhardt	" Airheard and Earhart.
Fischer	" Fisher.
Flemming.	" Fleming.
Foerster	" Foster.
Frei or Frey	" Fry.
Freimann	" Freeman.

Freund	to Friend.
Froebel	" Fravel.
Frohmann	" Froman.
Fuchs	" Fox.
Fuhrmann	" Furman.
Fuerst	" Furst.
Gaertner	" Gardner.
Gerber	" Garber and Tanner.
Gerth	" Garth.
Goetz	" Gates and Yates.
Goldschmidt	" Goldsmith.
Gottlieb	" Cudlipp.
Gruen	" Green.
Gruenebaum	" Greenbaum and Greentree.
Gute or Gude	" Goode.
Gutmann	" Goodman.
Hafer	" Haver.
Harbach	" Harbough.
Hardwich	" Hardwicke.
Hartenstein	" Hartenstine.
Hausmann	" Houseman.
Heid	" Hite.
Heilmann	" Hileman.
Heiner	" Hiner.
Heinz	" Hines.
Heiss	" Hayes.
Hermann	" Harman.
Herr	" Harr.
Herzog	" Duke.
Huth	" Hood.
Jaeger	" Yager, Yeager and Hunter.
Jehle	" Yahley.
John	" Jone and Jones.
Jung	" Young.
Kaiser	" Keyser.
Keil	" Kyle.
Kirchman	" Churchman.
Kirchwall	" Kercheval.

Klein	to	Cline, Kline and Little or Small.
Kloess and Kloss	"	Glaize.
Koch	"	Cook.
Koenig	"	King.
Koinath or Kunath	"	Koiner, Coyner, Koyner, Coiner, Kiner, Cuyner and Cyner.
Kohl	"	Cole.
Kohlmann	"	Coleman.
Koppel	"	Copple.
Kraemer	"	Creamer and Kremer.
Krause	"	Grouse and Krouse.
Kreutzer	"	Crozer.
Krueger	"	Crigger and Kreger.
Kuhn	"	Coon.
Kuntz	"	Coons, Kountz and Coontz.
Kuester	"	Custer.
Kurz	"	Short.
Lang and Lange	"	Long.
Laube	"	Loube.
Lauter	"	Lowther.
Lehmann	"	Layman.
Leibrock	"	Lybrock.
Lentz	"	Lantz.
Lieber	"	Liewer.
Loewe	"	Lyon and Lyons.
Loewenstein	"	Lovenstein and Livingston.
Lorenz	"	Lawrence.
Ludwig	"	Lewis.
Marschall	"	Marshall.
Matheus and Matthes	"	Mathew, Matthews and Mathues.
Mejo	"	Mayo.
Mertz	"	Martz.
Michel	"	Mitchel.
Moritz	"	Morris.
Neubert	"	Nighbart.
Neukirch	"	Newkirk.
Neumann	"	Newman.
Oppenheimer	"	Oppenhimer.

Puttmann	to Putman.
Reimann	" Rayman.
Reiner	" Riner.
Reiss	" Rice.
Ried	" Reed.
Riese	" Rees and Reese.
Roemer	" Romer.
Rothmann	" Redman and Rodman.
Sauer	" Sower.
Schaefer	" Shafer, Shepherd, Shepperd and Sheppard.
Scharf	" Sharp.
Schenk	" Shank.
Scheuner	" Shewner.
Schiener	" Shuoner.
Schmal	" Small.
Schmidt	" Smith.
Schmucker	" Smucker.
Schneider	" Snyder and Taylor.
Schoeplein	" Chapline.
Schreiber	" Shriver.
Schuermann	" Shurman and Sherman.
Schuessler	" Chisler.
Schuetz	" Sheetz.
Schumacher	" Shoemaker.
Schumann	" Shuman and Choohman.
Schwarz	" Sewards and Black.
Schweinfurt	" Swineford.
Schweitzer	" Switzer.
Seiler	" Siler.
Siegel	" Siegle, Seagles, Sycle and Sicle
Sniedt	" Sneed and Snead.
Spielmann	" Spilman.
Stahl	" Steel.
Staufer	" Stover.
Stein	" Stone.
Steinbach	" Stainback.
Steiner	" Stiner and Stoner.
Steinmetz	" Stinemetz.

Stephan	to	Stephens and Stevens.
Storch	"	Stork.
Tempel	"	Temple.
Thalheimer	"	Thalhimer.
Traut	"	Trout.
Uhl	"	Ewel.
Vierlaender	"	Verlander.
Vogel	"	Vogle.
Waechter	"	Wachter.
Wagner	"	Wagener, Waggener and Waggoner.
Wassermann	"	Waterman.
Weber	"	Weaver.
Weimar	"	Wymar.
Weise	"	Wise and White.
Werner	"	Warner.
Wieden	"	Weedon.
Wier	"	Wyer.
Wieland	"	Wyland.
Wilhelm	"	Williams.
Zimmermann	"	Simmerman and Carpenter.

SPECIMENS OF GERMAN-VIRGINIAN POETRY.

Die Letzte Predigt.

*Von Wilhelm Mueller.**)

Herbei ihr Männer, stark und schlicht,
  Die ihr getrotzt der Wildniss Schrecken!
Heut' ruft euch eine fromme Pflicht,
  Des Westens wetterbraune Recken.
Ihr Frauen, emsig und besonnen,
  Den Männern gleich an kühnem Muth,
Heut' lasst die Hütte rebumsponnen
  Getrost in eurer Kinder Hut.

Zum Kirchlein eilt am Waldesrand
  Das ihr erbaut, wie Juda's Söhne
Den Tempel, eure Wehr zur Hand
  Und auf den Lippen Psalmentöne.
Den Pred'ger gilt es, heut' zu ehren,
  Kommt aus dem Shenandoah-Thal,
Denn Mühlenberg wird euch belehren
  Mit ernstem Wort zum letztenmal.

Und wo man mit der deutschen Art
  Der Väter Sprache hoch gehalten,
Sind zeitig schon zur Kirchenfahrt
  Bereit die Jungen und die Alten.
Die würd'gen Siedler von den Farmen,
  Die Jäger von der Lichtung Saum,
Die Reichen kommen, wie die Armen,
  Das kleine Bethaus fasst sie kaum.

---

*) Prof. Wilhelm Mueller was born April 9th, 1815, at Heppenheim, Hessia, and came to America in 1866. He was principal of a school in Cincinnati, Ohio, and afterwards editor of the German "Puck," New York. Mr. Mueller published several collections of lyric and humorous poems, dramas and opera texts. In 1890—91 he was proprietor of a farm in Louisa County, Va., and now he travels in Germany. The poems reproduced here have been-published in "Der Sueden," Richmond, Va., 1891.

Als sich der Gläub'gen fromme Schaar
  Gestärkt durch kräftige Gesänge
Tritt Mühlenberg vor den Altar
  Und spricht zur andachtsvollen Menge:
"Oft hat mein Wort in euch entzündet
  Die Sehnsucht nach des Friedens Heil;
Den Segen hab' ich euch gekündet,
  Der frommer Demuth wird zu Theil."

"Ihr gabet willig der Person
  Des Königs die verdiente Ehre.
Gehorsam zolltet ihr dem Thron,
  Sowie es uns'rer Kirche Lehre.
Doch wenn mit heiligen Gesetzen
  Spott treibt der Herrscher Tyrannei,
Wenn sie der Völker Recht verletzen,
  Dann seid ihr aller Bande frei!"

"Empörung wird zur Mannespflicht,
  Gehorsam wäre Schmach und Schande,
Den König fordert vor Gericht
  Und zeiht ihn des Verraths am Lande.
Nicht länger singt des Friedens Psalmen,
  Stosst schmetternd in des Krieges Horn,
Verbergt die Sichel in den Halmen
  Und greift zum Schwert im Rächerzorn;

"Und wie ich euer Lehrer war
  Und euer Freund in Friedenszeiten,
Will ich in Stunden der Gefahr
  Euch in den Schlachten Donner leiten.
Steht treu zu mir in blut'ger Fehde,
  Die Freiheit ruft zum heil'gen Krieg.
Nun sei's genug der müss'gen Rede,
  Die Waffen führen uns zum Sieg!"

Der Pred'ger sprach's, und den Talar
  Liess er von seinen Schultern gleiten.
Gerüstet stand er am Altar,
  Ein Priesterheld aus alten Zeiten.

Des Staunens Bann lag auf der Runde;
Doch als der Pfarrer schlägt an's Schwert,
Da braus't ein Ruf aus jedem Munde:
"Mit Mühlenberg für Haus und Herd!"

Und wie's der Siedler Schaar gelobt,
So folgten sie des Führers Bahnen.
Wo heiss und wild der Kampf getobt,
Da wehten die Virginier Fahnen.
D'rum, wenn ihr jene stolzen Helden,
Die für die Freiheit kämpften, nennt,
Lasst auch von Mühlenberg euch melden
Und seinem deutschen Regiment.

Auf einem alten Fort.

Von Wilhelm Mueller.

Als deine Wälle rings von Waffen starrten,
Da botest du der Stadt und Küste Schutz.
Von jener Schanze wehten die Standarten
Und sprachen kühn dem Landesfeinde Trutz.

Jetzt deckt die steile Böschung frischer Rasen,
Am Schilderhaus sprosst Rittersporn empor.
Im Hofe seh' ich muntre Ziegen grasen,
Und Schwalben nisten an dem offnen Thor.

Der Bruderkampf, der Nord und Süd entzweite,
Liess an dem Strand die Schanzen einst erstehn.
Doch als der Friede kam nach heissem Streite,
Durft' auch des Krieges finstres Werk vergehn.

Und wo das Hornsignal zum Waffentanze
Mit dumpfem Klange rief der Krieger Schaar,
Da schmückt die Jugend mit dem Blumenkranze
Beim heitern Spiele sich das goldne Haar.

Die Pfähle, die das Bollwerk einst umgaben,
Vereint der Fischer jetzt zum starken Floss.
Und in dem Schanzkorb holen kecke Knaben
Der Tiefe Schätze aus des Meeres Schoss.

Columbia, du darfst dich glücklich nennen,
Bannst du der Zwietracht Geist im eignen Land—
An deinen Marken wird kein Kampf entbrennen,
Kein äussrer Feind droht jemals deinen Strand.

Indess die alte Welt der Völker Stärke
Den Furien des Kriegs zum Opfer bringt,
Uebst du die beste Kraft im Friedenswerke,
Die goldner Ernte Segen dir erringt.

Der Sueden.

Von Wilhelm Mueller.

Der Himmel trug der Schwermuth düstres Kleid,
Ein Wolkenzug schwebt' über meinem Haupt,
Wie eines Riesenkranichs graue Schwinge
Und barg des Tages flammendes Gestirn.

Der grimme Nord mit tödlich kaltem Hauch
Schnob durch des Land und zwang des Eises Joch
Den Strömen auf, und was da fleucht und kreucht
Erschauerte in seinem eis'gen Odem.
Mir selber drang er bis in's Mark und schien
Des Lebens Quell erstarrend zu durchkälten.

Da schwamm im Abendlicht ein Schwan dahin,
Von seinen Flügeln träuft' ein letster Glanz
Des Tag's und sank mir leuchtend in das Herz,
Gleich einem Gruss aus lenzbeglückten Zonen.
Und plötzlich rief's in meiner Seele laut:
Nach Süden, rasch dem Lüftesegler nach,
Hinweg, aus winterstarren Au'n nach Süden!

Und wie ein Zaubermantel trug das Ross,
  Das dampfbeschwingte, mich nach wärm'ren
Bald sah ich golden der Orange Pracht [Landen.
  Aus dunklem Laube schimmern und erging
Mich träumend unter glänzend blättrigen
  Magnolien, wonnig milde Lüfte athmend,
Und mit dem froh erstaunten Blick die Weite
  Des sonnig blauen Himmels kühn ergreifend.

O sanfter Hauch von harz'gem Duft geschwängert,
  O Sonnenblick, der in das Herz mir flammt!
Wie ihr den Sinn mir zauberisch berückt,
  Vermein' ich eine alte dunkle Sage
Mit einem Mal in klarem Licht zu schau'n.

Der Kastilianer, der den Quell der Jugend
  In diesen Landen sehend einst gesucht,
Ward nicht von seinem mächt'gen Drang betrogen,
  Nur springt der Wunderbrunnen der Verjüngung
Nicht aus dem Boden Florida's, wo Leon
  Nach ihm geforscht—er rauscht mit sanfter Macht
In Georgia's Fichtenhainen und umweht
  Dich stärkend in Lüften Carolina's,
Wo Dir aus reinem sonnenhellem Aether,
  Auf freien Höhen aus der Tannen Odem,
Im stillen Thal, aus murmelnden Gewässern,
  Wie aus dem Donnergruss der Katarakte
Ein neues Leben in den Busen dringt.

  Und jene Schätze, die voll Beutegier
Die Spanier einst zu heben kamen, ruhn
  Verborgen in der Erde dunklen Tiefen
In manchem sonnbeglänzten Hang des Südlands.

Und wenn das Erz aus Bergesschooss gewonnen
  Hell aufsprüht in des Ofens rothen Flammen
Und mit dem Pochen mächt'ger Eisenhämmer
  Die eh'rne Neuzeit ihren Einzug hält;
Und wenn einst auf virgin'schen Rebenhügeln
  Der Sonne Licht im Traubenblut erglüht

Und strahlend hell in dem Pokale funkelt,
Den Müden Stärkung, Kraft dem Siechen spen-
Dann ist die alte Sage wahr geworden, [dend,
Dann ist des Südlands goldner Schatz gehoben.

Die Landung der ersten Jungfrauen zu Jamestown, Va. Anno 1619.

Von Herrmann Schuricht.

"Ein Schiff in Sicht! Hallo — hallo!"
Ertönt der Ruf, — und flink und froh
Aus Jamestown eilt zum nahen Strand
Ein jeder Mann und junge Fant.

Noch war kein Einziger beweibt
Von Allen, die die Neugier treibt —
Und leicht begreiflich ist fürwahr:
Dass liebetoll die ganze Schaar.

Mit vollen Segeln biegt das Schiff
Jetzt um das nahe Felsenriff; —
Auf dem Verdecke ist zu schau'n
Ein Kranz holdseliger Jungfrau'n.

Sie lassen Tücher weh'n zum Gruss —
Die Mündchen spitzen sich zum Kuss —
Und jubelnd, — brennend vor Begier
Am Ufer steh'n die Pionier'.

Kaum legt das Schiff im Hafen an,
Als vorwärts dränget Mann für Mann;
Doch Captain Smith gebietet: "Halt!"
Und rufet, dass es weithin schallt:

"Zurück — ihr heirathslustig Pack —
Erst bringet fünfzig Pfund Taback,
Eh' eine Schöne Ihr wählt aus
Und führt als Eh'gesponst nach Haus!"

Das war, wie Jedermann ersieht,
Ganz niederträchtig und perfid —
Und ellenlang ward manch Gesicht,
Dieweil an Taback es gebricht.

Die Reich'ren aber schleppten schnell
Ihr Tabackquantum d'rauf zur Stell' —
Und wer zuerst kam, hatt' die Qual:
Denn heikel ist solch' Jungferwahl;

Die schönsten Mädchen gingen ab
Wie Marzipan — klipp-klapp — klipp-klapp —
Und auch die Aelt'ste, lahm und stumpf,
Führt heim zuletzt ein Lederstrumpf.

Genug — die Nachfrag' war so gross —
So lockend süss das Eheloos —
Dass noch manch' theure Mädchenfracht
Nach Jamestown ward zu Markt gebracht.

* * *

Wo ist sie hin, die schöne Zeit? — —
O Jammer und o Herzeleid —
Vergebens aus der Jungfrau'n Zahl
Sucht manche jetzt 'nen Eh'gemahl!

Widewilt's versunkene Insel.

Von Herrmann Schuricht.

In längstentschwund'nen Tagen,
Als Richmond kaum gekannt,
Lebt' an des Jamesstrom's Ufern
Ein Mann aus deutschem Land.

Am Fuss der wilden Fälle
Warf er die Angel aus —
Und Fisch und leck're Austern
Bracht' Abends er nach Haus.

Der Widewilt, — der Fischer, —
Ward ringsum bald genannt; —
Begehrt war seine Waare
Von Alt und Jung im Land.

Da schwoll nach Winterstürmen
Der Strom einst mächtig an,
Und brach durch Feld und Wälder
Sich schäumend neue Bahn.

Ehrwürd'ge Waldesriesen
Riss er vom Grunde los,
Trug sie hinab die Fälle
Zum wilden Fluthenschooss.

Und donnernd folgten ihnen
Sandmassen und Gestein
Und hüllten in der Tiefe
Mit festem Arm sie ein.

So wuchs im Stromesbette
Ein Inselchen empor,
Das Widewilt, der Kühne,
Zur Heimstatt sich erkor.

Er baute Pallisaden
Ringsum, der deutsche Mann,
Und legte Austernbeete
Auf seiner Insel an.

Sein Unternehmen blühte,
Gepflegt mit Fleiss und Muth —
Und trotzte Strom und Wellen
Und jeder Frühlingsfluth.

Doch Widewilt wurd' älter, —
Sein letztes Stündlein schlug —
Und eines stillen Abends
Man ihn zu Grabe trug.

D'rauf folgt ein strenger Winter —
Und hoch das Eis sich staut,
Wo kühn im Strom der Deutsche
Sein Inselland gebaut.

Kein Muth'ger wagt's zu schützen;-
Und als der Eiswall brach
Folgt ihm zermalmt,—geborsten,—
Des Todten Insel nach.

Jetzt decken Fluth und Wellen
Was Widewilt erstrebt, —
Dieweil er unvergessen
Im Volksmund weiterlebt.

Der See im Dismal Swamp in Virginien.

Nach Thomas Moore *von Herrmann Schuricht.*

Der grosse und berüchtigte Dismal Swamp liegt zehn bis zwölf Meilen von Norfolk, Va., entfernt und ein in der Mitte desselben gelegener See, welcher eine Länge von ungefähr sieben Meilen hat, wird "Drummond's See" genannt. Die Sage hat um denselben den Zauber der Romantik gewoben. Es wird erzählt, dass ein Jüngling um den Tod seines geliebten Mädchens den Verstand verlor, plötzlich aus dem Kreise seiner Freunde verschwand und nie mehr gesehen wurde. Er hatte oft behauptet, dass seine Geliebte nicht todt, sondern nach dem Dismal Swamp entflohen sei, und deshalb verbreitete sich das Gerücht, dass er gleichfalls nach jener traurigen Wildniss entwichen und dort verhungert, oder im Morast versunken sei. Thomas Moore, Erin's bewunderter und geliebter Sohn, weilte 1804 in Virginien, hörte die Sage vom See im Dismal Swamp und machte dieselbe zum Gegenstand der folgenden Dichtung:

Man grub ihr ein Grab,—zu kalt und dumpf,
Für ein Herz so treu und warm ; —
Und lenket, wo glüht der faulende Stumpf
Ihr Boot mit kräftigem Arm.

" Bald werd' ich sie schau'n im Mondenschein,
Bald hör' ich der Ruder Schlag ; —
Und zum See floh sie, durch Wald und Sumpf,
Ein Leben der Liebe wartet dort mein —
Und ich berg' die Maid im Cypressenhain
Folgt Todesgrauen ihr nach!"

Er hastet zum Sumpf und achtet's nicht,
Dass grausig und rauh der Pfad,
Den kühn er durch Dorngestrüpp sich bricht,—
Dass Schlangen sich bergen vor Tageslicht
Im Moor, das kein Fuss betrat.

Und sucht' er Rast, von Nacht umgraut,—
Und fühlt sich vom Schlaf geletzt,—
Da lagert er, wo verzaubertes Kraut
Mit giftigen Thränen sein Haupt bethaut
Und brennend die Haut ihm netzt.

Die Wölfin heult in dem nahen Rohr,—
Die Kupferschlang' zischt ihn an;
Wild schrickt er aus wüstem Traume empor
Und klagt: " Wo find' ich das dunkle Moor
Und Liebchen im weissen Kahn?"

Da schaut er den See;—jäh zuckt ein Strahl
Hellflammend und leuchtend weit;

"Willkommen Dein Licht—viel tausend Mal!"
Er ruft—und's Echo hallt durch Wald u. Thal
Den Namen der todten Maid.

Er höhlt einen Birkenstamm zum Kahn,
Stösst ab von des Ufer's Rand;
Ein Irrlicht nur leuchtete ihm voran —
Als jäh erbrauste ein wilder Orkan —
Und nie kehrt er heim an's Land.

Doch Nachts,—wenn die Rothaut jagt das Wild
Und rastet am Waldessaum,
Dann glaubt sie des liebenden Paares Bild
Zu schauen im Mondeslicht bleich und mild,
Im Kahn auf Wellen-Schaum.

Der Deutsche Tag im Jahre 1893.

Festspiel,

Der deutsch-amerikanischen Gesellschaft zu Richmond, Va., gewidmet

von Herrmann Schuricht.

Scene. — Eine Waldgegend. — Während der Vorhang sich hebt ertönen Glockengeläute und Trompetenfanfaren, — dann erscheint *Germania* freudig erregt und gefolgt von *Columbia* und *Virginia*, welche im Hintergrunde zurückbleiben und ihren Worten lauschen.

Germania (mit warmer Empfindung):

Trompeten schmettern und die Glocken hallen,
Zum Festplatz strömt das Volk von fern und nah,
Der *Deutsche Tag* bricht an,—laut hör ich schallen:
"Alt Deutschland hoch und hoch Amerika!"—
In jedem Auge leuchtet helle Freude
Und selbst die Hütte prangt im Festtagskleide.

Mit Wonne seh ich Deutschland's Söhne pflegen
Erinnerung an der Väter heimischen Herd,
Denn solche fromme Liebe ist ein Segen.—
Nur Selbstachtung macht And'rer Achtung werth ! —
Die deutschen Frauen preis ich, denn sie krönen
Des Festes Stunden durch den Reiz des Schönen.

Drum Heil dem Tage der im Freudenchore
Den deutschen Geist belebt im fremden Land !
Ein jedes Haus schmück' Deutschland's Tricolore
Und Blumen zieren jede Frauenhand ! —
Wir können froh, mit wachsendem Vertrauen,
Der Zukunft in das klare Auge schauen !

Columbia (von Virginia gefolgt, tritt sie an Germania heran):

Gruss biet ich Dir zum Ehrentage
Wo Dein Herz voll Jubel schlägt,
Wo empor im Flügelschlage
Himmelwärts Dich Hoffnung trägt. —
Doch in dieser grossen Stunde
Fall auch was uns störend trennt.—

E i n e n lass zum festen Bunde
Was sich "amerikanisch" nennt!
Ende Deines Stammes Irrung,
Bau nicht einen Staat im Staat —
Solch' Beginnen bringt Verwirrung
Und streut schlimmer Zwietracht Saat.

Germania (mit abweisender Handbewegung und in beschwörendem Tone sprechend):

O, halte ein und giess nicht Wehrmuthstropfen
In uns'res Festes harmlos stille Lust, —
Nur Lieb' und Treue sind es, welche klopfen
Mit mächt'gen Schlägen an die deutsche Brust!
Mit gleichem Maasse lass uns Alle messen: —
Die Heimath lieben, doch die alte nicht vergessen!

Mit ed'lem Stolz die Söhne Englands hangen
An ihrer Väter schönem Inselreich;

Der Pietät, mit der sie es umfangen,
Kommt nur die Liebe für die Mutter gleich; –
Und gleiche heil'ge Stimmen mahnen
Die Deutschen an die Stätten ihrer Ahnen.

Nicht als Erob'rer, nein, als Friedensboten,
Sie zogen ein in's jungfräuliche Land.
Den Boden brachen sie und halfen roden
Den Urwald mit geschäft'ger Hand, —
Sie pflanzten Reben an der Berge Hängen
Und füllten Thäler mit des Sanges Klängen.

Sie halfen kämpfen um der Freiheit Segen, —
Beschützten Weib und Kind mit Heldenmuth
Vor rothen Teufeln, — waren allerwegen
Dem Land getreu mit Gut und Blut.
So glücklich nur im opferfrohen Streben
Will in Amerika das Deutschthum leben!

Virginia (mit Begeisterung):

Ein weises Wort! — Ihm ist's gelungen
Jedweden Schatten zu zerstreu'n, —
Es hat mein stolzes Herz bezwungen,
Und fortan soll's Dein eigen sein!

(Virginia reicht der Germania lebhaft die Hand, während Columbia, wie versöhnend, ihre Rechte auf deren Schulter legt):

Virginien, die Mutter Kolonie,
Beut Dank dem deutschen Fleiss nur und Genie!

Nicht nur des Shenandoah Thales Fluren,
Oh, nein, fast jedes County in dem Staat
Zeigt deutlich deutschen Schaffens Spuren; —
Von mancher wackern Heldenthat
Erzählen die Geschichts-Annalen, —
Von Indianerkämpfen,—auch von Todesqualen.

Die Namen: Led'rer, Hermann, Stover,
Von Steuben, Gallatin und Mühlenberg,

Post, Hinkel, Buckner, Gist und Weisser,
Wirt, Armstädt, Kemper und so mehr,
Sind hellen Sternen zu vergleichen
Die hoch am Himmel stehn und nie verbleichen!

Columbia (zum Auditorium gewendet):

Gepriesen seid, geliebte deutsche Brüder,
Wir feiern mit Euch diesen deutschen Tag!
Einstimmen wollen wir in Eure Lieder
Und achten nicht der flüchtigen Stunde Schlag.
Die "deutsche Wacht" von weinumrankten Rheine
Wir sehen neidlos sie im Glorienscheine!

(Das Orchester, die drei Bühnengestalten und das gesammte Auditorium stimmen die "Wacht am Rhein" an)

Nach dem Deutschen Tage.

Von Herrmann Schuricht.

Der Tag ist vorüber, — das Lied ist verrauscht,
Dem fröhlichen Herzens wir Alle gelauscht:
Das Fest hat bewiesen, dass edel und wahr
Auch fern von der Heimath der Unseren Schaar.

In Lied und in Rede ward rühmend gedacht,
Was hier in dem Lande die Väter vollbracht:
Sie fällten den Urwald; — im blutigen Strauss
Beschützten sie Kinder, die Frauen und Haus.

Sie pflanzten die Reben am bergigen Hang
Und füllten die Thäler mit Frohsinn und Sang,—
Sie kämpften für Ehre und menschliches Recht —
Erzogen ein freies und treues Geschlecht!

Dass frei es stets bleibe und gross dieses Land,
D'rauf reichte der Deutsche dem Deutschen die Hand:
"Bleibt einig!" erklang es mit Kraft und mit Macht—
"Denn was wir erstreben, noch ist's nicht vollbracht!"

Zum 80sten Geburtstage des Fuersten Bismarck.

Festlied für den Bismarck-Commers der Deutsch-amerikanischen Gesellschaft von Virginien zu Richmond, Va., am 1. April 1895.

Von Herrmann Schuricht.

Melodie.—"Die Wacht am Rhein."

Ström' aus, o Lied, o Jubelsang —
Und glockenheller Becherklang!
Nur ein Gefühl, nur eine Lust
Heut flammt in aller Deutschen Brust;
||: Fürst Bismarck ist's, dem wahr und rein
Die Deutschen Dankesworte weih'n! : ||

Durch ihn das deutsche Vaterland
Zu neuer Lebenskraft erstand,—
Er schirmt' die heil'ge Landesmark
Durch deutsche Streiter, kühn und stark,—
||: Auch fern selbst, über Land und Meer,
Bracht' Deutschland's Namen er zu Ehr! : ||

Wir schieden einst vom heim'schen Strand,—
Sind Bürger jetzt im freien Land,—
Doch nimmer löscht die Sehnsucht aus
Zum unvergessnen Vaterhaus.
||: Die Heimathsliebe, treu und fest,
Der Deutsche wahrt im fernen West! : ||

Die deutsche Sitte, deutsches Wort,
Wir pflegen treulich fort und fort,—
Der deutsche Mann vergisst sie nicht,
Bis einst im Tod das Auge bricht;—

||: Sie sind sein stolz,—sein Hab und Gut,
Ein Stück vom eignen Fleisch und Blut. : ||

Fürst Bismarck hoch!—Für alle Zeit
Bleibt Dank und Achtung ihm geweiht!—
Des Reiches Schöpfer,—ruhmesreich,—
Gilt uns den grössten Helden gleich,—
||: Es schmückt sein Haupt im Silberglanz
Des Lorbeers immergrüner Kranz. : ||

Der Posten am Walde.

Im Lager bei Salem, Va., 1862.

Von Herrmann Schuricht.

Wenn Abends die Gattin bei Lampenschein,
Am trauten Herde,—verlassen,—allein,—
Dann zieh'n die Gedanken durch Nacht und
Zum stillen Posten am Walde hinaus. [Graus,

Wenn über die Eb'ne der Sturmwind jagt,
Und hohl in den Wipfeln der Bäume klagt,—
Dann schreckt sie empor aus freundlichem
Und denket desPostens amWaldessaum. [Traum,

Gar muthig wacht er im nächtlichen Schein,
In Sturm und Regen, der Theure—allein—
Und hält seine Büchse bereit zum Schuss,
Bereit zum Alarm und tödtlichem Gruss.

Wenn Feinde auch lauern in Schlachtordnung
Zu fassen die Beute im kühnen Sprung:
Schlaft ruhig Kam'raden, in dunkler Nacht
Getreu der Posten am Walde hält Wacht!—

Sie aber betet: "O du, der gebeut,
"Zerstreue die Wolken, wenn Wetter dräut,

"Damit auch in seine einsame Welt
"Des Mondes Lächeln und Sternenlicht fällt.

"Und füll' ihm die muthige Mannesbrust
"Mit Bildern der Heimath und Heimathlust,
"Und mal' ihm die Zukunft in Farbenpracht,
"Dem einsamen Posten auf stiller Wacht!"

Weihe-Sang.

Zur Einweihung der Saengerhalle am 24. September 1877.

Von G. A. Peple.

Stimmet ein, Gesangesbrüder,
In des Tages Festgesang!
Singet eure schönsten Lieder
Mit der Freude hellem Klang!
Denn das Haus, das schön erstanden,
Ist ja unsere Heimath neu;
Sie umschliesst mit festen Banden
Unsere Sänger wahr und treu.

Sei begrüsst, du gute Halle!
Sei begrüsst, du liebes Haus!
Denn der Sänger Herzen alle
Giessen Segen auf dich aus.
Und im Segen sollst du blühen
Wie ein deutscher Liederkranz;
Schön ist ja dein Morgenglühen—
Schöner wird dein Abendglanz.

Lasst in diesen Mauern schalten
Wie ein Lied die Harmonie,
Denn aus ihrem Friedenswalten
Steigt des Lebens Poesie.
Und die Frauen auch, die treuen,
Führt auch sie zum neuen Heerd;
Alles soll sich mit uns freuen,
Alles das uns lieb und werth.

Frohsinn, weil' in unserer Mitte,
Frohsinn—Frucht der Einigkeit;
Deutscher Sang und deutsche Sitte,
Euch sei dieses Haus geweiht.
Stimmet ein! Gesangesbrüder,
In des Tages Festgesang!
Singet eure schönsten Lieder
Mit der Freude hellem Klang.

Am Deutschen Tag 1896.

Von Pastor Dr. Paul L. Menzel.

Auf, auf! es rüstet sich alles zum Fest:
Der Deutsche Tag ist gekommen!
Die Jungen, die Alten—ein jeder verlässt
Mit Frohsinn im Herzen das heimische Nest,
Von deutscher Begeisterung entglommen.
Sie ziehen hinaus mit klingendem Spiel
In buntem Gemisch zum gemeinsamen Spiel:
Im Winde flattern die Fahnen,
Als wollten zur Eile sie mahnen.

Mein deutsches Volk! so seh' ich dich gern,
Voll Eifers und stolz von Empfinden.
Du verleugnest dich nicht, ob die Heimat auch fern;
Wie der Schiffer, so folgst du dem leuchtenden Stern,
Trotz widrigen Wogen und Winden.
Dein Stern ist die Liebe zum deutschen Geist,
Der alles, was niedrig, weit von sich weist;
Du strebest nach Idealen,
Die edeln, erwärmen und strahlen.

Es regt und bewegt sich von unten her
Die Gemeinheit mit frecher Stirne.
Sie frägt nicht nach Recht, nach Zucht nicht und Ehr',
Sie thut, als ob s i e allein Herrscherin wär',

Die schamlose, feile Dirne!
Politik, Religion und gesellige Freud',
Alles reisst sie an sich,—die Teufelsmaid!
  Und besudelt mit ihrer Berührung
  Was sich hingibt ihrer Verführung.

  Drum Heil dir, Germania, reine Braut!
Du zertritzt den abscheulichen Drachen.
Wer liebenden Herzens zu dir aufschaut,
Dem Geist deines Wesens sich anvertraut,
Du entreisst ihn dem gähnenden Rachen.
Mit deutscher Treu und deutscher Zucht,
Mit deutscher Kraft und deutscher Wucht
  Zerstörst du das Reich der Gemeinheit
  Und baust einen Tempel der Reinheit.

  Wo Wahrheit das ewige Fundament,
Und der Grundstein: nie wankende Treue;
"Ein Wort ein Mann!"—das sei der Zement,
Der alles verbindet, was deutsch sich nennt:
Wir geloben es heut' dir auf's Neue!
Ob Lug und Trug uns auch umringt,
Aus deutscher Brust der Schwur erklingt:
  Tod jeglicher Lüg' und Unklarheit!
  Unsre Losung ist: Treue und Wahrheit!—

  Auf solchem Grunde baut sich's gut;
Jeder Pfeiler ist dann eine Tugend:
Gehorsam und Ehrfurcht und Mannesmuth,
Und Keuschheit und reiner Begeisterung Gluth,
Das lerne vom Alter die Jugend.
Nicht Mammonsdienst und Heuchelsinn,
Nicht schnöde Wollust reiss uns hin:
  Ein Leben in Zucht und Ehren,
  Darnach nur steh das Begehren.

  Und dann fehlt auch das Höchste nicht,
Wo rein alles Denken und Sinnen:
Da funkelt im herrlichsten Sonnenlicht
Der Freiheitsgöttin hold' Gesicht

Hoch über des Domes Zinnen.
Sie weiht Germania's Tempel ein,
Zur Stätte voll Licht und Sonnenschein
  Für wahrhaft deutsche Seelen,
  Die ihren Dienst erwählen.

  Nun auf, mein Volk! und denke dran
An diesem Deutschen Tage:
Die Väter zogen dir voran,
"Fromm, frisch, froh, frei," auf Heldenbahn:
Folg' ihnen, kämpfe, wage,
Sei unverzagt! ein ganzer Mann,
Der im Kampfe den Drachen bezwingen kann,
  Dem winkt wahrer Freiheit Segen
  Auch hier auf all' seinen Wegen!

Zur Fahnenweihe und Stiftungsfest des Gesangvereins "Virginia," Richmond, Va., Juni 26. 1854.

Von B. Hassel.

  Auf ihr Sänger, hebt die Fahnen,
Laut erschalle froher Sang;
Mag sie führen uns auf Bahnen
Hin zu Spiel und Lust und Klang.

  Lasst sie heut' uns froh entfalten,
Reiht euch Brüder in die Reih'n:
Lasst die Freundschaft nie erkalten,
Der wir heut' auf's Neu uns weih'n.

  Nach der Freude lasst uns streben,
Die des Sanges Macht verleiht;
Mag' ein neues Band sie weben
Um den Sänger und die Maid.

  Liebchen küssen wir die Wangen,
Reichen froh dem Freund die Hand.

Vor Gefahr lasst uns nicht bangen,
Kühn die Stirn ihr zugewandt!

Hebt empor den vollen Becher,
Laut ertön' aus voller Brust:
Hoch die Fahne, hoch der Zecher,
Hoch das Weib, Gesang und Lust!

An Sie.

Von Prof. M. Schele de Vere.

Ich soll vergessen lernen,
Soll aus der Seele Grund
Das süsse Bild entfernen
Von dem das Herz mir wund?

Wohl seh' ich grüne Auen,
Maiblüthe, Sonnenlicht,—
Doch muss ich rückwärts schauen
Mit Thränen im Gesicht.

Wohlan, ich will verschmerzen,—
Vergessen kann ich's nie,—
Was dem gepressten Herzen
Einst Himmelswonne lieh!

Wer mag die Frommen schmähen,
Die betend, sehnsuchtkrank,
Noch starr gen Westen sehen
Wenn längst die Sonne sank!

Der Blumen Geheimniss.

Von Chr. Droste.

Die Blumen, die Du mir gepflückt,
Auf's Zimmer mir gebracht,
Die haben es mir zugehaucht
In heimlich dunkler Nacht:

Dass Du der Rose einen Kuss
Für mich hast anvertraut,
Dass Du sie dann mit feuchtem Blick
Noch einmal angeschaut.

"Mein Herz," so flüstertest Du leis,
"Ist bei Dir allezeit,
Doch weiss ich nicht, nenn' ich es Glück,
Nenn' ich es Herzeleid!"

Erinnerung.

Von Chr. Droste.

Ich fuhr im kleinen Nachen
Hinunter den heimischen Fluss,
Es rauschten mir Buchen und Eichen
Gar tönenden Wandergruss.

Vorüber an Dörfern und Städten
Ging meine einsame Fahrt,
An Hütten vorbei und Schlössern,
Und Menschen von mancherlei Art.

Vorüber an jener Terrasse,
Vom Abendroth sanft umglüht;
Dort sang eine Schaar von Mädchen
Das alte, uralte Lied.

Sie sangen von Liebe und Treue,
Vom Hoffen und vom Grab —
Es klangen die weichen Töne
Rührend zu mir herab.

Mein Nachen trieb langsam weiter,
Das Ruder entsank meiner Hand —
O Lied von Liebe und Treue,
Wie klingst du im Vaterland.

Turnerkraenzchen.

Dem Turnverein zu Richmond, Va., gewidmet im Jahre 1860

von Hugo Plaut.

Nun frisch! die Bänke weggeräumt
Und hurtig, Mädels, aufgezäumt!
Das Lustspiel ist vorüber;
Die P r e s s e sitzt schon bei'm Pokal —
Was thut's? sie hat vom letzten Mal'
Noch etwas Kritik über.

Ihr Musikanten! frisch d'rauf los,
Auf Instrumenten klein und gross
Ein Lustiges geblasen;
Spielt uns so etwas aus dem "F,"
Ich sag' Euch das nur im Betreff
Der Vettern und der Basen.

Die paaren sich schon hier und da,
Sie kommen an von fern und nah
In einer bunten Kette.
Husch! fliegt voran ein Schneiderlein,
Die Andern stürmen hinterdrein,
Als ging es um die Wette.

Sie wogen schaukelnd hin und her,
Ein aufgeregtes wildes Meer
Im lustigen Entrinnen;
Sie drehen wirbelnd sich im Kreis',
In hellen Strömen rinnt der Schweiss —
Mir schwindelt's vor den Sinnen.

Komm hurtig, Mädel, frisch und frei!
Zu sitzen hier wär' Narrethei, —
Hinein in's fröhl'che Streben!
Schon wiegen wir uns Brust an Brust,
Wir fliegen fort in trunk'ner Lust, —
So lob' ich mir das Leben!

Wie glüht auf meiner Wang' ihr Hauch,
Es wellt ihr Busen, blitzt ihr Aug',

Da — hat die Lust ein Ende!
Wie eine Mahnung schaut mich an
Mit ernstem Auge Vater Jahn
Von jenem Transparente.

O, Vater Jahn, du deutscher Mann,
Was hab' ich Böses denn gethan,
Dass Du heraufbeschworen
Die trüben Geister jener Zeit,
Wo ich mit schwerem Herzeleid
Mein Vaterland verloren.

Stossseufzer.

Von Hugo Plaut.

Sinnend am Geschmeidekasten
Stand der junge Juwelier,
Seine kund'gen Hände fassten
Einen glânzenden Saphir.
Seufzend seine Lippen hauchen:
Ach, Saphire, — ihre Augen!

Seinem Blicke strahlt entgegen
Röthlich ein Korallenband,
Und er nimmt des Meeres Segen
Traurig lächelnd in die Hand.
Traurig lässt er's wieder fallen:
Ihre Lippen, — ach, Korallen!

Ein Geschmeide gleissend funkelt
Jetzt vor seinem Kennerblick;
Und sein Antlitz sich verdunkelt,
Hastig stösst er es zurück;
Wild ruft er in seinem Schmerze:
Falscher Demant, — ach, ihr Herze!

Maasliebchen.

Von Hugo Plaut.

Die Sonne sinkt langsam hernieder,—
Sanft weht der Abendwind,—
Am murmelnden Wiesenbächlein
Steht spielend ein rosig' Kind.

Sie pflücket ein bleichendes Blümlein
Vom Grunde frisch und grün,
Und fängt es an zu entblättern
Nach altem deutschen Sinn.

"Er liebt mich von Herzen, mit Schmer-
Ein wenig oder nicht." [zen,
Das sind die magischen Worte,
Die leis' dazu sie spricht.

Mit banger, gespannter Erwartung,
Vollbringet sie ihr Spiel,
Schon sind an des Blümleins Kelche
Der Blätter nicht mehr viel.

Da rauscht's aus dem nahen Gebüsche,
Ein Jüngling tritt hervor,
"Er liebt Dich von ganzem Herzen,"
Klingt's traut an ihrem Ohr.

Es waren die Worte verklungen,
Ihr ward so wohl, so warm,
Sie fühlte sich liebend umschlungen
Von des Geliebten Arm.

SUPPLEMENTARY REMARKS TO VOLUME I OF THIS HISTORY OF THE GERMAN ELEMENT IN VIRGINIA.

Since the publication of Volume I the attention of the author has been called to the following supplements and mistakes.

On page 26, line 4, is to be added after the words: "ascertained to be in Norfolk," the name of the country: "England."

On page 40, referring to Governor Richard Kempe, and after the words: "President of this body in 1644," ought to be inserted: "1645 Lieutenant-Governor of Virginia."

On page 67, line 31, should stand: "In Stafford and Orange counties German settlements were built up at Germanna Ford," instead of only: "in Stafford county."

On page 68, after the words: "in picturesque language," ought to be subjoined: "Inconsistent with Colonel Byrd's statement and H. A. Rattermann's assertion ('Deutscher Pionier,' 8ter Jahrgang, Seite 106: 'Dem schottischen Edelmann [Spottswood] gefiel es unter den fleissigen und ruhigen Deutschen so wohl, dass er sich eine der deutschen Jungfrauen — eine Hannoveranerin Namens Theke — zur Gattin nahm,') — that the historian Campbell denies that Spottswood married a German lady and that he asserts: that Miss Thecky (not Theke) was Miss Dorothea Bryan or Brain, and that 'Thecky' was the diminutive or pet name of her Christian name. Campbell says furthermore: that Miss Dorothea was a sister of Ann Butler Bryan, who was Spottswood's wife."

The author is not convinced that Colonel Byrd's statement in regard to Governor Spottswood's wife and family-life are less trustworthy than Campbell's. Colonel Byrd visited Germanna and was a contemporary of Governor Spottswood.

On pages 70 to 73, referring to the Kemper family and to the settlements of Germanna, of Germantown, Fauquier county and on the Robinson river in Madison county, the author received the following explanatory emendations:

Mr. Charles E. Kemper of Washington, D. C., writes: "I have read with much interest your History of the German Element in Virginia. You make some statements, however, about my ancestor Johann Kemper, which are not in accord with family information and tradition. You state, that after marrying Alice Utterback he removed with others to the Robinson river section in Madison county. All our information is to the effect, that he settled at Germantown, Fauquier county, and probably died there, though as to this we are not certain."

A cousin of this correspondent, Mr. Willis M. Kemper, Attorney-at-Law, Cincinnati, Ohio, confirms by letter these remarks as follows: "Johann Kemper never went to live in the German colony in Madison county. When the colony of twelve families had their fuss with Governor Spottswood, the whole colony (I have their names, — taken from the diary of my great grandfather, James Kemper, a son of John Peter Kemper) — moved in what was then Stafford, after 1730 Prince Williams and after 1759 Fauquier county, — about nine miles southwest of Warrenton. — and settled Germantown. Descendants of all twelve of these families are to be found there today. John Peter Kemper's house, "Cedar Grove," was built with brick in 1745; it is still standing and inhabited by a member of the Kemper family. Governor Kemper's grandfather moved to Madison about the beginning of this century and in this way happened to be there."

The "fuss" the colonists had with Governor Spottswood, mentioned in the foregoing letter, has been alluded to in Vol. I, page 72, and after the words: "in the present county of Madison," — for the sake of better understanding, — ought to be added: "that the former good relations between the Governor and the German settlers had been seriously injured by these money matters, and the latter made bitter complaint of him." The evil final relations between Spottswood and the Germans are confirmed by the original manuscripts now on file in the State Library at Richmond, Va.

Partly alluding to the prenamed events, Rev. T. O. Keister of Greencastle, Franklin county, Pennsylvania, writes to the author: "For ten or twelve years I have been collecting material for a History of Lutheranism in Virginia. The history of Lutheranism in Madison county dates back to 1720, whose founders were evidently from the Germans who settled at Germanna and near there. The two colonies, the one at Germanna and the one at Spottswood's iron furnace near Germanna, for some reason moved up on the Robinson river and there in 1720 a deed was given them for their glebe lands. My data leads me to conclude, that their migration was made between 1719 and 1720."

Touching the same historical occurrence and in variance with the historian Dr. Slaughter, Mr. W. W. Scott, the present State Librarian of Virginia, writes: "I do not believe for a moment that it was these Germans (who settled at and near Germanna), or any of them who went to Germantown, Fauquier county, as stated by Dr. Slaughter."

These various data and conjectures do not settle the date and nature of the German settlements in Madison, Orange and Fauquier counties positively, but the author feels greatly obliged to the forenamed correspondents, as their letters throw some light on the subject and verify the main points of the historical facts he has represented in Volume I.

On page 71, line 15, referring to "the first German preacher in Virginia," Mr. Willis M. Kemper of Cincinnati writes on January 13th, 1899: "I think you are mistaken in saying that Gerhard Hinkel was the first German preacher in Virginia. I have always been claiming this honor for my ancestor Henry Haeger, who built his church at Germantown, according to James Kemper. John Peter Kemper did not marry a daughter, but a grand-daughter of Parson Haeger. You will find Parson Haeger's will on record in Prince William county, Will Book C, pages 108 and 117. By this will is apparent that the old gentleman had two daughters, — one of whom married a John Hoffmann, the other a John Fishbach, both members of the German colony of twelve families, brought over by Governor Spottswood. One of the grand-children, Elizabeth Fishbach, married Peter Kemper in 1738. Henry Haeger was the pastor of the twelfth colony, which, according to a petition quoted by Dr. Slaughter from Bishop Meade, came first and went to Germantown, — and therefore it must have been the twentieth colony that went to Madison county. Bishop Meade's petition says the second colony came in 1717; the date of the coming of the first colony is blank in Bishop Meade's petition. Not long since I wrote to the "Society for the Propagation of the Gospel in Foreign Parts" in London, from whose letter-book the petition was taken, and they write me: that this blank should be 1714." — But in another letter, dated February 3d, 1899, the same writer informs the author: "I don't know the exact date of Henry Haeger's coming *to Virginia*, or whether or not he had previously been at New Berne with Graffenried's Swiss and Palatines. I know the German colony settled at Germanna in 1714, and my great-grandfather says: their Pastor Haeger *came in after them.* He was certainly there in the summer of 1719, because the petition quoted in Bishop Meade says he was there when the petition was written and sent, and it must have left Virginia not later than midsummer 1719." — Thus the two letters of Mr. Willis M. Kemper appear to contradict each other in regard to the time of Rev. Haeger's arrival in Virginia. — Rev. Socrates Henkel, pastor at New Market, Va., states in his "History of the Evangelical Lutheran Tennessee Synod," page 67: "that his ancestor Gerhard Henkel came to Virginia about 1718," and therefore it is left in doubt, which of the two reverends came first. — In regard to the petition quoted is also reported: "A united petition from the two German colonies, one of fifty and the other of eighty persons, was sent to England in 1719, praying for an assistant to Rev. Haeger at Germanna," while others entertain grave doubt as to the very existence of such a document. General John E. Roller furthermore stated in a lecture at Richmond, Va., on January 9th, 1899: "The church erected at Germantown was the first *Reformed* church in America (not Lutheran.)"

On page 77, line 36, after the words: "Albemarle and Louisa counties," is to be inserted as stated by General Roller in his prementioned lecture: "Nearly two-thirds of the people of Virginia west of Fredericksburg trace their descent to the Germans."

On page 81, line 17, after the words: "of the foundation of Richmond," ought to be added: "In 1780 an act for locating the public squares to enlarge the town and for the purpose to locate the Capital, Halls of Justice, State House for Executive Boards and a residence for the Governor, etc., was passed. A committee of nine was appointed to lay out lots in such form and such dimensions as requisite, and the German citizen Rob't Goode (Gude), whose descendants are still living in Richmond, was elected a member of this important committee."

On page 94, after the words: "causing their own dissatisfaction," ought to be inserted: "For some years the Indians had molested the brethren and in July 1764 they broke up the settlements in the Shenandoah valley, and all of them, twenty-six persons, returned to Pennsylvania." — In his before mentioned lecture: "The Colonial German Element of Virginia," General Roller of Harrisonburg, Va., stated upon good authority: "The German Pietists under Kelpius visited Virginia in 1694 before settling in Pennsylvania, and Rev. Koster was the early Pietist pastor in Virginia." — Johann Kelpius was born in Siebenbuergen, was a follower of Phil. J. Spencer and Jacob Boehme and founded a community in the wilderness on the Wissahickon in Pennsylvania under the name: "Das Weib in der Wüste." He died in 1708, only 40 years of age." Accordingly neither Hinkel nor Haeger have been the first German preachers in Virginia, but the Pietist Rev. Koster.

In referring to the incident of Colonel Bowman's death, related on page 131, Mr. Wm. E. English, Vice-President of the Indiana Historical Society, a descendant of Joist Hite and connected with the Bowman family, writes: "The history states that in this glorious affair Colonel Bowman lost his life, plainly meaning Colonel Abraham Bowman, who succeeded General Muehlenberg in command of the Eighth Virginia Regiment. This is a mistake. Colonel Abraham Bowman settled in Lexington, Kentucky, after the Revolutionary War and was still alive when LaFayette visited this country the first time. There was another Colonel Bowman killed at Yorktown, but not Colonel Abraham. He, Abraham, was a brother of Colonel Joseph Bowman."

THE END.

INDEX OF NAMES

Volume II

-C-

-D-

-I-J-

-K-

-L-

-M-

-T-

-U-

-V-

-W-

-X-Y-Z-

GENERAL INDEX

A.

B.

C.

D.

E.

F.

G.

H.

I.

J

K.

L.

M.

N.

P.

R.

S.

T.

U.

V.

W.

Y.

Z.